Heaven Became Hell …
Hollywood Be Thy Name

Brent David Schroeder

ISBN: 978-1477481387

Book design by Christopher Peters
Cover Design by Lisa West

www.brentsbook.com

DEDICATION

I would like to dedicate this book to my parents for always being there for me, no matter what I did. I would like to thank my friend and one time body guard Keith Bramitt, for keeping me alive in the worst years of my life. And in memory of Robert Cruz, RIP, miss you bro! And to everyone else and to those who tried their best to keep me down, good luck next time.

● **Entertainment**

Local rockers look to the west

by Toni Griffith
The Vidette-Messenger

VALPARAISO — A band called Hap Hazzard will be out to rock Valparaiso Saturday.

The local group, whose lead singer describes their music as "a cross between Van Halen and a Pop-Tart commercial," says their 8 p.m. concert at Valparaiso University's gym is the first step on their road to superstar status.

The group is pulling up stakes and heading for Los Angeles at the end of the month. It's the route to go if you want to get anywhere in the music industry, says lead singer Bobby Hickle, 22, of Chesterton.

It's also a way to break out of the "straitjacket of conservative Valparaiso," he said.

"We're gonna shoot Valpo in the head Saturday night," says Hickle. "Let the kids have some good rock 'n' roll fun. A celebration of youth. No alcohol or drugs."

Hickle says good, clean fun is what the band's all about and what Valparaiso is sadly in need of for teens.

"They've shut down all the teen clubs. They want to keep the kids off the streets, but they don't want to offer them anything. Heaven forbid if the kids have some fun."

Hap Hazzard's brand of rock is definitely fun, says Hickle. Its attitude is "let's grab a bottle of Malibu rum, some girls in bikinis and sit around and dance."

Hickle characterizes the music as "good and positive. Heavy music with easy meaning lyrics.

"When you hear our music, you're gonna want to dance, smile, grab the guy's hand next to you and say aren't we having fun."

Bassist Brent Schroeder, 22, from Boone Grove, says their music is heavy on guitar, drums and bass and light on the singing.

Drummer Gary Nova, 18, and guitarist Michael Dee Marks, 23, both of Valparaiso, complete the band.

Hap Hazzard was born in May out of a group called Prisoner that featured all the musicians, except the drummer. Prisoner played around local bars and teen clubs for four years, doing updated versions of Ratt and Kiss tunes, before the guys decided to stop performing "copy."

Nova sparked the transition to Hap Hazzard and original material.

"Mike found Gary," said Schroeder. "He went into a drugstore to get batteries one

Hap Hazzard will be ready to hit the road and aim for the big time after a Saturday concert at Valparaiso University. The local rockers are, from left, Bobby Hickle, Brent Schroeder, Gary Nova and Michael Dee.

(V-M: Karen M. Dunivan)

day, walked by the magazine rack and sees a tall dude ripping pictures out of a rock magazine and sticking them in his pants. Mike asked Gary what he was doing and if he played in a band. Gary said he played drums and had just quit a band. The next day he came out and jammed."

That was the birth of Hap Hazzard. No more ripoffs of other bands' songs, says Hickle. It's all their own now.

"The way it happens is Mike comes up with a riff and starts messing around with it. Brent and Gary figure out the rhythm part and they'll play music till words come to me, then back and forth.

"It's like cooking. You put in a little salt, a little pepper, put it in the oven for awhile.

"It's really fun. We get to say what we want to say. I'm glad we're doing this."

Hap Hazzard is leaving for the West Coast Aug. 30.

"There are more options there," says Hickle. "It's where rock 'n' roll is. If we get signed by a record company, God bless us. If we don't, we still get the fun of playing."

"You're more accepted out there," says Schroeder. "Here, if you wear an earring, people

think you must be on drugs."

Schroeder's been out to the coast a couple of times, setting up an apartment, finding an agent and rehearsal space, making contacts.

The group's Saturday concert will be videotaped and edited to use in California.

"That way we let them hear our music and see what kind of

reaction we can get from a crowd. It'se a good way to do it," says Hickle.

The concert will be a farewell and thank you to Hap Hazzard's followers.

"It's for the fans who stuck by us through the craziness. This show's really for them"

Tickets are $4 at the door.

Introduction

As I strike the last match on an old matchbook from the Rainbow Bar and Grill on Sunset Boulevard in Hollywood, California, memories come flooding back -- some good, and some I want to forget.

During the late 1980's and early '90's in Hollywood, I could be found at the Rainbow five nights a week and at the Cathouse every Tuesday evening. The best food and drink, along with the best pieces of tail, could be found at these clubs. Every type of high-class criminal and illegal drug could also be found, along with other personal favors that could be obtained with a couple of whispers in a certain person's ear. I was that certain person -- if you could get a credible introduction. Hollywood was my town and my home for a decade of decadence.

Before you write me off, listen to my tale. Hopefully it will open your eyes to the ultimate American betrayal.

When my son asks me why I haven't been there for eighteen years, I hope he believes me when I say it hasn't been due to a lack of tears. I will try to explain how it used to be with his mother, an informant, and I, the notorious Hollywood figure, Mr. B, also known to various law enforcement agencies as the impeccable "Godfather of Club California" or the resilient "Bionic Man of the San Fernando Valley."

But that was a long time ago, though in my dreams, or should I say nightmares, it seems like yesterday.

Chapter 1

July of 1995 was one of the hottest summers on record, and I knew it was only going to get hotter. El Nino was the least of my worries. With the pedal to the metal I was speeding south down the I-5 freeway at eighty-five miles per hour. I was down to a quarter tank of gas; that was my life expectancy.

Following behind at seventy-five miles per hour were two black vans with tinted windows, filled with members of the satanic outlaw motorcycle gang, Heaven's Devils. They were armed to the teeth and wired out of their fucking minds on crystal methamphetamine. Their mission was to cut me down in the streets of Los Angeles. I would be unrecognizable at my funeral, they assured the underworld.

I was out-numbered, out-gunned, and standing alone. There was no talking my way out of this one. Words were useless, and a single AK-47 wouldn't be enough. My secret plan had backfired.

I thought I had come under the shadow of darkness and in disguise, but instead I had brought the fight to my enemies, who were harden and battle proven, and they were waiting in numbers.

I had been betrayed.

Their first attempt failed, so Christ was sending his elite.

Since it appeared that my life was about to end, I started thinking back to the past. I could only pray my loving parents would never find out about my secret life in Hollywood and how events led to this one moment. My undoing was partly my own fault, but some of the events were controlled by people who had been pulling the strings in the shadows for the last decade of my life.

I thought they were my friends.

~~

The four of us set out for Hollywood: September 1st 1987, with dreams of becoming the next Motley Crue. During the drive, we settled on a new name for the band. A band from Germany was already signed and using the name *Prisoner*. It was a great name; we used it for five years. We were famous in Northwest Indiana and Chicago as the youngest and hottest band on the heavy metal scene.

We had been arguing for weeks about a new name and were at each other's throats until Bobby Lee finally came up with *Hap Hazzard*.

The four-day drive to Hollywood was especially long because we were pulling a heavy trailer behind the van, carrying all our musical equipment and household junk. Michael and I took turns driving, switching whenever we filled up for gas and snacks. Bobby Lee hid in the back; he was now a fugitive, with a number of warrants for unpaid traffic tickets. Gary was one of the worst drivers I had ever seen, so he was just a passenger.

We drove thirteen hours a day, and with the heavy trailer, I didn't think we were going to make it up some of the really steep hills. I prayed that the Res-Trailer hitch I had personally welded onto the back of my van would hold.

Bobby Lee, an arrogant fuck, being his usual pain-in-the-ass self, decided he was going to learn how to play harmonica while we were all cooped up in the van. If that wasn't bad enough, he had eaten White Castle hamburgers the night before. The first day, when he wasn't in the van, I stuck the harmonica down the back of my pants and wiped my ass with it, and when that didn't stop him, I just ripped it out of his shit flavored mouth and tossed it out the window somewhere in Oklahoma.

"Why did you do that?" he yelled. "It was going to be part of the show."

"Another word, and you'll be out the window, fart-blossom!" I replied. "The next time we stop, you better wipe your rotten ass. You must have shit your pants on that last rip."

Michael lowered his sunglasses and just smiled at me as he drove the van. We had the same thought: <u>Shut up, asshole, and stop farting.</u>

"You guys got it lucky," Gary whined. "I'm stuck in the back. I want a window seat."

"Shut up," I said. "You're the new guy in the band. Suffer."

"You suck the big one," Gary muttered.

"Where's the love?" Bobby said as he burned another rotten, greasy, rancid-meat-flavored tasting fart.

Michael almost crashed the van as Gary tried to climb over me to stick his head out the window, while we sped down the highway rockin' to Van Halen.

~~

I found us an apartment in the Valley in Studio City, a modest two-bedroom on Bluffside Drive. It had a view of a brick wall in the rear and a view of the small swimming pool under our balcony. The pool was small enough that you could jump from side to side. I had never had an in-ground swimming pool before. I thought we were really living it up in the big city.

Across the street was our first celebrity neighbor, the guy who had played the part of Rob, owner of the diner, on <u>What's Happening</u>. I would say hi to him at the 7-11, and he would reply, "What's happening?" It made all of us laugh.

Moving to Hollywood was like having a second childhood. Not having to answer to anyone for once in my life, I went a little crazy. Plus, during this time period, it was cool to be the bad boys of rock-and-roll. The more obnoxious a band was, the more people talked about them.

Looking at the Hollywood sign, I quoted the Joker: "Wait till they get a load of me!"

I also started wondering what kind of trouble I could get into in this town. Living in Los Angeles meant you had complete freedom to express yourself in any way, and the opportunity to become anyone you wanted. Hollywood was the only city in the United States that accepted guys with long hair. Back in Indiana, you couldn't get a job at Burger King with long hair. You could have AIDS, that was okay, but forget long hair.

During this era in music, if you didn't have extremely long hair, you weren't considered a heavy metal musician. Image was what sold records. A rock band full of long-haired pretty boys might not be able to write a single song to save their lives, but screaming girls would flock to their shows. A band with excellent songs and real talent would get overlooked if one or two guys in the band were a little overweight or losing their hair. That was the reason we put up with Bobby's crap; he could sing and had looks that could kill.

Michael, Gary, and I had long hair, but it wasn't long enough or pretty enough for Hollywood standards, so I paid for us to get hair extensions. Then I dyed my hair jet-black and added a huge blonde streak down one side, through the hair that covered my eye. Gary and I both had headaches for two days because of the hair extensions; they were woven in so tightly it hurt to touch our scalps.

Michael, who had thick, bushy hair, didn't listen to the instructions from the hairstylist and washed his hair with hot water and lots of shampoo.

Standing in a wet towel in our apartment, he said with panic in his voice, "I think I have a serious problem."

"What the hell did you do?"

"I just washed my hair."

Michael sat down in a chair so I could take a closer look. I couldn't tell what was his hair and what was the extension; it was one giant wet mat.

"I don't know what to do," I confessed. "We might have to shave your head and start over."

"You are not shaving my head! Think of something else!"

"Relax," I replied. "I was just joking. But we are going to have to call someone for help."

Thinking back to my days of training horses as a kid, I bought some Afro Sheen, and with the help of six people working three at a time, we spent fourteen hours combing out his extensions. By the time we were done, the hair extensions looked like shit and had to be replaced, costing another $500.

The hairstylist was Lorien and her roommate was Tish. Lorien claimed she slept with secret agent Get Smart at the age of fourteen and Tish had gotten herpes from Robin Williams. I know for a fact, she blackmailed him for years to keep her mouth shut. Robin provided a nice apartment on Clark Street and gave her a sports car, but she would sell him out eventually to the Globe.

~~

Our first month in California, we went out to the Hollywood nightclubs every single night to make new friends and check out all the local bands. It was going to be difficult to be original and get noticed. Two hundred fifty thousand other musicians with the same idea had showed up in Hollywood at the same time. Every long-haired dude who could play guitar, bass, or drums or thought they could sing eventually ended up in Hollywood with dreams of stardom. It was like the California gold rush all over again. All the major record companies were based in Los Angeles and were only signing bands out of the Hollywood club circuit. It was their marketing test grounds.

The biggest club was the Country Club in Reseda, which held about 3,000 screaming fans. Only the big acts played there, or recently signed bands giving their farewell performances before going on nationwide tours.

The first club in Hollywood on the Strip was the Whiskey-a-Go-Go, where the Doors had played decades earlier. It hadn't changed a bit. Across the street was an AM/PM gas station that offered two hamburgers for a buck, packing the place every night after the Whiskey let out.

Two blocks west on the Sunset Strip was the Roxy, the biggest and most prestigious club in Hollywood. The Roxy had a twenty-five-dollar cover charge, and a beer cost five dollars. No brand names or bottles; you got it in a plastic cup. They were slinging so much booze, you got whatever they brought you and liked it. If you didn't tip the rude waitress at least a buck, you stood a better chance of hell freezing over than getting a second drink from the likes of her. The Roxy had a huge stage with red velvet curtains, and there wasn't a bad seat in the house. With a great sound system, it was the perfect place to see a band play.

One block west of the Roxy was the world-famous Gazzari's, which was owned by the godfather of rock-and-roll, Bill Gazzari. Bill was in his late eighties and always had hot, eighteen-year-old blondes hanging all over him like he was flypaper, making Hugh Hefner look like a boy scout.

Bill Gazzari had given Van Halen their first break after he recognized their talent and backed them. Van Halen played to sold-out shows every weekend at Gazzari's until they got signed, and the rest is history.

Two blocks south was Doug Wesson's Troubadour. It was old and somewhat rundown, but it had history. Elton John made his first Hollywood appearance at the Troubadour, which landed him his first recording contract. W.A.S.P. and L.A. Guns, along with many other heavy metal bands, packed the Troubadour every weekend for almost a decade of hard-driving rock.

The Whiskey, Roxy, Rainbow, Gazzari's, and the Troubadour were all within walking distance of each other. You could stumble out of one and actually fall into another without fear of the police giving you grief.

Orange County had Jezebel's, the best rock club in Anaheim, close to Disneyland. And then there was the Waters Club in Riverside, which had a huge stage. The main floor was divided in two, one side for minors and the other side with booze. Last but not least was one of my favorites, the FM Station. It was the best metal club in North Hollywood and sat, or should I say rocked, on the corner of Lankershim and Colfax.

All of these clubs made up the L.A. club circuit. Mötley Crüe, Ratt, Dokken, Great White, W.A.S.P., L.A. Guns, Bang Tango, Poison, Black-n-Blue, Guns n' Roses, and Warrant had all come from this club circuit.

These were some tough acts to follow. The fans in Hollywood were used to seeing the cream of the crop. I felt a little intimidated at first. Getting a chance to play these clubs wasn't that easy. In Chicago, our band got paid $500 a night or more, depending on the size of the crowd we drew. In Hollywood, right away I ran into a Hollywood scam called "pay to play."

I called After Dark Productions in Hollywood. I had sent them a tape and a video before moving there, and they expressed interest in setting us up with gigs. The promoter said, "How many shows do you guys want to play a month?"

"We're used to playing out four nights a week," I answered. "Once a week would be cool."

"All right, let me go over the rundown. If your band wants to play a Friday night at the Roxy, it'll cost two thousand for a forty-five minute slot at the beginning of the night, or thirty-five hundred dollars for the top slot of the evening."

I couldn't believe what I was hearing. "We have to pay you to play? I never heard of such a damn thing."

"That's the way it works in Hollywood. If you don't pay, you don't play."

"All right," I replied. "I'll get back to you."

If you didn't pay, you were told to fuck off, no matter how talented you were. Hollywood wasn't about the music, it was about crushing dreams and taking everyone's last cent in the process.

I did some checking around by talking with other bands on the Sunset Strip and found out it was true. These bands were playing every night of the week all over Hollywood, providing excellent entertainment -- and paying out their asses just for the privilege of playing in Hollywood.

So they could sleep at night, some of the promoters gave the musicians a couple thousand dollars worth of pre-sell tickets, so the musicians could try to sell them before their shows. They could then keep the money from the ticket sales, but that was really just a joke. Being a new band in Hollywood, you were damn lucky if someone would come to your show even if you gave them a ticket for free. There were so many shows going at once, it was sheer madness.

As a matter of fact, the hardest part about getting between all the clubs on the Sunset Strip was getting past the hundreds of long-haired musicians passing out band fliers advertising their next show.

"Hey, dude, take a flier," the musicians would say. "Take one for your friend."

Trying to get by, I would reply, "Thanks. I'll try to check out your show."

I would always take a band flier; it was an insult not to. Some people would take one, walk five feet, and drop it. There were so many band fliers being passed out and dropped, it looked like a ticker tape parade the next morning. It got so bad, the city of West Hollywood finally passed a law forbidding band fliers. They even made an example out of a band that didn't stop. It was costing the city a pretty penny to clean the mess up.

~~

We waited two months before playing out in hopes of being able to draw some kind of crowd. We were at the place where dreams came true.

In hopes of drawing a crowd and getting our name out there, we started the "flier wars." On Thursday, we would get ready around three in the morning and get our route planned out and our fliers and duct tape ready. Michael would drive, dropping Gary, Bobby Lee, and myself off at different locations on Highland Boulevard and Sunset Boulevard.

Running from lamppost to lamppost, we plastered each one with a flier about our up-and-coming show. If Warrant already had a flier up or Guns-n-Roses had a prime location, I would just put our flier over the top.

The next morning, when traffic came rushing into Hollywood, people saw Hap Hazzard fliers everywhere. If you got caught at any stop light, you could see the flyers plastered all over bus benches and road signs. The sign didn't read "25 MPH", it read "Hap Hazzard." Other bands saw how cool it was and started doing the same thing, eventually putting their fliers over ours. And so the wars began.

We had arrived, and I was making damn sure Hollywood knew we were here.

~~

Once we finally started playing the Sunset Strip, we drove our new apartment manager Norton totally nuts with all the late-night parties. He was awakened many times by the loud, drunken women who followed us home every night, their high heels echoing through the courtyard like they were hammering nails. They dropped cigarette butts everywhere, stained with bright ruby-red lipstick.

We lived toward the back of the complex, and it was easy to find us by following the beer tabs. Someone always managed to fall into the swimming pool fully clothed, letting out a shrilling death scream just before they splashed into the calm water.

The apartment complex only had thirty-three units, most of them joined in with us at the parties or liked us enough not to complain. My neighbor directly across the hallway was the world-famous guitarist Alex Mais, the fastest guitarist from Europe. He was in the United States on a record contract, and with the help of some money from his girlfriend's rich parents. Alex hardly spoke English, so his bizarre roommate Geno did most of the talking. With his long, dark hair, Geno resembled Richard Ramirez, the Night Stalker.

This was my first encounter with people who were into the black arts and occult doings. Every Sunday, like clockwork, they would have people over and they would chant and play bizarre music all day long, with incense burning. I knew if my mother found out I was living across from satanic worshipers, she wouldn't sleep a wink. For protection, I hung a huge golden crucifix on the inside of the front door to our apartment in hopes of keeping at bay any evil spirits that might be visiting next door.

Geno always liked to fuck with me and say, "Want a record contract? I'll draw up the papers. You'll have to sign in your blood."

I always said, "No thanks," but I had to ask, "What do you guys do every Sunday?"

With an evil-looking smile, just because he wanted to fuck with me, Geno showed me pictures of girls with upside-down Auks painted on their faces, all standing in a circle. It looked like fun . . . Not. If they had been bent over and naked, I might have been interested, or at least aroused.

Despite the weirdness, being neighbors with Alex and Geno had its upsides. Not all the musicians associated with Alex were satanic-worshippers.

The first time we played out and had a huge after-party, I banged on their door and invited them. A few minutes later, around two in the morning, Lars Ulrich and James Hetfield of Metallica came strolling in with our neighbor. This could only happen in Hollywood; the chances of Metallica showing up at my place in Indiana had been zero. The Metallica members were living on the success of their latest album, Master of Puppets.

I acted the same and treated them no differently, actually pretending not to know who they were. Even thou James Hetfield was wearing a Metallica t-shirt. Before coming to Hollywood, I had programmed my brain not to get excited around celebrities. I knew if you acted goofy, you would be treated as such, so I found it better to be rude and even a little insulting to become their friends -- not an asshole, but absolutely no ass-kissing of any sort.

I said to James and Lars, "There will be a twenty-dollar cover for each of you." They both looked at me like I was nuts. "Just joking. Come on in . . . Do you want a beer?"

They both laughed and replied, "Hell yeah, we alcoholics."

The drunker our drum roadie J.J. got, the funnier he became. He got in Lars's face, saying, "You look just like the drummer from Metallica."

Lars just laughed and replied, "This guy for real? Whatever he's on . . . I want some, too!"

Everyone laughed.

J.J. walked off to James and said, "You look like the guitar player in Metallica . . . seriously."

Everyone laughed again.

Then J.J. fell over with his hands in his front pockets, landing face-down on the living room floor like a cap-sized turtle caught in its shell.

Everyone started laughing, until Michael turned J.J. over and yelled, "He's is not breathing!"

Grant Stevens, our new band manager, yelled, "Pick that fat piece of shit up and help me get him into the shower . . . NOW!"

This was no easy task. J.J. was a full 280 pounds of pure baby fat, and since he was out cold, he wasn't helping one bit.

Working together, it took five of us to get him up and into the bathroom while Grant started running the cold water, hoping to snap him back into our world. Once the ice-cold water hit his face, and Michael slapped him on the back really hard, J.J. coughed, gagged, and filled the bathtub with what smelled like death. In reality, it was ten 7-11 chili dogs with cheese and chips.

I thought, <u>What a mess. I'm going to kill him when he sobers up.</u>

After babysitting J.J. for a while, Grant relieved me so I could venture back out into the party. Everyone in town was crammed into our apartment, and there wasn't a single inch of room to move without having your face planted into some silicone breasts. There were so many people that Stevie Rachelle, before he was the signer for Tuff, fell through the coffee table, and the couch was ruined after girls in high heels stood on it. The couch had seen better days and wasn't safe for anyone to sit on without fear of a spring sticking in your bum.

To avoid killing everyone's buzz, I said drunkenly, "Let's throw the coffee table and the couch away. I want to make more room." Looking around the party, I found a couple of drunken knuckleheads to help me pick up the old, heavy couch, which contained a hide-a-bed. I was too drunk, and it was too heavy to carry down the two flights of stairs. We were on the top floor. "Carry it to the back window," I ordered.

It barely squeezed through the window, so I had to run and give it a flying kick. The kick caused the couch to shoot out, hitting the apartment building across the alley like a small, out-of-control scud missile.

Thud!

Gary and a couple of other guys grabbed the couch when it finally hit the pavement and carried it to the back dumpster. They tried to pick up all the loose change that had fallen out as I dumped beer on them from above with a laugh. When they looked up, I pretended to pull up the zipper on my pants.

Every light in the next apartment building came on. I just knew that was going to be trouble, but since I was totally buzzed, it was still funny as hell.

A few minutes later, our apartment manager Norton was beating on my front door. When I was finally able to stop laughing and wipe the smile off my face, I opened the door and said, "What's happening?"

"Tell me you didn't throw a couch out the window!" Norton screamed.

I calmly replied, "Hell, no. That would be nuts."

Norton turned three shades of red. "Liar!"

"Cool off," I said with a hush of my hand. "It was the guys from Metallica." They were now standing where the couch had been. "It must be a rock star thing," I added, shrugging my shoulders like I didn't have a clue.

Norton clenched his teeth. "Tell those assholes in Metallica to chill out." Turning around, he left in a huge huff.

I looked over at James Hatfield and gave him the thumbs-up sign. He tilted his beer back, not knowing I had just used them as scapegoats. It had worked better than saying we were in the mob.

This same situation with band parties was happening every night of the week somewhere different all over the Valley and Hollywood. Anyone who wasn't a part of the music scene probably didn't appreciate the insane chaos. But all of us thousands of musicians who had come to Hollywood felt like it was our time to shine. Our attitude toward non-musicians was that they should move back to Indiana or some other normal state.

We cleared everyone out around five in the morning. Before I could get five minutes of much-needed sleep, I was rudely awakened by my first California earthquake. None of us had a clue about what was going on. I thought maybe the neighbors had thrown the couch back in retaliation.

Once I figured out what was happening, I jumped out of bed and ran out into the hallway, tripping over J.J., who was passed out on the floor like a huge, moaning speed bump.

"Get up asshole, it's a quake!"

The earthquake registered as a 5.5, which was nothing to someone who had been through one before, but it was a big deal to us hick kids.

Everyone in the apartment complex was standing out in front of the building, waiting for aftershocks. I stumbled over to the apartment manager Norton and said, "Bet you thought that was just another flying couch, huh?"

Norton looked at me and said, "Fuck off!" Before walking away. I just laughed.

J.J. slept through the whole event, and when he awoke a day later, he kept talking about this weird dream in which he had met the guys in Metallica.

I let J.J. think it was dream until I got the pictures developed.

When he saw the pictures, "Did I make an ass out of myself?"

I thought about it for a minute and said, "Yes, you did."

Everyone had a laugh, including the guys from Metallica.

DIAMOND IN THE ROUGH

Hap-Hazzard

"We're like the peanut M&M's of rock, one look at that yellow wrapper...

...and you know there are a few nuts in there."

Every once in awhile a band comes along that just makes you smile. Nothing political, nothing Satanic, nothing goofy, just plain fun. Hailing from (you guessed it) L.A., Hap-Hazzard is one happening band. As they state, "We play music because it's fun and we enjoy creating music that is fun. We are just concerned with having a good time and entertaining people with the best show we can put together,"

Hap-Hazzard, originally from Indiana, moved to the West Coast and are now playing the club circuit in Los Angeles. As lead vocalist Bobby Hickle says about their show, "We're very energetic, very fun. It's almost like going to the circus and the ringmaster has a machine gun."

Hap-Hazzard's demo *PSYCO-SYMATIC* cranks from cut to cut. The standout tracks are *'Shake, Don't Stir'* and *'Reminiscing Love.'* The demo is filled with great groove-filled rock. If any record companies need a good rock and roll act, check these guys out and sign them.

HAP-HAZZARD
 Michael deMarks: guitar and vocals
Brent Stoni: bass
Gary Nova: drums and percussions
Bobby Hickle: lead vocals

Fan club information: Big Time Production c/o Hazzard Patrol, 1147 E. Broadway, Ste 453, Glendale, CA 91203

Chapter 2

Gary and I worked the Hollywood club scene, going out every night of the week. We talked about our band to anybody who would listen. We made so many new friends that by the time we played our fourth show at the Troubadour, we were the headlining band.

A good and acrobatic band of brothers from Michigan called Lage opened for us, and local hotshots London closed the midnight slot. They were true rock-and-roll Hollywood bums with no jobs, they lived off of Hollywood women and slept in a motor-home.

The Troubadour was dark and mysterious; it reeked of pungent cologne and long-haired musicians trying to score with local chicks. It was mostly standing room on the main floor in front of the stage, with and a balcony going all the way around. There was a bar under the back balcony, where onlookers swilled drinks and fondled each other under the tables while making secret deals that would have been felonies anywhere else. But it was acceptable behavior in Hollywood, and no one feared being busted or even harassed.

We opened with the "Peter Gun Theme," hitting the stage like gangbusters. Our show got great reviews in all the local rock newspapers and started the ball rolling in the right direction. Guys in business suits were handing us business cards right and left, and girls were hanging all over us. I didn't know who I could trust, since everyone seemed so sincere.

In November 1987, we got really lucky and were picked up by a newly formed production company out of Burbank called Big Time Productions. Big Time Productions paid for us to record a new demo tape, and they also had connections at Capital Records.

Now that we had financial backing, every time we did a show it was advertised on L.A.'s number one radio station, KNAC. It gave me goose-bumps to finally hear our name over the airwaves. Meanwhile, a rock station in Missouri was playing "Reminiscing Love." It was getting requested all the time, and that was only because we had given one of our demo tapes to Joe Weber, a friend stationed in the military there. He got it on the radio station.

Before becoming rich and famous rock stars, though, we had to get jobs to pay for food, rent, and our beer habit. I wasn't going to mooch off of women, like so many Hollywood musicians. That was the norm. I was brought up to fend for myself and to be a man.

The first job we landed was really sweet. We passed out fliers for ten dollars an hour, working from nine in the morning until two in the afternoon. Bobby Lee, being a lazy lead singer, just threw his fliers in a dumpster so he could sit in a coffee shop. We all got fired, I was pissed!

Our band manager Gil Lopez, who went by the name Grant Stevens, also ran a telemarketing company in Los Angeles called Supply Distribution Center. Michael, Bobby Lee, and I went to work for Grant, while Gary went to work at McDonald's on Laurel Canyon and Venture Boulevard. Gary could speak both English and Spanish, so they made him manager within a week. They would have been better off saying, "Just take what you want and lock up when you're finished."

We all ate McDonald's until we could eat no more.

~~

The more we played in Hollywood, the more wild women came after us, making our apartment very crowded when it came time to go to bed. In the morning, I had to be very careful not to step on anyone sleeping on the floor or get anyone's clothes mixed up. There were carloads of horny sexy women, dressed to thrill, who came to Hollywood every weekend to do nothing but do guys with long, wild hair like they saw on MTV. There were ten women for every guy . . . great odds for getting lucky, if you had long hair. "Poser" were guys with long hair and the look, but weren't musicians. Real musicians, who practiced for many hard years, hated them for pretending. But they hung out just to score chicks.

We practiced every other day as a band at Atomic Sound in Burbank at a rate of fifty dollars an hour. The room had a sound-ready stage, including the lights. Many famous bands rehearsed there before going on tour or into the recording studio, making it a perfect place to make more music contacts.

On a daily basis, I was getting invited to more and more eccentric parties up in the Hollywood Hills and all over the Valley. The richer the party host, the more eccentric they were in entertaining their late-night guests. I attended a party where they had girls dressed in black thongs crawling around on all fours, offering themselves to the guests as "human ashtrays."

"What are they paying you?" I finally asked a girl named Fetish as the guy next to me ash his cigar into the crack of her ass. "Doesn't it hurt like hell?"

Fetish yelped. "Ouch! That's a big one. Twenty dollars an hour, and all the cocaine I want up my nose or my backside."

Every party I attended, people were constantly offering me cocaine and marijuana nonstop like there was an endless supply. I always turned down the drugs, causing people to look at me weird, like they couldn't believe I didn't want any. All the female guests at these parties could do as much nose candy as they could shove up their noses as long as they fucked somebody by the night's end. That wasn't a problem, as far as I could tell. Usually the girls were so high, they were just looking for a guy or girl to go down on. I had a girl almost chew through my underwear, she was so high.

From what I could tell, everyone in Hollywood had two very bad things in common. Everyone was on some type of illegal drug, and they were all into some type of black magick. Going to church was unheard of; it would have been a crime against Hollywood's unwritten laws of evil behavior.

Chapter 3

In December of 1987, IRS Records was showing some serious interest in signing our band to a recording deal.

Grant Stevens warned us, "This is a bad deal. If they make an offer, we shouldn't take it."

I asked, "Why not?"

"Record companies will sign a band at the end of the year," Grant explained, "but they won't invest any money or support the band."

"Why would they do that?"

"They'll just use you as a tax write-off."

I thought that was lower than rat's piss, but based on what I had seen of Hollywood, I wasn't surprised. We had put six years into this band, but to arrogant record executives, we were nothing more than numbers on a piece of paper.

Before signing a new band, especially a bunch of hicks from Indiana, a record company always checks them out. IRS Records appointed us a personal representative named Shelly Rears. Shelly was an attractive brunette in her mid-forties and spoke with a confident tone. She dressed very seductively, like a woman half her age.

"What's on for the evening?" Shelly asked as she kissed me on the cheek, while pinching my butt.

I hugged her back and cupped her seductive rear-end in my hands.

"Let's go to the Rainbow for dinner and drinks," I suggested.

"That sounds great. It'll be on the record company."

Gary and I replied, "Excellent! Let's get going."

When we stumbled into the apartment around three in the morning, Shelly opened her purse and pulled out a twenty-four-pack of condoms and three hits of ecstasy.

"Are you boys ready for the big time, or are you still farm boys pretending to be rock stars?" She asked with a seductive smile and a wink as she arched her back against the table.

I looked at Gary, and he looked back at me. We were both dumb founded.

She stood there waiting for an answer, looking very professional in her business attire.

I finally answered, "We're ready for the big time."

"Hell, yeah," Gary added.

With that challenge, I took my first hit of ecstasy. It was the first time I ever took any type of illegal, mind-altering drug.

"This is going to be really cool," Gary remarked with excitement.

I felt kind of weird and wasn't sure if I could perform. I couldn't even pee when another guy is standing next to me in the men's bathroom. Before I had a chance to back out, though, Shelly ripped off my belt and had my pants off, with her freshly powdered face buried in my crotch.

"Whoa, slow down," I stammered.

"I'll take the back half," replied Gary, as he pulled her dress off.

As the ecstasy started to kick in, 20 minutes later, I could feel my mindset starting to dramatically change. If I closed my eyes, nothing else going on around me mattered. It was like a blur and my hearing was highly effected.

"I want a turn in a few minutes," Gary said.

"It might be a while," I replied with a moan.

Gary, with his teeth, he pulled off her black g-string and tossed them up to me like a souvenir.

"What a nice ass," Gary remarked. I just nodded my head.

Gary smiled and playfully spanked her behind for five minutes, which only made her moan louder. She managed to moan loud enough so everyone could hear our sexual activities.

"Is everything all right in there?" Michael asked as he banged on the bedroom door with a laugh that followed.

"It's cool," I replied. "We will keep it down."

"It sounds like someone's being killed."

"No, just having a good time," Gary answered with a smart-ass laugh.

I had never seen such a high class woman turn into such a raging minx the minute the bedroom door was closed. She was the first woman I had been with who was seriously, and I mean seriously, into anal sex.

Sticking her derriere up in the air, she rubbed baby lotion onto herself and started begging, "Fuck my ass -- now!"

Gary said, "No problem."

"Show no mercy," Shelly begged.

For the next five hours, Gary and I would take turns pounding her rear-end until she came, over and over again as we would tag off like in pro wrestling.

"High five," Gary said as we slapped hands.

I couldn't believe how great I felt. I had never done drugs before, and this was just like a scene out of a Ginger Lynn Porno movie.

In the past, I had thought of back-road screwing as somewhat distasteful, I had never tried it but now I understood what a turn-on it was. It was tighter and felt like a good blowjob combined with the physical act of screwing.

The ecstasy allowed us to have sex for five hours straight. We used up the twenty-four-pack of condoms between the two of us.

The ecstasy transferred all our adrenaline to our sexual organs, making us sexual supermen.

"I'll see you boys later," Shelly said. "Thanks for the great evening."

We both smiled. Shelly blew us a kiss and was out the door with a bounce in her step.

"At least we don't have to worry about her being pregnant," Gary said.

"She'll be wearing Depends by fifty," I remarked.

We both laughed before passing out.

~~

While Gary and I were doing our part, Bobby Lee went to the Rainbow the next night and disappeared. Two weeks went by before we got a phone call.

Michael answered the phone. "Hello?"

"Miss me?"

"Where are you?"

"I'm in Denver," Bobby replied, "partying with my new girlfriend."

"When are you coming back?" Michael asked.

He didn't know when he was coming back; he wasn't in any hurry to get back to the couch in the living room. The thought of having to get a job had turned him off from Hollywood. He had never had to work, girls always supported him.

Michael and I had been putting up with him for almost six years. I'd had enough. We were so close to our ultimate goal, and I was watching our opportunity slip right past as fast as it came. IRS Records got tired of waiting and signed a band named Seduce, which got a slot in the movie <u>The Decline of Western Civilization</u>. That could have been us. I was pissed!

Michael, Gary, and I had a business meeting with Grant Stevens, our band manager.

"We seriously need to shop for a new singer," Grant said. "This type of behavior isn't professional and shouldn't be tolerated from anyone."

"I'm sick to death of Bobby's crap," I said. "I hate the motherfucker."

"I'm sick of kissing his ass, too," added Gary.

"I agree," replied Michael.

So it was agreed.

Grant spent a couple thousand dollars putting out huge ads in all the rocker magazines and newspapers all over the United States, without mentioning the name of the band. We didn't want Bobby to find out.

Grant got a lot of calls and a shit-load of tapes and pictures. Everyone in the country wanted to try out for a band in Hollywood. The singers who answered the ads couldn't sing a single note in key and were even more flakey than Bobby. They all looked great, but couldn't sing a single note in key.

"It looks like we're going to have to take Bobby back," I said to Michael.

"This really sucks."

"I know. I wanted to be rid of his lazy ass, too."

Bobby Lee moved back to Hollywood a couple of months later with his new girlfriend. He never knew we tried to replace him.

I just bit my tongue and welcomed him back.

Chapter 4

<u>Christmas Eve 1987</u>

Hollywood spared no expense in decorating Hollywood Boulevard with bright lights and Christmas trees all topped with fake snow, creating the impression of a winter wonderland. Everyone in Hollywood was trying to use the Christmas season to their advantage; even the street people were dressing like Santa in hopes of scamming some goodwill cheer.

We had the best table at the Rainbow, right in front of the fireplace. The fire blazed. We ordered the Rainbow's famous Italian pizza and gulped down ice-cold Michelob out of fancy glasses like millionaires. After dinner, we ventured upstairs into the Rainbow's loft, wishing Clarence a Merry Christmas. Clarence nodded his head in return without cracking a smile, but it was understood that he meant "Merry Christmas."

The Rainbow had quite a history and high-class clientele. Everyone in the music business could be seen having dinner or getting drunk on a regular basic without the media bothering them. It wasn't permitted. John Belushi ate his last meal at the Rainbow, more than likely scoring the drugs at the Rainbow that he overdosed on.

Most nights after ten o'clock, a line formed to get in, and it wasn't just for the food. The Rainbow also doubled as a human meat market.

It didn't look like much from the outside -- just a small, red neon sign with a small parking lot, sharing the limited spaces with the Roxy next door. The entrance was a small door on the side of the building, where Steady the doorman, who was always cool and friendly, asked the men for ten dollars. Females, if somewhat attractive, would easily slide through for free and could count on rich men buying them drinks for the rest of the evening. Guys had to be twenty-one to get in. There was no age limit on the women as far as I could see, as long as they weren't wearing braces. On many occasions, I met girls seventeen or eighteen upstairs in the loft, just giving their asses away for the next line of cocaine.

Once inside, there was three choice: turn right for the downstairs bar, go straight back into the kitchen for a private table, or turn left into the downstairs dining room. In the dining room, a wall-sized fireplace faced forty assorted table and booths done in red leather. On the walls hung many framed pictures of famous rock and movie stars hanging out at the Rainbow before they were famous and after they had made it big.

Around the corner behind the fireplace was a set of stairs that led up into a world of deception, sin, perversion, and acts of debauchery, better known as the Rainbow loft.

The stairs leading up to the loft was decorated like an old pirate ship, with mess nets hanging from the walls and ceiling.

To get into the loft, you had to pay Clarence another ten dollars to get by him. Clarence was a 7'2" black Superman, and when he spoke, everyone stopped and listened, even in their most drunken state.

Clarence seldom spoke; he usually just stood there like a giant statue and nodded his head. On a rare occasion, he had to reach into the crowd to straighten out someone from out of town who was being unruly. Anyone who lived in Hollywood knew better.

The loft was rather small, not much bigger than my parents' basement. It featured a sunken dance floor and a private room above the dance floor, overlooking the rest of the bar, for rent at a hundred dollars a table upon reservation. The dance floor was usually crammed with at least a hundred people, sweating and rubbing up against each other without a single inch of space to breathe.

I found out fast that once you were under the Rainbow, you were in another world, with no rules or moral values.

That was why I loved it.

All the women in the Rainbow were fair game; they all had the same thoughts about sex as the men. The women -- or should I say, the vixens -- wore as little as possible, usually skin tight black leather miniskirts with fishnet stockings and high heels. If they wore underwear at all, it was only a g-string, and they often flashed each other on the dance floor to get the sexual excitement brewing even hotter.

Working my way through the crowd, I ordered my first drink from Apache, my favorite waitress. Before I could finish it, a drop-dead gorgeous blonde resembling Marilyn Monroe sidled up to me in her skin tight black miniskirt. She was so close, I could smell her lipstick.

"Do you want to slow dance?" she seductively asked.

I thought, <u>No, I'd like to do something else</u>, but instead I replied, "Yes."

Her name was Jenny; she was in town stripping at the Body Shop for the holiday season. She was a stocking stuffer, all right. Jenny was from Oceanside, California, and was traveling with her girlfriend Birdie, who, unbelievably, was from my hometown. Since everyone in Hollywood was a liar, I didn't believe her at first.

"Look," Birdie said, showing me her Indiana driver's license. She wasn't lying, so we bonded instantly: two Indiana kids in a big, strange and fucked-up city.

After a couple of dances, Jenny and I went downstairs and took a seat at the bar. We downed two more Long Island iced teas before I grabbed Patty by the arm and said, "Get me a can of whipped cream."

We finished our drinks and stumbled out of the Rainbow onto the

Sunset Strip. We headed toward Gill's Liquor store, then down to my green Ford van, parked on Dolheny Avenue.

We climbed into the back; it had tinted windows and was private. I locked the doors and slid my Colt .380 under the seat within reach.

With a kinky look, Jenny said, "Give me the can."

While I quickly undressed, she took the can of whipped cream and filled her black lace panties until they were expanded like a cream filled pastry. Jenny, being the aggressor, grabbed me by the back of head and pulled me into a lap dive.

Before I could eat half a pie, the inside of the van lit up as if Rudolf the red-nosed reindeer had landed on the hood with good old fat Saint Nick.

I came up with whipped cream all over my face and said, "What the fuck is going on?" I thought it was some wise guys messing around. I started to reach for my gun, but then I heard the authority in their voices and realized I was having my first encounter with the LAPD -- and I had my pants down.

Banging on the van, they demanded, "Open the door, now!"

I yanked my pants up and unlocked the van door. They pulled the door open and shined their flashlights on us. The two cops had their 9mm pistols drawn.

Both started laughing and holstered their weapons.

"Don't you look stupid," said one of them.

"Yes, I do." I replied.

The cops were really cool from that point forward. I was surprised; their mentality was quite the opposite of Indiana law enforcement.

"Get dressed, go back to the club, and sober up before attempting to drive."

"Yes, officers."

They both chuckled to each other as they walked back to their cruiser parked around the corner. They were just fucking with us.

When Jenny and I returned to the Rainbow, Steady the doorman passed us through the front door very quickly, asking, "Did you have a good time?"

As soon as we got inside, we darted past the bar and through the kitchen to the private bathroom. While standing in line, I noticed that Jenny had whipped cream running down her legs and I had whipped cream in my hair and on the front of my pants. Now I knew why everyone outside was laughing.

~~

At the end of the evening, around 2:00 in the morning, Jenny asked, "Can Birdie and I spend the holiday with you?"

I thought about it.

"We'll make it worth your while," she added.

"Alright. Let's go!"

When I pulled the van up in front of the Rainbow, the girls were waiting with two huge traveling trunks filled with stripper clothes and sex toys.

"Have trunks, will travel."

I didn't know they meant to move in.

I had threesomes every night for the next month. The girls cleaned and made dinner every night for everyone in the apartment. It was the rock-and-roll lifestyle dream come true. Hell, I was a virgin 4 years ago.

Jenny was the first girl I had been with who shaved her vagina completely clean -- not even a landing strip or a forehead rest. Girls back where I came from didn't do this, it was unheard of. I didn't like it at first, but it grew on me and is now the norm.

Having sex with bisexuals definitely made me a better lover with more understanding of the female body. Since they were both completely shaved, it was much easier to find the right spots. If I didn't find the right spot, they would make sure I did.

When the girls came home after stripping, they headed straight for the bedroom, dropping clothes along the way.

The first time I went down on Jenny, she said, "Let Birdie teach you the right way." I hadn't realized I was doing it the wrong way, so I swallowed my Leo pride and listened and learned. I guess I wasn't as good as I thought. It was a little knock to the ego, but I listened. Birdie taught me to first give the love-muffin gentle loving kisses, followed by a stiff, yet tender, flickering tongue.

"You must warm it up," Birdie instructed, "instead of just diving in face-first like a drunk driver. Don't be shy about sticking your tongue in her cute little backdoor either."

I laughed to myself. I was usually drunk when I had sex; the two always happened at the same time.

They stayed for a couple of weeks, until a drug dealer from Hollywood named Wolf picked them up.

"Have trunks, will Travel."

I would hook up with them off and on for the next ten years.

Chapter 5

<u>March 1988</u>

We finished recording our second CD, <u>Pocket Rocket,</u> with the financial help of Big Time Productions. When the CD was finished, we started playing the Hollywood club scene again. Our first show out was at the Whiskey-a-Go-Go on Friday night, a prime spot for any band in Hollywood. The show went great, and it felt good to be playing out again. This was my dream and the only reason I had come to Hollywood. I could see no other reason for being here.

After the show, still wearing my black leather pants, I stopped at the Rainbow to have a few more beers and to invite more girls back to the apartment for heavy drinking and petting until the wee hours of the morning. Later, staggering out of the Rainbow with a hell of a buzz, I heard a snide remark from a familiar, annoying voice.

"What, no strippers or Rainbow girls tonight? You must be slipping."

Turning, I almost told her to fuck off, but since I was in a really good mood, I stopped myself and answered, "No, unless you're willing to come home with me."

"Dream on," she replied. "You've been with too many Rainbow girls."

Her name was Angel Ray. Her long brown hair was hair-sprayed bigger than mine, and she couldn't have been more than 5'2" and a hundred pounds when wet. <u>What a little shit</u>, I thought, and came up with a smart-ass comeback.

"What makes you any different? You're standing in front of the Rainbow."

"Just for your information," she snapped, "I have never been in the Rainbow, and I don't have one-night-stands. But my friends do. Maybe you can score with one of them."

She stood there staring at me defiantly. I already knew everything about her two friends, Terri and Wendy. They were both into band guys and had fucked Gary on many occasions. Wendy had once told me, "I'm not afraid of getting AIDS. I hate condoms, and I'm very confident . . . I know what AIDS looks like."

"We'll put that on your tombstone," I'd replied.

"We loved your show at the Whiskey," Terri was saying. "You guys rocked."

"Thanks," I replied.

"You were all right," Angel said, "I've seen better."

Paying no attention to Angel, I said to Wendy and Terri, "There's a party going on at my apartment in Studio City. You're welcome to come, and you can bring her if you want." I jabbed my thumb at Angel. She gave me a snide look back.

I thought Angel was a little cutie; she didn't dress like a tramp and was always looking for a reason to backtalk me. I didn't mind her ribbing . . . it was cute.

I can't remember how it happened, but somehow, by the time the sun had come up, I had slept with Angel and promised to call her during the week.

Of course, I didn't.

By the next weekend, I was back at the Rainbow for my weekly fix; it was my Hollywood addiction. As Gary and I stumbled out of the Rainbow onto the Sunset Strip with a stripper under each arm, I saw Angel coming toward me. She had just exited the Whiskey-a-Go-Go. I pretended to not see her.

She let me know she wasn't too happy by punching me in the chest with her bony knuckles, without breaking her stride.

"Did that girl just punch you?" the stripper asked.

Thinking quickly, I replied, "That was just my younger sister screwing around. We play that way." Meanwhile, I was thinking, What a little shit. I almost felt guilty, but I was already committed for the evening and wasn't going to turn down a chance to drive in the fast lane.

By the next weekend, however, I was walking up and down the Sunset Strip, looking for Angel. I just couldn't get her off my mind. Finally I spotted her hanging out in front of the Roxy. There she was, all decked out and ready for an evening on the Sunset Strip. Spiked hair, short dress, attitude and heels to rock.

I came up behind her and gently stuck the chrome tip of my cowboy boot in the crack of her butt, giving her a Hollywood goosing.

"Hey! You asshole! Watch where you put that thing."

She tried to smack me playfully, but I managed to grab her and hold on until she had cooled off long enough for me to give her a kiss on the cheek. She smelled wonderful.

"Yuck. Hope I don't catch anything," she said.

I could only reply in a smart-ass tone, "It ain't easy being' sleazy."

Terri started to give me shit, until I reminded her of her own Hollywood reputation as the queen of blow-jobs. She went silent.

I could tell Angel was different from the rest of the Hollywood girls. She was intelligent and didn't use drugs or drink. That was very uncommon in Hollywood. I also knew she wouldn't take any of my crap, and for some reason, that attracted me. Maybe I was ready for a normal girlfriend, or at least one who only took her clothes off for me.

As time went by and I got to know Angel, I found out she went to school part-time and cut hair at a salon during the day in Pomona. She was eighteen and had just rented her first one-bedroom apartment with two stinky cats.

Angel's father was a retired Air Force colonel who had served twenty-eight years with military intelligence. Angel had been born in Germany on a military base. That made her an Air Force brat.

The first time I met her parents, I could tell her father didn't like me, and I wasn't surprised.

"Don't take it personal," Angel said. "It's the hair and the idea that you might be screwing his precious little Angel." I was, and I understood. In time we would become good friends.

Angel's younger sister was a cutie, and her younger brother Scooter and I became lifelong friends. We both played guitar and studied martial arts, so I always had something new to show him.

Angel's mother liked me instantly, even though my answer to her first question was a lie. She asked me, "Why are you wearing a patch over your eye?"

"I got an infection from a dirty contact lens I didn't wash properly," I answered. In reality, I had passed out while going down on her daughter and awoke the next afternoon with my eye swollen shut.

The eye doctor removed the pubic hair and said to Angel, "I think this is yours."

I laughed . . . She blushed.

Since I enjoyed eating muff pie and Angel didn't want to date a guy who looked like a pirate, I got out the razor and shaving cream once we got home and taught her a new trick I had learned from Birdie.

Since Angel lived in Rancho Cucamonga, sixty miles east of Los Angeles, I could only see her on the weekends. With the heavy traffic and chances of gridlock, the drive could take anywhere from an hour to six hours, if there was an accident.

During the week, I was still trying to earn a living. The telephone sales job wasn't going very well. I was only making $150 a week, and my savings account was slowly dwindling down, since I was paying most of the bills around the band apartment.

Since the phone job didn't look like it was going to pan out, I went on a few welding job interviews. I turned down three jobs in a row. I had been making fourteen dollars an hour back in Chicago, I was a union boilermaker, all position welder and the best offer I was getting now was six-fifty an hour.

When I looked around the shipyards and the welding shops, all I saw were illegal aliens working for minimum wage. I would be damned if I was going to weld in the extreme heat for chump change, risking my life and eyesight. It made me cop a real shit attitude towards Los Angeles.

It was hard to make any real money at Grant's company; he did everything by the book, making everyone follow the sales pitch perfectly. If you didn't follow the pitch, you were fired. The calls were taped and monitored by the office manager. When it comes to sales, truth isn't usually involved.

Hanging out at the Rainbow, I got an offer from another telemarketing company. The salesmen who worked there said, "We can say anything we want to get the sale."

Their company didn't follow the telemarketing rules or laws; the money came first, and the consequences later.

"How much money do you guys make?" I asked.

"Enough, that I could wipe my butt with dollar bills."

"Then I'm interested."

"Welcome to the circle."

Chapter 6

Copy Supply Warehouse was located on La Brea and Olympic Boulevard. The customers, or should I say victims, in the business world referred to us as "toner pirates" or "toner phonier," along with many other nasty words. This business was known as a "boiler room."

Toner, for anyone who doesn't know, is the dry black ink poured into photocopiers; it also comes in cartridge form. It was worth its weight in gold, the way we marketed it -- or should I say, crammed it down the customers' throats.

Selling toner was the perfect job for a Hollywood musician; we only worked five hours a day. The only drawback was that we had to be there at 6:00 in the morning. The alarm would go off at 5:15, and I would roll out of bed, throw on some shorts and a tank top, brush my teeth, pull my hair back into a ponytail, pop in four earrings, and put on my lucky baseball cap that read, "Mustaches ride for free -- no fat chicks." I had to be out the door by 5:30, just in time to beat the traffic jam on the 101 Hollywood Freeway. If I was ten minutes late getting on the road, I could be stuck in traffic for hours. The average speed of a car in Los Angeles during the morning rush was only eleven miles per hour.

Once I got to work, they always had fresh, hot coffee with boxes of sugar donuts covered in rich chocolate to boost the sales peoples' energy levels. Many of them were popping speeders or doing lines of cocaine to jump-start their systems, but hot coffee and fresh donuts were enough to get me wired.

My first day at Copy Supply Warehouse was a real trip. Rob, the manager, was standing out in front of the building drinking a beer at 6:00 in the morning. He looked like he had been up all night and smelled of stale sex.

"So, you're B," he said. "I've heard a lot about you." He shook my hand and, after wiping his mouth, added, "Welcome to the family."

"It's great to be working here," I replied as I took a look around the parking lot filled with cars I could only dream of owning.

"Forget everything you learned at Grant's company. We do it completely different around here."

To make me feel right at home, Rob gave me a desk with a huge leather swivel chair right next to the window on the top floor, with a great view of downtown Los Angeles. It made a country boy feel real important, and I mean real important.

As I was looking around the office and taking everything in, Rob handed me an application. I started to fill it out, but Rob stopped me and said, "Don't use your real name or address. This is just in case someone asks."

I looked at him kind of funny. "Seriously?"

"Yeah, seriously!"

Nod-nod, wink-wink, and I understood.

Rob tore up the first application and gave me a new one. "Make up a fake name. Use a name that you feel comfortable saying on the telephone."

"Okay." I felt like I was selling my soul.

This was the first time in my life I had ever used a fake name. I chose Bill Davis.

"What about taxes?" I asked. "I don't want to get fucked at the end of the year."

Rob just laughed, like I was stupid for not knowing the rules of the game. "Don't worry about it. You'll change your name next year. My name isn't even Rob." He continued laughing as he walked away, sharing the joke with other people in the office. They looked at me and laughed as well.

Sitting at my new desk, feeling stupid for not understanding the rules, I started looking around the office. The room was filled with hot-looking rock-and-roll chicks and other Hollywood musicians I recognized from the Sunset Strip. The downstairs office was packed with bubble-blowing chicks dressed in miniskirts. All these girls wanted to be models and actresses and were waiting for their big break . . . much like myself.

I found all this a bit weird. I wasn't sure if I was ready to start messing around with the government. I didn't want to get into serious trouble and considered not coming back after the first day. Pulling pranks and stupid jokes was one thing, but being part of a criminal network was another.

Sitting back and watching everyone make money all day, I just couldn't believe the money that was being handed out like sheets of toilet paper. The owner and boss, Mickey Rathe, walked around with $30,000 in his front pocket like it was chump change. Never in my life had I seen such a huge wad of cash being handled like it was nothing. He gave cash to people as they got their sales, just to make everyone work faster. He handed out ten dollars in the morning for breakfast, ten dollars for being on time, and ten dollars for lunch. The funny thing was, we went home before lunch.

I think the man actually liked handing out money; it made him smile.

~~

Roland Mackay was the trainer; I spent a week listening to him pitch over the telephone with an extra headset. Roland made sale after sale with just the right amount of confidence in his voice and by being very pushy.

Rob, the office manager, told me, "There are around five-hundred different models of photocopiers out on the market. Learn them." He handed me a thick book with all the listings.

In time, I memorized every number and could recite anything about the copier and the special features that made it work, just like one of the repairmen who worked on them. After two weeks of training, I got settled into my new desk. As I eased back in my leather chair, Rob handed me the legal sales pitch authorized by the Better Business Bureau.

I looked at Rob expectantly.

"Hang it up next to your phone and forget about it," he instructed.

"What the hell does that mean?" I asked.

"It's just for show," he replied. "Got it?"

Seeing how things worked around here, I said, "Got it!"

With the legal sales pitch, we wouldn't have made any money. We were supposed to inform the customers that we were calling from Southern California and tell them the real name of the company. Usually, if they heard "California," they would hang up or say, "We buy locally."

I can remember my first phone call. I was scared to death; I think I hung up without even pitching. I knew what I was doing was morally wrong. During this period in my life, I still believed in Heaven and in a place called Hell. Any way I looked at it, I just knew this activity was wrong. In time, however, I convinced myself it was cool, as the money corrupted my soul.

I started out at 6:15 a.m. calling the East Coast. They were three hours ahead and already into their day, but still somewhat asleep. I called business offices first: doctors, insurance companies, and my personal favorite, banks.

While the phone was ringing, I thought out my sales pitch.

"Hello, law offices of Howard, Fine, and Howard. How can I help you?"

"Hi," I said. "This is Bill Davis calling about the photocopier. How are you doing today?"

"Good morning, Bill," the secretary replied. "What can I do for you?"

"I need to find out how much toner you have on hand for the photocopier," I asked politely. "Can you take a look in the cabinet?"

When calling, I had no way of actually knowing if the business had a copier. It was a hit-or-miss pitch.

If they said, "We don't have a copier," we were instructed to slam down the phone in their ear. It was just tradition around the office. The sound of slamming phones brought laughter and lifted our spirits.

While waiting for the secretary to check the photocopier, I prepared to continue the sales pitch.

"We have four bottles of the dry ink," she said.

Even if she said "ten bottles," I responded the same way. "Then I'm glad I called, because the price of the toner is about to go out of sight. I'm going to send you a couple of boxes at the old price, that way you'll be stocked up for quite a while."

"Thanks, Bill. Have a nice day."

"You're welcome. You, too."

Sometimes it was that easy. Most of the time, however, the calls went like this:

"Hello, this is Bill Davis calling about the copier --"

"We don't have a copier. Take us off your list, asshole!" Then they slammed down the phone in <u>my</u> ear.

To get the business accounts, I used out-of-state phone books. I would go down the list, crossing them off as I went and making notes about the business on index cards for future use.

We were supposed to ask for the person in charge of ordering, but I didn't, in case they knew what was going on. Instead, I pitched to the first lackey who answered the phone. I never gave out the name of our company, unless they bought toner. Otherwise, they had no idea where we were calling from.

By the second week, I was making a thousand dollars in cash. After that first thousand, I really got into the job and looked forward to going to work every morning. It felt a little strange and rather cool at the same time to be carrying a black briefcase like a lawyer. Once I got known around the office, I began competing to try to out-sell the other salesmen.

On Wednesday, all the salesmen in the office would have a contest to see how many times in a single conversation with a female customer we could tell her to "bend over." The female salesman did it too. We had to say it in such a sweet and innocent way that the secretaries wouldn't catch on.

"Hello, this is Bill Davis calling about the photocopier."

"Hi, Bill. What can I do for you?"

"Could you bend over and check to see how much toner is in the cabinet under the machine?"

"All right . . . Two bottles."

"Thank you. Could you also bend over and double-check the model number for me?" And so it went.

Out of the hundreds of times I did it, only once did a secretary stop and ask, "Did you just tell me to bend over?" I started laughing. "You did," she snapped. "While I'm bent over, maybe you can kiss my ass!"

"If you come to Hollywood," I replied, "I'm sure someone will want to fuck it!"

She slammed down the phone.

John Shell had the office record; he had managed to say it twenty-five times during one conversation before getting caught. Sure, the game was totally childish, but it was fun and paid very well. The boss encouraged it for office morale. We were a couple of thousand miles away, so we felt safe that the people we made mad weren't going to show up and beat the hell out of us.

There were six toner companies hidden in Hollywood that were selling toner in this fashion. All of them were part of a Hungarian Mafia. All the secretaries thought it was the same guy calling all the time and would threaten to call the police. We just laughed. If we got someone on the telephone whose insults and arguing were really entertaining, we would call several times a week just to get a rise out of them.

It was a well-known fact in the sales world that people in New York were the rudest and the hardest to sell; they would tell you to fuck off or threaten to shove the bottle of toner up your ass. Southerners were a bit on the slow side, falling time and time again for different scams. The people of the great state of Texas were the most hostile. One guy from Dallas said, "If you ever call here again, I'll give you a Texas chili bowl."

I had to ask. "What is a Texas chili bowl?"

"It involves hot sauce, your telephone, and your anus."

I laughed. I got others to call him back for fun.

All the phone lines leaving the building went through a computer system that made the calls untraceable. The phones in the sales office were reprogrammed every morning with a new code. Copy Supply Warehouse employed computer hackers to supply them with stolen phone card numbers. All the calls we were making were charged to some huge corporation's phone bill. The computer hackers also hacked into Xerox, Cannon, Minolta, Sanyo, and other photocopier companies and retrieved sales records of who had bought which copiers and their model numbers. That would give us more of an edge when we called, since we already had the information we could easily pull off the act of their supplier.

If someone asked, "Are you with Xerox?" I would just hang up. I never lied, if asked; I just talked as if I knew what the hell I was talking about. I never wanted to get caught lying on a phone line that could be tapped by federal agents. As long as I never outright lied, I could never be charged with a crime. But I could talk as if I worked for Xerox.

I would say things like, "How's that machine running for you?" and "That's a really nice unit. It's the same one we have in our main office. But I have to give ours a kick every now and then." That would usually get a laugh.

One office lady said, "The machine isn't running right. What should I do? You did a shit job last time you worked on the copier." She thought I was the repair guy who had worked on the machine last.

Feeling like being a little shit that morning, I replied, "If I were you, I'd get a hammer from one of the guys in shipping and give the machine a couple smacks on the side. That should loosen up any toner that might be stuck."

"Okay." She put down the phone, and I could hear her walking down the hallway. A few minutes passed before she picked the phone up again and said, "I have the hammer. Where do you want me to hit it?" By this time, I had her on speaker phone, and everyone was listening.

"Hit it on the side of the machine."

"All right, if you say so . . ."

Bang, bang, bang, bang, CRASH!

"Hello, Bill."

"What was that?" I asked.

"I smashed the glass top by accident."

Everyone in the office was rolling on the floor. No one could believe I had actually talked someone into beating their copier with a hammer. I couldn't believe it myself.

Deciding to take it one step further, I asked, "Is it running any better?"

"No," she replied. "The copies still look too light."

Trying not to laugh, I suggested, "Get those guys in the shipping department to help you turn the copier on its side to loosen up the dry toner."

"Are you sure?"

"I'm sure, or my name isn't Bill Davis."

"All right, I'll get the guys."

A few minutes passed. Everyone in the office was gathered around the phone to see how far I could take it.

Finally, a man picked up the phone and said, "You want us to do what?"

"I need you to turn the copier on its side and whack it with a hammer to loosen up the dry toner. Haven't you done this before?" I made him feel stupid for even asking the question.

I had to keep the mute button on; everyone in the office was rolling on the floor.

"Turn it on its side," the guy said to the other employees.

They got the copier on its side, and I could hear them arguing. The secretary picked up the phone and said, "What should I do now?"

"Hit that thing," I replied. "Stop screwing around."

She hit the copier several times, and I yelled through the phone, "Hit that thing harder!"

CRASH!

She picked up the phone. "They dropped the machine, and it smashed."

"What do you mean, it smashed?"

"It's all messed up now and leaking fluids."

Holding the mute button down, I laughed until tears flowed out of my eyes. Regaining my composure, I let up on the mute button.

"See the number on the side of the machine, where it says 'service'?" I asked.

"Yes."

"Call that number, and they'll come out and fix it properly."

"Thanks, Bill."

"No problem. Glad to be of help."

I thought I'm going straight to hell for that one.

~~

The toner we were selling was the real stuff; it was just marked up to an unbelievable price. They could probably get a box of toner from their local supplier for fifty dollars a box, and we were selling it to them for $298.50, plus shipping.

"Plus shipping" always made me laugh.

The major photocopier manufactures sent out notices to their customers, warning them about the "toner pirates." The TV show 60 Minutes even ran a special about it. I thought we would be out of business when I read the article in Time, but it hardly made a dent. I couldn't believe that after all the attention, people would still fall for the scam . . . but I was wrong. Everyone I sold to had at least a four-year college degree.

Since we were buying toner directly from the manufacturers by the semi-truckload, it wasn't too hard to figure out who the toner pirates were. They still sold to us. It was comically, they were as much in on it as us.

This scam had already been going on for fifteen years before I got to Hollywood. I would have thought that after the first time a company got burned, they would wise up and not get hit again . . . but again, I was wrong, underestimating the general public's stupidity.

I sold to one lady named Betty at a lawyer's office a couple of times before she realized she was paying way too much for her toner. The last time I called her, she was really mad and told me not to call again before hanging up. I thought, Good for her -- someone with an actual brain. I marked down in Betty's account file that she was hip to the deal. I set her account to the side and tried back every few months to see if someone new had taken over her position. Finally, after I had called about a dozen times, someone new answered the phone.

"Is Betty there?" I asked. If Betty came to the phone, I just hung up. But this time, a new girl answered, "She doesn't work here anymore. Can I help you?"

Bingo!

"This is Bill Davis. I'm calling about the Xerox 1065 photocopier -- you know, the photocopier in the office by the water cooler."

"Yes, all right. How can I help you?"

"I was just calling Betty to inform her that the back-order of toner has come in and is being shipped today."

"Betty didn't tell me about this."

"She placed it a couple of months ago. I'll just mark the order to your attention."

"That would be fine."

Since I had used Betty's name and already had all the information about her photocopier, I could send her four boxes. My commission would be

$300 in cash that day -- in my pocket.

Within a couple of months, I was making thousands a week and quickly becoming the star salesman. In time, I could look around the office and tell who were the better salespeople just by the way they held the phone. Anyone who held their phone in their right hand and put it to the left ear or vice versa was usually lazy, while those who cradled the phone so they could write while talking were the good salesmen.

In the back, behind the sales office, there was a room of employees who did all the re-loads of accounts that had paid more than twice. They pitched to the office managers by offering them a free gift for their business. This was a pay- off, and certain office managers were in on the deal. Mickey Rathe, the owner of the company, would send them free tickets to Hawaii or free TVs just to keep the moochers on the hook. Mickey sent the gifts to their home addresses.

The computer hackers who worked for our company made up profiles on the office buyers so we would know how far they would go before blowing the whistle. We had files with all of their personal information, including a driver's license photo. We knew what these people looked like, which gave us another edge. I kept thinking this invasion of privacy must be illegal, but everyone around the office acted like it was normal.

The only thing that helped my conscience was that when it came to the toner, none of the customers had to pay for it if they chose not to. We had no written contracts and were in no position to take anyone to court. If they had the balls or the brains, they could have had it for free. I sent my cousin in New York toner for years and told him not to bother paying for it. He didn't.

Another rule I kept to help my conscience was that I only scammed the big, evil corporations . . . no little guys. I knew the companies I was calling could afford it and would fuck anyone the first chance they got. I'm talking about companies like State Farm, Allstate, Firestone, Banks, and so on.

Copy Supply Warehouse wasn't just a job; it was a meeting point for some of the greatest criminal minds in Hollywood to gather and recruit new membership. Through Copy Supply Warehouse, I met big-time players who worked out of the Rainbow, which became their personal office where they conducted illegal activities. I hadn't noticed these people in the past; I was there for the women. But the evil noticed me.

~~

Alexis had long, jet-black hair spiked eight inches off the top of his head. He wore enough make-up to be in the rock band Kiss, as long as it didn't rain. His business activities consisted of selling cocaine and making fake birth certificates. That enabled anyone who had gotten in trouble for getting high to change their identity as easy as they changed their underwear -- if anyone in

Hollywood wore any. The Rainbow loft was his office. As I got to know Alexis, I found out he had a connection at one of the hospitals. In exchange for cocaine, his connection gave him birth certificates with all the information on dead newborns.

Alexis was the type of guy who would say or do anything to get a chick into bed. He had every type of business card in the world in his wallet. On different occasions, I heard him claim to be a movie scout for MGM, owner of a modeling agency, and a music producer. Once the girls found out he was a fake, they would want to kick his ass -- or worse.

One night, while we were drinking in the loft at the Rainbow, a pissed-off female set the back of his coat on fire and threw a drink in his face, causing his make-up to run.

Another angry woman drove up on the sidewalk and ran him down one evening. That explained his limp and the cane.

Alexis was a guy's guy; he knew all the ins and outs of Hollywood. He was cool to you if you were a guy . . . as long as you knew a lot of chicks.

"If you like the Rainbow, you're going to love this other club I hang out at."

"Let's go," I replied.

"Follow me. I'll show you where to get a membership card."

I became a member that night, and my membership card got me in the door for free.

The *Cathouse* was only open one night of the week: Tuesday. It was owned by Taime Downs, the lead singer of Faster Pussycat and his partner Rickie Rackman, lead singer of the band Virgin and host of the MTV head-bangers' ball. I saw many famous rock bands play there, including Guns n' Roses, while Hollywood actors like Mickey Rourke and Nicholas Cage watched from the crowd, standing right next to me. Axle Rose and Vince Neil sang a song together.

The Hollywood clubs all had bright lights and plenty of flare and glamour, but the neighborhoods surrounding most of them were places where you wouldn't want your car to break down. Freaks and the mentally ill hung out on the famous Hollywood Walk of Fame on Hollywood Boulevard, where all the famous movie stars had their names encased in gold stars on the sidewalk. It was a total tourist trap with all the Hollywood stores and was somewhat safe during the daylight hours, if you were careful to guard against pickpockets. After dark, however, it resembled a scene out of Night of the Living Dead with all the crack-heads walking up and down the side streets off Hollywood Boulevard like zombies trying to find a dealer with the best deal for the buck.

Don't get me wrong; there were plenty of live demonstrations of insanity during the day for out-of-towners looking for photo opportunities. Usually by noon, a lunatic dressed like a priest -- and he might have even been a real priest -- would appear in front of the Scientology building on Hollywood Boulevard and scream verses straight out of the Bible at you if you dared to walk anywhere near him or make eye contact.

The priest had competition on the north side of Hollywood Boulevard. Another lunatic walked up and down the street carrying a huge wooden cross on his back like Jesus, except that his cross wasn't nailed on and it had rollers on the bottom to help with the weight -- making him a cheater in my book.

There was also the Button Lady, who was covered with thousands of pins and buttons from head to toe that flashed as she walked up and down Hollywood Boulevard twenty-four hours a day, talking to herself.

In front of Manns Chinese Theatre was an older, weathered-looking fellow in dark glasses, playing guitar for loose change from tourists. He never said he was blind; he just sat there and let everyone assume. He made about $300 a day.

Out in the Valley there was one group of homeless people who worked out of Studio City. I referred to them as the "Gasoline Gang." The Gasoline Gang would hang out on the corner of Vineland and Ventura Boulevard with an empty gas can, asking for money. Their sales pitch was, "Our car ran out of gas, and we need to get home. Our baby is alone."

I gave them five dollars the first time, before I found out they didn't have a baby or a car; they lived under the overpass of the 101 Freeway and Vineland. The second time, I gave them a hundred dollars and a sack of clothes the band members had donated.

Hundreds, maybe thousands, of homeless people lived in Hollywood behind all the glamour. Some of the homeless were angry at the world and quite dangerous, while others were just down on their luck, living out their last days hand-to-mouth. Most of them had watched their dreams get crushed by the meat-grinder known as Hollywood. Their souls had been stolen, and only an outer shell remained. In many ways, they were already dead. They were just waiting for the Reaper. It would be the only bright light in their life.

Chapter 7

Because of certain laws, Los Angeles became known as the "boiler room" capital of the United States. They were known as boiler rooms because in the beginning years of telemarketing, they set up the telephone rooms in the boiler rooms of office buildings. They hid the telemarketing operation from the public while tapping into business phone lines and making the calls for free. Everyone coming to work at a boiler room operation had to do it in secret, sneaking in and out of the building to avoid drawing unwanted attention. Now they were so bold they set them up in big fancy offices and passed them off as legal businesses.

Anywhere else in the country, long-haired white guys were treated like losers, unless they were rich enough to shove it back down people's throats. But at Copy Supply Warehouse, we were treated with all the respect in the world. The Hungarian crime family saw past the long hair and learned to tap into a good source of loyal employees. All the long-haired musicians spoke professionally, and the people on the other end of the line had no idea what they looked like. They probably had no doubt that they were talking to guys with college degrees and short hair, dressed in suits.

As far as the job was concerned, I was happy and having a good time, but the apartment life and the band were another matter. Bobby's new girlfriend hadn't put up with his lazy ass and bad attitude for long. She got rid of the deadbeat, and he moved back in with us. When I heard he was coming back, I was sick -- sick of his crap. I couldn't stand seeing him lying around all day, doing nothing but eating all my food and drinking everything in sight. He used three clean towels every day without ever offering to do laundry.

On top of it all, he was being a total dick-smack. In his mind, Bobby thought he was David Lee Roth. I hated to inform him that everyone in Hollywood was sick of David Lee Roth's crap also and didn't need a replacement.

After he moved back in, I started being a dick-smack right back to him. But Bobby went to work on Grant, the owner of Big Time Productions, kissing his ass in just the right places and making it very hard for me to voice my opinion during band meetings. Six months earlier, Grant had thought Bobby was a lazy piece of human shit, but now they were cocaine party buddies. Grant had the drugs, and Bobby had the chicks.

When I told Grant I thought he was a fucker for bringing cocaine around, it didn't go over too well. I pissed off Grant. I didn't care.

~~

On June 1, 1988, Angel took the summer off from school and moved to North Hollywood to share an apartment with a girl from Germany she had grown up with. I got both of them jobs at Copy Supply Warehouse in the downstairs office, doing filing.

After Angel had been working there a week, she said, "Do you know what kind of people we're working for?"

"I have a weird feeling."

"They're making a couple hundred thousand dollars a day or more."

"Just from the toner?"

"That, and they're also taking bets on dog races and ponies." In a whisper, she added, "They have a guy who does the serious collections, and he looks like a real nutcase."

I knew what she was saying was absolutely true, but I didn't want to believe I was being drawn into the world of organized crime. I knew, but I didn't want to believe it. The money was too damn good.

Mickey Rathe, the owner of Copy Supply Warehouse, was probably in his late fifties. His hair was as white as snow, and he barely spoke English. But as far as I could tell, he treated everyone like gold. I knew for a fact that many of his office managers had at one time been living on the streets.

Our manager, Rob, was also a musician and had been so broke at one point, he had made a gay video just to put food in his mouth . . . along with a few other things. Rob wasn't proud of it, and it wasn't a subject that could be discussed around the office. Not unless you wanted your teeth knocked out.

At first, all the senior officers in the organized crime group appeared to be tough guys, but once I got to know them, I found out they were all bisexual. I had never heard of a gay Mafia; it didn't fit the profile. When The Godfather was made, no one was using cocaine. I think they were all bisexual because their heavy use of cocaine confused their brainwaves.

Mickey had two sons. Peter was my age, with long dark hair. He played drums in a Hollywood band with the "Gook Boy," so we got along. The other son, Stevie, was a party-boy. He was fucked up every time I saw him and he liked to bet on the ponies. They had it all: the houses, the cars, and the women . . . if that was what they were into.

Everyone at Copy Supply Warehouse offered me cocaine, marijuana, and beer at work. From the time I got up until I went to sleep, it seemed like someone was always tempting me with cocaine. There seemed to be an endless supply.

Joe Shermie, who was once the bass player for Three Dog Night, worked in the downstairs office. He had been a millionaire rock star in the 1970's, but because of his cocaine problem, he now had nothing and was living paycheck to paycheck, to the point of getting busted for shoplifting

Twinkies at the 7-11 on the corner of La Brea and Pico Boulevard.

~~

Monday morning, right around 6:30 a.m., the sun was shining like it could only shine in California. I was in my upstairs office gazing at downtown Los Angeles, thinking I was glad not to be stuck in traffic as I downed my espresso.

From my office window, I could see several blocks in two directions. I noticed the RTD bus swerve through traffic abruptly, almost causing an accident to get to the curb half a block shy of the bus stop. The bus door opened, and Nick Stanley emerged and ran for the parking lot of Copy Supply Warehouse -- covered in blood.

Nick wasn't freaked out; he was calm as he stripped his clothes off in the back parking lot. His bloody clothes were tossed into a black trash bag, and he was hosed off by one of the guys in the shipping department as they cracked jokes about getting him behind the ears. Nick slicked his hair back and dressed quickly while they got a car ready for his departure.

Nick had stayed with us for a couple of months as a roadie for the band and was a good guide to the streets of Los Angeles. Nick made a good first impression, but in reality, he was probably one of the most cold-hearted individuals I would ever encounter.

As an example, Nick had befriended this dumb but nice Russian kid nicknamed Lock-Va. His family had just moved to Los Angeles from Russia and had put an ad in the newspaper to rent out their spare guest house. Nick answered the ad. Being very slick, he started taking this Russian kid to all the parties and clubs, making him feel cool, but in reality he was making fun of him without him even knowing. After spending an entire year eating dinner and celebrating holidays with the family, Nick sprung his scam. By this point, the Russian kid's mother was even doing his laundry.

The entire time Nick lived there, he kept talking about getting the opportunity to buy his own business.

"I want to open my own toner room," Nick said. "I'll make your son manager if you back me financially."

Knowing their son was a fool, they said, "How much do you need?"

"Hundred thousand dollars."

"We only have seventy-five thousand. It's our entire life's savings."

"That will work," Nick replied. "I'll go with a smaller operation." The deal was made, or so it seemed. "I want you guys to meet me on Highland and Franklin. Bring the money in cash."

"Why is that?" asked the father.

"I'm getting a special deal. The guy doesn't know I have a backer, so you're my silent partner. He's paranoid about meeting new people."

They trusted Nick and did as he asked.

Standing on Highland, waiting right out in front of Toner 2000 and dressed in his three-piece suit, Nick looked like a new business owner.

The Russians pulled up to the curb and rolled down the window. "How's it going?"

"Great. Do you have the cash? Everything is ready to go."

"Yes, it's in the briefcase."

"Good, hand it to me. I'll go in and make the deal. Once it's done, I'll come back out and get you."

"Okay. We will wait right here."

Nick walked in the front door of Toner 2000 and out the back door to a cab that was waiting. Toner 2000 was not for sale; they didn't even know Nick. He took a cab back to the Russians' house, got his belongings, took what he wanted of theirs and was off to Palm Springs for a vacation. He ran through their entire life savings in six weeks.

The Russian family sat outside Toner 2000 until the store closed. The Russian kid's mother cried her eyes out, when they arrived home.

I thought, <u>How could someone be so cold and heartless?</u>

Nick answered another ad for an apartment. By flashing large sums of money, he talked the apartment manager into giving him all the rent money. He convinced him he could double the money and have it back before Monday.

The apartment manager got two years in prison for embezzlement.

Watching Nick, I learned a lot. The trick was to flash large sums of money, which blinded people and made his words sound like the truth.

~~

I rushed down the stairs to the parking lot. "What the fuck happened?" I yelled.

"I was on my way into work," Nick replied with a grin," when three gang members tried to rob me at knifepoint." He smirked.

"Are you all right?"

"I'm fine, never been better."

Wrong move on the part of the gangbangers; they had crossed a veteran criminal of Los Angeles that had no regard for human life.

"Those little bastards tried to stick me, it was funny, but I took it away, and they're stuck," he boasted. He was quite proud of himself. Still, he thought it would be good to leave town for a while. I could understand, that was common street sense. Plus Mickey ordered him gone for a while.

By Wednesday, everyone in the office had already stopped talking about Nick. The main topic of discussion was the Lakers. These criminals were tight; they took care of their own. Nick was a great salesman and had made them a lot of money, so he was of value. Everyone covered for him when the police came snooping around.

~~

Roland Mackay, the trainer at Copy Supply Warehouse, had come to Hollywood from back East to be a rock star and just happened to fall into Copy Supply Warehouse, much like myself. He went to the Rainbow and met a hot chick who was also from back East, trying to be a model. Roland let her move in and was really excited to be getting a steady piece of ass.

After work on Friday, Roland and I went out for drinks with people from the office. I dropped Roland off at home around four o'clock, he went in and crashed out on his couch.

For no reason, other than being insane, his girlfriend walked in while he was sleeping and shot him six times, emptying the gun into his chest and sleeping face.

The funeral was closed-casket.

While sitting there during the eulogy, I thought about how fast things happen in Hollywood. You were forgotten before you were even a memory. It was always the same story time and time again: rags to riches, riches to rags, and then finally to body bags. At least he never knew what hit him.

Some people wouldn't be so lucky.

Chapter 8

<u>June 1988</u>

By now, my entire life was dedicated to the band. Everything I did was because of the band, and I was now seriously considering quitting the one and only thing in my life I truly loved.

We were finally being evicted from our apartment because of too many parties. Norton, the apartment manager, hated Bobby's attitude with a passion.

I truly hated Bobby more than Satan himself. I fantasized all the time about wrapping my hands around his throat.

It was bad enough that I had to pay all his bills, such as rent and electricity, but he also ran up large phone bills that were in my name. I had to hide my food in my bedroom if I wanted it to be there when I returned. I had basically given up on keeping anything; Bobby had drunk all the booze out of my liquor cabinet and refilled all the bottles with water. It was damn embarrassing when I offered someone a shot and they downed room-temperature water, slightly flavored like alcohol. They only made a comment about it when I offered a second round.

I had to make a quick decision.

~~

The weekend of June 13th, I was down in Hollywood hanging out on the Sunset Strip with Gary. We were passing out fliers about our show coming up at Gazzari's the following weekend.

I hadn't made my mind up about quitting the band for sure until that weekend, when I had a conversation with Hollywood's newest pretty boy, Stevie Rachelle. He was the bleach blonde lead singer for Tuff, one of the hottest bands currently playing the Hollywood club scene. I had known Stevie before he became a rock star and still considered him my friend.

"Look, its Friday night," Stevie said, "and every singer in Hollywood that wants a record deal is out here on the sunset strip promoting his band. Where's Bobby?"

I shrugged in disgust. "Sitting at home and watching TV."

"I have never once seen him out here in the trenches, kissing ass. He's a good singer, but full of himself."

I thought, <u>You don't know the half of it.</u>

I knew Stevie was absolutely right. There was Jani Lane, the lead singer of Warrant, right down the street passing out fliers and shaking hands.

The members of L.A. Guns, who were already signed to a record deal, were talking up their new record with local fans, while the lead singer of my band was too great in his own mind to grace anyone on the Sunset Strip with his royal presence.

"I know a band from New York that just moved here," Stevie said. "They need a bass player. Do you want me to give them a call?"

"Sure. Have them check me out at our show next weekend."

"I'll do that."

When I got home around 3:30 in the morning with a buzz, I immediately saw Bobby lying on my couch, watching cartoons while eating my food. He'd found the food I'd hidden in my bedroom, which meant he had gone through my underwear drawer. That sent me into a rage!

"I'm sick of your fucking lazy ass sponging off me!" I yelled. "Either get off your fucking ass and help me move this band forward, or I swear to God I'm going to beat the living shit out of you!"

Michael and I had sworn to each other that we would never let Bobby come between us. We were both intelligent enough never to fall under Bobby's spell. But that time had finally come to pass.

"Get off his back," Michael said. "I'm tired of you always bitching about Bobby!"

"Fine!" He's your responsibility, and from this date forward, you can pay his way, because I'm done. The free ride is over. Far as I'm concerned, he can starve to death! Fuck you, Bobby, you lazy, cock-sucking whore." I slammed my bedroom door.

Bobby knew when to keep his mouth shut. I respected Michael and would never physically do anything to him, but Bobby was a different case. If he had said a single word, there would have been bloodshed.

As I lay on my bed, feeling devastated, the room started to spin. I couldn't believe Michael would take that bum's side. As far as I was concerned, our next show would be my last show. I would rather die and go straight to hell than have to live with this fucking prima donna a single day longer.

It would be hard to quit Hap Hazzard. I spent countless sleepless nights tossing and turning, unable to decide if I was making the right decision. Quitting would mean I had failed and blown my entire life's savings. Basically, I would have come to Hollywood for nothing.

On the other hand, if I didn't quit the band, I was going to commit murder -- I just knew it. I understood what Eddie and Alex Van Halen put up with.

I had thought Michael and I would be friends for life and would raise our children together in some huge mansion. It had been our dream to make this band huge, I was so sure it would happen I banked everything I owned on it.

Once I got over being sad, I was extremely pissed.

I had stuck up for Michael many times over the years when Bobby had bad-mouthed him behind his back. Bobby would always remark, "Michael's a good guitar player, but he doesn't have the look." Once, Bobby wanted to replace him because he'd had to cut his hair to keep a job in Indiana. I never sided with Bobby against Michael, and I never repeated what Bobby said. I knew it would only hurt Michael's feelings and knock his ego. In this business, you had to have complete confidence, or the game was over.

Michael wasn't an ugly guy, he just didn't have the pretty-boy look. He was tall and very skinny, with no muscle mass, even though he was hung like a donkey. Bobby, on the other hand, with his perfect pool side tan and long flowing thick blonde hair looked perfect; he was flawless, except for his personality. He judged people purely by their appearance. If Bobby thought he was better looking than you, which was just about everyone, he treated you like a servant and wanted you to wait on him.

By the way Michael was acting, I could tell Bobby was talking behind my back. He should have stuck up for me, but he didn't, and Gary let me know it was true. He hated Bobby, also. Michael hated Bobby also, but he thought he needed him in order to make it. He was wrong, and lost a good friend.

~~

The final show came, and Gazzari's was packed. Seeing the crowd, it made it even harder for me to leave the band. The guys from New York were in the crowd, they were standing in the front row. I was ready to put on a good show.

Bill Gazzari, the godfather of rock-and-roll, came backstage with a blonde under each arm to say hi to the band.

"Are you boys ready to put on a good show?" Bill asked.

Eyeing the two blondes, I said, "Yeah, we're ready to rock the house!"

"Great! Glad to hear it. I don't let just any band play my club. Only the best and hottest-looking bands can play my club."

"Thanks, Bill," I replied. "We won't let you down."

"Have a great show. Let's go, my sweets."

We had two opening acts. When we finally hit the stage, the Hollywood crowd was there to see us. I gave the sound man a hundred dollar bill, but I ripped it in half and said, "We better sound great if you want the other half. I will hold on to it until after the show."

It was our best show ever; we had constructed a stage with ramps and high risers with special effects to make our show even bigger than life. During the last song, "Red Ball Jets," Bobby Lee had roadies behind the stage started throwing huge red beach balls out into the crowd. The crowd was throwing the huge red beach balls back and forth while the fog machines kicked into high gear, covering the front of the stage in three feet of fog.

The show was going so well, I was having serious second thoughts about quitting the band; it was our finest hour. No one in the crowd could feel the hate going on during our show.

I was wearing black leather pants that tucked into snakeskin cowboy boots with four earrings and my left nipple pierced. Black skull leather suspenders were holding up my black leather pants. My bass strap was made of thirteen steel handcuffs I had welded together, and I always had my back hot-waxed before any show. Back hair was a Hollywood no-no. With my hair extensions, my hair was more than halfway down my back and light brown, with blonde streaks and spiked high. My favorite bass was airbrushed with a naked centerfold of Marilyn Monroe. In hot pink letter across the black bass it read "Sleazy Please, Please Me" above the whamming bar.

At the end of "Red Ball Jets," I jumped down from one of the risers, which was about five feet in the air, just as someone in the crowd threw one of those huge red beach balls back onto the stage. With my perfect luck and timing, I landed on it, knocking my feet out from under me. I flipped through the air and hit the stage hard.

I managed to protect my bass, but I injured two fingers on my left hand. Jumping back up like a pro, I kept playing, using my thumb over the top of the bass to hit the notes and finish the song.

Eventually I noticed that everyone in the front row of the crowd was pointing at me. I kept playing until I realized what they were pointing at. Looking down, I saw that my chest was covered in blood. The nipple ring had gotten caught in the steel handcuffs, and now my nipple was ripped and hanging by a thread.

Still playing, I ran off stage, handed my bass to Stroths, and grabbed a couple of napkins and a roll of duct tape out of my gig bag. I took the nipple ring out and pushed my nipple back in place, then put the napkin over my nipple and wrapped gray duct tape completely around my chest until it felt secure. I put my bass back on and finished the song covered in blood.

There were so many people around after the show, after I got back from the hospital I just couldn't quit the band. Everyone was excited, and I couldn't ruin the mood. I was having too good of a time. The after-show party was huge, with plenty of booze and women. We drank ourselves into darkness.

When I awoke, I was out at Angel's for a day of rest away from Hollywood. I spent the entire day deciding what to do. Then I got a call from Gary. "Hey, how's it going?" he asked.

"I'm fine. I'll be home tomorrow."

"That's cool. Bobby has been talking shit about you. He said you made us look really stupid when you fell."

"Fuck that asshole," I yelled into the phone. "He's the one who filled the stage with beach balls. I got seriously hurt." That pissed me off and sealed the deal.

When I got back on Monday, I rented a suite. I had a meeting with Grant Stevens, our band manager.

"I quit the damn band."

"Why?" asked Grant. "The show went well?"

"If I have to spend one more minute around Bobby, I will kill him."

"Can't you just ignore him?"

"No. No way. I'm also mad at Michael for not sticking up for me."

"I thought you and Michael were like best friends, brothers."

"I thought so, too, but I guess that's not the case, from what I'm hearing. Michael has decided that he needs Bobby more than me, I'm done."

"That really sucks. Sorry to hear that. You guy are so close to a record deal."

"I don't care anymore."

I reached out and shook Grant's hand. "Bobby's your problem. Good luck."

Walking down the hallway on the tenth floor, I felt like a burden had been lifted off my shoulders. The faster the elevator got me to the ground the better. The band from New York wanted me, they thought I kicked ass. I was ready to move on and they were already signed with Capital Records.

Chapter 9

My new suite was at a complex called Studio Colony. I had watched it being built over the course of the past year. It was a city within a city -- six buildings with sixty units in each building. The style was futuristic, with everything painted white, mauve, and teal. A five-story clock tower stood in the center of the courtyard. The complex was like a giant fortress, taking up an entire city block. Twenty-foot walls surrounded the place, and cameras scanned the property at all times.

To get into the complex, you had to get through a security station manned by two armed guards, which required a pass. If a guest arrived, the guard would call up to the suite before letting them enter, which gave you the option of seeing or not seeing the person attempting to visit. The guards were discreet.

In the center of the complex was an Olympic-sized swimming pool, with girls lounging around in g-strings every afternoon, tanning their voluptuous backsides. Next to the swimming pool were a barbecue pit and two huge Jacuzzis, surrounded by palm trees. In the main building, there was a full-size weight room with a sauna and two racquetball courts with a glass viewing room for spectators.

Many famous Hollywood figures lived in this complex because of the security. Just to name a few, I remember Tone Loc, the Nelson twins, the Barbarian Brothers, Brett and Bobby from Poison, Steven Percy of Ratt, and Fred Curry, the drummer from Cinderella lived above me. Many cast members from soap operas lived there as well, since it was only two blocks west of Universal Studios. I parked my car next to the guitar player from Wang-Chu and the girl next door, her father was the guitarist for Elvis Presley. When Angel and I attended her wedding in Woodlyn Hills, we got to meet the rest of the band.

The new suite was $1500 a month. I decided I needed some roommates to help out so I wouldn't be stressed for money, considering the way I spent it while living the Hollywood lifestyle. I let John Shell, the best toner salesman in all of Los Angeles, move into one bedroom. He made as much as a Beverly Hills doctor and helped me a great deal in my sales techniques.

I also let Mia sleep on the couch and store some of her belongings in my bedroom closet. Mia was a girl Gary had brought home one night, using and abusing, so I took pity when I found out she was sleeping in her truck in Hollywood. I let her move in with me as a friend, because I knew she needed one. She was a cute little redhead who passed herself off as Molly Ringwald's little sister. It worked; she looked like a younger version of Molly's character right out of <u>Sixteen Candles</u>. I also got her a job at Copy Supply Warehouse in the office with my girlfriend Angel, which was a mistake. They hated each other, and I heard it nonstop from both ends.

When I told John Shell he could move in, I didn't know he was a crack addict -- a $2000-per-weekend addict. The first weekend, he took Mia's truck without asking and wrecked it during a drug run. The next time, he took my car in the middle of the night while I was sleeping, ran it out of gas, and lost the keys on the 101 Hollywood Freeway. John made $200,000 per year and didn't even have a car, and now I knew why. Before coming to live with me, he had stayed in a $100-a-week hotel with a mattress on the floor and a black-and-white television on a plastic milk crate.

I couldn't deal with it; he had to return to his environment.

~~

While trying to get my living situation straightened out, I also realized that the band I had joined wasn't what I was looking for. They were trying to imitate Aerosmith with their New York attitude. The lead singer of the band was already reminding me of Bobby Lee, and without Michael there, my heart wasn't really into the music. I could have remained in the band, but I said no thanks to collect my thoughts, even thou they had a record deal.

As soon as everyone in Hollywood heard I wasn't in Hap Hazzard, I was bombarded by phone calls with offers from other Hollywood musicians, which I thought was cool at first. It boosted my spirits, until I figured out that everyone I tried to play with was too hard to get along with. Every musician in Hollywood was the best from their Small Town, U.S.A., and none of them would compromise their egos long enough to form a long-lasting band. And forget about agreeing on a band name.

Months went by, and I went through band after band before finally teaming up with two guys I had met at Copy Supply Warehouse. Gary agreed to quit Hap Hazzard, too. He hated Bobby Lee so bad, he fantasized about strangling him.

Allen was the lead guitarist. He was a long-haired loudmouth from New York with the talent to be one of the best guitarists in rock history, if he could ever get his shit together. Allen could play any lead off Van Halen's first album, along with any of the late Randy Rhodes licks like it was second nature -- forwards and backwards with his eyes closed.

The other guy was Doug, a bleached blonde long-haired singer from Minnesota. He looked so much like Vince Neil of Mötley Crüe that Vince's own mother would have taken a second look.

I let Doug and Allen move into John's old bedroom.

I also let Cyn, a friend from Boone Grove, Indiana move in. Cyn and I had been friends since we were kids, she was the niece of baseball player Ron Kittle. She was trying to break into modeling.

Chapter 10

Summer 1988

Toward the end of the summer, Angel and I had a falling out.

I was feeling depressed about leaving Hap Hazzard. They had already replaced me with a new bass player and were still playing songs I had written on the Sunset Strip. That made me extremely furious. I was very angry at Michael; we had been like brothers. He was letting Bobby spread all kinds of slanderous rumors about me and why I had left the band, telling people I had gotten kicked out. After hearing all that Hollywood crap, I wasn't very pleasant to be around. I was angry all the time.

When Angel and I broke up, we agreed to be friends and not to date anyone we were both friends with. We were going to respect each other, since we both traveled the same Hollywood circle. But the very next day, Angel started dating Roger. They had been working together at Copy Supply Warehouse. I had never worried about Roger hitting on her because I thought he was gay. He looked like Prince, or the artist formerly known as Prince.

I was the last to know.

Completely clueless, seeing Angel every day at work after we broke up made me think that maybe I had made a mistake. I tried to get back together with her, but she kept making up reasons why we couldn't. Meanwhile, Roger just sat there in the same office with us, saying nothing.

What a chicken-shit coward, I thought later.

When Doug finally told me, I was shocked and disgusted at the same time. Around the office, I tried to act like it didn't bother me, but it did. It was practically impossible for me to work, knowing they were in the downstairs office.

Part of me was really sad and felt betrayed, and the other part wanted to take Roger's head and shove it up his own ass. I had never liked him, anyway. I was really mad at Angel; I couldn't even look at her or get one word out if I crossed her in the hallway at work. It wasn't a classy move on her part.

The more I thought about it, the more it got to me. The office jokes started, and my sales fell to zero. I turned to heavy drinking and returned to the Rainbow for love and companionship for the next month. I took time off from the office to get my head straight, but instead I screwed it into the ground upside-down.

When I finally returned to work, I was on my last dollar. Two months of partying had drained me down to nothing. Before I could get my first paycheck, though, the pirate ship was boarded and the crew was forced to walk the plank.

That Friday morning, I went through the normal procedures for entering the building. To get to the upstairs office, I had to be buzzed in through a set of steel doors, which protected the salesmen from violent customers or curious homeless people who wandered the streets of Los Angeles. Selling toner over the telephone wasn't illegal, but we were using stolen phone codes, as well as taking bets. So the authorities were looking for any reason to bust Mickey. All the phones were equipped with an instant erase button, and everyone was instructed to hit the erase button to destroy the evidence if a raid ever occurred. The FBI had raided Mickey a couple of years prior and come up with nothing. They still had a hard-on for him after he had shoved the last charges back down their throats.

Around 9:30 on this Friday morning, as I walked down the hallway toward the bathroom, I heard what sounded like a small army running up the stairs leading into the office. As I paused to listen, I noticed the new female employee, a hot-looking young lady in her early twenties, leaving her desk and opening the main door to the office.

As she slipped through the door, the FBI came running in, yelling, "Raid!"

Dropping my hot coffee, I quickly turned around and took off down the hallway toward my desk, with the FBI hot on my heels.

They had their guns drawn and their badges out. They yelled, "Put your telephones down and your hands up!"

I made it back to my desk and hit my erase button, just like everyone else in the office. I barely had time to stuff my pocket knife into the cushion of my chair before they grabbed me.

Like Judge Judy, the FBI officers demanded to see our identifications. "Anyone who doesn't have an picture identification goes straight to jail until you can prove yourself."

It appeared that the FBI, along with Postal Inspector Jim Do-Gooder, had been watching Copy Supply Warehouse for some time and had placed an undercover female agent in the office as a new employee -- probably her first assignment right out of the academy in Virginia. The FBI had been camped across the street in a huge work van, taking pictures of all the employees as they came into Copy Supply Warehouse.

The agents lined us up against the wall and took our pictures. Since there were a couple hundred employees, they fingerprinted everyone right there in the office, as if it were a booking station. Those who had outstanding warrants went straight to jail, and cars in the parking lot with unpaid tickets got booted and towed. None of us got our paychecks.

Agent Do-Gooder warned us, "If I catch any of you selling toner anywhere else, I will arrest you and take you in."

Everyone nodded their heads in agreement, but when Agent Do-Gooder turned his back, more than half the people up against the wall flipped him the bird.

Later, as the feds were rolling out filing cabinets, Mickey told everyone to go home. "Copy Supply Warehouse will be closed for a few days, but I'll straighten everything out," he assured us with a smile. "We'll be back open again, just like last time."

Mia, Doug, and Cyn had all worked at Copy Supply Warehouse as well. Rent was due in two weeks, and none of us had saved any money because we were making so much. The FBI had closed down toner rooms all over Hollywood, and the ones that hadn't been hit weren't hiring anybody. The word had gotten out about undercover agents being involved. I had no idea what to do for work, but I had to find something fast, or I was going to be living under the overpass with the Gasoline Gang. The band had emptied my savings account, and my broken heart finished me off with the help of the booze I guzzled at the Rainbow to drown my sorrows.

I was qualified to do many types of work. I could go back to welding or working on cars, but after working in a plush office, I had become spoiled. I couldn't imagine going back to welding for pennies in the heat, I just couldn't.

Although I worried about getting the rent paid, I avoided calling my parents. I couldn't tell them I had run through my money like toilet paper. I was ashamed of my irresponsibility. Everyone back in Indiana was already pressuring me to move back, assuming my dream was over and it was time to come home. I didn't see it that way. Death before dishonor my father always said.

A week before the FBI raid, I had kicked Allen out of the suite -- not for being loud and rude, but for selling marijuana. At first I didn't mind, but he became very sloppy and stupid about it. He would say anything over the telephone and talk real loud in the hallway about pot. Anybody could have heard him and turned us in. I warned him several times, but he was usually too damn high to understand.

When I asked him to leave, he understood, and we remained good friends. Alan agreed that Studio Colony was too fancy for his loud, rude New York attitude.

Between all of us in the apartment, we only had $800 towards rent, and we needed $1500. The apartment complex was corporate-owned and very strict. They would start evictions right away because there was a waiting list to get in.

I lost many nights of sleep thinking about the situation I had gotten into. Finally, I made a decision, feeling I had no choice if I wanted to stay in Hollywood. I knew what could happen, but I did it anyway.

I explained to my roommates, "I'm going to buy $800 worth of marijuana and take over Allen's pot business in the valley to make our rent."

"Are you sure that's a good idea?" said Doug.

"After we all start working again, I'll gladly stop."

This wasn't something I wanted to do, but if I gave up and moved back to Indiana, Bobby Lee would win. I would be the first in the band to give up and come home, meaning I was nothing more than a mere country hick.

Since I didn't smoke, the marijuana sales would be pure profit, unlike Allen, who smoked liked a chimney. What really scared me, though, was the thought of my family back in Indiana finding out. I would be a total disgrace and would have to explain my actions if I ever wanted to show my face again. I would feel like an even bigger loser.

Since I hadn't been a dick toward Allen, he agreed to set me up. I would take care of his valley customers, making his job easier.

Once the first deal was ready, Allen told me to meet him outside the front gates of Studio Colony. He was getting a ride from Hollywood and didn't want to come into the complex because he'd had a previous altercation with one of the security guards.

As I walked out the front gate of the complex, I noticed they were filming an episode of <u>Murder, She Wrote</u>. There were cops everywhere for crowd control. That only added to my paranoia, and I walked out the front gate already looking guilty. I took another look around before jumping in the car with Allen.

"Get in the car, dumb fuck," Allen said. "What the hell are you looking for?"

"Shut the fuck up, asshole. I'm just being cautious."

"Cautious for what? Get in the car!"

As we went for a ride around the block, Allen passed me two pounds of weed. I tried to back out of the deal.

"I'm not sure about this," I said. "There are cops everywhere. They're filming a shoot."

"Shut up and have some balls," Allen snapped. "Just act normal, if that's possible. They're not that bright. You live there, and they're only around for stalkers and crazed fans."

"I know, but maybe another time would be better."

"If you don't act like a total idiot and bother anybody for any autographs, you'll be just fine."

I squirmed in my seat. "Another time would be better."

"The time is now. I'm not coming back!"

"Alright! Chill your ass out!"

Not wanting to look like a total pussy, I stuffed the bags of weed down the front of my baggy sweats, leaving my shirt out to cover the bulge. Allen stopped down the street, and I jumped out.

"Thanks, asshole! Catch you later!"

"No problem. Remember, no autographs, dipshit!"

In a way that only Allen could see, I flipped him the bird and turned and waved at the security guards as I passed through the gates. The guard waved back and passed me through with no problem. I had made it through the first checkpoint.

I started down the hill toward my apartment building only a hundred yards away. I was freaking out mentally, thinking about what would happen if one of these cops knew what I was carrying.

I didn't want to act nervous, but I was practically defecating in my pants. I kept thinking, <u>What have I gotten myself into?</u>

I passed through the second security check for the TV shoot and showed my pass. As I stepped over the blockade, one bag of weed somehow managed to slip through my underwear and was working its way down my pant leg.

<u>Oh fucking shit!</u> I thought.

I stopped and bent down, pretending to tie my shoe. As subtly as possible, I tucked the bag into the top of my sock.

Before I could make it across the walkway, a police officer stopped me and said, "You'll have to wait. Once the camera starts rolling, just walk like you would normally. Don't look at the cameras. You're going to be on film in the background."

"What did you say?" I thought. <u>Shit. I'm going to be on film the first time I score weed.</u>

By the time I finally got into my suite, I felt like the entire LAPD was hot on my heels and would be kicking down my front door at any moment. Sitting in my bathroom with the door locked, I was ready to flush the weed the second the door came crashing down. I stood there frozen in time for an hour until one of my roommates came home, breaking the silence.

I had been playing the famous Black Sabbath song "Paranoid" for over fourteen years in cover bands. I never really understood the meaning of the word until now.

I had absolutely no idea how to sell marijuana or what kind of weed was good and what was garbage. Since I didn't have a scale, I just divided the bags into smaller bags, tripling my money on the first batch within three days. I paid the rent on time and had extra money to spend. I couldn't believe it; it was too damn easy. I became a natural in a very short time and my clients loved my new secret services.

I figured if I stayed low-key, didn't get greedy and did just enough to get by, no one would notice. I had no plans to become the next Tony Montana. I was just going to do this until we all went back to work.

~~

In the toner world, I had been Bill Davis. Now, in the weed world, I was Bill Greenleaf. Stoners actually thought it was a conspiracy that I had the last name Greenleaf.

One stoner said, "It's like your calling, man."

I shook my head and replied, "Don't read that much into it. It's just a play on words."

"Greenleaf . . . That's cool," slurred the stoner, winking at me with one bloodshot eye.

Everyone I sold a bag of weed to offered to get me stoned. It was an unwritten law to offer out of respect and to ensure you always got a good deal the next time around. I always declined, until one late afternoon when a stripper from the Body Shop, named Candy Cane, remarked how much she loved doing the wild thing while being stoned.

Looking at her sexy legs and her perfectly shaped behind that showed no sign of panty lines, I said, "Candy, believe it or not, I have never smoked a cigarette or a joint in my entire life. I only took over Allen's business to make extra money until I can find another job. When I go back to work, you'll have to drive back into Hollywood to score from Allen."

"I hate going into that part of Hollywood," said Candy. "It's such a shithole. Coming to see you is so much safer, and with your gentleman manners and classy accommodations . . . So let's see if I can talk you into staying in the business, at least for me."

She said it with such a sexy tone in her voice that it got me thinking with the wrong head. Smiling, she ran her tongue over her glossy red peppermint-flavored lips.

I smiled back as blood rushed to my groin.

I found myself considering it. This was the first time in my life that I didn't have to be anywhere or answer to anyone. I was free of all responsibilities. Plus, I figured that if enough people kept offering to smoke me out and I kept turning it down, it would cause paranoia. The stripper standing in front of me talking about hot, kinky sex, sealed the deal.

I couldn't roll a joint to save my life, so I tossed Candy Cane a bag of weed and said, "Roll up a joint and join me in my bedroom. I'm going to grab us a couple of ice-cold beers."

As I finished my last beer, I turned up the stereo on White Snake's latest release, and Candy started a sexy striptease. By the time she bent over and grabbed her ankles, she was down to her birthday suit, wrapped only in garter belts and nylons.

Looking at me seductively, she sparked up the rather thick joint she had just rolled and laid down on my bed. Putting each high-heeled shoe on each bed post, she rubbed her kitty with her left hand. With her right hand, she took the joint out of her mouth and parted her lower lips, inserting the doobie.

I watched in sexual amazement.

Then she put it to my lips and said, "Taste."

I leaned forward, lured in by the scent of female hormones. I thought I would cough and gag, but I guess I had become immune after all those years of welding and living in the smog of Los Angeles. Then the worst thing that could have happened, happened: I loved it.

The pot calmed my nerves, while at the same time making me even hornier than I thought imaginable. Anything that made sex better was a plus in my book. We pounded for the next hour.

I couldn't roll a joint to save my life, so one of my customers made me a homemade pipe out of a Bud Light can. He dented one side, making it flat, and poked tiny holes with a needle into the can, forming what looked like a screen. Then he poked a hole in the side of the can, which he called the carburetor.

I hid the can under my bed and took a few tokes before going to sleep every night. That sent me into a new world I hadn't been to before, creating new ideas and views of the world that seemed to unfold before my naked eyes.

Since I didn't die and nothing bad happened, everything I heard about weed was false. The chemical changes in my body were already starting the transformation.

It was the gateway drug.

Chapter 11

<u>November 1988</u>

I joined a rogue group of former salesmen from Copy Supply Warehouse who were selling toner out of a small company hiding in a building behind Yum-Yum Donuts in North Hollywood.

Even though I had returned to work, I decided to keep my weed business going. My frame of mind toward marijuana had changed with the introduction of THC into my bloodstream. I had been infected.

Shopping at the Sherman Oaks Galleria, I took the glass elevator to the top floor. As I stood there enjoying the view of the shops mixed in with palm trees, I kept thinking, <u>I must be losing my mind. What the hell am I doing?</u> I was defying direct orders from the FBI, and I was sure the DEA wouldn't be too happy that I wasn't giving them their cut of my weed business. But the way I looked at it, I was only doing what I had to do to survive in a ruthless city that was already full of crime and corruption. I was hardly making a dent.

When I got home from the mall, I noticed a flier on the bulletin board by the entrance to the elevators for barely used black furniture. "Moving Sale. Everything Must Go," it announced. Usually, I wouldn't have paid attention to the bulletin board, but the handwriting style on the notice caught my eye.

When I got up to my suite, I called and was surprised to find out she lived in Studio Colony in the next building over. After a quick shower, I walked to her place.

I rang the doorbell, expecting to meet an older lady because of the handwriting style. But to my surprise, a beautiful young woman with baby blue eyes answered with a welcoming smile. I had seen her once before, lounging by the swimming pool. As I walked in, she turned just so that her long, flowing blonde hair moved with the surrounding air, brushing my face. It reminded me of ripe peaches and was so arousing I could hardly think straight.

I could tell by her furniture and her mannerisms that she had class. She wasn't a Rainbow girl, by any means. Five years earlier, I wouldn't have had the nerve to talk to a Harvard graduate, but after being a top Hollywood musician, I felt I was as good as anyone. I laid on the charm, and thick.

"My name is Eve," she said.

"Nice to meet you. My name is Brent." I gave my real name to people I trusted . . . and that was only a few.

"I'm a Hollywood musician and an all around knuckle head, anyway you look at it. I used to raise horses as a kid in a small ass-backwards town called Boone Grove, Indiana."

She laughed and replied, "I'm accountant, but I love heavy metal music. I recognize you from the ads in the rocker magazines."

I smiled, it was nice to get credit for all the years I spent practicing alone in my bedroom to learn my trade. I wasn't a Poser.

I bought all her furniture just so I could come back and ask her out.

After picking up the furniture, I asked her out, and she accepted. Unfortunately, she moved to England two days later on a job transfer.

~~

Three weeks later, I noticed a moving van parked in front of Eve's building. There she was, standing with her long blonde hair blowing in the California breeze, just like in the movies. I couldn't believe my eyes.

I parked my car and walked over to give her a welcome-home kiss. I thought about pinching her butt, but I didn't press my luck and remained a perfect gentleman.

"England was cold and foggy," she explained. "After living in Sunny Southern California, I couldn't wait to get back. I even took a pay cut." She smiled. "I also couldn't stop thinking about you. I knew the minute your arrogant attitude walked through my door that you were trouble, and I've always been attracted to trouble."

I laughed and thought, Arrogance was something I learned from Bobby Lee. Nice guys finish last; it was sad but true.

Eve and I both had many dark secrets, and it took a few weeks of dating for everything to come out into the open. I was afraid to tell Eve what I did for a living, fearing she wouldn't dig it. I told her about the telemarketing business but left out some of the details, making it sound more legitimate than it really was.

Eve worked as an accountant for an entertainment investment company. They handled many famous Hollywood actors' investments, including Joyce Dewitt, Larry Hagman, and Grandpa from the Munsters.

Once I found out Eve smoked weed, I told her about my second business, and we became smoking buddies. That connection bonded us instantly. Every day after work, we would play racquetball, go for a swim, and workout in the gym until dinner. We shared dinner every night outside by the grills, enjoying the Southern California weather, since we were both young and still able to absorb the sunshine.

Eve told me how she had been raised in upstate New York in a town called Bingington. She had already gone through one horrible divorce with a biker who had gotten them involved in a satanic cult on the East Coast. Looking at Eve, so beautiful and innocent-looking, it was hard to believe that anyone would sell their soul for the short period of time they had to spend on the earth. She didn't look the way I imagined a witch looking. I couldn't detect an evil bone in her body or a blemish on her soul. She didn't have a witch's wart on her nose, nor did her skin glow in the dark.

We were still only friends, after spending every day and evening together for a month. Finally, I asked her, "Are you attracted to me? What would get you in the right mood?"

"I haven't had sex with anyone since my husband," Eve replied, "so I would feel kind of weird. But a couple lines of cocaine would break that barrier, I'm sure." She gave me a shy smile.

Shocked, I thought about her comment for the rest of the evening as we ate dinner and started watching a movie. Eve got up several times to go into the kitchen and use the bathroom during the course of the evening, and my eyes followed her every move like a loving puppy dog.

During the movie, in the middle of a sex scene, I got up and said, "I'll be right back." I had never done cocaine, but it was everywhere around me. There was a cocaine dealer named Jay living in my building, so I made him a quick trade. It was that easy. Within five minutes, I returned with a gram of cocaine in my hand. I was about to do one of the stupidest things in my life. This would change everything -- forever.

As soon as I opened the bindle in front of Eve, I saw the expression on her face. Her eyes changed in size and color. I could actually see the chemical change in her body once she knew the cocaine was in front of her.

To me, it was just plain white powder.

I didn't know what to do with it, so I handed the fold to her. Eve opened her purse and pulled out a brown leather pouch, retrieving a chopping razor and a flat stone the size of a medium pancake. She crushed the cocaine boulders with a cigarette lighter, chopped the pile into very fine powder, creating lines about four inches long across the chopping stone. The lines of cocaine sparkled under the bright lights of the bathroom. I checked twice to make sure the door was locked.

"This is a very special event," Eve said, retrieving a brand new crisp hundred-dollar bill from her brown leather wallet. She smiled as she rolled the bill into a straw and handed it to me. Trying to be as cool as I could, I handed it back, insisting that she go first.

Eve put the toilet lid down and took a seat, placing the chopping stone in her lap, between her lovely legs.

"Hold my hair back," Eve said.

I pulled her long blonde hair behind her head as she put her face to the stone and snorted the first line through the hundred-dollar bill. The powder disappeared up her cute button nose without any effort or pain. She tilted her head back, and I let her golden hair fall down. It waved from side to side as she enjoyed the instant wave of pleasure rushing through her bloodstream to that special pleasure zone in her brain.

With a sexy look of desire, Eve ran her fingertip across her gums, tasting the cocaine. Then she once again handed me the hundred-dollar bill.

"You're up to bat, Mr. Rock Star."

I took the bill and looked at the chopping stone in her lap, still having second thoughts about doing it.

"Is it getting you horny?" I asked.

Eve picked up the stone with her left hand and pulled her dress up with her right hand, flashing me a quick peek of her beautiful blonde muff encased in transparent black panties. I could see she was already starting to get wet. With seeing that, I knelt down on one knee and put the bill to my nose, placing my face directly into her lap.

The first line was incredible, like nothing I had ever felt before in my life. I couldn't believe how the cocaine made me feel, and since I was smoking weed at the same time, the high was out of this world. Drinking beer suddenly seemed foolish and rather immature. I thought I had found Heaven on Earth, but I had actually opened Pandora's Box, letting the demons out. Once out, they are almost impossible to put back, if ever.

The cocaine increased my libido, making me even more aggressive in bed. By the time the night was over and the cocaine was gone, we had worn ourselves out and settled into a days-long sleep.

When I awoke, I felt like a young vampire after his first taste of human blood. My body was still tingling. Although I didn't plan on doing it again, the cocaine had awakened a sleeping monster in Eve. I just didn't know it yet.

Chapter 12

With the federal indictments and the made-up charges that had been leveled against Mickey Rathe, my former boss and his sons from Copy Supply Warehouse, it wasn't looking too good. They had thumbed their noses at our government for too long, and this time they were going to make something stick, even if the FBI had to make up charges. Copy Supply Warehouse would never re-open.

But not all was lost. The night before the FBI raid, Mickey had been tipped off. He had at least one Fed on his payroll. Boris, his right-hand man and enforcer, downloaded all the account files and customer lists onto floppy disks the night before the FBI raid. Mickey then made a secret deal with another Hungarian boss, selling him all the files from Copy Supply Warehouse for a huge chunk of traveling money and a percentage of future profits.

I was only one of a few employees whom Mickey's son Peter liked. I might have been a smart-ass, and a wise-cracker, but I was trustworthy and always showed him respect. He knew I didn't use drugs . . . at least, I hadn't the last time I saw him.

The new toner company was going to be the same company, just under a new name and location, along with a new puppet-master pulling the strings. That would be me, "Bill Taylor." Some high-ranking criminals were shocked; such an arrangement was almost unheard of. I wasn't Hungarian. I was just a white boy outsider from Boone Grove, Indiana. Nevertheless, I'd proven myself, so I was given the power to set up my own office. I quickly became the manager and recruiter of the new pirate ship called West Coast Suppliers. I received a good weekly salary and thirty-five percent of my sales, propelling my income to six figures my first year.

The first time I met with my new boss, Zolie, he said, "I need good salesmen, no fuck-ups or drug addicts. I'm not letting the things that went on over at Copy Supply Warehouse go on here, making us vulnerable to the DEA. The FBI is enough of a pain in the ass, but at least we have a friend on the inside."

"I understand."

"We're going to run a smaller pirate ship so we won't draw as much attention from the Feds. We should make some good money in the process. No more fucking around, no cussing people out or screwing with them. If they don't want to buy, say thanks, and hang up quietly. Got it?"

"That really sucks," I replied. "The salesmen will feel like they have a real job, and it might kill morale."

Zolie looked at me with a look only a boss could give.
"Relax, I'm just joking. No problem, don't have a stroke."

~~

With Tony the bruiser's help, I set up Zolie's new office at the corner of Santa Monica and Fuller Avenue. The office was located above a pool cleaning business and an auto parts store. The parking lot below the new office served as a meeting point every morning for male hookers who dressed up like women. I didn't know it when I signed the lease for the office space one afternoon. Every morning I had to chase transvestites out of the parking lot like stray cats as they were shooting up drugs or blowing early-morning customers.

I liked Zolie for the most part, but he was no Mickey, and the salesmen didn't like him. It often seemed like I was the only one who could get along with people that others considered assholes. But I understood where the salesmen were coming from. At first he really got on my nerves, but I soon learned his bark was worse than his actual bite. Zolie was a little man in height, resembling Scrooge, but he carried himself like a boss. When he yelled, and I mean when he yelled, everyone jumped.

I told Zolie many times, "If you want me to run the office and keep the salesmen happy, it would be better if you stayed in your back office and stop yelling like Danny DeVito." My suggestions went in one ear and out the other. It was like talking to a brick wall.

My secretary was a Russian woman named Mary. She was cool but thought Americans were pigs. I joked with her all the time like a American smart-ass.

"Mary," I asked, "what do they call good-looking women in Russia?"
She just rolled her eyes. "What?"
"Tourists."
Everyone in the office laughed.
Mary replied, "Shut up, you . . . American pig dog."
Gary got under her skin every time he came to the office to visit. He would hit on her and remark how much he wanted to hear her moan in that heavy accent.

"Tell that asshole Gary to stop coming by the office," Mary suggested. "Or I will show him a Russian back-hand." I laughed.

Everyone at the new office knew the FBI was trying to keep track of everyone who worked at Copy Supply Warehouse. However, with all the fake identifications and false addresses on our job applications, we managed to give the government the slip. The paper trail led nowhere.

The FBI was trying to get former Copy Supply Warehouse employees to testify against Mickey in court, but no one was cooperating. There was a rumor going around that the Feds had something on an ex-employee who was helping them out, but no one knew who it was . . . yet.

~~

When Mickey's court date arrived, we all watched from a distance. I couldn't show my face in court, I didn't want to be photographed and have anything else added to my FBI file. It didn't go well for Mickey. The government charged him with mail fraud, tax evasion, racketeering, and other made-up charges.

Soon we found out that the rat was Roger, Angel's boyfriend. He had made a deal with the government to testify against Mickey. They had Roger on the wiretaps when he was threatening customers during his collection attempts and making cocaine deals with Hollywood drug dealers. To save his miserable ass, he squealed like a stuck pig and gave the government the pieces of the puzzle they needed to put it all together.

Mickey got twenty years, and his sons got ten. The judge gave them two weeks to get their things in order before reporting to the prison.

The night before they were to report to prison, they threw a huge going-away party at his mansion with booze, cocaine, and hookers for all.

They knew the Feds were probably watching, so at the end of the party, Mickey and his sons snuck out of the house with the caterers. They escaped to Mexico City, and by the time anyone even knew they were gone, they had caught a flight back to Hungary. They forfeited almost two million dollars in bail money and three huge mansions in the Hollywood Hills, but they had millions of American dollars stashed in banks overseas -- more than enough to live like kings in a third world country. They would never again step foot in the United States.

Since they hadn't killed anybody -- or gotten caught for it -- Hungary wouldn't extradite them back to the United States. The FBI had wasted their time and serious tax dollars. Shutting down Copy Supply Warehouse had done absolutely nothing to the toner business; it had only created a bunch of smaller and harder-to-find toner companies. The Feds had, however, seized ten million dollars in assets.

It showed me that you could still beat the system and that crime could pay. They made off like bandits and still thumbed their nose at our government for a second time.

Chapter 13

My roommates, Mia and Cyn, got out of the toner business. Mia got a job in another field of telemarketing known as phone sex. Cyn got a job as a cocktail waitress at a bar on Ventura Boulevard called "Moscow Nights."

I had known Cyn since we were kids. She had moved to Hollywood a couple of weeks after our band arrived. She was trying to break into the modeling.

Every week for the past sixty years, hundreds of unsuspecting beauties from all over the United States and the entire world had been coming to Hollywood in the hope of becoming the next superstar. All the models had photo albums with their pictures and all their statistics, such as height, weight, bust size, age, and contact information.

As soon as the models arrived in Hollywood, whether it was by car, bus, train, or plane, they looked up the modeling agencies in the phone book. The agencies with the biggest and most glamorous ads were usually the scammers. The real agencies didn't advertise, and without a credible introduction, you would never get past the rather in creditably rude receptionist at the front desk, who herself was probably a wannabe model who had failed.

The models who were new in town made appointments with the fake agencies that put on a good front. They always rented fancy offices with nice black leather furniture and pictures of famous models plastered all over the walls to make you think they had something to do with the models' success. In reality, they had no connection with anyone in Hollywood, other than other scum-bags.

The interview always went well for the unsuspecting model. They would tell her what she had been waiting to hear. Even if the girl had a horn growing out her forehead, the line would be the same. Most of these girls were fresh off the farm, much like myself, and to hear someone in glamorous Hollywood confirm what they had always thought about themselves, they'd do anything.

This was the way it worked. The modeling agent would tell the young model, "The only thing I can see that's holding you back in your career is your portfolio. It's outdated and not glamorous enough for Hollywood. "To be frank, it is a joke. No one will take you seriously."

"What can I do to get a better one?" the model would ask.

"Well, lucky for you, my young lady, I just happen to be friends with a Famous Hollywood Photographer who owes me a favor."

"Do you think you could set me up with him?"

The fake modeling agent would walk around his office and look through his book; it was all part of the charade.

"Normally, a photo shoot with this Famous Hollywood Photographer would cost $5,000 to $10,000, but since we're friends, he'll do it for twenty-five-hundred." If they can get away with it, sex would also be added to the deal.

He would promise to get the model work and get back in touch real soon. In reality, however, they had no connections, and in a couple of months they would move the office and change the name of the agency.

I went through this scam with Cyn three times before she finally listened and stopped wasting her parents' money. I saw the disappointment in her eyes when she finally realized that everything about Hollywood was a bunch of bullshit. It was the same look I had seen in the mirror.

She turned to cocaine.

~~

It was around three in the morning when I was awakened by loud noises in the living room. I rubbed my eyes and reached for my pistol. Then I heard laughter, which calmed my nerves -- but pissed me off instead.

Eve asked, "What's going on?"

"Stay in bed," I said. "I'll take care of this."

I opened my bedroom door and saw a completely naked man on all fours, heaving and dumping his guts out on my carpet. Glancing toward the kitchen, I saw Cyn hiding behind the icebox door, attempting to conceal her nakedness.

I reached my limit. This was the third night in a row I had been awakened from a dead sleep. I still worked for a living.

I grabbed the guy by the back of his head with every intention of tossing his drunken disorderly ass out into the hallway naked. Then Cyn yelled, "That's Neal Scheol of Journey. Please don't hurt him."

She said the right words; I stopped. I didn't have my contacts in, so I rubbed my eyes again and looked at him a second time. I was a huge Journey fan up to that point. Once my eyes focused, I realized it was the famous lead guitarist I had envied for many years, acting like a complete jackass in a drunken state of utter stupidity.

Neal had cut his hair short and was in town recording with Bad English, so I let him go and shut my bedroom door without violence.

Eve asked, "What was going on?"

"Go back to sleep," I replied. "It's just a drunken rock star acting the part of a dumbass."

~~

Before I left for work in the morning, Cyn and I had it out.

"I don't have a cocaine problem!" Cyn yelled. "Get off my fucking back."

"Yes, you do!" I snapped back. I'd had enough. "The all-night parties are over. Next time, I'm going to get up and toss everyone out. I don't care who they are or who they were, and that includes Billy Idol, Big Gunns, or any of those guys that roadie for Ratt. I have to get up early in the morning."

"You can't tell me what to do, you don't own me."

"As long as you're in my place, yes, yes I can!"

When I got home later that day, I found Cyn passed out on the couch with a bottle of wine in one hand and a lighter in the other. The telephone was off the hook right next to her head, and a glass crack pipe had melted into the carpet, right where she had dropped it. She was damn lucky the suite hadn't burned to the ground.

Before I could start yelling, I felt the building start to sway. The whole building rocked back and forth for half a minute, followed by every alarm in the city going off.

Once the quake stopped, we headed out into the courtyard for safety, just in case the building wasn't able to handle an aftershock. As we stood outside, I looked over at Cyn. She still had the lighter in one hand, and she had picked up her crack pipe in the other, as if it was natural. There must have been a couple of hundred people standing around, so I immediately grabbed her by the back of the arm and dragged her back into my apartment.

Big Gunns, the cocaine dealer from the club, had showed Cyn how to free-base cocaine, which only sent her deeper into her addiction. The difference between smoking cocaine and snorting it is like choosing between doing it or not doing it -- there's that much of a difference.

To Free-Base cocaine is to purify the cocaine from the "cut." Cut is usually anything white that will mix with the cocaine, like speed, baking soda, B-12, or even baby laxative.

I didn't smoke it, I tried it once before having sex, and my junk didn't work. I had spent the next two hours licking instead of sticking.

~~

When I came home later in the afternoon the day of the quake, Mia said, "Cyn has been locked in the bathroom since three o'clock, and she won't come out."

I heaved a sigh. "Wonderful!"

I beat on the bathroom door for a few minutes without getting a response. She didn't even yell "Fuck off," so I got worried.

I opened the door with a credit card and looked around the bathroom. A gallon of water was next to the bathtub, and the telephone was on the back of the toilet. I pulled back the shower curtain and found Cyn passed out in the bathtub with a needle dangling from her neck. I thought she was dead.

I slammed the bathroom door and yelled, "Call 911!"

The slamming of the door awoke Cyn; she wasn't dead after all. "Don't call 911!" she said, jumping out of the tub.

My temper flared. "That's fucking it!" I yelled. "You're going back to Indiana tonight. Pack your suitcase, and I'll ship the rest. You're not going to die in my apartment and leave me to explain to your parents that I knew and did nothing. Sorry, but that's not going to happen!"

"I don't have a problem!"

"Yes, you do," I yelled. "Why can't you just stop?"

At this point, I still didn't fully understand cocaine and its power, because it hadn't yet affected me personally.

Cyn stormed into her bedroom and slammed the door. "I'm not going!"

"You're going, or I'm calling your parents. I'll tell them everything."

"Fuck off," she yelled, opening and slamming the bathroom door.

"Slam that door one more time and you will wish you hadn't!"

I put Cyn on a plane that night and shipped her belongings home by mail. I saved her life but ruined our friendship, especially when her mother called and asked, "Why is my daughter spending all the time in the bathroom? And who's sending her packages every other day from Hollywood?" I told. Cyn hated me.

Chapter 14

I was quickly realizing that Los Angeles was like a giant meat grinder. One by one, everyone I knew and cared about was getting chewed up and spit out in tiny pieces. It was hard to prepare for broken dreams, and even harder to defend against false promises made with fake smiles by people with no souls. The soulless were very tricky and sinisterly clever.

I thought it would never happen to me. I would be stronger and smarter. I would beat the system of a down.

Before my roommate Doug moved in, he had lived in Hollywood on Fuller Avenue with two rock-and-roll chicks who screwed every rock star in Hollywood once they became rich and famous. These two girls could be found in their videos and bedrooms for the better part of the late '80's. They filled Doug's head with all kinds of mumbo jumbo that couldn't be proven true or false . . . but Doug believed with all his heart what he heard from the lips of women who sucked famous rock stars' cocks.

These two rock-and-roll vixens told Doug a chilling tale of how Nikki Sixx of Mötley Crüe had sold his soul using black magick to become rich and famous. Mötley Crüe's first album had done very well locally, but not enough to make them rich or famous. According to these girls, Nikki Sixx had hired a coven of witches to help him out, and their second album, titled <u>Shout at the Devil</u>, put them over the top. They were now in the minds of every metal-head and groupie, it literally happened overnight. Just like magick.

Vince Neil, the lead singer, killed someone in a car accident and only served twenty-one days in jail. Nikki Sixx, the bass player and brains of the band, overdosed on heroin, and was dead for ten minutes after his heart stopped. He only came back to life after a second shot of adrenaline was pumped into his heart, inspiring the song, "Kick Start My Heart." The paramedic was a fan and refused to let him die.

Mötley Crüe seemed untouchable. No matter how bad they fucked up, they remained on top of the metal scene, while Tommy Lee banged one babe after another. To Doug, the members of Mötley Crüe were like gods. He believed the girls' words were true with all his heart and watched the Mötley Crüe uncensored live video over and over again.

~~

Coming home from the office, I had a weird feeling as I inserted the key into the door lock. Doug had stayed home that day, saying he was sick.

Opening the apartment door, I felt a cold chill come over me, a sensation I had never felt before. I smelled incense and exotic candles, mixed with a weird smell, leaving a lasting impression. I didn't like what I smelled, so I knocked on Doug's bedroom door.

No one answered.

I retired to my bedroom with a horrible feeling that something was oh-so-wrong, but it was his room, and I had to respect his privacy if his door was shut.

A day later, Doug finally said, "I did the deed. Mia helped me with instructions she got from Geno and Eve."

I asked, "What deed?"

"Just think. . . We're going to be rich and famous. I did it for the band."

I shook my head. "You stupid fuck. I'm not doing it."

"If you really want to make it, you will."

"I guess I won't make it."

I went to my bedroom, feeling deeply sad. I still believed in Heaven and a place called Hell, not knowing it could be a place on Earth.

Sitting back in my bedroom, thinking about what Doug had just told me, I remembered all those church assholes protesting our concerts back in Indiana, saying we were playing the "Devil's" music. Maybe they had been right all along, and I was the stupid fool.

I thought surely not all of these bands could have sold their souls . . . but maybe they did. Most rock stars seemed to die horrible deaths, choking on their own vomit. I really couldn't see "Warrant" doing the deed.

~~

A couple of days passed, and to my relief, nothing happened.

Doug thought he was going to be receiving magical powers from the master of darkness. I think he actually expected someone to show up in a cloud of smoke, but nothing happened. No ghostly aberration appeared dressed in black, with contracts for a huge record deal.

After nothing happened and his singing didn't become the best, he said to me, "Maybe I shouldn't have done that."

I didn't know what to say, so I just shook my head. Wanting to help, I read the books he and Mia had used and went over the ritual for selling his soul. I figured out that they had made a few mistakes in the ceremony. To write the deal with Satan, you were supposed to follow the proper instructions perfectly and have some knowledge of the black arts. It all takes practice and is not for amateurs or musicians.

The deal must be written down in your own blood on the skin of a king. The skin of a king means the skin of any type of animal that is king of its kingdom, such as a lion, ram, bull, or buck. Good luck finding that. I convinced Doug that white paper written in black pen hardly sealed the deal.

After the FBI raid and the soul-selling episode, Doug finally broke away from Satan's grip. "I've had enough cocaine and enough of Hollywood," he told me one afternoon. "I'm moving back east to try and get my life together."

I understood and wished my friend well.

With Doug leaving, there went another band project down the tubes, and another year wasted.

Allen, our guitarist and my weed connection, quit the office . . . or should I say, Zolie banned him from the office for being all freaked out on a new drug called "Ice." Allen was so high, he thought he had tiny bugs crawling out of his fingernails. Several times I caught him in the bathroom pouring rubbing alcohol over his hands and fingernails until his skin burned red.

"What the fuck are you doing?" I asked.

"I got bugs from sleeping on the floor," he said.

"You do not!"

No matter how many times I tried, I couldn't convince him it was just in his mind, and I watched another friend rot from the inside out.

I would grab him and yell, "Get it together! You're losing your mind." He would just look at me like I was nuts.

~~

Later that week, Eve and I ran into Gary at the Rainbow while having dinner. We hung out and partied until dawn at his apartment in Hollywood. Gary told me he finally couldn't take anymore of Bobby's crap and had quit Hap Hazzard. Once again, we were a team in search of a singer and a lead guitarist.

Gary was living with an old high school buddy known as "Shitfield." I had cruised muscle cars with him back in Indiana. I thought Shitfield was really cool, even though he had blonde hair that was all one length like the Dutch Boy on the side of the paint can. Gary and Shitfield had been living in a one-bedroom apartment down in Hollywood on Bronson. The only nice thing about Gary's apartment was the top-floor location and a view of the Hollywood sign.

Gary's building was rundown and the elevator didn't work, so we had to walk up four flights of dimly-lit stairs, with bums sleeping in the corner shadows. The hallways smelled of damp carpet, mildew, and bum piss. I was afraid of getting an infection from touching the doorknobs.

After hanging out for a few hours, Gary said, "Do you want to see something entertaining?"

"Sure Chet. Let's see something good!"

Having no idea what he was doing, I watched as Gary filled up a five-gallon bucket of ice-cold water and walked out on his balcony.

"There is a real art to doing this," he said with a stupid look on his face.

"You have to throw it fast enough that all five gallons stay together, creating a giant water ball."

"Why would you want to do that?"

Gary looked over the balcony at a bum sleeping on the bus bench below. I shook my head. "Don't do it, seriously, don't do it."

Gary smiled at me and threw the water. It hit the bum square in the head like a giant watery cannonball, soaking him. The bum opened his eyes, licked his lips, turned over, and went back to sleep.

"We're going to have to use something heavier," said Gary.

We both laughed. I felt guilty for laughing.

I was appalled and would have smacked Gary, but the bum actually needed a bath, so the water wasn't going to hurt him.

"Gary, tell him what else you like to do to the bums," Shitfield said, suggesting that I wouldn't approve.

"What else could you possibly do to these poor street people?" I demanded. "What the fuck is wrong with you, anyway?"

With a sinister smile, Gary replied, "Watch, and I'll show you." He showed great pride in a new game he called "Bum Baiting."

"What is Bum Baiting?"

Gary walked out on the balcony and spotted two bums on the opposite street corner. "This is where the fun really begins," he said.

"What kind of fun?"

Gary threw a bright, shiny quarter up into the air. It touched down in the middle of Hollywood Boulevard amid heavy traffic flowing in both directions. By the second bounce, the two bums had spotted the lucky change like it was a gift that had fallen from Heaven. Scrambling to their feet, they darted after the money without even looking for oncoming traffic. Cars blew their horns and dodged to the side, their angry drivers screaming obscenities.

"Did you ever see one get hit by a car?" I asked.

Gary shrugged and, with his usual stupid, boyish smile, said, "No, they always get the money. No one wants to hit them for fear of getting sued. They'd rather crash into another car that's insured than hit a bum."

Un-fucking-believable.

Back inside the apartment, Gary continued laughing and snorted a five-inch rail of cocaine out of a huge pile on the dining room table.

"It's cheap entertainment," he said. "It only costs a quarter." Shitfield shook his head, but smiled and laughed.

Although I found their behavior disturbing, I said, "I want you chets to move into my place out in Studio City. That way we can start working on the music for the new band, and you can help me pay the high rent. The bums won't miss you!"

They both agreed and moved in with me at the end of the month.

~~

Gary was working at a different toner room, making really good money, and Shitfield was installing cable television around Los Angeles, making all kinds of new friends. Shitfield hooked up anyone who wanted free cable with all the channels for $200 a pop, clearing thousands a week, plus salary.

I asked Shitfield, "Can I advertise to my customers that this cable service is available?"

"Sure," he replied. "Why not? A buck is a buck."

Everyone who smoked weed and sold toner also wanted free cable, so the orders started coming into the suite as if it was a real cable office. We split the two hundred bucks for every order I got.

Shitfield also found out how much power the cable man had; everyone was always offering him gifts and bribes. If Shitfield smelled like marijuana when he showed up to do a cable installation, he usually got weed as a tip, thereby making all kinds of valuable connections in different neighborhoods all over Los Angeles.

Through Shitfield, I met one of my dearest and most loyal friends, who helped me survive in L.A. like a guardian angel. He would be with me through the worst and the best of times, and I would be there for him to the end.

~~

After the guys got all moved in at Studio Colony, Shitfield came home one night and broke out some of the sweetest-smelling green weed I had ever seen in my entire life from Humble County.

After the second puff, I asked, "Where did you get this shit?"

"I hooked up a guy's cable down in the Hood, and he gave it to me for free. Guess what?"

"What?"

"I got his number, and he said he could hook us up anytime."

"That's cool. Let's invite your new friend over for a cookout down by the swimming pool this weekend. I want to meet him."

Shitfield set it up. I was properly introduced to Rudy Valentino Roberto Cruz.

Rudy had a lifetime of experience in dealing with the underground world of Los Angeles. It was his town -- and I mean it was _his_ town. Some people called him Totie.

Rudy belonged to a certain group of organized Hispanics who had been running their neighborhoods since they were children. Rudy was the oldest one still alive, 29, making him "King Rudy."

Rudy was a Leo like me but had a completely different upbringing.

Somehow, we both ended up in the same place at the same time . . . making us new partners.

I was very lucky to have great parents. Rudy's mother was an alcoholic who was into voodoo, and his father was a safe-cracker who was in and out of prison most of his life. Rudy had grown up in tiny apartments filled with cockroaches and filth and had to move every time his mother flipped out or started a fight with a new boyfriend, bringing the police. In a violent rage, his mother would physically wreck the place while young Rudy and his siblings cried for her to stop.

Rudy really took a liking to us and treated us to free tickets to all the L.A. Kings hockey games. He also introduced us around the "Hood." I had never been around gang-bangers before and didn't know how to act, so I just acted like my goofy self. Rudy's friends liked me and welcomed all of us in, since Rudy was speaking on our behalf. Most of them were covered in tattoos from head to toe, some had tattoos of the number thirteen encircled in a devils pitch fork. Some, but not all, sported black teardrops, which were considered street medals that proved you had killed someone in street battle.

Rudy was the only one in his family to graduate from high school. After graduation, he had joined the Highway Patrol and proudly served on the force for a number of years. Married his love from El Salvador and bought a house to raise his family. One day, while cruising down the I-5 freeway, he got cut off, sending his motorcycle into a death roll. He suffered road rash over his entire body and serious back injuries that prevented him from further motorcycle duty.

While he was recovering, the LAPD screwed him out of his disability and benefits for unknown reasons -- probably because of Reagan cutbacks. He also suspected it had something to do with the fact that he was a minority.

Deeply disappointed in the system he had thought he was a part of and trusted, Rudy switched sides to survive.

"I know what to do and what not to do to attract attention," Rudy told me. "If you listen to me very carefully, without ever doubting my words, I'll keep you out of jail. As long as you don't draw federal attention, we're covered locally." He gave me his word, and that meant something in the City of Lost Angels. "We only make deliveries during LAPD shift changes and I know the times when there are no cop cars on the roads.

Although it was hard for me to believe, here I was, hanging out with gang-bangers who dressed like businessmen. They survived many street battles in the shadows of Los Angeles skyscrapers and did business right before the eyes of the authorities. I quickly realized that they owned the streets of Los Angeles and probably outnumbered the police force fifty to one. There was power in numbers.

While hanging out with Rudy, I learned he had a huge family and that quite a few of them worked for the city. Two nephews served with the

LAPD, giving us access to several computer systems for information. Rudy even had cousins who were border guards, making trips to Mexico very profitable. Rudy would walk back across the border with a huge smile, a wore out penis, carrying enough contraband to send him to prison for the rest of his life. The border guard would say, "Welcome home, Señor Cruz.

"I'll supply you with anything you need," Rudy told me, "and that means that you are now under my personal protection. If anybody messes with you, I will be glad to have the boys take care of it. They love street missions and any chance to impress me for street credibility."

"Thank you." We shook hands and he hugged me.

"Rule number one: Never talk over the telephone about anything in any way, shape, or form. We'll set up code words that will fit into normal conversations. If you ever say anything over the telephone, I'll hang up, and we will be done doing business."

"Okay."

"Do you understand? Not even once will I let it slide."

"Yes -- crystal clear." I already had that rule in place.

I was quickly losing my Indiana boy innocence and becoming an active part of the Hollywood underground world of crime and corruption. Still, it didn't seem like I was doing anything wrong . . . compared to what I saw others doing.

Chapter 15

Gary and I started putting a new music project together by teaming up with a veteran of the Hollywood heavy metal scene -- a lead guitarist named Darren Murakami. We hoped this would finally propel us into rock-and-roll stardom.

Darren was an excellent lead guitarist. Within three weeks, we had written ten metal tunes that flowed together with a magical rhythm, as if we had been playing together for years. I was damn lucky that Darren had a good sense of humor. I called him names like "Gook Boy," "Low Pan," and "Hung like a Gnat." He was part Japanese, Hawaiian, and American, but somehow he stood six feet tall with long dark hair.

Darren said in his defense, "I'm too damn good-looking and too tall to ever pick rice, you stupid fuck." He fought back by calling me a "shit-kicking redneck ass-backwards Indiana stupid fuck." Everyone in Los Angeles thought people from Indiana were like the guys in the movie <u>Deliverance</u>. I assured them, I was more of a Chicago guy and that I'd never fucked my cousin or any sheep . . . but I couldn't vouch for Gary.

The three of us rented a thousand-dollar-a-month rehearsal room in an old, dilapidated building on the corner of Hollywood Boulevard and Vine, said to be the most dangerous corner in all of Hollywood. The place was called the Hollywood Billiards, and over a hundred Sunset Strip bands rehearsed there on any given night.

On one corner, across the street, was an old hot dog stand that served as a front for drug sales. Next to it was an adult bookstore with live nude shows in the back and ass for sale in the basement. On the other side was a liquor store and a burned-out building which housed homeless who were using crack. Black gang-bangers sold crack out in front of the Hollywood Billiards, and outlaw bikers sold meth in the downstairs pool hall. It was the perfect setting for a murder, drawing all the wrong elements.

There were eight floors above the pool hall and thirty rooms on each floor, which were open twenty-four hours every day. Bands could practice anytime, as loud and as long as they wanted. The building should have been condemned many years earlier; there was only one working toilet on each floor -- if you were lucky. Some of the Hollywood musicians who were still trying to make it big actually lived in their practice rooms at the Hollywood Billiards. They slept on the floors and took showers on the roof by hanging a garden hose over a drainpipe.

After the first week of practicing at the Billiards, I went around and put a flier on every band's door, offering a job to any musician who wanted to get

Heaven Became Hell ... Hollywood Be Thy Name!

off his lazy ass and work to get out of the these ghetto-like conditions. By the end of that week, I had hired twenty-five Hollywood musicians from the Sunset Strip and put them to work on the telephone, selling toner . . . It was the perfect job for a Hollywood heavy metal musician.

~~

One night after rehearsal, I burned a couple of joints and walked out into the hallway with the smell of weed on my clothes. On my way to the bathroom, hoping to find one that works, I was stopped by a famous Hollywood musician. He has asked not to be named. He has kids now and lives a normal life.

"Hey, I was wondering -- do you have any more weed?" he asked.

"No problem," I replied, handing him what I had. I knew he wasn't a cop. I had his albums back at my suite. Thinking quickly, I added, "If you want more, here's my number." I pointed to the door that read "Bottoms Up" and said, "That's the room I practice in."

After I had hooked him up a few times and was very discreet when I came to his Mansion in the Hollywood Hills, he told several other big-name musicians about my services. Within a couple of days, nine different signed metal bands were calling me and wanting me to take care of them . . . and so I did. I began thinking this could be the perfect way to get more music contacts.

These guys spent big so I was calling Rudy every other day for more weed.

Grinning, Rudy told me, "Bubba, you're becoming my star student and my only connection into the Caucasian land."

I thought that was funny; I knew I was helping Rudy expand his reach way out past the Hood.

My old roommate J.J. was now working for a IRS Records; his job was to take care of anything the musicians needed when they came to town to do a show.

I gave J.J. a good deal but told him to stick it to them. R.E.M. and Georgia Satellite could afford it.

~~

Everything in my life seemed to be going smoothly, and I was adjusting to my new, eccentric lifestyle, until I noticed Eve had developed a serious sweet tooth for the fine white powder known as cocaine. In fact, she was doing it every day.

I still had control over cocaine; I could do it one day and go a few weeks without. But I saw the same pattern in Eve that I had in Cyn: she was smoking it behind my back and would no longer spend the night. I knew she was back in her apartment with the glass pipe pressed to her lips, instead of mine. It made me extremely sad.

If I wanted to hang out with Eve, I had to let her get high, which led to me getting high. After doing large amounts of cocaine, going to sleep or getting any serious rest was out of the question. When I tried to lie down or fall asleep, I started hearing strange sounds . . . that I had never heard before. I would hear every creak and tweak, and sounds that were similar to a helicopter's blades or the sound of voices coming over a police radio. But none of it was real . . . it was just what they call paranoia. And believe me, when you have it, no one can tell you there's nothing there. Your brain is racing so fast, everything is amplified ten times.

Finally, after months of partying, I told Eve, "We have to stop. This is getting way out of control. I don't want to die of a heart attack."

After hearing my speech, Eve finally agreed to let me check her into a rehabilitation center. She finally admitted she couldn't do it on her own.

It took me two weeks to get her admitted; all the beds were full in all medical centers within a hundred miles. There was a great need for drug rehabilitation in Hollywood. Since we were white, we couldn't take any of the free programs the city offered. I had to pay top dollar to get her treatment. All the money I had made from the weed sales went into fixing my girlfriend. One drug paid for the damage of another drug.

The only drug rehabilitation center that had an open bed was fifty miles away. The hour drive was an argument and a final plea to turn the car around. Eve tried her best to seduce me into changing my mind. But I held firm and said, "There's no turning back if you want to save our relationship, along with your own life. If you're not going to do it for me, do it for yourself."

"All right, I will go. But please grant me one last wish. Let me do one more line, real quick, before they lock me up. Please, just one more!"

I thought, What the hell, she's going into treatment. What harm would one more do? I really didn't want our last time together to be a fight. I wanted her to go willing and happy.

When we pulled into the rehabilitation center, I said, "Do your line real quick while I get your things out of the trunk."

"Thanks," Eve replied, "I love you."

"I love you, too."

Before I knew what she was doing, she had dumped the entire bottle out, making one giant line.

"What the fuck are you doing?" I screamed. "I said a line, not the entire bottle, god-damn it!"

In extreme anger, I grabbed Eve's belongings and escorted her very quickly into the center. I told the check-in nurse how much she had just done in the parking lot. I feared she might overdose in the waiting room while they messed with the paperwork.

The nurse started giving me shit. "Why did you let her do that much cocaine?"

I snapped. "Listen, lady. She's got a problem -- that's why she's here. If I could have stopped her, I would have. So shut the fuck up and admit her before her heart stops! NOW!"

Eve wasn't allowed to bring anything but a few personal objects. The staff of nurses went through her belongings with a fine-toothed comb looking for drugs, and discovered some hidden in one of her tampons. After that, they strip-searched her, including a full body cavity search, violating her most private parts -- all with my permission, once I had signed the forms. I knew Eve would hate me for that, but after seeing her snort one gram of cocaine all at once into her ninety-eight-pound body, I wasn't taking any chances.

The staff of nurses who appeared after I'd signed the papers really gave me the creeps. They looked like a bunch of thick-necked lesbians who couldn't wait to tear Eve's clothes off.

The head nurse said to me, "No phone calls or visits. You can call every other day, and the nurse on duty will give you progressive reports on Eve's condition."

My heart sank. "Why is that?"

"We enforce the 'tough love' program. I'm sure you've already tried the nice way. Let us have her, and come back in fifteen days."

As they shut the door in my face, I felt like I had left my girlfriend in prison to serve a sentence. I was locked outside, trying to look in.

I had told Eve I would take care of her plants and feed her fish. I also planned to pick up any drug paraphernalia, such as pipes, razor blades, dirty straws, that might be lying around her suite. I fed her fish and watered her plants, but at first I couldn't find anything lying around. Then, remembering what the nurses had found at the center, I started digging.

With a little more effort, I found cocaine hidden in a bottle in her medicine cabinet and some more hidden in the salt shaker, wrapped in a tiny plastic bag. I found her pipe hidden in a tampon in the box in the bathroom closet. There was probably more somewhere, I just knew it.

~~

When I called the rehabilitation center the second day, the nurse said, "We're having a real hard time with her. She isn't going along with the program. She is throwing a fit."

"Is she going to be all right?" I asked. "I want to talk to her."

"No way," the nurse replied. "She's angry with you for bringing her here. This is why we say no contact. She's just lashing out at everyone and everything because her body is going through chemical withdrawal. It's not a pretty sight."

"Will she be all right?" I asked with panic in my voice.

"It'll take time for her to detoxify," the nurse explained. "The worst isn't over yet. Just keep your faith and say an extra prayer for her tonight.

~~

I called the center back on the fourth day and learned that my prayers hadn't been answered . . . In fact, they'd been slammed!

"I don't know how to say this," the nurse told me, "but Eve took off. She escaped in the middle of the night with another addict."

I slammed down the phone.

When I got to the center, I screamed, "What kind of place are you running? How incompetent is the staff, if they can't keep track of a ninety-eight-pound female!"

No one had any answers, other than that she was missing, along with her roommate. For the next four hours, I drove around, checking all the bus stops without any luck. Finally I headed home, thinking that would surely be her final destination.

I called into the office and told Mary I wouldn't be coming in today.

"No problem," Zolie said. "If you need anything, let me know."

I waited all day in my apartment for Eve to show up, without any word. As the second day passed, I began thinking the worst. I knew something had happened, or she would have been home by now or called for a ride. Being alone on the streets of Los Angeles was like swimming in shark-infested waters with your wrists slit.

I sat by the phone for three days, when I wasn't walking back and forth to her apartment to check for her return. While I was waiting, my parents called.

"How's it going on the West Coast?" asked my father.

"Everything is peaches and cream."

"How's the music business going?" my mother asked.

"Fine," I replied. "Just taking a break." I had to pretend everything was all right and life couldn't be better, since they hadn't approved of me living in California. They wanted me home and made it clear.

I pulled it off. They thought nothing was wrong. I should have been an actor. I couldn't tell the truth, how could I.

I hadn't slept a wink in days. The phone rang around two in the morning, and I picked it up.

"May I speak with Brent?" said an unfamiliar voice.

"Yes, this is he. Who is this?"

"This is the hospital calling to tell you we have Eve."

I sat up in bed. "Is she all right? What happened?"

"We want to keep her overnight."

"What happened? When can I come get her?"

"Come in the morning. The doctor will talk with you when you get here."

Since the nurse wouldn't tell me anything, I had the rest of the night to think the worst thoughts. At least I knew she was alive and it appeared my prays had been answered.

~~

"I'm here to pick up Eve," I said to the nurse at the front desk of the hospital. "I'm her boyfriend." "We've been expecting you," the nurse replied. "I'll have the doctor come out and talk with you. Please have a seat." By the look on her face, I knew something was wrong.

Sitting there in the waiting room, I was reminded how much I hated the smell of a hospital -- a chemical smell of death in the air, of clean death.

A man with gray hair in a white coat and tennis shoes strolled up and put out his hand. "Are you Brent?"

"Yes, I am." I stood to shake his hand.

"I'm Dr. Covey. I worked on Eve last night. You might want to sit down."

"What's going on? What happened?"

"She's in stable condition; she's lucky to be alive."

"What happened?" I repeated.

"The LAPD brought her in late last night. They found her stumbling down the street naked and battered."

"What do you mean, naked?"

"Eve was raped and almost beaten to death," the doctor said solemnly. "She needed serious medical attention."

"What kind of medical attention?"

"I had to stitch her private parts. She was beaten badly, but she will heal."

"How is she doing now?"

"She's up and walking around, wanting to go home."

"Can I see her?"

"Yes, after you speak with the police. They want you to help them with the report. They'll be here in a few minutes."

I sat there with my hands over my face, barely believing what I had been told. How did I let this happen? I kept thinking over and over again. This couldn't be true.

When the police arrived, I was still in shock and didn't hear them when they called my name. A large police officer, standing at least 6'6" and wearing a bulletproof vest, reached out and grabbed my shoulder. "Hey, buddy, are you Eve's boyfriend?"

I looked up and nodded my head. "Yes."

"We need to talk about what happened to Eve."

"What happened?"

"Your girlfriend made friends with her roommate, and she talked Eve into escaping during the middle of the night."

"What roommate?"

"Her name is LaRhonda, but she gave a false address when she checked into the treatment center, and we have no idea who she really is."

"You didn't catch the people who raped Eve?"

The officer shook his head. "No. Eve couldn't remember where she escaped from."

"Why not?"

"Apparently she was all doped up and out of it when she escaped."

"Do you have anything?"

The police officer flipped through the pages of the police report. "Monkey Knuckle, Tin Tin, Low Down, and Ramrod, those are the names Eve gave us. They are not known gang members to us."

"Do you have any idea what actually happened?"

"Eve and LaRhonda took a bus to Englewood, where they went to a crack house to get high. Eve told us everything was cool until she tried to leave. Four large African-American males grabbed her, threw her to the ground, and took turns raping her for two days."

"What happened to LaRhonda?"

"Nothing, she was in on it. We believe she sold Eve out for cocaine."

I took a deep breath. "Anything else I should know?"

"Eve has rope burns on her wrists and ankles. They tied her up and whipped her with a coat hanger while they were getting high on crack.

After the officer left, I just stood there helplessly as my world crumbled around me.

After a few minutes, Eve appeared with a nurse walking close behind. I grabbed her hand and escorted her out to the car. The ride home from the hospital was silent and cold; Eve never said a single word. She wouldn't make eye contact with me. I certainly didn't know what to say, so I said nothing. I figured she would talk about it when she felt like it . . . if ever. I had been told to give her as much space as possible.

She was so book-smart that it intimidated me, but on the other hand she had no common sense, like most college-educated people.

The event had been so traumatic, Eve just sat in her apartment with a blank look on her face and the drapes closed. She wanted to be left alone for days. When she didn't answer the door, I finally stopped by and let myself in with my key. Eve was fast asleep on her bed. Looking around the room, I noticed her witchcraft books were out. I could only guess that she was probably casting a spell of death on the men who had raped her. Every time I looked at the whip marks and cigar burns on her back and the coldness in her eyes, I knew I was going to take these sadistic rapists out if I could ever find them. I knew the police weren't going to investigate it any further, since Eve was alive and a drug addict.

I conducted my own investigation by asking Rudy. He had contacts everywhere. I gave him the names Tin Tin, Monkey Knuckle, Low Down, and Ramrod, and a general area of their location.

"I'll do some checking," he said.

"Thanks."

"No problem, Bubba."

~~

My relationship with Eve ended a week later when I caught her doing cocaine again. I lost it.

"You didn't learn a damn thing, did you?" I yelled!

Eve didn't respond; she just looked the other way, absorbed in her own world -- the world she had shut me out of. I couldn't take it anymore. I gave her an ultimatum: choose between me and the cocaine.

She chose the cocaine.

Every time I came up against cocaine, it won hands down.

Chapter 16

<u>March 1989</u>

I wasn't having very good luck with any of the women I had attempted to date in Southern California. They were breaking my heart left and right, making me a mental wreck with their bullshit.

I was afraid to fall in love again, so I spent many lonely nights cruising the Rainbow for Hollywood one night stands, just to get my rocks off without any emotional ties. The sex was always kinky, but very impersonal and uncaring. I couldn't even remember the last time I'd gotten a loving kiss above the belt.

I also learned within the first year of living in the city limits of Los Angeles that their main source of income was parking tickets. No matter where you parked, it seemed that they gave you a ticket for some stupid reason. The posted sign was usually hidden behind thick greenery. Every ticket was at least fifty dollars, and the cost doubled after thirty days. There was no way to contest or beat the system! After your fifth ticket went unpaid, parking enforcement would put a Denver Boot on your car, locking the car's tire and preventing the car from moving. You had a week to pay all tickets before they towed your car, and thirty days to pay after that before they sold it at auction. If you were slick enough to avoid being booted, they would hold your new license plates until all tickets were paid in full.

I wouldn't pay, so I had four cars, but I could only drive the van and my new Trans Am. The Z-28 and the Audi 5000 had a couple thousand dollars worth of tickets, so the plates were expired. Since I knew I was being ripped off, I preferred not to drive the cars until I figured out how to beat the L.A. parking system.

By doing some research, I found out that when you buy or sell a car, all the parking tickets stick with the name of the person to whom the car was registered at the time of the parking tickets. They have since changed this glitch because of me; I did affect the system. Using my friend Alexis to obtain fake names and Social Security numbers, I sold all my cars back to myself under a fake name, clearing all the parking tickets for that year and giving the car a clean slate.

That put a smile on my face, and I quickly taught it to others. It was cheaper to pay a small sales tax and to change ownership than it was to pay all the parking fines. Plus, I got a real kick out of screwing the system. Now my real name was used for nothing. The first tickets, were my last.

I also went out and purchased four pairs of C.O.S. clamp cutters and kept one in the trunk of each car. If I got the Denver Boot, I could just cut it off within seconds, throw it in my trunk, and be on my merry way without much discomfort to my schedule.

Every Denver Boot I acquired I threw in the Los Angeles River on Vineland by my complex. The homeless people living under the 101 overpass were using the Denver Boots to weight down their tents against the Santa Ana winds.

~~

While hanging around the weight room in my complex, which was more like a social club, I met a guy with short, dark hair and a medium athletic build named Louis Anthony Furre. He told me to call him Chino.

I had seen him around the pool and racquetball courts for the last year before I finally struck up a conversation. Chino lived alone and asked me to play racquetball while I was waiting for Rudy one afternoon. After that, we started playing every week for several months.

After our game one day, we went up to his suite on the top floor. I liked the apartment layout and we did some rails. Then we both started talking. The cocaine always made you talk your head off; it could be used as a truth serum. I told Chino about my weed business and the office I ran for the Hungarians.

"I know who the Rathes are," said Chino, "and I know all about the Hungarian crime families of Hollywood."

"What do you do for a living?"

With a laugh and sinful smile, Chino answered, "Legally, I'm a freelance advisor, but that's not what pays the bills."

Chino was an independent contractor, trained by the U.S. military and Special Forces. His services were for those who could find him and afford him.

"So who do you work for?" I asked.

"I never discuss that," he replied, "but believe me, they're famous and crooked, with many faces -- pretending to be the good guys."

Evil white men.

Chino added, "Any moron can walk up and pull a trigger. That's for fools, and doesn't pay very well. But if you can make it look like an accident, that's where the big bucks come into play. The rich elite don't go around shooting people like Kennedy and Martin Luther King anymore -- that draws too much attention and public prying into the business that should be kept a secret. Everyone has to die someday. No one lives forever. And if it appears to be an accident or natural, like a heart attack or a car crash, what can someone say?"

Chino also warned me about the telephone; he didn't have one. He called the telephone the eyes and ears of the intelligence world.

Once we knew what we could do for each other, a partnership was formed. From that point forward, I got cocaine for Chino, knowing I might need a favor from someone like him someday.

It was just good business being in the business.

~~

This time when Chino contacted me, his request was a hard one to fill, since two of my connections had just gotten busted. I only had one source that wasn't in jail or too strung out to answer the phone.

Chino was stopping in Burbank to see me while passing through, giving me only a couple of hours notice. I was to meet him at the Burbank airport, and he would make it worth my while.

Trying to maintain Chino's level of professionalism and not disappoint him, I broke down and called Big Gunns. I hadn't been over to his high-rise suite since Eve had moved in with his roommate for free drugs. She had finally hit rock bottom and never returned to work or called me. She had stopped smoking cocaine, only to start shooting it into her tiny veins, since her new boyfriend was a paramedic and would supply her with needles.

Now I knew where Cyn got her needles.

Out of last-minute desperation, I made an appointment to pick up the usual, just knowing the emotional risk it would cause if I saw Eve. Hearing that someone had taught her how to shoot up made me want to kill him.

~~

As I entered Big Gunn's building, an alarm went off inside my head, warning me to just keep walking through and not to get anything. I felt I was being watched, just like I'd felt the day the FBI raided Copy Supply Warehouse. I hadn't known what I was feeling then, but I felt the same right now.

I started to head for the elevators, but that feeling made me walk past to the stairwell and hike up four flights of steps very quietly. Entering the hallway from the stairwell, I ducked down and crawled under the window that faced the front of the building. I felt stupid doing it, but I did it anyway.

Knocking on Big Gunn's penthouse door, I kept my hat pulled low and my sunglasses in place.

A girl named Tomorrow answered the door and let me in with a smile and a kiss, while rubbing my crotch. Tomorrow was a <u>Penthouse</u> centerfold and a permanent fixture at Big Gunn's. As soon as she got high, she liked walking around in nothing but a g-string and a bra.

"See anything else you might want while you're here?" she asked seductively.

Being polite, I said, "Maybe. What do you got to eat?"

"How about this?" She bent over and pulled her black g-string to one side to show off her recently shaved snatch.

I paid no attention. I had seen this act many times before, and I wasn't going to give her the gratification of ogling her like some of my friends did when she pulled this stunt at my suite.

"Very nice, I will have to eat another time," I replied. "Take me to Big Gunns!" I gave her butt a slap with the palm of my right hand, which put a smile on her face and hand print on her ass, but started us in the right direction.

Looking across the living room, I saw Eve standing in the other bedroom, looking at me through a reflection in a mirror. I couldn't believe how she looked -- like death warmed over. She had truly hit rock bottom and was jobless and penniless. The thought made me feel even more guilty for being at Big Gunn's penthouse.

I looked away, feeling the sadness in my heart and the missing part of my soul that she had taken. I pretended not to see her; I had nothing to say. Instead, I went about my business like a professional, not letting my emotions get in the way of conducting my transaction. When dealing with people in this business, being emotional might make someone nervous, and that would be bad.

Walking down the hallway with all of this on my mind, I struggled to block it out. If I didn't . . . things could go seriously wrong. I was back on the clock and strapped.

Big Gunns was doing his usual thing, watching pornos and playing cards with a stripper. Some girls dressed in miniskirts were doing lines on the countertop in the bathroom. Sledgehammer, Big Gunn's bodyguard, was sitting in the corner watching everything with his .45 caliber holstered under his arm, ready to draw at the first sign of any trouble.

Tomorrow followed me into Big Gunn's bedroom and, pinching me on the butt, said, "I've been trying to get it on with Eve, but she's not into girls."

Big Gunns snarled, "Shut the fuck up!" and pointed to the door. Tomorrow was yesterday. "Sorry about that," he said.

"Don't sweat it; I'm beyond that. Let's do business."

I handed Big Gunns a thousand dollars, and he handed me two ounces of cocaine. Chino would in turn pay me three thousand without any questions.

I took my baseball hat off and stuffed the ounces into the inside liner, going all the way around the brim. Turning the hat around backward, I put it back on my head.

"Thanks," I said. "But I gotta go. I think you understand."

"It's cool, man. Just be careful getting that home. No speeding in your red sports car, sonny boy."

"I won't. See you later." I was in and out the door within five minutes.

I couldn't hang around knowing Eve was in the other bedroom. It was eating me up inside. After what happened to her, I had no business doing this deal.

On my way out, that tingling alarm in my head went off. I listened, so I avoided the elevators and took the stairs down to the first level. I looked around and saw no one watching. Jumping over the back wall into the alley, I made it to my car without anyone seeing me leave the building, just like a ninja on a secret assassination mission.

The ride home was doubly unpleasant. The sun was hot and the traffic was heavy, and I was paranoid about getting pulled over. At the same time, I felt really depressed after seeing Eve in that condition. It made me want to go back and kick in the door to rescue her from herself, but that would have been very foolish. I knew I couldn't help her if she didn't want the help.

~~

Later that night at the bar in the Burbank airport, Chino had no idea the hell I had gone through to make this happen. I wasn't going to be a little bitch and tell him, either. Instead, I delivered him his package without any trouble.

We spent an hour having drinks and dinner before making the transaction. During the meal, we switched envelopes under the table. No one could see . . . not even me.

"There's some extra for short notice," Chino said quietly.

Trying to be cool, I replied, "Thanks, anytime."

I opened the envelope and counted $5,000 -- $4,000 profit.

As we exited the bar, I said, "Here." I handed Chino an envelope back, minus $3,000.

Chino asked, "What's this?"

"Keep the other two thousand on account for your services someday."

Chino gave me a funny look.

I thought, Maybe I pissed him off.

He finally laughed and replied, "That's fine by me."

Chino was off on a flight to Arkansas -- to do what, I didn't know and wasn't stupid enough to ask. He spent a lot of time there during the late '80's and early 90's.

For the next decade, I would do the same deal with Chino every couple of months, building up a huge account of special favors. It was just an eccentric gesture on my behalf, since I was dealing with such a dangerous man. I wanted to seem as dangerous in his eyes.

~~

The next morning, there was a loud knock at Big Gunn's door. Before anyone could answer, the door came crashing in, and a police battering ram followed close behind. A SWAT team dressed in black bulletproof jackets with M-16s cocked and drawn came through the front door like storm troopers invading the Imperial Cruiser.

"Search warrant!" they screamed. "Up with your hands, motherfuckers!"

They rounded up everyone in Big Gunn's penthouse at gunpoint. One by one, they were strip-searched in the living room like convicts, including Eve. They got Big Gunns with one kilo of cocaine. He was lucky; he usually had much more. He was sentenced to two years in prison.

"I'll be out in seven to nine months or sooner, if the jails get overcrowded," he said confidently.

"I'll see you then," I replied.

Big Gunns never made it out; he got scanted in the shower and bled to death.

Eve got sentenced to a rehabilitation center. I was done with her.

I hoped I could forget and move on with the next chapter in my life, I wanted to close this one quickly.

The party at the penthouse was over.

Chapter 17

<u>Summer 1989</u>

I spent the entire summer and into the fall cruising the bars of Southern California, looking for the answers to my life and in search of a female companion who wasn't crazy. I should have gotten my head examined for looking for love in Hollywood.

After Big Gunns went to prison, I started seeing some of the girls from his penthouse cruising the Rainbow and looking for somewhere to hang out all night after the club closed.

One Friday night, I went to the Rainbow for a pre-Halloween party. I had made a cool costume out of clothes I had bought on Melrose Boulevard. I went through several secondhand shops and found old-style black stitch-up pants and a white, long-sleeve shirt. Stopping at a yard sale, I bought a silver necklace that I wore around my neck to complete the costume. The necklace featured a giant pentagram with the names <u>Berkaial</u>, <u>Amasarac</u>, <u>Akibecc</u>, and <u>Asaradel</u> engraved on the back in each corner of the star. I looked like a real vampire, with my long, dark, streaked hair.

Halloween had always been one of my favorite holidays, and I was really looking forward to seeing the Rainbow girls dress up even more sexy for Halloween, given the chance to be even more devilish.

Around midnight, as the secondhand on my smoke-black Movado watch proved it was the witching hour, I was in the upstairs loft of the Rainbow, downing my third Long Island Iced Tea. Elizabeth, an attractive, alterative-looking blonde with a pierced tongue and a tattoo in black ink above the crack of her derriere, invited me to a Halloween party up in the Hollywood Hills after the Rainbow closed.

"What does your tattoo mean?" I asked after she caught me checking out her ass.

"I'll have to show you."

"No, seriously -- I really want to know."

"It says, 'In through the out door.'"

I assumed she was a Led Zeppelin fan.

"Too bad about Big Gunns," Elizabeth remarked.

I agreed as we drove up a steep incline into a private driveway in the Hollywood Hills. The house overlooked Tinsel Town and could have been defended like a fortress. I couldn't imagine what a house like that might cost and what someone would have to do to call it home for a lifetime.

The valet who parked my sports car had a goofy look; there was something odd about him. I suspected that he had shaved his eyebrows off and painted them back on. He took my keys and handed me an envelope that read, "Welcome to the Party." I opened the envelope. It contained three joints and a gram of cocaine as party favors.

The drugs were normal, but the shaving of the eyebrows wasn't . . . Nor was the tattoo of a pentagram behind his left ear.

When we entered the mansion, it was packed with all kinds of Hollywood weirdos. Taking a closer look, I realized they weren't all wearing costumes. Everyone there knew Elizabeth, and she introduced me to the host and owner of the house. He was probably in his late fifties but was surrounded by people in their twenties or younger, who were all kissing his ass to the point of making me sick. I wasn't impressed, I wasn't an actor. I had real talent.

I knew who he was; he produced movies and had the palest skin of any man I had ever seen. You would have never guessed by his complexion that he lived in Southern California. I had heard one of the Hollywood madams complain about him getting rough and being weird with some of her girls. He was into heavy bondage and heavy use of cocaine.

After mingling with the guests for a couple of hours and drinking several more drinks, Elizabeth and I went into a back bedroom and snorted some more lines, getting really high. Lying there on the bed, I looked around the bedroom and was compelled to ask, "Whose bedroom is this, anyway?"

There was a variety of strange objects in the bedroom that I had only seen in occult bookstores, and many symbols of the black magick I recognized from my past.

"It's my bedroom," she said. "I live here with my uncle. You met him earlier."

I wasn't really sure if I believe he was her uncle. By this time, Elizabeth was starting to give me the creeps. I was sick of seeing this ignorant witchcraft crap everywhere. To me, praying to a fallen angel only indicated signs of mental illness or lack of self-esteem. If you play with fire, you will get burned, I always said. I had plenty of experience in that department.

Elizabeth locked her bedroom door and bent over slightly. "Do you want to get really kinky with me?"

She looked hot bent over. Forgetting about the witchcraft junk, I replied, "What do you have in mind?"

"I'll show you," she said with a sinister smile.

Reaching into her dresser drawer, she pulled out a wooden paddle and laid it on the bed. Then she pulled out a vial of powdered cocaine and a tiny funnel with a rubber tip.

I asked, "What the hell is that for?"

"I want you to fill my rear end with a gram of cocaine," she said without shame, "and then paddle me until I orgasm."

95

That was new and original.

"Sure," I said. "Bend over." I was glad she didn't want to paddle me.

Heavy metal music blared in the background, and patchouli incense burned around the bed. The mood was just right and I would do anything she said. Elizabeth's seductive tone of voice and hot body got me really horny, and the cocaine made me feel uninhibited. She instantly got up on the bed like a cat in heat.

"How's this look?" Lifting up her dress, she stuck her derriere up in the air while putting her face down into the pillow.

"It looks good enough to eat."

"Have a taste, don't be shy."

Thinking there was nothing sweeter than a nice piece of blonde pie, I knelt down and placed my face between her luscious cheeks, getting a good face-full, really working it.

"Yeah, baby, that's it," she moaned, grabbing the back of my head and pushing my face even deeper into the sweet wet pie. "Ohhhh!" Elizabeth screamed, her whole body shaking.

"Did you like that?"

"Yeah, baby. Let's do that other thing."

"All right."

Remaining on all fours, Elizabeth pulled her cheeks apart. Using one finger, she smeared lubricant into her tight, pink rectum with gentle loving care. I opened the vial of cocaine.

"The whole thing," she said. "I have more, don't worry."

I inserted the rubber tip of the tiny baby blue funnel into her tight pink anus very carefully.

"Make sure it's inserted all the way," she instructed.

She arched her back, even more as I emptied the vial of cocaine into the tiny funnel, filling her rectum until the bottle was empty.

"Blow on the end. Make sure all the cocaine is out of the funnel and take it out slowly. I can feel it tingling."

I set the funnel down and picked up the wooden paddle from the bed. Elizabeth reached for the headboard and retrieved a glass pipe, a lighter, and a rock of cocaine about the size of a dime.

"I'm going to take a huge hit off this pipe," she said. "When I exhale, paddle me until I come -- please!"

"If that's what you want." Never knowing what a woman might actually want, I agreed.

Elizabeth put the rock of cocaine into the pipe and melted it, then put the glass pipe to her voluptuous lips. She hit the lighter and put the flame to the glass pipe. It crackled. After sucking hard on the glass penis for forty seconds, she finally set the pipe down into the glass ashtray on the headboard. Bracing herself, she stuck her ass out for easy targeting.

Elizabeth exhaled and commanded, "Swat!"

I struck her ass with the wooden paddle and continued paddling as she screamed, "Harder!" I really let her have it, one smack after another, with enough force that she had to keep repositioning herself. Her bottom turned a bright shade of red. Finally her legs started shaking and she yelled, "Stop!" and fell to the bed.

I watched in amazement as she shook with multiple orgasms, her juices flowed down both her legs. Wiping the sweat from my own forehead, I felt the strain of the zipper on my pants. She had a amazing body.

Lying there with a sexually satisfied smile, she rubbed her backside, enjoying the feeling that had brought her to multiple orgasms. Looking back over her shoulder, she threw back her thick blonde hair and said with a kinky smile, "Put your cock in my ass . . . please!"

Always wanting to be the perfect gentleman and always accommodating my female lovers, I broke out a condom and did as she asked, betting that she wouldn't do much sitting the next day after the numbing effects of the cocaine wore off.

Once we finished with our kinky sex games, we got dressed and walked down a long hallway to a back stairway that led to the basement under the house.

"Where are we going?" I asked.

"Be quiet."

She led me into another room with a giant two-way mirror on the wall, looking into what appeared to be a giant bathroom with a huge marble hot tub. Hundreds of candles burned around it. Many people dressed in dark robes encircled the tub.

"What the fuck is going on?" I asked.

Elizabeth explained, "My girlfriend Kathy is being made a full member of my coven. My aunt is the high priestess performing the ritual.

"Can they see us?"

"No," she said, and pointed out her friend Kathy. She was in the hot tub with the high priestess, who was bathing the younger witch for the ritual. It wasn't uncommon for rich people to have two-way mirrors or hidden cameras in their bathrooms in Hollywood.

After a few minutes, the high priestess got out of the hot tub naked. She picked up her magic athame and waved it in the air many times before entering a circle formed on the floor in the center of the room.

The high priestess commanded the forces of the East, South, West, and North to attend. Then she began dancing around while the other members started to chant unfamiliar words. Finally, after jumping around like a chicken on acid, the old witch approached Kathy, reached out her hand, and helped her out of the hot tub naked.

The high priestess said some words and they both responded together,

"Perfect love and perfect trust."

Blindfolding Kathy, the high priestess stepped behind her and towered over her like a captor, gently giving her a sinful kiss on the lips.

She accepted with great pleasure.

Standing behind Kathy with her silicone breasts pushed up against the young girl's naked back, she pushed Kathy into the circle drawn on the tile floor.

Taking a piece of rope from the altar, she bound Kathy's hands behind her back and ran the rope around her neck, making a perfect triangle on her back. Kathy was then led around the room like some prize catch, and some more words that I didn't understand were said while the other members started chanting.

Everyone then became silent, and the high priestess said, "Take heed, O spirits of the dark, Kathy has been properly prepared for this day and will be made a priest."

She struck a bell thirteen times and said more words to her gods of nature. She then stepped in front of Kathy and started kissing her feet, knees, vagina, breasts, and finally lips to seal the deal.

Kathy was then led to the altar, made to kneel, and tied by the neck and ankles, causing her to bend forward.

The high priestess struck the annoying bell another few times until it became silent.

The high priestess said, "Art thou ready to swear thou will always be true to the Black Arts?"

Kathy responded, "I will!"

The high priestess struck the bell three more times and said, "Thou first must be purified."

I didn't know what to think of what I was being shown, and I didn't know why Elizabeth was revealing these secret rituals to me. So I kept one eye on what was going on and the other watching my back, constantly checking my surroundings.

The high priestess picked up a sacrificial knife from the altar and held it above Kathy's head, as if she was pointing to the full moon shining through the skylight. That was the only source of light in the room, other than candles burning in medieval holders surrounding the room.

Everyone in the secret room was robed and their faces were covered, so I couldn't tell if they were male or female. I assumed they were all female witches, but I could be wrong.

Suddenly, with the knife in her hand, the high priestess spun around and for a brief moment stared directly at me through the mirror. A chill went through my soul.

I knew from that point forward that our presence wasn't a secret.

I was mentally freaking out, but I didn't move as the high priestess put the knife down and picked up some type of wooden rod.

Gently at first, the high priestess stroked Kathy's buttock. Each stroke got harder, until red welts started to appear. Elizabeth got turned on.

"I want some of that, too," she said.

She started rubbing my groin, but with all the cocaine and the thoughts of being sacrificed to Satan, I just couldn't get into achieving another hard-on. It had taken witchcraft to finally kill my constant erections.

When the high priestess was finished, Kathy's backside looked like someone had ice-skated across it.

"Are you ready to protect, help, and defend any brother or sister of the black arts?" asked the priestess.

Kathy answered in a sinister voice, "I am."

"Say after me: I solemnly swear in the presence of the Evil One, of my own free will, that I will keep the secrets."

Kathy replied, "I swear and may my weapons turn against me if I break this solemn oath."

The high priestess untied Kathy and made her stand, as she rubbed her hands all over Kathy's naked body, feeling her up and down while kissing her on the nipples and lips. She ended the ritual and consecrated Kathy by touching her vagina and both breasts with holy oil. Then she did the same with red wine.

Elizabeth said, "The ritual is almost over. Let's get going."

We took off and went back to her bedroom for more cocaine and sex until dawn. I never slept a wink. Instead, I kept an eye on the bedroom door. My pistols were not more than an arm's reach away at all times.

Elizabeth said, "You have absolutely nothing to fear. Why are you so uptight? I know you're into all this type of stuff. Eve was, and I know you loved her. She said you were cool."

"I'm cool," I replied. "The cocaine has just gotten me freaked out." I tried to cover and explain.

As soon as the sun came up, it was a breathtaking sight. I felt safe in the sunlight; the darkness and the evilness had passed and everything looked different in the daylight.

I skipped out without awaking Elizabeth. This mystery mansion was huge and I thought I might need a guide to just find my way out. This was the perfect place for a murder; no one would have heard a damn thing.

Strolling down the hallway, I was met by a maid who called me by my fake name, "Buster Rears." She showed me to my car and handed me the keys.

My sports car was parked up front, freshly washed and cleaned for me to leave.

The sun hurt my eyes, and my sunglasses were missing so I had to stop at the first gas station to buy a cheap pair.

Then I noticed a dark car following me. I recognized the car from being parked around the side of the mansion. I knew someone was following me . . . I didn't like it.

They must have gone through my glove box and saw the fake name on the car's title. That was why the maid called me Buster Rears. The address on the title was also fake. After seeing the ritual in the basement last night, I didn't want these people to know where I lived. I knew I had to lose them.

I gassed up the car to half a tank and bought an extra large cappuccino with two shots of espresso. Walking outside, I downed the coffee real quick to get myself wired and my blood pumping to the stage of alertness.

I pretended I didn't see them; it was part of the game.

I put on the cheap plastic pair of no-name brand sunglasses to cover my eyes and started my car and proceeded onto Laurel Canyon at normal speed. The traffic was thick, but I waited, and when I got the chance, I abruptly passed a car on the curve and hit the gas so I could beat them down the canyon into the Valley.

They weren't able to `pass. I gave them the slip.

That gave me the creeps, so I never called Elizabeth. I avoided the Rainbow for a while.

Chapter 18

My neck and jaw had been bothering me. All the cocaine and stress had brought back a lot of pain that had been caused by the trauma of the car accident and the serious beating I'd taken from a biker before coming to Hollywood. I made an appointment with a doctor in Hollywood to see if he could adjust my jaw and neck.

To my surprise, Angel was the doctor's receptionist. It had been a year since I had last seen her. This was just too weird; I figured it must be fate.

After the Copy Supply Warehouse raid, I had lost track of her and what was going on in her life while I was dealing with Eve. So much had happened in the past year, I wasn't sure if she could deal so I decided to keep my mouth shut.

Angel's hair had really grown; it was a foot longer than mine without extensions. She was dressed conservatively in high heels, which made her look very professional, yet sexy.

I stared for a few seconds, then cleared my throat and whistled as she bent over to pick up some papers.

Angel turned around with a shocked look on her face, but then she returned my smile and gave me a big hug. She felt wonderful.

"Still a smart-ass, I see," she remarked.

"Nothing has changed," I said. "Why would it?"

"I guess there's just no hope for some people, is there?"

"Nope." We both laughed.

Her hair smelled wonderful and brought back a lot of good memories of a time when Satan and drugs weren't involved.

I invited her to go to Knott's Berry Farm for Halloween, and she accepted. I left the office feeling pumped. Things were finally looking up after a year of drugs, depression, and demon possession.

~~

We had a great time at Knott's Berry Farm, and by the middle of the night, we were holding hands just like we had been last year. I wanted to get back together with her, but I couldn't tell her about my weed business. When I had last dated her, I hadn't been doing any drugs. I knew she wouldn't stand for any criminal behavior, especially after getting busted at Copy Supply Warehouse.

I drank beer and hid my weed-smoking for a while because I was ashamed. I didn't mess with the cocaine with her around.

~~

Seven months passed by rather quickly, and my relationship with Angel was going well. I decided to move out of my suite in Studio City for several reasons. First, the place was giving me the creeps, and I wasn't the only one who felt that way. Everyone thought the suite was haunted. I never told anybody about what Doug had done. Witchcraft wasn't a subject I wanted to discuss.

Everyone who stayed over had the same experience: they would wake up screaming from a terrifying nightmare. When I asked what they were yelling about, none of them could remember. Guests also saw strange shadows forming on the walls of Doug's bedroom, where he had done the satanic ritual. I thought everyone was just nuts, until I started seeing the weird shadows myself. Then I knew what my friends were talking about. It was frightening, and I couldn't explain it. To this day, I still remember the dark shadows forming and the whispering in my ear every night.

I also felt that too many of the wrong people knew where I lived. I was getting a lot of weird phone calls. Someone would call and just listen, without saying a single word. They would stay on the line until I hung up. That was just pure intimidation -- from whom, I didn't know. I got an air horn and tried to blow their eardrums out.

We all agreed it was time to go.

Gary, Shitfield, and myself moved from the Valley into the concrete jungle known as Hollywood. The new place was at the top of Fuller Avenue, right up the hill from rock-and-roll Ralph's.

I left no paper trail for anyone to follow; I didn't forward my phone number or my mail. Instead, I rented a P.O. Box on Sunset Boulevard as my address.

~~

My new building was called The Pinnacle. It was one of the most expensive and prestigious buildings in Hollywood, sitting on top of the Hollywood Hills just below Errol Flynn's burned-out mansion. The set for the old Bat Cave was up there also.

I could see the entire city of Hollywood from my balcony and on a clear day I could see the ocean. Because of the thick smog, those days were very few.

Quickly, I learned that The Pinnacle was filled with rich and eccentric people who had nothing better to do than get high all day and act as weird as possible. I knew we were going to fit in quite well. Within the first week I was already in an upstairs bathroom doing cocaine with Steven Percy and Amir, lead guitarist of Rough Cut, and most recently of Orgy.

Tammie Downs, the lead singer of Faster Pussy Cat, lived upstairs, next to the asshole singer of the band Cat and Boots. Steven Percy of Ratt lived there sometimes, when he needed a couch to crash on. If I was unlucky enough to get caught in the elevator with him, I was reminded of how much I hated the smell of hard liquor and day-old sweat.

The complex was also filled with drug dealers dealing in many different types of drugs, and everyone was willing to trade.

The Pinnacle had seven floors and featured a hot tub and swimming pool on the roof with a spectacular view of Hollywood. Three high-priced call girls lived on the third floor and sunbathed naked on the roof by the pool in the late afternoon every day.

A couple of dipshits who lived on the second floor pretended to be vampires. They were ugly guys who needed makeup to look Hollywood-pretty, but once I got to know them, I realized the vampire act was just another scam to get girls. A lack of pussy would make some guys do anything. I just couldn't believe they dressed like vampires all the time; they actually slept in crates with dirt. Their pale white skin was a serious contrast to the dyed jet-black hair. They had even gone as far as to go to some dentist in Hollywood, who added "fag caps" to their teeth. With colored contacts, they looked like vampires right out of The Lost Boys.

"Fang" and "Thirst" were always making jokes about prowling the Hollywood nightclubs in search of that perfect human meal, and nighttime was known as "feeding time." The vampires tried to fix me up with a female vampire, but I said, "Sharp teeth and my privates don't go together any better than zippers and foreskin."

"Too bad -- vampire girls really suck!" Fang said with a fake European accent.

"Thanks anyway, but I hate dead fucks," I replied with a laugh.

After a couple of weeks at my new apartment, with my outgoing personality I had gotten everyone in the building accounts concerning weed and cable television hookups. It was a social building, where everyone hung out at the pool and the Jacuzzi, so it was easy to tell who was into a good time: everyone.

Timbo, my new neighbor and now second guitarist in the band, introduced me to the "Wild Boyz." I'm talking about the original wild boyz of Hollywood, not a couple of MTV jackasses running around in thongs. I'm referring to Shane the Pain and his sidekick, Bow. They were the craziest non-thinking motherfuckers I had met up to this point in my life. I had met people who were more dangerous, but these two guys would steal and scam anything that wasn't nailed down like a couple of pack weasels.

Before being properly introduced to Shane and Bow, I had seen them run a scam at the liquor store at the bottom of Fuller Avenue and Sunset Boulevard. While Angel waited in the car, I had walked into the store and noticed two shady-looking characters looking around. I could tell they were up to something and thought they were going to rob the store, so I reached into my jacket and unfastened my pistol from its holster. I wasn't going to stop them from robbing the place, but they weren't going to get my money or wallet.

Shane was at one end of the store, and Bow was at the other. They walked toward each other, bumped shoulders, and started an argument.

"Watch where you're going, asshole!"

"Fuck you right back, asshole!"

Then the fists flew, and it turned into an outright brawl. The Korean working behind the counter had to come out to break up the fight. I thought they were just nuts until I saw their third partner in crime, Baron, grab three bottles of whiskey and a couple cases of beer and stroll out the front door before the owner had any idea what was going on. Shane and Bow stopped fighting and left the store, while the Korean was happy that nothing had gotten busted. I said nothing as he bagged up my beer.

For some reason, I took a liking to Shane and Bow. Shane was always beating up on Bow, using him like a punching bag, but Bow did deserve it sometimes for acting stupid.

The Wild Boyz had many ways of making money without working. Sometimes they sold beer out of a cooler on the beach or sold fake mushrooms to Marines who came to Hollywood on the weekends from San Diego. It was always some sort of low-level scam.

Shane was the brains and the muscle of this two-man operation. He was six feet tall and slender, with a solid muscle build and long blonde hair that any girl would have envied. His right shoulder was decorated with a big tattoo of a flaming Phoenix. Shane, meanwhile, resembled a young Iggy Pop and would have been considered a pretty boy. But with the crazy look I saw in his eyes, I knew it would be a mistake to say that to his face. His father was a truck driver from Ohio with a bad temper and a drinking problem. He had beaten Shane for most of his childhood, creating a permanent problem for society.

Bow stood 5'8" and had shoulder-length jet black hair. He had been living on his own since he was eleven. He was a little slow from being stoned all the time but was very likeable. Bow was always trying to get on my good side by stealing things for me. I would say, "Stop doing that. I don't need power tools or a shopping cart."

The Wild Boyz also did a lot of shit jobs for a man called Uncle Paul; he was the under boss for the Bulgarian Mafia. Uncle Paul had been linked to many murder investigations. His income came from three main sources: cocaine, counterfeit money, and jobs as a contractor. It cost five thousand a hit; ten thousand if you wanted it done with a knife, making it really messy; and fifty thousand to make an entire family disappear.

I had never seen counterfeit twenty-dollar bills before, and I was amazed by how good they looked. I could barely tell the difference, other than the slightly lighter color of the counterfeits. The way the funny money was floating around, it seemed that Uncle Paul had an endless supply.

I asked Shane, "Where the hell is he getting the fake money?"

"Someone got a tip and stole the plates they used to make counterfeit money in the movie <u>To Live and Die In L.A.</u>" The movie was about counterfeiters, and now these guys were spending the fake money just like in the movie. Now it had made the transition from screen to street.

Every single night -- since this city never slept -- Uncle Paul would send Shane, Bow, and a crew of twenty other street kids out to break fake twenty-dollar bills. They would go out and buy small items, like a cup of coffee at an all-night donut shop, just so they could get $19.50 in real change. They also bought items out of the local newspaper and would pay the people in fake money, then pawn the items for real cash. This was the way the system worked; for every dollar of real, you could purchase three dollars in fake, tripling your money. You had to take the risk of exchanging it, but that risk was minimal.

To achieve the necessary ugly shade of green ink, they used kiwi-lime Kool-Aid and mixed it with a dark-colored tea. The wet sheets were dried out in the sun. Once dry, the sheets were laid out on a table and cut with a flat board cutter. To give them a crinkled look, it was tossed in a dryer with dozens of poker chips.

I passed on the counterfeiting operation; I was already involved in enough illegal activities. I had a cousin who had been a Secret Service agent. He had died in the line of duty, guarding the Queen of England. To show respect, I didn't want to mess with that branch of the government.

"Thanks . . . but no thanks."

Chapter 19

June 1990

I had fallen asleep in my office chair and was awoken by Eve, who placed her hands over my eyes and said, "Guess who?"

I was very surprised to see her alive and looking so well rested . . . back amongst the living.

"I'm off the drugs," she said, "And I landed a sweet job as an accountant for a firm that's representing Warrant and Smashing Gladys.

"Great." I was glad to hear it.

"I bought a brand new truck, and I paid all my back bills. My credit is restored and perfect."

I was happy for her. Eve stayed for dinner. While we were eating, Rudy stopped by and dropped off the usual.

"It's nice to see you, young lady," Rudy said with his usual gentle manner. "I'm also glad to see you're doing so well."

Eve smiled.

I shook Rudy's hand, and he said, "I'll call you later."

~~

Later that evening, Rudy called and asked me to come to his house in the Hills. "Come alone," he said. That was the first time he had requested my presence. I thought that was a little strange, so it put me on edge. I thought I did something wrong.

When I arrived at Rudy's, he was hanging out with a few of his crew. They were getting rowdy and having a good time. After shaking everyone's hand, I sat down and sparked up a joint.

"You're not thinking of getting back with Eve, are you?" he finally asked.

"I don't think so. Angel and I are getting along really well. I don't want to screw that up."

"That's cool," Rudy replied. "I wasn't going to tell you what one of my people found concerning the guys who raped Eve last year, but I feel I have to."

My heart stopped for a brief second. "What did you say?"

"Through a few different deals, a guy named Monkey Knuckle sold us this tape."

"What tape are you talking about?"

"I just found out about these guys myself. They make snuff films."

I thought, <u>What is he talking about?</u>

"I don't want to see anything like that!" I replied. "I'm kinky, not completely twisted."

"The first part of the movie they sell as hard bondage," Rudy explained. "The second part of the movie, when the girl is all used up . . . they kill her."

"Who would buy something like that?"

"Rich people in Beverly Hills are known for paying big bucks, and they're popular in the heroine trade."

"What does this have to do with Eve?"

Rudy put the tape into the VCR. "This one is called <u>The Dungeon</u>."

On the television screen, I saw a girl that looked like Eve tied to a bed, being raped. I only watched a few seconds before demanding, "I want to know where I can find these motherfuckers!"

I will never forget the glazed look on her face and the sheer terror in her baby-blue eyes as she was being raped by four muscle-bound, drug-crazed animals that probably hadn't had their rabies shots. It brought back all the nightmares, plus new ones, as if I had witnessed it myself. I felt helpless to stop it, like a guardian angel locked in another dimension.

I snapped inside.

"Rudy," I yelled, "I want these fuckers retired!"

"I had to make sure it was the right guys before I gave the green light."

I took the next two days off from the office while I turned it over in my mind. I couldn't think about anything else. I felt different, like I had never felt before. Could I actually do what was expected by the rule of the streets of Los Angeles?

As days passed, Rudy accumulated all the information about the animals that had raped Eve. He knew where they lived and found out they were not part of any gang. They were freelancers from Detroit. Their lifestyle didn't sit right with Rudy once he found out what they were doing in his city. Rudy and I were high-class criminals, and animalistic behavior didn't jive with our sense of honor. We were only criminals against a system that tried to enslave us. We didn't go around hurting people . . . unless they did something to bring it on.

I still believed in Heaven and feared even more for my mortal soul. What I had done in the past could be forgiven, but breaking the 6th commandment would close the gates to Heaven forever.

Many thoughts ran through my mind as Rudy and I walked around McCarruther Park. The pond was filled with ducks that were being poisoned by the empty plastic lighters the homeless would toss in when the cops came around to stop the crack-smoking.

I was thinking about my life in Los Angeles. This was what it had come down to.

"Bubba, you got two choices," Rudy said to me in his Latino accent.

"You can take care of your business, or you can go back to Indiana. After shooting your mouth off, you'll have to prove to everyone that you deserve respect and the right to live in our world."

I nodded. "I understand."

"Our world is not like your world, where fine-bred lawyers settle law and order . . . where a fat ass wearing a powdered wig slams a gavel."

"I know that," I replied. "It's just that . . . this is a line I thought I would never have to cross."

Rudy continued walking. "If you want this type of life, it doesn't come cheap or without self-sacrifice. If your heart's not in it, then you'll never survive in Los Angeles. Nothing is free."

"I know."

"If you want to belong, if you want the respect, if you want the power and the money, you'll do what has to be done, without fear or hesitation. You'll do it with all your heart, like a lion in the jungle being challenged."

"I want your respect -- I do. But I'm not sure if I can do what's expected of me."

We walked some more as I thought.

"If I call it off," Rudy said, "my boys will never back you. Some of them think you're just a white boy out of your neighborhood. But I know you can prove to them you're one of the elite. I know you're a Leo like me."

That was true. I was a Leo, and I wanted the respect. I wanted to be a part of the crew. There was strength in numbers, and nothing went down in Los Angeles without them knowing about it.

Above all, I wanted my revenge.

I thought about all the ways I could have Chino take care of these animals. But if I did, it wouldn't get me street respect. I would be just another rich white asshole paying a minority to do his dirty work.

"I'm not trying to pressure you into doing anything you don't want to do," Rudy explained as we left the park. "You have to make up your own mind. Either your legend starts now, or it ends."

~~

When we arrived at Monkey Knuckle's house, I was scared shitless, although no one could have known by looking at me. I kept a straight face and stayed focused as we knocked on the front door of an old, dilapidated house -- the usual for this type of neighborhood.

A big black guy wearing no shirt answered the door and let us in. The place smelled of crack cocaine, mold and death.

"I'd like to introduce you guys to my friend," Rudy said casually. "This is Bubba. He wants to do some business with you."

"Come in, niggers!" There was some laughter.

I was already crazy-looking, with my long dark hair and the single white streak down the side. The name Bubba hardly fit my appearance, but it put them at ease. That was their last mistake.

"I'll be outside," said Rudy. "I need some fresh air."

"No problem," I said with confidence. "I got this handled."

The door shut behind Rudy, and there I was, in the same room with the guys who had beaten and raped Eve.

"So," I remarked, "you guys are into making films, I hear?"

"Yeah," Monkey Knuckle replied. "Have you seen our work?"

"Yeah," I replied in a different tone, hardly able to hold back the anger. "I have, up close. You guys are some sick motherfuckers. What is wrong with you?"

"What the fuck does that mean?"

I didn't answer; I showed them.

Low Down yelled, "The white boy is strapped!"

Chapter 20

I had proven myself way beyond what was expected of me. I still couldn't believe who I had become. My Latino friends had given me the nickname "Mr. B." They said it with full respect, as if I was one of their own. I was.

The bullet hole in my right bicep had almost healed. The scar that remained was from the cigar they had used to seal the wound once the bullet was removed. The burned flesh hid the hole. Digging out the slug was no vacation.

I was so traumatized, I never told Eve what happened. I just blew her off. I didn't want to get any more involved emotionally. I had done too many bad things because of Eve, and it appeared a witch's spell had already damned me to hell. I could only hope for forgiveness.

I had chosen Angel as my current girlfriend, but I couldn't tell her about the situation, either. Instead, I bottled it up and stored the memories in the back of my mind. They would always be there to haunt me.

No one came after me, nobody cared, especially the LAPD, and in time, it was like it had never happened. But I relived the event over and over in my mind, knowing I had made the wrong decision about moving to Los Angeles. There was no turning back now. Going home a loser after Hap Hazzard would have been a better choice.

~~

I enjoyed living in the Hollywood Hills, but I couldn't get any rest or privacy. I was living too damn close to all the Hollywood nightclubs. Every night, a different group of friends would stop by after the clubs let out, keeping me up until sunrise. I was still running Zolie's company, and it was hard to get up and go to work every day after absolutely no sleep.

There was so much cocaine flowing through Hollywood that the people around me were shaking when they tried to stand still and couldn't talk at a normal speed. Words like the and and were no longer parts of sentences.

Uncle Paul had been making a lot of really huge cocaine buys using the counterfeit money and now proclaimed himself the new "King of Cocaine." He was probably sitting on 100 to 150 pounds of cocaine, hidden in a couple of storage units in Hollywood. I drove past the storage units every day, knowing that the only security measure protecting the hundreds of pounds of cocaine was a single padlock I could cut off in a second with my clamp cutters. But I wasn't a thief and took great pride in saying that.

Shane the Paine became Uncle Paul's right hand man. He would take many dangerous risks and do really big deals with the Russians for $20,000 and $40,000. They were the new crime group trying to move in for a piece of the Hollywood pie.

Since the Russians were prone to violence and were military-trained, Shane started carrying a 9mm pistol under each arm at all times. One morning I watched him put on his tank top and strap on the pistols, covering them with a long-sleeved shirt.

"You're nuts for doing these big deals," I said. "My Hungarian friends won't even do business with the Russians."

"I got it handled," Shane replied. "The most they can do is kill me. Let them try."

I figured Shane must have a death wish, based on his heavy drug use and the fact that he was just looking for a reason to shoot it out with someone like "Mad Dog Cole."

In a six-month period, I watched Shane go from being a petty thief to one of Hollywood's most feared and deadly enforcers as he started using crystal meth. His reputation preceded him.

An enforcer was someone who did all the dirty deeds that someone else wanted done, like drug exchanges and strong-arm collections. An enforcer would enforce someone else's laws for money, without concern for human feelings. An enforcer had the ability not to have pity. Shane was young and very strong and didn't give a shit about anyone who got in the way of his goal of making a fast buck. No one stood before him and got away with it.

It seemed like we had it all, like there would be no end to the party. But in the back of my mind, a voice kept warning me like a broken record, <u>It's going to be one hell of a trip down.</u>

~~

On the nights when Angel wasn't around and I didn't have band practice, I hung out with Shane if I had a moment of boredom. He knew all the underground Hollywood clubs. One night, he talked me into going to a mobile club called "Club Fuck." Club Fuck had to move every week because of the activities going on within the club. You could only find the new location through a member, and it wasn't revealed until a couple of hours after dark. Phones rang across the City of Lost Angels as people passed along the secret address. Only the elite of Hollywood belonged to this club.

As we entered Club Fuck, I noticed a huge, bald biker with two dozen piercings and tattoos sitting to the right on a stool, giving free hits off his base-pipe if he could spank you in return. The line was forming around the door, and girls were already dropping their bottoms in anticipation. I couldn't believe they were doing drugs out in the open without any fear of getting busted.

Most of the female club-goers walked around practically naked and were so fucked up they could barely stand on their six-inch come fuck me high heels.

Shane fit in well. It was his environment.

I was somewhat shocked and walked around in a daze, checking out the sights. I watched a couple of lesbians get their bottoms spanked a nice shade of bright pink. Then my attention was drawn toward the center stage as a loud roar rose up from the crowd.

On the stage stood a breathtaking femme fatale with long auburn hair. Her hands were tied together over her head. On each side of her was a long-haired musician, one lifting her dress while the other whipped her backside with a cat-o'-nine tails. Her backside arched to meet every slash; I could tell she was getting off on each stroke of the whip.

Fascinated, I couldn't take my eyes off her. She had the ass of a Greek goddess and a sinister look about her. The mesmerizing expression in her eyes turned me on with each slash.

George, the lead guitarist of Tuff, told me her name was Anna. "She's a black witch that's into Wicca and other forms of black magick, stay way, she's bad news," he explained.

"Great," I replied. "That ruined the fantasy, almost." I'd had enough of witches to last a lifetime. I finished my drink and went home alone. I had a real girlfriend who wasn't on drugs or into worshiping Satan. She was an Angel.

Chapter 21

The talk show host Sally Jessie Rafael had flown out from New York to interview musicians who lived at the Hollywood Billiards. The show she aired afterward was titled, "Guys Who Want To Be Rock Stars." Timbo and some other guys I knew flew to New York to be on her talk show.

Sally Jessie Rafael lowered her trademark red eyeglasses and asked Timbo and the other musicians, "Why can't you guys work and hold regular jobs to pay your bills, like normal people?"

"I'm always playing my guitar," Timbo replied, "and I can't take the time away from my music career to work."

Timbo might as well have said, "I'm too lazy and too busy getting high to have a real job."

Sally Jessie didn't buy that excuse and made them look like lazy, long-haired losers.

~~

While Timbo was in New York, Angel and I went to Las Vegas and had a nice weekend away from Hollywood. When I got back home, I didn't see any bullet holes in the walls or bloodstains on the carpet, so I assumed the apartment had been quiet while I was out of town. But before I could even get my bags unpacked, Shitfield walked into my bedroom and shut the door. He had a serious look.

"Gary let Shane and Bow hang around while you were gone," he said. "Look out on the balcony."

I opened my drapes and saw two brand-new Lifecycle exercise bikes hidden under a blanket.

"Bow brought them in here the other night," said Shitfield. "I'm letting you know I'm moving out today. And fast."

"Why? What's the big deal, I will get rid of them."

"Gary and Bow also ordered pizza and Chicken Delight a couple of times while you were gone and paid for it with funny money."

"Fucking assholes! Anything else?"

"When Timbo got his van fixed a couple days ago, he paid the mechanic six hundred dollars in fake money."

I went ballistic and stormed out into the living room. I was ready to start chopping off some heads.

Grabbing Bow by the collar, I yelled, "Where did you get those fucking Lifecycles?"

"I found them in a back alley. They were just going to throw them away."

"Yeah, right," I yelled. "Those look like the Lifecycles from the gym downstairs! You stupid fuck, I have to live here."

"I knew you liked them, so I grabbed them for you," he answered sheepishly.

"I didn't want them in my apartment, you fucking moron! Put them back after the apartment manager leaves for the night."

"Okay, okay. I will."

I looked at Gary as he tried to sneak out of the room. "Gary, you fucking asshole, if I find one counterfeit bill in this apartment, I am going to pummel you to a bloody pulp!"

I didn't even bother unpacking my suitcases; I had to move fast. Within twenty minutes, I was looking for a new place to live . . . somewhere not so close to Hollywood.

"Start packing," I told Gary. "We're out of here tomorrow morning."

When I had moved in, I had used a fake name and Social Security number so I felt safe. As long as we moved, it would be cool. I had a bad feeling, we had to move fast. Lazy equaled jail.

Meanwhile, the Secret Service was already trying to track down the counterfeit money. Luckily, they moved at a turtle's speed. When the mechanic deposited all the checks and the fake cash at the end of the day, the bank caught it right away. With the Secret Service standing over his shoulder, he pulled Timbo's bill and gave them his license plate number. The Secret Service ran the plate number and went to his last apartment in the Valley. By tracking his mail, they ended up at the Pinnacle ten hours after I moved out.

The apartment manager told them we had been there the previous night. But I left no clues; their lead ended at the Pinnacle.

Chapter 22

My new house on Coldwater Canyon was around five thousand square feet, with four bedrooms and a nice pool and heated Jacuzzi outside. All around the swimming pool stood stone statues with water shooting out of their mouths and into the swimming pool. The backyard was surrounded by an eight-foot brick wall, providing total privacy from everyone except airplanes and satellites. The house had also come with a live security system named Duke. He stood 6'3" and weighed a couple hundred pounds. He was an eating machine that never stopped -- he was a big yellow Great Dane named Marmaduke.

Every Friday night at the new house after getting home from work, I dumped a couple of cases of beer into the swimming pool. While sitting in the hot tub, I grabbed floating beers with the pool net whenever I wanted one. Usually, I would grab a beer for me and one for Duke. I would pour his into the bowl next to the tub, and before I could get two sips, he would be done and after my beer, slobbering all over me.

"Get off me, Duke," I'd yell. "Get back, dammit!" He would try to box me, so I would have to sit in the middle of the tub, out of his reach.

On a couple of occasions, Duke got so drunk he fell into the swimming pool while trying to steal an ice cold beer. He was like a bull in a china shop, howling in embarrassment as he tried to get out of the pool.

"Bet he won't do that again," said Gary with a laugh.

"I bet he does," I replied. "He's a hops hound."

Everyone laughed.

~~

I was really enjoying my new house out in the Valley, especially since it was far enough away from Hollywood that no one knew where I lived. I had peace and quiet for the first time in several years.

Unfortunately, I only got a couple of months of peace and quiet. I hadn't moved far enough away, and one by one, certain people I didn't want to associate with found their way to my new house and began stopping by unannounced.

Boris Jackoffski from Copy Supply Warehouse was one of those people. "I need your help," he said.

I thought, Great.

Boris had been Mickey's personal enforcer and had been hiding from the Feds for the last two years because of his role with the Rathes. He was probably one of the only men I was actually afraid of. I never knew what he was going to do. He was huge, and his hands could easily palm my head and crush it like a grape. He was more violent than Shane after two large coffees and a couple of rails of speed. The heavy amounts of cocaine he was shoveling up his nose made him very unstable and easily spooked. When around Boris, it was always best to make no sudden moves. Tapping him on the shoulder could produce the same results as spooking a horse from behind.

Boris made me an offer that I couldn't refuse. "I got a shitload of uncut cocaine I've been sitting on, and I need to unload it quick."

I mulled it over. "I'll take a couple eight balls," I offered.

He shook his head. "No. I'm talking about the whole stash. I need the money to split the country."

Fuck, I thought, I don't want any part of this. But . . . He was asking me for help. Or should I say, he was still asking at this point. Boris had always treated me with respect, and it was much better to have him as a friend than an enemy.

I had two choices. The first choice was to do what he asked and make a lot of money. I would also gain more credibility in the underworld. My second choice was to say no and hope he dealt with the rejection in a humane fashion, but I didn't think he would. He was very desperate and he knew I could help.

"Okay, I'll help," I finally said. "Show me what you've got."

"You made the right decision," Boris said with a snide smile.

The minute I agreed, I knew the paranoia would come back and I would have more sleepless nights as I worried about getting busted. If I got caught with the amount Boris was delivering, I would surely spend time in prison. I remembered being a little kid and saying to myself many times that I would never be stupid enough to do anything that would take away my freedom and put me in a cell.

I had done more things in my few years of living in Los Angeles than I could have ever predicted in my wildest dreams. And I was considered one of the good guys among the group of people I called my friends. Going behind bars would mean entering a world where I was the minority and prey for many gangs that hated whites. Rudy told me he had connections on the inside that would protect me, if that ever happened.

Since my house wasn't a secret anymore, I threw a huge Halloween party and got rid of enough cocaine to pay Boris in full and get rid of him. I liked moving weed; it was a harmless drug. No one died or lost everything over it. It made people relaxed and happy. But messing with cocaine made me feel extremely guilty. I knew that every time I came up against it, I lost.

The day after the party, I took Boris to the Burbank airport. He was looking guilty and dangerous at the same time; I could feel a vibe coming off of him as we had drinks in the airport bar. I bought him a ticket under a fake name and shook his hand, and that was the last I saw of him.

At the price I had just paid for the cocaine, I could be everyone's best friend and still make a bundle of untraceable cash. I didn't want to be in this business, but then again it was exciting. I loved the power and prestige that came with the title of party dealer. In Hollywood, a party dealer was an honorable job and well respected, as long as you had a good product -- because the party in Hollywood never stops. Now I had it 24-7. I had stopped doing it.

Going through the sacks of cocaine, I noticed what appeared to be bloodstains that someone had attempted to wipe off. I just shook my head, imagining how Boris had obtained the cocaine . . . and paying for it didn't seem like a likely option. Holding the sacks in my hands, I wondered how many lives it had already ruined before it reached my hands and moved on to the victims of this plague.

I knew that if I didn't chill out after the Halloween party, I wouldn't get to stay in my new house for any length of time.

My neighbors were mostly Asians and Mexicans who were all pretty well off. The other white people in the neighborhood were scared and living behind locked doors with steel gates -- but not us. My friends were always racing up and down the street on their Harleys, drinking and smoking funny little cigarettes. It didn't leave a good impression, but I didn't care. My new neighbors had hated me from day one because I was white with long hair and carried a guitar case. I tried to make friends with neighbors on both sides, but since I was renting, they were assholes. So I was an asshole right back.

My metal band practiced in the studio at the new house, and we were ready to start playing the Sunset Strip when our lead singer got some stripper pregnant. He wanted to keep the child, so they moved back to Seattle to have the kid. The band broke up for the meantime while Brady was gone. I'd had just about enough of dealing with musicians. We spent more time practicing than ever getting to play out because of constant member changes.

It wasn't even fun to play in Hollywood. The people in the audience were all fellow musicians with broken dreams, who were miserable and cynical. All the negativity made everyone hate each other, and instead of boosting the music, it killed it. When *Anna Black* didn't get signed, I knew the scene was over.

So I stayed home most of the time. Pretty soon, I found out the only people in our neighborhood who were louder than my metal band and ruder than my friends were the garbage men who picked up our trash once a week. They came every Sunday morning with their stereo blasting and the bass so loud it shook our house from four houses away. As they emptied the trash cans, they smashed them on the back of the truck so hard I was replacing cans every other week. Sunday morning, I was pretty hung over, but I dragged myself out of bed to ask them to take into consideration that I was sleeping and to stop wrecking my trash cans. They basically told me to fuck off and were even louder the next weekend.

In an act of revenge which I found very pleasurable, I went out and bought a new trash can from Home Depot that sealed airtight. I put it out back by Duke's doghouse. Duke shit like a small horse, it took four weeks to fill the entire trash can to the top with fifty pounds of stomach-turning, maggot-infested dog shit covered with flies. It looked like a giant bucket of chocolate pudding with a serious yeast infection. It looked alive as the maggots and worms were always moving.

When my best friend Johnny Boy came out for a little vacation, I talked him into helping me carry the trash can out to the curb.

Johnny Boy and I each grabbed a handle on the side of the can and walked a few feet while holding our breath.

"Got to set it down," said Johnny Boy. "I need some fresh air."

"What a puss."

"Fuck you asshole. This smell is worse than rotten ass."

"Reminds you of your wife, huh."

"Fuck you, I should stick your head in the can."

We set the can down and stepped back to get a breath of fresh air before continuing. Once we got it out to the curb, I opened it and placed some newspaper across the top to hide the big surprise.

We stayed up all night doing blow until we heard the garbage truck coming down the street with the music blaring. We rushed to the front window. Johnny Boy, Gary, and I peeked through the blinds to enjoy the show that was about to unfold. I wanted the Gook Boy to see, but he passed out.

"Someone go and wake up that slant-eyed bastard," said Gary.

I replied, "Dock that chink a day's pay." We all laughed.

"This is going to be good," said Johnny Boy. "I can't wait to see the looks on their faces."

"Me, too," said Gary. "I've waited weeks."

The sun had already come up, and it was going to be in the nineties, making the shit-bomb in the can ready to go.

There were three trash cans. I had placed the special can last in line.

The garbage men grabbed the first and second cans, bouncing them extra hard off the back of the truck. We waited in anticipation.

When they came to the third can, it was so heavy it took two of them to lift it. They let it fall with such force onto the back edge of the truck that it looked like a giant green pimple exploding as the plastic crinkled under the heavy weight. Dog shit flew in all directions. Some got in the truck, about half. Guess where the rest landed?

We all laughed until we cried.

"You haven't changed one bit," Johnny Boy said. "I'm glad I'm your friend. I wouldn't want to be on your bad side!"

"That was worth staying up for," Gary added.

"Who's going to clean up the mess that spilled?"

"It was your idea," everyone answered.

Chapter 23

<u>Christmas 1990</u>

Angel and I flew back to Indiana for the holidays. We had a very merry white Christmas, and I'm not referring to cocaine. I was reminded how much I loved the snowy Indiana winters. We spent time with my family and enjoyed my grandmother's Lithuanian cooking. My entire family adored Angel, and my local buddies thought she was a total knock-out. They told me to not let her get away or they would be calling her . . . and they would.

It was the best Christmas I had ever had. I had a real loving feeling, and for the first time, being a rock star just didn't seem that important.

~~

The Gulf War began right after the New Year in January of 1991. We all thought it was going to be a long and bloody war, just like Nostradamus had predicted. It sure seemed like the prophecy was coming true by the way the government was taking the Army Reserves away from their families and shipping them overseas under the "Bush Plan." I wasn't worried about getting drafted . . . I was well hidden from the government. They could never find me.

I was already starting to think about dumping this house and moving to an apartment, since there was at least one thief living among us. Weed had gone missing from my bedroom and money off my dresser. I was pissed that I had to lock my bedroom door while sitting by the swimming pool.

When I had rented the house in the beginning, it was supposed to be for the four band members only, but everyone except myself moved their girlfriends in, causing total chaos. More than one woman under one roof is too many. Darren was the only one I really trusted, but then he moved in his hillbilly girlfriend and her blind dog Dickie. Between the dog always yapping and the hillbilly girlfriend screaming in Southern slang, I was ready to knock their heads together.

On the weekends, Timbo's girlfriend would invite all her Swedish girlfriends over and they would lie out by the pool nude. In their country, there was nothing shameful about their naked, tanned, well-toned bodies. That caused a lot of tension among the other guys' girlfriends. Angel never said anything, but if Darren even looked in the direction of the swimming pool, his girlfriend would go nuts, as if someone had shoved a live chicken up her ass without K-Y!

"Darren," she yelled, "what the fuck are you looking at? Get your ass in here, motherfucker!"

I said to Darren, "Knock that crazy bitch out, or I am!"

"I'll tell her to keep it down, Hap."

"Just do it... ass-nip!"

Gary had a very nice girlfriend named Jennifer, she had a normal job and a level head. Gary somehow talked her into getting a boob job and got her to start stripping after her day job, while Gary sat around drinking beer by the swimming pool.

Jennifer's father was a famous Hollywood actor named Stewart Daemon who played the part of the young, good-looking doctor Alan Quartermine on General Hospital.

When she finally dumped Gary for constantly cheating, he sold pictures of her stripping to the Globe for $500, totally embarrassing her famous Hollywood family. I thought maybe hit men would come for Gary. If it were my daughter, I would have sent them.

~~

By the end of March 1991, everyone was relieved that the war in the desert had ended so quickly without many American deaths. As I was watching CNN, the third name that rolled off the list of dead soldiers was my brother's full name. It wasn't really my brother, but I was freaked out seeing his name roll across the screen as one of the first Americans to be killed in action. By 2004, over 12,000 Gulf War vets would be dead from chemical agents used on them, which were manufactured in Texas and Florida before the war.

Now that the war was over, I threw a record release party for a punk band called Snare, who played in my living room. Their album was titled Left, Right, Left. It was like Metallica had met the Ramones.

Angel and I had gotten into a fight the week before after I caught her on the Sunset Strip checking out her old boyfriend's band. She had told me she had too much homework to come out for the weekend. It really upset me; I hate being lied to. It made me feel like a fool for even putting money down on an engagement ring. I was the guy who always said, "I'll never get married," and here I was actually doing it. I was glad I hadn't opened my mouth.

The party was huge and out of control. It doubled as Timbo's birthday party. Mia's roommate, Laura, really had the hots for me, but I had always turned down her advances in the past because of Angel. Tonight was different.

As she bent over to snort a line off the mirror, Laura said, "You can do anything you want. There are no no's." She smiled.

I thought, No no's, huh?

Mirrors surrounded my bed on three sides, along with red track lighting that shone on the bed from the cathedral ceiling. I had a king-size waterbed with red and black satin sheets, which would usually end up on the floor by morning. The wall next to my bed served as a display of my martial arts weapons, num-chucks, syses, karmas, a half-dozen swords of different lengths and thicknesses of steel. All the bladed weapons were very sharp and very deadly.

To add a '90's touch, I had mixed in bondage toys, including crops, leather paddles, and a cat-o'-nine tails that Bow had shoplifted from the Pleasure Chest on Santa Monica. Every guy who walked into my bedroom had to test the sharpness of the blades by running the tip of his finger down the blade, usually drawing blood before I could warn him. The women would always feel the leather whips and smile with a kinky grin. Everyone thought Angel was a kinky sex kitten, but that wasn't the case. The toys were for guests.

As Snare finished their last song, I was getting ready to start kicking drunken guests out. Eight hours of dealing with idiots was more than enough. Laura and I had been doing cocaine all night and she had already given me two blowjobs, but I was ready for something a little kinkier. Just as I got Laura bent over in my bedroom, and seconds before planting my face, I heard <u>bang-bang-bang</u>!

I knew instantly what it was. I could hear the bullets ripping through the garage door and embedding in the inner wall like the sounds of hail hitting the roof on a warm Indiana summer night.

I grabbed my Colt .380 out of my Bible with an extra clip. Throwing on a bathrobe, I charged out of my bedroom door and tripped over J.J., who had once again passed out in the hallway.

"Goddammit," I yelled, "get off the floor!"

Hurrying to the front door, I looked out the peephole and saw a low-rider speeding away. I opened the front door to investigate and was almost mowed down by Mad Max Mason, running for his life. Mad Max Mason was so drunk he couldn't even tell me why they were shooting at him. I thought the police would show up for sure, but they didn't.

Reentering my bedroom, I found Laura stretched out across the waterbed, with the stereo playing Lynch Mob's first album at a good volume. She looked very sexy dressed in white lingerie, with her long brown hair pulled back into two ponytails with pink bow ties. That gave her a sweet, innocent baby doll look that only fooled others; I knew better. Laura had a great tan, making the white silk panties even more appealing. We smoked another joint and snorted a couple more rails while toasting with two glasses of champagne.

"Hand me the vial," said Laura, while licking her lips.

Laura dumped out a line across my penis and then went down on it. I thought I was in Heaven. Laura had the sweetest, most talented mouth of any female I had ever been with. If she were a James Bond villain, her name would be Golden Lips.

Laura and I played all types of kinky sex games. We took turns tying each other up and licking cocaine off certain body parts that were stimulated. It made for a great final party in the house, as I spanked, danked, and thanked Laura until she left around eleven in the morning.

Afterward, I went into the kitchen to get something to drink -- something cold and without alcohol -- only to find someone trying to hide in the refrigerator. He had removed the shelves and items and was totally hidden inside, except for his feet hanging out. When I pulled the door open, the look of fright that came across his face was funny.

"What the fuck are you doing in the icebox?" I demanded.

He looked up at me. "It's the only safe place to hide . . . from THEM."

I yelled into the living room, "Someone give this asshole a ride home." I hated people who couldn't handle their shit.

Mia was still in the living room with a couple of drunken fools who were trying to screw her, but I could tell by the look on her face that she had no interest in either one. They were playing with that Ouija board. That brought back a lot of bad memories.

Back when I was with Eve at Studio Colony, I had come home one day to find her and Mia playing with the Ouija board in the living room. I started laughing and mocking them. I thought it was dumb.

Eve got extremely angry, "You're very naïve, and you will anger the spirits of the board and break our connection!"

"Great," I said. "Tell the spirits to get the hell out of my apartment, and take Casper with them." I added. "It's just you pushing that thing around the stupid board."

"Ask the board a question, smart-ass!" said Eve.

"Alright." I thought for a minute and replied, "What was my grandmother's maiden name before she came to the United States in 1917?"

Without hesitation, the Ouija board immediately spelled out the correct name. That freaked me out. There was no way these two could have known. I didn't have it written down anywhere, nor had I ever spelled it correctly.

~~

Later that night, while Mia was out, I took the Ouija board out of the closet and threw it in the trash bin in the lower garage, thinking it was gone.

When I got up in the morning, the Ouija board had been slide under my front door and was lying there like a floor mat. I was freaked out. I figured it had to be one of the girls fucking with me, so I put it in a black trash bag, walked over to the next building, and threw it in their trash bin, making sure it was hidden under trash.

Before going to bed that evening, I smoked a joint and was just about to pass out when I heard a strange sound by the front door. I jumped up and poked my head out of my bedroom. I could see that the Ouija board had been slid under my front door again.

Grabbing my pistol and my bathrobe, I opened the front door and took off down the hallway only seven or eight seconds behind whoever had slid the board under the door. There was no one in sight, but I could feel them, as if they were watching me.

The clock said 12:13. I had to be up in five hours, so I went back inside to get some sleep. Instead, I lay awake staring at the front door with my pistol cocked, waiting for my uninvited guest to attempt to turn my door handle.

When the paperboy slammed my newspaper against the door, I almost jumped him before realizing what time it was: 5:13. Time to go to work with no sleep . . . Fuck!

I put the Ouija board back in the closet and decided not to mess with it anymore. I thought about burning it, but Mia said they didn't burn and it would only curse me if I messed with it anymore.

Watching Mia mess with that damn Ouija board had brought back creepy memories of what had happened to Eve, ruining the good thoughts I had had of kinky sex.

I didn't freak out on Mia; I just nodded and went back to bed to get some desperately needed sleep.

Chapter 24

I knew the drive-by gang shooting might just be the beginning of the problems. So Monday morning, bright and early, I set up a new place eighteen miles away. I needed to put a little distance between me and my old place and move into a different police district. That was an important part of counter-surveillance. Plus, once I moved I couldn't leave a paper trail and couldn't order any food from old restaurants -- which sucked, since I lived on take-out.

When I got back later that afternoon, I noticed a white sedan parked halfway down the block. Two suspicious-looking white men sat inside and appeared to be watching my house with binoculars. Thinking quickly, I wrote down their license plate number and drove straight to a pay phone to page Rudy with the special code that indicated a security breech was in effect. "9-11."

Rudy called me back within a minute and agreed to meet at Studio Colony. We still had our gate pass from the time when I lived there. Anyone following us wouldn't get past security without the proper clearance, giving us a chance to have a secret meeting. I always kept a set of security keys to the buildings where I had lived in the past so I would have several secure places to go if followed. Even if they changed the locks, I had friends and customers who would give me the new keys. I had security keys to over thirty different complexes all over Los Angeles.

When I arrived at Studio Colony, I saw Rudy already waiting in the courtyard under one of the palm trees. Looking cool as a cucumber, he was drinking iced tea and wearing his favorite dark sunglasses so he could check out the sights.

"Enjoying the sights?" I asked.

"What's up, Bubba?" "What do you think, some nice backsides."

"The house got shot up the other night by some assholes shooting at Mad Max Mason, and now I think I'm being watched. I want you to run this license plate number to find out who's onto me and why."

"Give me the number."

Rudy strutted over to the pay phone to make the call to his connection at the Los Angeles Police Department. It rang and someone answered. I loved having access to their computer system.

Rudy came back and said, "My nephew will call back within the hour. Are you up for some racquetball?"

"Yeah," I replied. "Got any money?"

Just to show my gratitude, I let Rudy win three out of four games, until the phone finally rang. Rudy answered, and I could hear him agreeing and nodding his head in a manner that assured me he understood what was going on.

After hanging up, he walked back over and said, "Both your neighbors called the police about the shooting. They also reported a loud noise during your party. But since you didn't call the police and it was your house that got shot up, they want to know who's living there and what's going on. They want to know if you're affiliated with the gangbangers or if it was just another random shooting."

I realized that my lack of fear had caused a royal screw-up. I should have acted scared like a normal frightened citizen, instead of a tough guy who couldn't wait to eat some pussy.

"Your phone is probably being tapped," Rudy continued. "Don't give any hints that you might be moving. Pretend nothing is wrong, and move very quickly!"

"How am I going to ditch the surveillance?"

"Get a moving truck, and leave the rest up to me."

After the meeting with Rudy, I picked up the moving truck with Gook Boy's help. Darren and his girlfriend were moving in with his father in East Los Angeles, since Darren's girlfriend was not only barefoot but also pregnant. Gary and Timbo were moving in with some chicks.

Nothing at the house was in my real name, including the license plates on my cars, so I had that to my advantage.

I had to get Duke a new home; he was way too big to live with me in an apartment. I had put out some ads a month earlier with no response, but I was finally contacted by a guy who was coming over that night around seven to see Duke.

~~

With the Van Nuys police watching from down the street, I brazenly took a smoke break in the living room around five-thirty after packing the moving truck. The interior of the house looked like London on an average day, but it smelled like a cross between fresh green hay and a smashed skunk impaled on a Christmas tree, slightly burning over some chestnut coals.

As time slipped by, I melted into the couch, watching Spider Man on the boob tube along with my friends. Around six o'clock, I heard the sounds of a Harley pulling into the driveway, and then the doorbell rang. I was too wasted to get up, so I yelled for one of Timbo's Swedish girls to answer the door.

She yelled back, "It's the guy about the dog."

"I'll be right there."

Instead of waiting for me, the stupid Swedish girl let the guy in and led him into the living room, all the while topless.

The guy turned out to be a California Highway Patrol officer in full uniform. He was at least 6'5" with a bright blonde buzz cut; he looked like a Nazi storm trooper, right down to his leather motorcycle boots. He stood there with a goofy look on his face.

The officer looked around the room like it was a scene out of a Cheech and Chong movie: a bunch of long hairs lounging around on couches wearing only jean shorts, combat boots, and tattoos, and smoking like they were living in Amsterdam.

If this had happened back in Indiana, I would have expected the cop to start beating us. But it wasn't, so I quickly remembered the rules for dealing with California police: Stay cool, and usually they would be cool in return . . . unless you just happened to get a rookie or if you were black.

The officer smelled the weed and saw the water bong, but he pretended not to notice as he stepped forward through the cloud of thick smoke. Waving it out of his face with his left hand, he said in a deep tone, "I'm here to talk with Buster Hymen about a dog named Duke."

I sobered up real quick without laughing, stood up, and shook his hand while trying to pretend everything was normal. Everyone else in the living room went into their own personal comas and didn't dare make eye contact until I introduced everyone by their nicknames to just break the ice. It was very uncomfortable.

"My name is Jack," he said. "Where's the dog?"

I took Jack outside, knowing he could use the fresh air and introduced him to Duke. They hit it off instantly, since Jack was big enough to roughhouse.

Jack said, "I'll take the dog. I'll be back in an hour with my truck to pick him up."

"Sounds good."

About an hour later, after airing out the house, Jack returned with his truck and asked, "How much were you asking for Duke... was it two hundred dollars?"

"Jack," I said, "is he going to have a nice home?"

Jack, now in street clothes and looking less intimidating, replied, "Yes, my wife and I have a nice ranch at the bottom of the hill with plenty of room for Duke to run and to tear things up."

"That sounds ultimately cool," I replied. "I don't want any money. Just take care of him. Duke likes to drink beer and has been known to smoke on a few occasions."

Jack just laughed and said, "I will have to break Duke of the smoking habit, but I always need a good drinking buddy. I hope Duke likes Budweiser."

"Duke will drink anything in a can, and you don't have to open it."

I gave Duke a final hug goodbye. He whipped me in the nuts with his long, thick tail one last time, then climbed into the back of the truck.

Jack said, "Since you have been so cool, here is something I came across today." He handed me a bag with something wrapped up real tight inside.

"What's this?" I asked.

"Nice meeting you, Buster," Jack replied. "Take care, and enjoy." He backed out of the driveway with a weird smile on his face.

I looked down the street at the white sedan, wondering what the Van Nuys surveillance team thought about a cop coming into my house twice -- once in uniform and once in street clothes, and now handing me a package out front. It must have looked just like a dope deal.

I walked inside thinking, It must be something his wife cooked up.

To my surprise, it was two ounces of marijuana. One ounce was good green buds, and the second was Mexican dirt weed.

I couldn't believe it.

Never looking a gift horse in the mouth, I took the presents and laughed.

When we finally left with the moving truck, we drove straight to Studio Colony where I knew the surveillance team couldn't follow us into the complex. I saw them in the rear-view mirror but pretended not to notice, hoping Rudy's plan would work like he promised.

I had already informed the head security guard what I was up to, and he replied, "I will do this last favor, but I don't want to lose my job or end up in prison."

"That's cool," I said. "I need two hours inside the complex." I tossed him the ounce of Mexican weed.

As I backed the moving truck into the last building in the back of the complex, out of sight from the outside world, Rudy's crew of muscle were waiting in four panel vans with tinted windows in the underground parking lot.

As fast as humanly possible, we unloaded all my belongings from the moving truck into the four smaller moving vans with magnetic signs that read, "Juan's Plumbing." Within an hour, we were driving out the back gates, leaving the original moving truck behind. It wasn't in my real name, and I made damn sure to wipe all the fingerprints from the truck.

Rudy's plan worked brilliantly. I ditched the surveillance team and moved into my new apartment on Colfax Avenue in North Hollywood, California.

Hotel California.

Chapter 25

Once I finally got settled into my new apartment, I patched things up with Angel. I really missed her and figured we were even. We planned on spending the summer lying out by the swimming pool in the courtyard of Club California while snacking on cold shrimp, or shopping at Venice Beach and eating cups of fresh sliced fruit. Angel always looked really hot in her black bathing suit, making me feel proud to be seen with her by my side. She was a Leo like me.

When we got back together, Angel decided she was going to get me a cat. We went to the animal pound in North Hollywood, the place smelled like a giant turd. We walked through the dog kennel to the cat section in the back. What a treat that was, especially during mid afternoon heat.

The cat section was run by some crazy old man who had spent too much time out in the hot sun or was sniffing glue; I couldn't be sure what his deal was. He thought of his stray cats as his lost children and talked to them in a stupid baby voice that got on my nerves real quick. All the cats were in one huge room. There were thirty cats of various sizes and colors on one side of the room, and on the other side was this one long-haired, wild-looking cat all by herself.

The first cat I picked up was cute and cuddly, but the old man said, "That cat has been returned twice. It likes to pee on rugs."

"No thanks," I said, setting the cute cat down. Suddenly, like a lightning strike, the wild cat from across the room attacked the cute cat at the bottom of my feet.

"Wow!" I exclaimed. "That cat is ferocious, like a miniature bobcat! Look at the way her hair is standing on all ends."

"That cat likes you," said Angel. "It got jealous."

I looked down at the wild cat. It was looking up at me with a weird expression. We both shook our heads of long hair at each other, thinking, We look alike. We both had black and white hair.

Being around animals my entire life, I knew how to act. I reached down very slowly and let the cat smell my hand. The cat hissed at me and took a defensive position like a badger. I backed off.

"What is that cat?" I asked the goofy old man. "A manx?"

"No," the old man replied. "It's an American bobtail. They first appeared in 1902. She is a rare mix . . . half-domestic shorthair, half bobcat.

The American bobtail had long, black, beautiful fur, with four white socks and a tiny tail only an inch long, if that. She was all torn up from fighting.

"What's her name?"

"Boots," the old man replied. "Her tail will spin around a hundred miles per hour like a helicopter's blade when she gets mad, similar to the warning of a rattlesnake before striking."

"Why don't you take that cat?" Angel suggested in her usual smart-ass tone. "It's the only one tough enough to last in your eccentric lifestyle and be able to defend its self against your stupid friends."

The idea made some sense, considering it had come out of a female's mouth. But the cat looked like it had the mange from fighting.

Now that I showed some interest, the old man said, "Boots isn't quite a year old. She was raised on the streets of Hollywood and got caught behind Popeye's, going through the dumpster." The old man continued the sales pitch: "She only has a week left before we put her under, since she's always fighting with the other cats. It's a shame . . . She is very rare."

The old man was quite the salesman, laying it on thick so I would take this wild cat off his hands.

I thought, <u>He's afraid of Boots.</u>

I walked over to Boots, reached down, and gave her little tail a tiny tug. That was a big mistake. She turned around and laid into my foot. Sitting back on her butt, she was ready to box me with her two front paws, armed with deadly claws like a wolverine. If I hadn't been wearing Doc Martens combat boots, she would have bitten my ankle, but instead she chipped her first tooth.

<u>What a fucking mean cat</u>, I thought.

"I don't want that cat," I declared. "I'll check back in a week to see if you have anything new." I gave Boots the middle finger.

As I walked away, Boots meowed sadly. I stopped and looked at her again. She was rare, indeed, so I said, "That is the only cat that could survive my lifestyle. I'll take her."

I couldn't wait to sick her on a few of my friends.

The car ride home was nothing compared to the fight for authority once we got home. It would be some time before we both finally came to terms and I established the rules of the house.

My friends nicknamed her Combat Boots, and later, when she got fat and filled out, they called her Land Shark.

It got to the point that every time I ordered food, I had to order that cat her own dinner from Mr. Jiffy's Chicken if I wanted to eat in peace. Even if I locked her in another room, she would open the door or tear something up in retaliation. It worked, so now she got her own dinner of breast, wing, a half slab of ribs, and three shrimp and fries. I always kept her drink; she didn't like soda, but that was about it.

In time, Boots began sleeping at the foot of my bed, like a sentinel guarding her master, alerting me to any strange noises. She would eventually grow from a skinny street cat to a fat, twenty-three-pound party animal that enjoyed living the Southern California lifestyle.

~~

Angel had no clue how big I had become in the underground world of the black market. She knew nothing of my deals and never asked. I'm not saying she was as dumb as Lois Lane -- she just looked the other way. She wasn't your normal female; when her mouth opened, only intelligent things came out.

Nevertheless, to make it easier, everyone was under strict rules not to come over or to stop by if they saw Angel's car parked out front. She came first, no questions. Everyone followed that rule accept for Shane, who showed up at the house a couple of days before I moved. I wasn't surprised to see him; I had heard that a bunch of bad things had gone down in Hollywood.

Shane said he was on his way to Seattle to hide out for a couple months and to check out the new "grunge scene" created by Nirvana. The Hollywood music explosion was over. "Teen Spirit" killed the metal scene. Pretty boys were gone and had been replaced by dirt, gloom, misery, sickness, and depression about hating your parents. I didn't get it. That wasn't the life I wanted to live or sing about. I loved my parents; they were the people I trusted above anyone. And I wasn't into heroin.

Shane said, "I have some extremely bad news. They found Bow in a dumpster in Hollywood a couple days ago with a Colombian Necktie."

A "Colombian Necktie" was what they called it when four guys hold all your limps down, cut your throat, reached in through the opening, and pull your tongue out through the slit in your neck, letting your tongue hang down on your chest like a red necktie. The victim is still alive long enough to realize what has happened while they spend the next few minutes choking on their own blood and gasping for their last breath.

"Why, and what happened?" I asked.

"The Colombians we ripped off with the counterfeit money sent a kill team to Hollywood to wipe us out and anyone involved with Uncle Paul."

I shook my head in anger. "I told you guys a thousand times this was going to happen, but no one would listen. I'm really glad I'm moving in a couple of days!"

I floated Shane a couple thousand dollars I would never see again, and off he went. I was rather upset about Bow. I liked him, even though he was a stupid fuck at times, but he had a good heart for a petty thief. Since they were my friends, I declined not to tell Angel about any of this and acted like nothing was wrong as we sat by the swimming pool at Club California, drinking ice-cold homemade lemonade.

It was my business, she would never understand. I wouldn't expect her to.

~~

Club California was the hottest apartment complex for single partiers in North Hollywood. They weren't the newest or the nicest units, but everyone who lived there was a rocker or a full-time partier, creating the perfect atmosphere for definite trouble. I found the place by accident one day when I was dropping off Robert Sarzo, the lead guitarist of "Hurricane."

A lot of famous people lived in the complex, and some of them were in the adult film industry. In time, I got to know and love many of them.

Club California had been owned back in the '80's by a California senator until he got busted for tax fraud. He had to sell the complex to some corporation to pay his legal bills. When the senator had owned the complex, it had been stocked with hookers for all his rich buddies to party with on the weekends. But his time was over, and my time to run Club California was at hand.

I rented an apartment in the back of the building so I could have total privacy and peace and quiet for a while. There were three hundred apartments in three separate buildings touching corner-to-corner, forming a perfect Bermuda Triangle with the swimming pool in the central courtyard. The giant swimming pool was in the shape of the letter Z and surrounded by three-story palm trees, giving excellent shade to the barbecue pit and outdoor tables.

There was a recreation center in the courtyard with an indoor ping-pong table, two pool tables, and a small gym. Behind the gym was a mirrored room for private workouts. There were two tennis courts out back and volleyball nets built into a huge sandbox to give it that beach effect. All the equipment that you needed could be checked out from the twenty-four-hour security guard at the front desk in the main lobby.

The residents of Club California hung out at the FM Station, a rock club on the corner of Lankershim and Colfax, owned by a guy named Filthy McNasty. They only went to work to pay rent and to buy booze. They took drinking very seriously; it was their main source of entertainment, with twenty-four-hour access to beer right across the street. For once, I wasn't the loudest tenant. It was a non-stop party. The tenants would just walk -- or should I say stumble -- from one apartment to another as if they were in a college dorm. It wasn't uncommon for someone to stop by at three in the morning if your lights were on for a beer or to share some type of illegal substance. I was seeing potential.

Once I got in with the Club California crowd, I started throwing parties down at the barbecue pit and inviting the entire complex, making my presence known. I couldn't handle the peace and quiet for too long. By the end of the summer, I was everyone's best friend. The apartment manager even offered to warn me of any type of law enforcement snooping around.

After talking with the manager, I began to realize that the longer I lived in the lights and glamour of Hollywood, the more I was becoming one of the people known as a "lost angel." I was not on the path I had come to Hollywood for. I was now a criminal in the eyes of the authorities, but a hero to civilians and celebrities and too many in the underworld.

Club California was just too sweet of a deal; there was no reason for the police to ever come there. Everyone in the place was in on what was happening, and people started to move there just for the convenience of living near me.

~~

Then the shit hit the fan.

Some Russian assholes involved with another organized crime group moved into the back of the complex. They rented four apartments under false names, and the management of Club California didn't realize who they were until he had let them in. They were involved with weapons, cocaine, weed, stolen credit cards, and chipped cellular phones. These guys had to be the outcasts of their group, because they were really stupid and attracted unwanted attention.

The four Russian families had a shitload of kids who were so rude and unruly, many people I knew fantasized about drowning them like rats in the swimming pool. It wasn't very pleasant or even possible to sit by the swimming pool anymore; the Russians had literally taken over the courtyard with all their friends and criminal cohorts. They were always hitting on everyone's girlfriends and acting like jackasses, doing belly flops and getting everyone's belongings all wet.

The Russian men had no manners or class and learned their pick-up lines off Saturday Night Live. The Russian women needed a bush-trimming, back-waxing and an appointment with Jenny Craig.

Sammy the Fat Slob, as we called him, was the head of the four families. He was in his mid-fifties and probably weighed 350 pounds. He spent most of the day sitting by the swimming pool under the shade of one of the palm trees, watching the girls while smoking cigars that stunk like a hairy rat's ass. Sammy wore so much gold that between his necklaces and wrist chains, if he had fallen into the swimming pool, he would have caused a tidal wave that would have flooded the courtyard before he sank like the Titanic.

I didn't care what anyone did, but Sammy wasn't very careful about his business. On several occasions I saw him sneak a line of cocaine at one of the poolside tables and even offered one of the guys in the building a huge sack of cocaine if Sammy could do his girlfriend. Since I wasn't the only tough guy in the complex, that incident got ugly, and the police got involved.

Two days later, the apartment manager came by my apartment. "The

FBI contacted the office about setting up surveillance on the Russian families tomorrow," he said. "It's part of an ongoing international investigation linked with Interpol."

"How much time do I have before they arrive?"

"Twelve hours," he replied.

<u>Fuck -- not enough time to move.</u>

Since I didn't have time to move before the FBI arrived, I decided to study their methods of operation concerning surveillance and their ability to blend in with the civilian population that lived at Club California. The apartment manager told me which apartments they were moving into, so I set up my own surveillance teams to watch their every move from beginning to end. I had already set up wireless cameras in smoke detectors in the hallways to spy on the Russian criminals. I just moved the cameras so I could see who the agents were as they moved in. I also planted hidden transmitters in the wall-outlets, so I could hear their secret conversations from within the apartments occupied by the FBI.

As the FBI moved in surveillance equipment, I took pictures of all the agents and their cars and followed them back to their base of operations on Ventura Boulevard in Tarzana. They were using a front office under the name Alta Services.

In a couple of days, I started seeing the different agents hanging around the swimming pool, pretending to be civilians. Watching the agents, I noticed that they acted much like myself. They were very laid back and never started a conversation unless someone engaged them. They mostly just listened and watched . . . especially the girls by the pool, I noticed. At least that told me the government agents were still human, not evil robots or clones of Hoover.

Late night, when they thought no one was watching, the agents bugged the entire swimming pool area with hidden microphones in the light sockets. After that, I couldn't sit by the swimming pool anymore in fear that someone might come up and say something stupid, drawing unwanted attention to myself.

Even though the FBI had set up base camp, I still ran my operation in quiet mode. Meanwhile, I started to look for a new place to live.

Chapter 26

While dealing with the FBI and Russian criminals, I started seeing a decline in my relationship with Angel. She wouldn't tell me what the problem was, and it was driving me insane. When she drove her boss's $80,000 car out one weekend, I figured it out quickly.

As a last-ditch effort to save the relationship, I agreed to travel to San Francisco to attend the Exotic Erotic Halloween Ball with David and Nora for the weekend. As shy as Angel was about kinky sex, I just couldn't believe she would want to go to an event with this level of sexual debauchery.

The Exotic Erotic Halloween Ball was held in a huge convention center with three indoor rooms the size of football fields. Every weirdo in San Francisco was at the party . . . including us. Some of the guests attending the party came wearing only a mask, while walking around with limp dicks and dry snatches. I thought, <u>Anyone that out of shape needs clothes.</u>

There were a lot of gay couples, women and men, along with transvestites and masters showing off their slaves. Some people were there to watch and others to perform as part of their kinky sex play. We were just watchers.

On the first stage stood a priest with three hot chicks, dressed up like Catholic schoolgirls in black and white uniforms. With their pigtails, they looked like Brittney Spears look-alikes.

The priest was huge and dressed in black, literally towering over the sexy, terrified schoolgirls as he waved his heavy wooden ruler -- his instrument of the Lord. Looking at the schoolgirls, he smacked the palm of his hand, warming up the ruler.

As the show started, the priest sat on a chair in the center of the stage. He pointed to the first schoolgirl, and she walk over and laid across his lap. "Pull up your skirt -- now!" he demanded.

The girl reached back and lifted her dress to reveal white cotton panties. The priest grabbed the cotton panties and pulled them up the crack of the school girl's behind, showing off her tender backside. She jumped.

The crowd watched in excitement.

The priest teased her, playfully giving her love taps. He started off slow and easy with the wooden ruler, working up to a good, solid-sounding punishment. He smacked her hard for a good five minutes. The schoolgirl kicked and screamed, but she was getting off at the same time.

The priest stood up and turned her around for the crowd to see her well-disciplined rear-end.

I smacked Angel on the rear end and said, "You're next!"

"You wish."

Looking around the outlandish party, I noticed everyone in the place was high on something illegal or well on their way to being totally drunk.

In the last room, porno stars were hosting a wet T-shirt contest, which seemed rather tame after the last two rooms of perverted entertainment. But a hard-core punk rock band came on after the contest and kicked ass for an hour.

Along the back wall were twenty hot-looking Filipino chicks in black miniskirts, looking like models. They were searching the crowd for guys to blow, giving out free blowjobs to any guy who would drop his pants in the area of their mouths. Two of the chicks were lying on their backs on a table with their heads hanging over the edge. Guys would walk up and just start pumping their mouths.

Angel laughed and said, "Go over there and stop bothering me!" I started to walk over, but she grabbed my arm, and we both started cracking up.

Nora and David informed us that they had seen these women the previous year, and they were not chicks at all, but rather guys messing with straight guys who were drunk and horny.

"No way," I argued. "They're too hot."

"Look a little closer," Nora said. "See the Adam's apples in their throats as the cocks go in and out?"

She was right.

It was entertaining until a Marine pulled one of their wigs off and another stuck his hand into a pair of panties stuffed with dick. The fight had to be broken up by security as cameras flashed. The transvestites were holding their own; they had been through this drill before. It appeared that taking a punch in the eye to get a strange cock in the mouth was an equal trade, since they didn't stop after the fight was over; it was business as usual.

When we got back to the hotel room, it was around four in the morning. I was ready for some hot, kinky sex -- I wanted to eat Angel alive.

"I'm tired," she complained, turning into the Ice Queen.

I was pissed. All we had done was watch other people have sex all night long, and now . . . nothing.

I was so horny, I drew a bath, did a couple of rails, and took care of business without her.

~~

The eight-hour drive south on the Pacific Coast Highway toward Hollywood was a cold ride. I stared out the window, watching the waves of the ocean break against the shoreline. When Angel dropped me off, we were broken up, and I didn't know why.

Entering my apartment, I was really depressed. I went straight into the bathroom, shut the door, and threw down a pile of blow onto the mirror. I cut a couple of rails, snorted them, and then sat in the dry bathtub with my hands over my face, not wanting to deal with the real world for a while.

Being in love sucked. It hurt worse than being shot, stabbed, and hit by lightning . . . all at once. I was someone that would know.

Chapter 27

Thanksgiving would have been really depressing, but I threw a huge weekend party with my Club California friends, who were becoming my second family. They knew I was miserable about Angel, but they were happy because that meant I was available every night to party.

A week earlier, while spying on the FBI, I had seen a pizza delivery guy pull up to the curb in front of the apartment complex. He sat in his truck for ten minutes without getting out.

I thought, <u>What the fuck is he doing?</u>

I tuned my night vision into the pizza truck to see the guy jacking off onto the pizza. I was disgusted!

When he was done, he closed the lid and headed up the front steps of Club California with a bulge still in the front of his dirty jeans and a sick, perverted smile on his face.

I called the security guard and told him what I had seen, and he called the police. He stopped the pizza guy on the front steps as he was leaving the building after his delivery. The police took the pizza as evidence.

The security guard called me back and said, "Do you know who almost ate that pizza? A guy named Glen, his roommate is Otis Day."

"No shit." I was a huge fan. <u>Animal House</u> was the first R-rated movie I had ever seen. It was the first time I saw huge tits.

When I found out that Otis Day lived only a couple doors down, I figured I would invite him for Thanksgiving. I knocked on his door a few times before he finally answered. I was persistent.

He opened the door slightly and said, "What's up?"

"Otis Day?"

"That's my stage name, but yes, what's going on?"

"I'm having a party," I explained with a smile, "and your presence is wanted. "I'm not taking no for an answer.”

"I'm not in any shape for a party." Otis opened the door a little wider. "You're the new guy down the hall, the heavy metal musician -- and a little more, from what I hear."

"That's right. I was the one who made sure you didn't eat that pizza."

Once I had gotten Otis to smile, I knew he was going to the party.

When everyone saw him come into my apartment, the level of excitement rose. They wanted him to sing "I Think I Want to Scream and Shout" and "Shamalama Ding-Dong." He did, after a few drinks.

Later that evening, I played a game of chess with the world heavyweight champion Tony Tucker, who had come with Cindy from Detroit. He beat me in the game, so I joked about punching him in the eye. Tony Tucker was one of the biggest men I had ever seen; he barely fit through my front door. His hand was still in a cast after his last fight with Mike Tyson.

~~

Trying to get over Angel, I took Eve out to dinner two weeks after Thanksgiving with some of her co-workers to the Moonlight Tango on Ventura Boulevard.

Jani Lane, the singer of Warrant, and his new wife, model Bobby Brown, joined us for dinner. She was pregnant and kept asking Jani to sing to the baby. I knew Jani from the days of standing on the Sunset Strip passing out fliers. He seemed happy, but I knew she would break his heart. I had already heard many stories about her when he was on the road with Warrant. I knew she was an all-around pain in the ass and a Hollywood tramp.

Eve wanted to get back together, but this time I was using cocaine and she was clean. I wouldn't be able to hide it from her and would only end up drawing her back into that world. I couldn't do it to her. I still had enough sense.

"I can't right now," I said. "Things in my life aren't right." I left it at that. I didn't explain.

I was still in love with Angel.

~~

The third week of December, Angel called and then drove out for the evening to have dinner with me at the Rainbow. She knew I was really depressed about our breakup, and she also knew that I had been partying. My skin looked like hell, and I shook when I tried to stand still. I felt it was better to get high and forget, than to be sad and wonder what she was doing, and with whom. I could only imagine based on our past.

When Angel arrived, I could tell she still had some feelings for me, but she had already made up her mind: our relationship was over.

As soon as we got to the Rainbow, I ordered a drink and downed it while I walked to the back bathroom to do a couple of rails. I did the lines, sniffed some water up my nose, and slipped out the door, knocking heads with Vince Neil of Motely Crue.

"Sorry," I said, pointing to the blow I hadn't done still lying on the countertop. He just nodded as he rubbed his forehead.

I was so upset, I couldn't eat a bite of my steak dinner, so I pushed it to the side, just wanting to get the hell out of there. The lines of cocaine made me dwell on thoughts of Angel being with someone else, and that was all I could think of when I looked into her eyes.

I wanted to ask her all kinds of stupid questions, but I refrained and kept my mouth shut while people stopped by our table to say hello. Everyone thought we were a couple again.

When Angel noticed I hadn't touched my dinner, she took her shoe off and placed her foot in my crotch. "I promise to spend one more night with you," she said, "if you cheer up and eat your dinner."

I ate my dinner very quickly and shared one last night with my Angel. I accepted that and loved her enough for one lifetime, but in the morning she asked me to come out to her parents' for Christmas. I thought about it for a few seconds.

"No," I answered, not wanting to ride my emotions like a roller coaster any longer; it was making me look weak.

Angel gave me a really sad look.

~~

The day before Christmas Eve, I drove into Hollywood to one of my many safety deposit boxes. Looking over my shoulder to make sure no one was following, I entered the bank and got my key ready. Opening the box, I took out the engagement ring I had bought for Angel the previous year.

I didn't know what to do with the ring. I had never mentioned it after our relationship became rocky. But I wanted to get the ring before the bank closed for the holidays, thinking I might use it in a last-ditch effort to win her back.

~~

Christmas Eve, I drove out to Angel's parents' place. I really wanted to be with her, and I could only hope she wouldn't be with someone else when I arrived. If she was, I would just get back in my car without causing any trouble and leave. I respected her parents. I actually loved them too.

During the long drive to Rancho Cucamonga, I couldn't make up my mind whether to give her the ring or just forget about it and spare myself from looking like a complete loser.

When I arrived at the house, I walked up the sidewalk and knocked on the front door. I could hear the sounds of Christmas music and the aroma of Italian cooking. I had really become attached to her family; I was losing more than one person in my life.

Angel's brother Scooter answered the door. "Merry Christmas!" he said, and yelled for his sister.

Angel was alone and was glad to see me. "Come in," she said with a smile.

I gave her a hug and kiss on the cheek.

I kept hoping all night that she would want to rekindle the flame as her parents took family pictures that included me, but she didn't, and I left around midnight feeling really depressed. I wanted to be with her in the worst way, but my Leo pride wasn't going to let me beg.

Walking to my car in the moonlight, I had to put on my leather trench coat. It was getting a bit chilly; I had an icy feeling all the way around.

I tried to give Angel a kiss goodbye, but she pulled away and said, "Let's just be friends."

"I can't," I replied. "We've been lovers for too many years." I opened my car door with a heavy sadness in my heart. I looked at her one last time and said, "I won't call. I will respect your decision."

She nodded.

"I'll be moving in the next month," I reminded her. "After that, I'll be a ghost."

She nodded again.

I took one last look, pushed in the clutch, and rolled up the tinted window.

The long drive back to North Hollywood gave me plenty of time to reflect on my life in California. The feelings I had about this year were the total opposite of the feelings I had had last Christmas in Indiana with my family. Last Christmas I had been sober and happy; this year I was depressed and stressed out on cocaine, marijuana, and booze, mixed with greasy fast food.

Twice I had let the same girl break my heart. I swore to God I would never give her that power again.

As I topped the mountain and began descending into Los Angeles, the song "Under the Bridge" by the Red Hot Chili Peppers began playing on the radio, and the words seemed to speak directly to me. The song stuck in my mind forever, reminding me of Angel.

With Angel gone, I had no one I could truly trust. I was now alone in a city of ten million lost souls. I was as lost as any.

As the song ended and the sadness passed, my Leo pride took over. Instead of getting off at the Hollywood exit, I stayed on until I arrived at the Santa Monica Pier. I did a couple more blasts out of the glass bullet and got a drink on the beach. I ended up sharing my drink with a homeless guy.

"Merry Christmas," he said.

I walked down to the end of the pier. Staring out into the ocean, I wiped my tears and downed my drink. Finally, I reached into my pocket and pulled out a box wrapped in gift wrap.

The funny thing was, I had never stepped a single foot into the ocean during all my years in California. Jaws had ruined it for me. I had a fear of getting my leg bitten off.

I opened the box with the ring. It was beautiful as it sparkled in the moonlight. The diamonds were forever . . . my love for Angel would never be.

I wound up and threw the engagement ring into the ocean, along with my heart. Both were now gone forever.

Chapter 28

Even though the FBI was conducting surveillance on the Russians while occupying three apartments, I was still able to do business right under their noses. They were hardly an inconvenience. It was almost comical -- they would have felt awfully stupid knowing they themselves were under surveillance.

Everyone who came over lived in the complex. There were no cars coming or going, just people walking through the inner hallways. The few people who came over hung out for a couple of hours for the free home party. Nothing out of the ordinary.

Everyone except the Russians knew about the FBI. If they had been cool, instead of being creeps, I would have informed them -- but I wanted them gone. I was hoping the FBI would clean them out for me like exterminators, so I could continue my current lifestyle at Club California.

Everyone liked the way it used to be, before both groups arrived. We missed living freely, out in the open.

When I walked through the hallways of Club California, I felt like I owned the place. I really did, since I knew everything that went on and everything about every single person who lived within its walls . . . including the federal agents by their first names.

After thinking it over, I decided to start slipping the FBI the information they needed to get their job done so they could get rid of my problem and get out of my home. Since the pool area was bugged, I used it as my way of talking to the FBI without actually speaking to them directly. I wrote up a script for two strippers to read at the pool. It went like this:

"Is this chair taken?" said one of the strippers to the other.

"No," she replied. "Have a seat."

They got settled, opened their drinks, and talked about meaningless shit. Then it started.

"Did you hear what the Russians are doing?"

"Are you referring to the cocaine they move into the complex during the early morning, or are you talking about the chipped cellular phones they're getting from that guy over on Lankershim, who's posing as a real cellular phone dealer?"

"No, I'm talking about the AK-47's they store in the trunk of their car in the parking garage."

"Which car?"

"The one that never moves. They just keep it washed to remove the dust."

"I didn't know about that, but I heard that the one Russian kid tried to rape one of the maids."

And so on it went.

I thought, That should do the trick. I couldn't have made it any easier.

I was supposed to be moved out by the end of January, but now it was the first of March.

Rudy said, "Bubba, what are you doing? Snap out of this depression and get the fuck out of your apartment, now!"

"I will."

"Stop fucking with the FBI," Rudy demanded. "Pay no attention to them and move out."

"Alright."

"Get the hell out of Dodge before you bring attention to our operation. She is not going to call. Get over her and move on!"

I knew Rudy was right; I was putting our operation in jeopardy. I found a new place that day and prepared to move. As much as I didn't want to go, it was time to disappear again. Out of desperation, as a last resort, I called one of Angel's friends and asked her what Angel was up to. For some stupid reason, I was hoping to hear that she missed me.

Teri said, "She is already with someone else."

I acted like it didn't bother me; I didn't want to give her the pleasure.

When I got off the phone, I snorted two huge rails of cocaine, picked up the telephone, and threw it through my smoked glass coffee table.

SMASH!

I snorted another huge rail of cocaine and then went into my dresser drawer and took all the pictures of us together that I had collected over the last four years. In a jealous rage, I threw them into the kitchen sink and sprayed them with lighter fluid. I grabbed a pack of matches and lit them, sending everything up in flames.

The smoke detectors started going off, and the apartment filled up with smoke very quickly. The ringing in my head from the large amount of cocaine I had snorted, and the constant buzzing alarm of the smoke detectors sent me further into a rage. I stormed out the door into the hallway and put my right foot through the glass container, smashing the glass, and retrieving the fire extinguisher.

I came back in and sprayed the sink to smother the fire. But the smoke detectors wouldn't stop buzzing, and the smoke was so overwhelming. I started choking. Furious, I threw the fire extinguisher through the glass sliding door.

SMASH!

My new secretary, Jennifer, came running in and yelled, "What the hell are you doing? Are you nuts?"

"Fucking nuts is right!" I turned to tell her to get the fuck out of my apartment, but suddenly I felt a heavy throbbing pain in my chest and got dizzy. The lights went out as my head hit the floor.

When I awoke, Jennifer was shaking me while I lay on the floor with what felt like a bad case of heartburn. My chest was tight, and I could only get small breaths of air. I tried not to panic. I could barely move my hands and feet. There was an intense tingling all over my body.

Jennifer's eyes told me how serious it was. She wanted to call 911, but I grabbed her by the ankle and prevented her from reaching the telephone. I would have rather died than have an ambulance show up with the FBI surveillance. They would want to know what was going on.

After a couple of days, some of the feeling started to come back into my arms and legs. I lay in bed for two more weeks recovering, hoping I wasn't going to have permanent damage. But instead of getting better, my lungs started to fill with fluid and a fever began that ran so hot, I started seeing hallucinations.

Jennifer called Rudy.

~~

Rudy came over and took one look at me and left. An hour later he returned with a doctor carrying a black medical bag.

The doctor, with his round-rimmed glasses and slightly balding head, didn't look like a savior of life but like an alcoholic. I got two injections of medicine and a bottle of antibiotics that finally broke the fever. The doctor suspected that I'd had a heart attack, but that was a guess from a man who drank booze like bottled water.

~~

Still laying in bed going on the fourth week, Jennifer knocked on my bedroom door and said, "You have someone here that wants to talk with you. He insists on coming in. His name is Shane. Do you know him?"

"Fuck, yeah!"

"What's up, my brother?" Shane said. "You don't look so good."

"I've seen better days."

I was glad Shane was still alive. Nothing had changed, and he helped himself to my beer supply as usual. I didn't object.

"I'm living out in Agoura Hills with my new girlfriend in a gated community," Shane said. "I have a new job. That's what brought me to you."

"What kind of job?"

"I'm a scout for a certain group of bikers out in the Valley."

"Scout?" I asked.

"These bikers send me out to find drug dealers, and then they dress up like cops and raid them for drugs, guns, and money. These guys had heard

145

about you and sent me to check out your security. I'll tell them that you went out of business and you're not worth the time or the risk involved." He shook his head. "You have no idea how close you came to getting fucked over in the worst way. They always beat the hell out of everyone after duct-taping everyone's hands and feet together during the raid. Most of the drug dealers have no idea they've been ripped off until it's too late. What are they going to do, call the police?" Shane laughed.

"Shane," I said, "this place is under surveillance by the FBI. That would have been a real cluster fuck. The FBI would have come to investigate their unscheduled raid, and they would have had a double bust, or a firefight."

"That would have never happened, Shane replied, an informant that drives a gold BMW always runs the addresses before the raids to make sure there are no surveillance operations. This informant/computer hacker has all the federal agents under wiretaps to track them at all times."

"A federal agent is helping them?"

"Yup, the bikers have a couple old houses in the desert where they stage fake raids, using police tactics with live ammo."

"I want to know who these low-life bikers were."

Shane said, "Don't push your luck. Just move." He wouldn't tell me who his new employers were, so I didn't fuck with him about it. He didn't have to save my ass, but he did.

In the Land of Actors, I was learning that just because someone was wearing a uniform or had a badge, it didn't mean they were real.

~~

The move went smoothly. My friends had me moved and relocated within four hours. The FBI paid no attention to me; I was clear.

My new place was a two-bedroom suite with three balconies and three different views of the Valley. Being on the top floor, I would sit back on my couch at night and shut off all the lights, get stoned, and watch small aircraft cruising the skies of the San Fernando Valley.

The last item I removed from Club California was my answering machine. I knew once I unplugged it, I would never talk with Angel again.

I looked at the phone for a few minutes . . . and then pulled the line.

I was now a ghost. New name, new location, same face, different day.

Chapter 29

<u>April 1992</u>

I had learned a lot about the FBI by watching them from a short distance at Club California. By tuning into the hidden transmitters on my police scanner, I could also spy on the Russian criminals by listening through the "bugs" hidden in their apartments, placed there by the government.

I noticed that on all of the apartments the FBI occupied, they always installed a third deadbolt lock. That was to prevent a maintenance man or an apartment manager from getting in and disturbing their surveillance equipment. It was a dead giveaway.

~~

The first night of living in my new apartment, I found out why the apartment was available. During daylight, the neighborhood was cool, but after dark, things got really dangerous . . . even for my lifestyle.

The apartment manager was a young white girl in her mid-twenties, and she was totally cool when I looked at the suite. I had smelled weed on her when we signed the lease, so I didn't think there would be any problems. But I found out later she had a black boyfriend who sold crack out of the building.

My new bedroom wall faced the inner stairway. When people coming down from their crack high couldn't wait for the elevator, they would run up the stairs, sounding like a herd of elephants.

Jennifer, my secretary, had moved in directly below me. She was afraid to leave her balcony door open at night. Hookers hung out on the corner of Lankershim Boulevard, flapping their big lips and making all kinds of racket.

I yelled a couple times from the top floor, "Shut up, you fucking sluts!"

The whores screamed back, "Fuck you, white boy! Make us!"

That meant there were all kinds of weirdos cruising up and down the street looking for two types of crack. I would always have to walk female guests to their cars after dark, fully strapped.

During the daylight hours it was fine. Across the street was a recording studio. The band Ugly Kid Joe were recording their first album and took breaks to eat at the Funky Dog.

I didn't do any business out of my new apartment. With all the other crap going on, I didn't want to get lumped in with that mess.

Even though I didn't live at Club California, I still had my safe at Gene's apartment. Every night was business as usual. By seven o'clock, I would be dressed to do business in black dress pants, button-up shirt with long sleeves, and snakeskin cowboy boots with one silver spur that was sharp enough to cut your throat.

I would put my Colt .380 pistol in the swell of my back and my new fifteen-shot 9mm in my front belt, pulling my shirt over both. I was ready to do business the American way, making sure my .32 caliber was stuck neatly into my boot.

Standing in front of the full-length mirror, I spun around to make sure no weapons were showing. I pre-rolled ten joints and placed them in my gold cigarette case, which never once, I was proud to say, contained tobacco.

I took the elevator down to my red sports car in the parking garage. I then hit the automatic door opener and drove to Club California, pulling into the underground parking garage as if I still lived there. The security guards were still my friends and would cover for my presence in the complex if anyone was to inquire.

All my orders came by pager, with secret numbers: the amount and the apartment number. I would go through each building, making all my stops and making sure to go around the apartments that I knew the FBI agents were staying.

I made damn sure to stay out of their lines of vision, using back stairways and cutting through the underground parking garages unnoticed. I knew the complex better than anyone, always traveling the corridors close to the walls and very quietly.

Rudy was the only weed connection I needed, but I had to find new cocaine connections all the time, since they didn't last long. The closest, and most reliable, was a guy who worked at a car wash in Van Nuys. Big Gunn's bodyguard, Sledgehammer, set me up with Paco after Big Gunns got busted a couple of years ago. When I needed to score, I paged Paco at the car wash.

He would page me back with a "go" or "no" code.

If it was a "go," I would place the money under the front seat, get out of the car, and make myself a cup of hot, fresh Columbian coffee with a lot of sugar and non-dairy mix. They would run my sports car through the wash and hand dry it. I would pay for the wash, finish my coffee, tip the guy who handed me the keys, and get back in. The money would be gone and the cocaine would be under the front seat.

I spoke with no one and saw nothing. I didn't even know which guy out of the ten guys who washed my car was Paco; I had never met him in person. I was introduced by the description of my car and my code number.

As I got settled in, I let two of my close friends move into my new suite. I hated to live alone and was always willing to share space. Tim Thaw, a trusted friend, took the far bedroom. He supplied me with endless free rental videos from the Odessa in North Hollywood. Tim was the total opposite of myself, but we looked enough alike that some people thought we were brothers.

Then there was Mad Max Mason, the guy the gangbangers had shot at when I lived on Cold Water Canyon. Max looked like Charles Manson with a Jesus Christ edge. He had very long, dirty, hippie-like hair, a full beard, and goofy-looking sideburns. Max was harmless, unless you were hurt by words.

I had met Max through his wife Apache, my favorite waitress in the upstairs loft of the Rainbow. She had convinced me a couple of years earlier to give Max a job, sparking the friendship. The first time I saw Max, he just looked dirty and unkempt, and he was, but I gave him a chance anyway, just like everyone else in my life.

He started off selling toner for me, but now Max's job was to stay at my place when I wasn't there to make sure no one came in to plant hidden transmitters or snoop through my belongings. I couldn't risk leaving my place empty, even for ten minutes. Government agents worked that quickly; I had seen them in action.

I gave Max my philosophy: "Only scam the system that's in place to scam you -- no little people or civilians." I took from the corporations and shared with everyone, to the point of almost being broke most of the time. My generous Leo heart led to an empty wallet, but it made everything seem all right, as long as greed wasn't involved.

Besides being a drunk, Max was a bigot. If I had to compare his views to anyone, I would pick Archie Bunker. When I took Max to parties, he would get really drunk and started yelling, "I'm white, I'm white! And anybody who's not white can fuck off!"

Max's stunts never got him any chicks, so I didn't see the point. There was even a flier being passed around Hollywood for a party that read in fine bold print, If you know Mad Max Mason, don't bring him to the party.

I thought that was funny as hell, and so did Max. He went anyway.

After the first week of living in my new apartment, my buddy Shitfield stopped by with a Hispanic guy who fancied himself a ladies' man. I could tell by his gold and the smell of his cologne.

"Did you bring me my new illegal cable box?" I asked.

"You know it," replied Shitfield.

Now I had all the channels, and so did half a dozen other people in the building.

"Do you still need a new coke connection?" Shitfield asked.

I nodded. "Yep." Something happened to Paco at the car wash, he stopped answering my pages."

Shitfield smiled and turned to the Hispanic guy. "This is my new connection. He has the best in the entire Valley."

"Oh really."

"I would like you to meet Dougie."

"You can call me the Kid," he said.

I stood and shook his hand. <u>What a grip.</u>

After pumping weights for many years behind bars, he was built like Fort Knox. It would have taken a serious bullet to even penetrate the solid wall of muscle in his chest. As part of the Kid's probation, he had gotten a regular job at a cable company in Glendale.

The Kid accepted the beer I offered, and Shitfield accepted Jennifer. He took her into my bedroom while the Kid and I talked business. That was the way things went on in Los Angeles.

"As much as you want," the Kid said. "I'll even deliver it to your hands, any time, twenty-four-seven."

"Sounds pretty sweet. Got a sample?"

He smiled.

"Let's try it."

Now that I was thinking, my new apartment was actually the perfect setup for business, since there was already a ton of illegal activity going on. No one would notice me having a few parties.

I had a sit-down meeting with the apartment manager. I let her know that I knew what her boyfriend was up to. She was shocked that I was so forward.

"I'm not here to complain," I said. "Let's do business."

I figured if they were going to keep me up all night, I might as well be making something for all the trouble.

I told her boyfriend, "I will supply you."

With Shane standing next to me, looking all fucking crazy, he replied, "All right, I guess."

Now I was running the building; they were taking orders from me and taking all the heat. I didn't even have to pay rent anymore. It came out of their end, since I lost weeks of sleep.

I was learning fast how to play the game and was making up my own rules as I went along.

Chapter 30

No matter how good things seemed or how fast one problem got solved, something else always happened in Los Angeles that made me say to myself, "Why in the hell do I live in this fucked-up city nicknamed the Meat Grinder?"

The extremely nice weather blinded people to the evil and hid the true nature of Los Angeles. It was not a good place, but appeared like the Garden of Eden to a tourist because of the palm trees and endless sunshine.

We all knew there was going to be a major riot because of the Rodney King beating, equal to the Watts riots of the '60's, if the white cops who did the beating didn't go to prison. The jury was still out on deliberation. All over Los Angeles, citizens were bracing themselves, fearing the worst and preparing.

With the riot talk all over the Los Angeles, I went down into the Hood and picked up an M-16, a crate of .223 ammo, and plenty of rounds for my pistols. I was lucky enough to get some pepper spray grenades that had been stolen from the Army Reserve.

"You better be ready," said Rudy. "I'm hearing it straight from the Hood. Everyone is stocking up on ammo and gasoline, the riot is going to be brutal."

Seeing the old news footage of the Watts riots, I added a folding stock to my M-16 assault rifle, making it small enough to hide under a trench coat. For perfect shooting, I installed a laser sighting system and added a homemade silencer and flash suppressor for shooting rioters without attracting attention.

I thought to myself, I'm not going to be burned alive or beaten to death by some rioter just because I'm white. My building will be their last stop.

While working at my office in Hollywood, I had a meeting with some of my Hungarian criminal friends. I came up with the idea to rent three buildings, opening fake businesses real quick before the riot. Jewels thought it was a great idea, and we went ahead with the plan. One building was an adult warehouse, and the other two were labeled as drug companies just to attract the attention of the wrong people. The buildings were insured and were supposed to be stocked with merchandise . . . or so the fake paperwork claimed.

I can remember the beginning of the riot like it was yesterday. Mad Max Mason, Gary, Shane, and I were sitting around my living room like a bunch of pirates, drinking a few brews and smoking fat joints. The sun was about to set over the top of the Hollywood Hills. It was so peaceful, like the calm before the storm. Then all of a sudden . . . all hell broke loose!

There was a break in the television programming and for the first time, I saw the instructions of an emergency broadcast come across the screen.

It wasn't a test. They were warning people of the riot in progress.

The news commentator said, "Get the hell out of Los Angeles, and fast!"

As we gathered in front of the television, the news commentator went to the live cameras in the news choppers. We started seeing live footage of the riot in full force. The camera zoomed in and showed in great detail the truck driver, Reginald Denny, being pulled from his truck and tossed to the street like a rag doll, for no other reason than being white. The black attackers encircled Reginald like wild jackals, kicking and poking him like the L.A. cops had done to Rodney King. Then one of the bastards smashed Reginald in the head with a giant cement block.

Shane jumped up and screamed, "That wouldn't have happened to me! I would've shot every one of those motherfuckers. Let's go down there and kill those fuckers! Who's with me?"

"Fuck that," I replied. "If they come here, I'll fight to the death, but I'm not playing hero today."

Shane reached into his black duffel bag and pulled out two 9mm submachine gun pistols. "Come if they dare. They'll never leave the Valley alive!" We all smashed our beers together and geared up for the evening.

White people all over Los Angeles were being pulled out of their cars at stop lights and beaten with clubs and bricks. All this was happening because the cops who had beaten Rodney King were found not guilty. The riot had broken out within minutes of the verdict being read.

Shitfield and the Kid were down in the Hood on the corner of Crenshaw when the riot broke out, which wasn't a good place to be at any time. They tried to make it to Rudy's place but were cut off and had to make a mad dash through Hollywood. They blew through stop lights and stop signs until they reached the 101 Freeway.

"They were throwing rocks and beer bottles," Shitfield said, "and even taking shots at us as we fled from South Central."

"I had my pistol at my side," the Kid added. "I was ready to pop the first asshole who dared to open my van door!"

Looking at Shitfield's cable van from my balcony above, I said, "Look, there are three bullet holes in the top of your van. You were damn lucky to escape alive!"

Shitfield shook his head, knowing he had gotten lucky.

The riot started at 5:15 sharp, and by seven o'clock the sun was almost blocked out by the thick smoke from all the buildings that were burning out of control in Los Angeles. It was almost like a prophecy out of the Bible. The sun was turning different colors of red from the smoke . . . a sight I would never forget.

By eight o'clock, the riot was in full force, and the streets of Los Angeles were covered with looters acting like mad ants. The rioters were carrying bats and wooden boards, smashing out store windows and beating anyone who got in their way.

Most of the people caught in the riot locked themselves in their homes out of fear of being burned alive. They waited for the LAPD to come to their rescue, but that didn't happen. Instead, the LAPD retreated as rioters threw gas bombs from rooftops and unseen snipers shot everything in sight, including firemen and paramedics.

Standing on my balcony, looking through binoculars with my M-16 slung over my shoulder, I could see the fires in the distance, coming closer every hour.

Looking around my neighborhood from my balcony, I saw that my neighbors were also on their rooftops, carrying automatic weapons in an attempt to save their belongings.

I told everyone at Club California I wasn't making my run tonight, so everyone came to stay with me. My place was high in the sky and like a fortress. I had a solid steel fire door that would hold up against an elephant.

Chuck, the guy who had made and installed the steel doors, said, "It would take the LAPD ten minutes to get through the door if they had the right equipment." In that amount of time, I could have everything flushed down the toilet. I would even have enough time to fix them eggs and bacon, since I didn't eat donuts. "It would be easier to go through the wall," Chuck claimed.

The steel door looked just like any other door in the building. By also installing a solid steel door frame, he had made kicking in my door impossible.

Chuck came over to my new place every time I moved to take new measurements. He would duplicate the door and paint it to be exact. We would switch the doors in the middle of the night, when we knew we were the only people up.

Chuck started doing this service for me back at Club California after Shane told me about the bikers who liked dressing up like cops. Chuck was one of Rudy's trusted friends.

By nine o'clock, I had seventy-five people at my apartment. They were drinking, smoking, and snorting while watching the riot on several televisions. It was total anarchy in the streets. Anything was fair game, and if you couldn't run fast enough, you got eaten. It wasn't just black people rioting; it was everyone who wanted "free stuff." Stolen cars that had been hot-wired were being used like weapons, crashing through the storefronts along Hollywood Boulevard and opening them up like cans of tuna. Once everything was stolen, the thieves would set the store to the fire.

A brave, or should I say stupid, newscaster was stopping looters and interviewing them about why they were rioting. A couple looters actually stopped for the camera and did an interview and told their real names. I couldn't believe the stupidity on both sides.

Police Chief Daryl "Dipshit" Gates didn't lift a finger to stop the riot. He had been heavily criticized after the Rodney King beatings, and for that, he was letting the people of Los Angeles suffer.

The LAPD set up barricades protecting certain rich white neighborhoods, such as Beverly Hills and West Hollywood. Everyone else was on their own. Korean store owners were patrolling the tops of their stores with AK-47s, shooting warning shots into the air to scare looters away. Believe it or not, the police started arresting the people who were defending their property. As the Korean store owners were being handcuffed and tossed into the backs of squad cars, looters with bricks and gas bombs devoured their defenseless stores.

Finally, by midnight, when everyone saw how the LAPD had been over run, the National Guard was called and put all of us under martial law. That meant that anyone out after dark would be stopped and arrested on sight. Anyone who didn't comply would be shot while law and order was being restored to the City of Lost Angels. They weren't fucking around anymore. We were under siege, with helicopters and Army troop carriers bringing soldiers into the city by the thousands to restore order. Seeing that only reminded me that the government was still in charge, no matter what the people thought or wanted to believe.

The news clips on television looked like scenes out of the movie Escape From New York, with all the buildings on fire at the same time: ten thousand fires burning out of control.

It took five days to restore law and order, resulting in a few looters being shot to thin the herd. Once the National Guard pulled out and martial law was lifted, the LAPD went to work using computer lists of all the items that had been stolen during the riots. They ran the numbers off empty cardboard boxes rioters had left outside on the street curbs in front of apartment complexes. That evidence gave the LAPD warrants to enter and look for stolen property within the housing projects and rundown complexes. Doors were getting knocked on and kicked in all over the city. With the help of the police videos, they captured over twenty thousand license plates of looters that had come from all over Los Angeles to join in the quest for "free stuff."

In the end, the LAPD convicted fourteen thousand people for looting and stealing. Most of the businesses in Hollywood were burned out, and the only houses that were untouched were the crack houses. No one dared fuck with them.

A couple of days after the riot was over, I took a drive with Rudy through the war zone. Everything was burned out. It reminded me of Gary, Indiana, where I was born.

The riot ruined a lot of people's lives, but I made enough money to quit my job at Zolie's. Fifteen hundred bucks a week wasn't enough to inspire me to get up in the morning anymore. I would rather stay up all night partying with strippers and sleep until the next afternoon. The office was a place people could find me. It wasn't good counter-surveillance.

Plus, I was done taking orders. I was now giving them and everyone was listening.

Chapter 31

Walking through the courtyard of Club California, I saw Sammy the Slob, the father of the Russian families, sitting by the swimming pool eating a fat sandwich like it was feeding time at the human zoo. I thought, <u>I'd like to whack him myself</u> and fantasized about him choking to death on his own sandwich.

Suddenly, out of nowhere, guys in bright yellow windbreakers with the words "Federal Agents" in bold print started screaming, "Put your hands up!"

I thought, <u>Fuck!</u> I didn't have any drugs, but I was armed to the teeth.

I stopped in my tracks and started to put my hands up as the agents ran past me and grabbed Fat Sammy and his family members. As the last federal agent passed me, he said, "Put your hands down and go about your business."

"No problem," I replied. They didn't even know who I was, and I liked that very much.

A few minutes later, listening through my police scanner,

I heard the Feds searching the Russians' apartments. They found several pounds of weed and a kilo of cocaine, but the real prize was the twenty-five AK-47s they found in the trunk of Sammy's car, along with boxes of chipped phones.

The arrest of Fat Sammy pleased me so much, I decided to throw a party in honor of the FBI. My plan worked like a charm.

~~

A few hours before the party, I went down to Jennifer's to make sure she had called everyone about the party, and I got shanghaied into helping her new roommate move some of her belongings into the apartment. She had just driven two days straight from Florida. Jennifer introduced her to me as Brittney.

I could tell that Brittney was into fitness, since I had to carry a workout machine and boxes of health food supplements into the building. Brittney had pulled her blonde hair back into a bun and was wearing dirty sweats from the two-day drive and no make-up, but she seemed cute with her Southern accent. Still, I really didn't give her too much attention.

I had a party to plan.

Later that night, when I saw Brittney, she was dressed to kill. Her red lipstick made her lips look like melted strawberries glazed with liquid sugar. I was stunned. I hardly recognized her with her long blonde hair down; she looked like an airbrushed centerfold right out of the pages of <u>Playboy</u>. She looked very classy, the way she wore her make-up and carried herself in high heels. She was out to impress, and I was definitely impressed.

I found out quickly that Brittney knew how to play the game. She knew how to get my attention. While walking out of my bathroom, wiping my nose, I saw Brittney and Jennifer lying on top of each other across my waterbed with their tongues buried in each other's mouths like it was a love scene on some daytime soap opera. I stopped dead in my tracks and said, "What are you, a couple of dykes?"

Brittney snapped back, "It was the only way I could get your undivided attention."

I lifted Jennifer by the arm and led her to the door. "You're in charge of the party," I said, and kicked her out of my bedroom.

Tossing Brittney back onto the bed, I shut the drapes to the outside world. Nothing else mattered as I turned on the red lights and turned up the stereo to a good volume, cranking out the first album from Alice in Chains.

Brittney stood up, and I slowly unzipped her dress, letting it fall to the floor and revealing dark black garter belts and stockings that set me into ecstasy. I started kissing her on the back of the neck, working my way down her back to her perfect behind, which was still wrapped in sexy dressing. I chewed through her g-string until it snapped in my mouth like a piece of dental floss.

Starting to map my new territory with my tongue, I noticed that Brittney's body was flawless, with not a single ounce of body fat -- just those 38 double D's, Southern raised and untouched in California so far.

Once I undressed, we climbed into bed and kissed passionately, fondling each other until we both fell out of bed and hit the floor with a thud. The last thing I remembered was Brittney saying in a low voice, "Tomorrow would be much better . . . Yeah, tomorrow."

I agreed, as we both passed out.

We didn't wake up until the late afternoon, still on the floor with my satin sheets pulled over our naked bodies.

I asked, "Did you have a good time last night?"

"I don't remember," Brittney replied. "Do you have any aspirin? I've got a rippin' headache."

~~

I was very attracted to Brittney, so we started dating. It had been five months since Angel.

Brittney was the first woman I had ever dated who was taller than myself. She towered over me by six inches when she wore high heels. Brittney was a Leo like me and could make a hell of an entrance.

Born in Alabama, she had gone to college in Florida for the past four years and earned a degree in business and psychology. She talked with a

Southern drawl and used out-of-date words like <u>groovy</u> and <u>far-out</u>. She had beautiful strawberry blonde hair in both places; one was teased and hair-sprayed, the other trimmed neatly into the shape of a cute, edible heart.

Brittney didn't do cocaine or smoke pot, but she liked to drink . . . and I mean, she really liked to drink.

~~

During the party, everyone was saying that they wanted me to move back to Club California. I was informed that the FBI had pulled out after busting Sammy the Slob and his crew of classless thugs.

I rented three separate apartments two days later, but they wouldn't be ready for ten days. I had time to pack with no hurry. But I could be packed and gone within four hours, if necessary.

~~

The entire time I knew Shane, he was always talking about a stripper named Trisha. I had heard about her for years; she was supposed to be the hottest thing in Hollywood without wheels. I thought Trisha was just something Shane had made up, until he said he was picking her up at the LAX International Airport one night. She was returning from a two-year dance tour in Japan.

When Shane walked through the door with a beautiful blonde in an extremely low-cut red evening dress, the whole room seemed to light up like the Fourth of July.

Before we could be properly introduced, she pushed past Shane, tripping on her six-inch heels, and said, "I'm going to be sick."

"By the way," Shane said, "this is Trisha."

During the twenty-three-hour flight from Japan, Trisha had taken full advantage of the free champagne, and after Shane's reckless lane-changing on the way home, she was ready to let loose.

I somehow managed to catch her in my arms before she hit the floor and carried her to the bathroom like a knight in shining armor. I could have really used armor, we didn't make it to my bathroom before Trisha let loose down the front of my shirt and dress pants.

Like a complete dumbass, I just stood there smiling as Trisha got down on all fours and hacked her brains out for at least three minutes, like a sick puppy dog. I held her blonde hair back while Shane asked, "Can I get a beer?"

When she was finished, I was very relieved that her head didn't start spinning around or start cussing at me in Hebrew.

"Do you have some sweats I can put on?" Trisha asked. "I want to wash my dress off in the sink so it won't stain. Give me your dress pants. I'll clean them off, too." She reached over and undid my belt. "Hurry, before it stains."

Within five minutes of meeting Trisha, I was standing there in my underwear and she was totally naked in front of me, hand-washing the clothes in the sink. I had to force all my thoughts in a different direction to keep from popping a boner.

Trisha had no shame about her body. She was proud to show it off and thought nothing that I was standing there. She had three tattoos that could be covered by a single g-string. At the top of Trisha's mound were a set of black clouds, the type you would see in a werewolf movie, floating through the small patch of blonde pubic hair. On each side of her inner lips were two vampire bites, with a few drops of red blood trickling down out of the bite holes.

At the top of her butt crack was a tattoo of a little pixie fairy with its wings extended across both her butt cheeks, like it was showing the way to Heaven.

Once Trisha showered and felt better, she never stopped smiling. Her bubbly personality was like a breath of fresh air. She was smart, sexy, funny and could speak Japanese and held a license to fly an airplane.

"Shane told me all about you," Trisha said. "You're going to be the guy running Club California? That's interesting."

"Interesting in what way?"

Trisha just smiled and replied, "Time will tell."

Chapter 32

<hr>

July 1, 1992

This time, when I moved back to Club California, I rented what I thought was the best apartment available in the complex. I sat on the top floor at the corner of the courtyard, overlooking the entire swimming pool.

The previous tenants, Krazy Kurtis and Benny the Mean, who had been gone already when I had moved into Club California the first time, had left the apartment a total wreck. Oil stains had completely ruined the carpet. Unattended cigarettes had left huge burn marks on the countertops. The apartment had to be literally gutted.

For some odd reason, the apartment had been empty for several years. With the best view in the complex, I couldn't understand why, but I wanted it and rented it. The perfect view of the pool area allowed me to indicate my preferences. If I opened my sliding glass door and turned on the living room lights, that meant I was up and having people over. If I shut my drapes and kept only my bedroom light on, everyone respected my privacy.

Krazy Kurtis and Benny the Mean, along with a group of wild women, knocked on my apartment door the first time I had a party and introduced themselves.

Knowing their reputation, and since they had the porno star Falen with them, I invited them in and we hit it off. They were glad to see I was keeping up the reputation of their old place.

I asked Benny, "Why did you and Krazy Kurtis move out?"

"Our female roommate went into the bathroom and shot up a rather large dose of crystal meth, then walked out and collapsed on the floor. She died at the foot of where your bed is now. After that, we were being watched by the DEA, so we split back to Texas until things blew over."

Now I knew why my new apartment had remained empty: bad karma. That bothered me; I didn't like living where someone had died in an untimely fashion.

~~

Jennifer and Brittney moved back to Club California also, taking the other two apartments I had rented. Jennifer was my personal secretary, and Brittney and I were dating off and on, we fought a lot. I wouldn't speak to her for days, until we ran into each other by the swimming pool. Once I saw Brittney 98% naked, I always forgot about what she had done to piss me off.

~~

On Fourth of July weekend, Jennifer, Trisha, Debra-Do Wrong, and twenty other close friends went to see Mad Max Mason's metal band, called the "Dispossessed Majority," play some shithole bar south of Hollywood Boulevard. The bar was in a really rundown neighborhood, like any neighborhood in Hollywood. We were risking our lives just to make the trip after dark.

Gary, Shitfield, Shane, and I got ready in my bedroom for the trip into Hollywood. Everyone was carrying at least one gun with extra clips of ammo, along with steel blades just in case we ran out of bullets. It was a bit over the top, but the weapons made us feel safe in a dangerous, unpredictable city.

By the time we all got to the bar, Mad Max Manson was already out of his mind drunk and ready to tear the place down. It might have been Max's night to shine, but the poor guy who went on stage before Max's band probably crawled under a rock after his show and died. It was his first show, and with his extremely bad luck, he had Mad Max Mason as the heckler from hell in the crowd.

As the comedian finished his first round of jokes, everyone clapped, except for Mad Max Mason. He just stood there cross-eyed drunk and glared at the stage.

I thought, Oh no. I could tell by the strange look on his face that there was going to be some kind of trouble.

As the comedian waited for the laughter to stop, Mad Max Mason stood up and yelled, "Are you fucking black?"

There was dead silence, like in one of those E.F. Hutton commercials. Everyone's heads twisted in all directions to see who would be stupid enough to make such a remark.

With his long hair hanging in his dazed face, holding an ice-cold beer in each hand, Max yelled again, "Are you FUCKING BLACK? Because I'm white, and that's my stage!" He continued yelling at the top of his lungs, "I'm white! I'm white!" I couldn't believe it; I never thought he would pull such a stunt outside the safety of my apartment.

The shocked and intimidated black comedian didn't have a response to that one. He was totally freaked out, and the look on his face was the funniest part of the show. He thought he was going to be lynched by members of the Hell's Angels.

I thought we were going to be knifed, until I noticed that the comedian onstage was the only black guy in the bar, besides his mother and Otis Day -- who had that shocked look on his face like in Animal House.

"Otis, that's kind of funny?"

"Shut up Brent, you idiot."

161

I laughed.

Shane did the honors and grabbed Max by the back of the neck, forcing him to sit down and shut the fuck up -- or get knocked out. It was kind of funny, for a brief second. I wished the comedian could have worked it into his show, but he didn't and left the stage. Being a Hollywood performer, I knew that had to suck, and I mean really suck bad, so I went backstage to apologize for my friend's rude drunken behavior.

"Hey, dude," I said, "don't let that get to you. My friend is just a mean drunk."

"I thought I was going to get killed," replied the comedian. "I bet Jerry Seinfeld never ran into that."

"You're probably right," I said. "They probably called him a Jew."

The comedian thought that was funny and felt a little better when I told him Mad Max Mason was totally crazy and a raving drunk.

"Don't take it personally," I added. "He would have done it to any black guy. Sorry."

"Thanks for coming backstage," he said. "I'll try again on another day."

"Don't give up. I'm sure you'll never run into a heckler like Max again."

"You're right about that."

I reached into my wallet and dug through my stack of business cards. "Call Jimmy the Z. Tell him I told you to call. He handles comedians."

"Thanks." We shook hands.

To smooth things over and make him feel a little bit better, I finished with, "My friend Max's parents were killed by a couple of black guys. That's why he hates blacks."

"Sorry to hear that. We're not all that way."

What I had told him wasn't true . . . Max's parents had both drunk themselves to death, and Max was well on his way to upholding the family tradition. Max told me the best memory he had of his childhood was one year on Thanksgiving, while saying grace, his father turned his head and threw up into his aunt's lap before falling out of his chair drunk.

When I heard stories like that, I realized what good and decent parents I had. It made me feel even more guilty for living the way I was living, but this was what I had to do to keep living in Los Angeles. Many times, I had wanted to give it all up while I still could and move back to Indiana, but I would never admit to my parents that being a musician had been the wrong choice. I was too proud to ever let them know how bad things really were. How could I tell them I was risking my life every second that I stayed in Los Angeles?

I still wanted to be a musician, if I could only stop partying and playing the game of counter-surveillance. I didn't want to live like this much longer; it was very nerve-wracking. I really just wanted to be a musician . . . The dream was still there, somewhere in the back of my mind, being clouded by everything else that was going on.

~~

Once Max's band hit the stage, the place came alive. Max was more outrageous than usual, stage-diving and screaming, "Go, white man, go! Go, white man, go!"

On his many stage dives into the crowd, Max grabbed drinks off people's tables and smashed his way back through the onlookers to the stage. The crowd loved Max, and the show was a smash, along with all the band equipment and part of the stage. His band-mates ran for cover.

The owner of the club yelled, "Someone stop that fucking lunatic from throwing that goddamn bass drum!"

It was too late.

We were having such a good time, I invited about fifty people from the bar back to my place for an after-party, which lasted for two days before everyone finally came down and went home.

When Rudy came over the next day to do business, he said, "Did you know that Max is passed out by the swimming pool in one of the pool chairs?"

"Hmm. I wondered where he went."

"You might what to go down there and turn him over," Rudy suggested. "He looks burnt to a crisp."

Max was so burned on his arms and face, I had to have him taken to the veteran's hospital to be treated for heat stroke and alcohol poisoning. His liver was so swollen, it stuck out of his side like a potato and caused his skin to turn shades of yellow. At the end of the party when we ran out of beer, Max would take a coffee filter and pour almost empty cans of old beer through the filter so it would catch the cigarette butts, then drink the warm beer.

"Bubba, I know Max is your friend," said Rudy, "but he's drawing too much attention with his stupid antics. It could harm the business. Get rid of him before he brings us down."

I knew that Rudy was absolutely right; my current lifestyle was running at full throttle. Nothing was in my real name, and nothing I did was legal. Still, I didn't consider myself a criminal . . . more of a rebel living in the badlands, settling everything with lethal force just like in the old Wild West.

The Kid, my cocaine connection, had expanded. He had climbed to the number two spot on the cocaine ladder in the Valley and was working his way into the Hollywood hip-hop and techno music scenes. I kept telling him like a broken record, "You're getting too damn big. Scale back."

"I know what I'm doing," he snapped. "Worry about yourself."

"All right, fine," I fired back. "But greed causes mistakes."

"Yeah, I know. Shut the fuck up."

The Kid talked on his cellular phone about everything, and I would have a fit when I heard him do it. I tried to tell him that anyone with a scanner could pick up his conversation. He also talked over the ground lines, so I wouldn't let him use my phone anymore.

"What do you mean I can't make a call?" growled the Kid.

"You talk over the phone line," I replied. "I can't have it."

"You're fucking paranoid."

"Damn right I am. I don't want to get busted."

That caused us to get into many arguments. To add fuel to the fire, the Kid bought a couple of sports cars and a 4-wheel-drive monster truck that might as well have had plates that read, "Drug Dealer."

He also bought his mother a new house and a nice boat on the ocean, which I thought was foolish, since he didn't even like the ocean. This was where greed took over and stupidity stepped in.

The Kid told me, "I'm flying to Ohio to do a two-kilo deal. I'll be back in two days."

"Are you nuts?" I replied. "They don't have L.A. gang-bangers walking around dressed in gold in Ohio. You'll stick out like a turd in a punch bowl."

He laughed and said, "It's cool. Don't worry."

"You don't need the money that bad. Why take the risk?"

"I got my business handled. Do you have the killer green weed for me? It's for Tommy Lee."

I handed him the smoke. "Give Tommy my regards."

"I will." And out the door he went.

I had always wanted to meet Tommy Lee but had never had time to make the run out to Topanga Canyon with the Kid.

~~

The deal went sour in Ohio, and the Kid came back with the cocaine.

During the flight back, he called his people on his cellular phone to tell them what had happened and that he was bringing the cocaine back.

"They" heard the call and were waiting for him. The second the Kid grabbed his bags at LAX, the DEA arrested him with the kilo. When I heard that, I shut down that part of my operation.

I really needed a break from the Hollywood lifestyle, so I took a two-week vacation in Indiana to visit with my family and attend my ten-year class reunion. I was really looking forward to eating my mother's home-cooked meals. I usually ate out two to three times a day at fancy restaurants all over Hollywood, and most of them just gave me a stomach ache.

I had bought two plane tickets and was planning on taking Brittney, but we got into another fight and broke up a couple of days before the flight. I called Mary Olsen, who was filming her last scene as an extra on Baywatch and needed a break, so she went instead.

The flight was smooth as we flew into Chicago's Midway Airport. Johnny Boy picked us up in his black Cadillac and delivered us to my brother's house, where a welcome-home party was already in full swing. The beer keg was tapped, and some drunk guy was molesting the blow-up doll in the corner. The stereo blared Guns n' Roses in the background, as everyone got fucked up.

My brother's house was packed with old friends that I hadn't seen in many years. They weren't sure what to think of my new L.A. style. I was wearing jean shorts, a tight-fitting shirt, Doc Martens combat boots with eighteen laces and steel toes. My hair wasn't spiked like it had been in the glam days; now it was long and one length. Once every guy got a good look at Mary's legs and backside, they couldn't care less what I was wearing.

Mary and I partied until dawn, and I was afraid I was going to feel like shit at the class reunion. But after a few lines the next afternoon, Mary and I were ready to rock the town.

Most of my high school friends had gotten married at least once, some twice, and had a couple of kids by several different women. I was one of the only ones who were still single. None of them, other than Johnny Boy and Mullins, had a clue as to who I was. They all thought I was still playing in a band back in Hollywood, and that was what I let them think.

My best friend Johnny Boy got married for the second time while I was home, and for the second time, I stood up as his best man.

It was a nice ten-day break from Hollywood. Part of me didn't want to go back, but I couldn't admit I had failed in the music business. I would rather die than look like a loser.

Sometimes, Leo pride is a killer.

Chapter 33

I started spending a lot of time hanging out with Trisha while Brittney and I were fighting. Trisha was breathtaking, and it really pissed off Brittney. Trisha wasn't into cocaine and kept suggesting I try some meth because it would help stop the craving for cocaine.

Shane loved meth; it was his drug of choice. The meth only made him stronger and meaner than humanly possible. "Cocaine is for credit card yuppie pussies," he liked to say. He wasn't afraid to let his opinion be heard.

Speed, or should I say crystal methamphetamine, came in a much harder form than cocaine. It had to be crushed flat, then cut up with a very sharp and dangerous knife just to enhance the visual effect. The bigger the knife, the better, and no size was considered too big.

I didn't like meth at first; it burned the shit out of my nose and made my eyes water. It wasn't sweet smelling like cocaine and had an unmatchable chemical taste of its own. But once the meth high kicked in, it was better then cocaine. It didn't have that instant rush, but after it took effect, I could stay up days goofing off with Trisha.

Trisha was like a trophy I had earned with the title.

"Where did you get the meth?" I asked.

"I shouldn't say," Trisha replied. "From a biker friend . . . His name is Christ. Maybe someday I'll introduce you, if I can catch him in a good mood."

The more crystal meth I did, the better it made me feel. I was happy and had more energy than I'd had in many years. Once my body adapted to the new drug, the craving for cocaine went away instantly.

I couldn't believe it was even possible.

~~

Weeks turned into months as I avoided cocaine altogether. I thought crystal meth was a gift from Heaven, but in reality, it was a curse from Hitler that would affect my life forever.

It is now a known fact that Hitler shot up with meth and gave it to his soldiers in the form of chocolate bars. That was why his storm troopers were so ruthless and could march and fight for weeks without food or water. Meth had been developed by a Japanese scientist in 1920 and was probably the cause of World War II, making the Japanese think they were invincible as they shared their invention with Germany in 1932.

The meth didn't cause paranoia like cocaine. I could stay up for two to three days straight like a superhuman, without a fear in the world. Since it had helped me stop the cocaine, I started turning all my friends on to it, and they loved it. No one wanted cocaine. They wanted meth, and as fast as I could get it.

On the street, meth had many names, including speed, crank, glass, rocket fuel, lemon drop, and gack. It was all basically the same, just different grades and homemade brands that differed slightly. It was nothing but pure chemicals, nothing natural, and none of the ingredients by themselves would have been safe to ingest. Several poisons were required to produce a strong batch.

I had been using a few hundred dollars' worth of cocaine every day, but now I used only twenty dollars' worth of meth, and it kept me twice as high for twenty times longer. Meth was much cheaper and went a hell of a lot further, and the best part was, it was made in the good ol' U.S.A.

The meth that Trisha had was pure and very refined, made in a lab in controlled conditions by someone who knew what the hell they were doing as they cooked it down. A good batch of meth had such a strong chemical smell, it would make you gag if you stuck your nose into the plastic bag holding it. Gack!

Once I figured this was a good thing, I talked Shane into becoming my right-hand man. He set me up with a new meth connection and started another business venture that I knew would be very lucrative. I had a jump on the market; it was a brand new product in my circle. I could handle the stimulant without losing it. It had been a biker drug so far, but I would change that.

Shane also introduced me to a bunch of new computer hackers who had grown up in the Valley. They were local boys . . . home-grown criminals. Their names were Matt the Ratt, "the profiteer with the biggest nuts," or so his business card claimed. Then there was Joey the Mumbler, who always mumbled and quoted Metallica songs like they were words of wisdom straight out of the Bible. Then there was Silva the Irritator, who could drive anyone absolutely nuts with his endless stupid questions, designed by his twisted mind to get under your skin so he could get pleasure from your mental frustration. The brains of the bunch was Mike Dollar, known to law enforcement agencies as Dr. Doom.

These Valley hackers were different from the other hackers I had been dealing with. They were into low-life types of crime. They used their skills to commit fraud, forgery, and many other kinds of electronic crimes. Dr. Doom could duplicate anyone's checks and go out on shopping sprees with no remorse.

Dr. Doom was my first connection for meth. He traded stolen credit card numbers to Valley bikers who made the meth somewhere in the north end of the Valley towards the desert, where the smell of the cooking meth couldn't be detected.

I was one of the first entrepreneurs who switched to meth, cutting out the South American cartel by keeping the money in our country. Everyone in Club California switched to meth within a couple of months, like a virus that had infected the entire population of people living under one roof. The meth was a brand new drug to everyone around me. I didn't know anyone who had done it for any length of time, nor did I know what side effects might result from daily use.

I was making more money than ever because I didn't use that much and didn't give away much to friends mooching. A little went a long way. In a very short period of time, I became one of the biggest meth suppliers in the Valley, or at least in North Hollywood.

All the strippers did meth to keep their weight down, and so did a majority of the porn stars, whom I was more than happy to supply . . . which caused more friction with Brittney. I had friends who had been overweight all their lives, even while using cocaine, but when they started using meth, the pounds melted off and stayed off as long as they continued to use. I even lost what Angel called my love handles. I was pure muscle, unable to sit still for a minute. I always had to be doing something, physically and mentally.

Within six months, if you offered someone a line of cocaine in my scene, it would have been an insult and an indication of your bad taste in drugs. You couldn't even give the shit away. That made some people angry.

Chapter 34

Whenever I tried to get some rest, it was damn near impossible. The amount of crystal meth Shane was using wouldn't let him sit still for a single second. He was up all night doing laundry and going in and out of the apartment, slamming the solid steel door. When he stayed in his bedroom, that only drove the neighbors nuts because he would rearrange his entire bedroom every night. His waterbed would stay in the same position, but everything else in his bedroom would move around it, including the pictures on the walls. Re-hanging the pictures, he used large nails that needed to be pounded into the walls, as if he were Thor, the God of Thunder, with his mighty hammer.

My new neighbor, Pool Table Joe, shared a bedroom wall with Shane's bedroom. One night, Shane was doing his normal thing when the doorbell began ringing furiously. I opened the door to see Joe and Club Kevin, all flustered as if they had been sleeping, with their long hair pressed flat on one side of their faces.

"If that fucking asshole pounds one more nail," Joe yelled, "I'm going to shoot him through the goddamn wall!"

"It's only one in the morning!" Shane yelled back. "Don't be a puss."

"No problem, Joe," I replied, jumping between them. "I'll take care of the situation."

I gave Shane a look.

That could have gotten ugly, but I cooled things down between the two tough guys.

Pool Table Joe had an interesting apartment that gave him the nickname. He had no furniture, just a pool table in the middle of his living room . . . nothing else, other than a dozen barstools and a television hanging in the corner next to the makeshift bar. How he had gotten the pool table up to the third floor, I would never know.

Joe was an independent biker associated with many different groups, much like myself. We became instant friends, despite the fact that he wanted to shoot my roommate. I really didn't blame him. Shane was one of Hollywood's most deadly enforcers, but sometimes you had to treat him like an out-of-control child to keep him from destroying the place and everything around it. I was the only person who could yell at Shane, because he still respected me. If anyone else were to raise their voice toward him like I did, they would be dead. I knew it, and so did everyone else.

"If I can't pound nails," Shane declared, "I have to find something else to do."

That thought was almost frightening.

"Great," I said, "just as long as you're quiet. I don't give a fuck what you do. Count the carpet fibers or something, anything that doesn't bother anyone else. Is that possible?" He didn't answer or appreciate my remarks.

After wondering for hours what the rattle of the spray can was, I figured it out as soon as I was almost overcome by paint fumes. Looking at the clock, I saw that it was four in the morning. <u>Fuck!</u>

Pissed, I got out of bed to open all the windows and the sliding glass door. I had to stand out on the balcony until the place aired out.

Shane walked out onto the balcony and said, "Can't sleep, huh." He then proceeded to wash his hands with gasoline, spilling it all over my bare feet.

I looked at Shane and said, "You should just put up a bright flashing neon sign that reads, 'Drug Addict Up All Night.'"

He didn't get it, and I wasn't going to explain.

Chapter 35

Knowing the hammer would eventually fall, I started looking for ways to invest my money. I invested in the carpet-cleaning business of my friend Kerry, a former Hollywood musician.

"I have the knowledge and experience to run a carpet business," Kerry pitched, "but I don't have the financial backing."

"Not a problem," I replied. "Here's a stack of bills to get you going."

I loaned another Hollywood musician money to start a swimming pool cleaning business, making me the silent partner.

That was all good and legal, but I was looking for a business that I would enjoy doing. I knew I couldn't live like this forever . . . I already wanted out.

~~

On Halloween in 1992, my friend Jake from Burbank stopped by.

"Can my wife hang out with you for the day?" Jake asked. "I have to go somewhere, and she can't know."

"No problem," I replied. "Why can't you take her with you?"

"I'm doing a scene in a porno today. We need the money, and she can't know where it's coming from."

"I understand. I'll cover for you."

"Can Sophie sell candles to your friends when they stop by?"

"No problem." I knew they needed the money. They had just had a baby.

As the day went on, Sophie sold every candle in the huge box and made a thousand dollars cash. I couldn't believe how many people loved candles, especially the strippers. What made these candles really unique, was that they had hidden charms, stones, and other surprises buried deep within the wax, like prizes in a Cracker Jacks box.

All the "tweeters" who did meth loved to burn candles and play with the hot wax. They loved to pick out the secret charms like little children on Christmas Day, opening their gifts. Some tweeters were so impatient they put the candles in the stove to melt the wax and find the hidden treasures.

Some people did even dumber things.

Rob the day-trader complained, "I put one of those candles in the microwave to melt the wax, but it exploded like a bomb. I should sue you!"

"You better be kidding," I snapped, "or your head will explode like a bomb."

Shane just shook his head and added, "Shut up, asshole, if you know what's good for you!" He smacked him on the back of his head, Benny Hill-style.

All my friends who bought candles from Sophie wanted more, like it was a new addiction. Jake was the manager of the company that manufactured the candles. It was located in Burbank by the airport.

He told me, "It won't be a problem to sell you seconds -- candles with small chips or defects -- for really cheap."

"I accept."

~~

Christmas season, 1992, my apartment was stacked with boxes and boxes of candles. Everyone was buying candles for Christmas presents.

These were very expensive candles.

It would cost as much as forty dollars in an outlet store for one of the pyramid shaped candles.

All of the candles in the beginning were seconds, that had small defects like small scratches and chips. Since I was good with my hands and very crafty, I would touch up any defects with paint and Jennifer would re-wrap them in the plastic wrap.

Jennifer asked, "How many days have we been at this?"

"We are on day four of being up," I replied. "Here's another line. Let's do another hundred candles."

"That sounds good. Put in a porno video and I'm set."

"Between the Cheeks, Part Two," I replied, "that is your favorite, right?"

"Yep!"

The meth made Jennifer a nymphomaniac. Every couple of hours, I would have to take her in the next room and give her a playful spanking.

I could always tell when she was in the mood. When she bent over to do her line, she would stay bent over and lift her dress, revealing her tight behind.

Since we were just friends, and I wanted it to stay that way, we never went all the way.

But that would get her juices flowing, so when we went back out, she would grab the first guy willing, and fuck their brains out in the next room. It could be Shitfield, Steve, Pat McCormick, Neighbor-Dan, any guy who was willing. There was no jealousy among anyone.

~~

Once Jake ran out of second candles, he started stealing the perfect candles without my knowledge, until he got caught and fired!

"Dude," I said, "I would have paid more. You shouldn't have been stealing them."

"It just got out of hand, and I couldn't stop."

I felt bad that Jake had lost his job, so I put up the money to open our own candle company, since I already had the market for the product. This might be something I want to do.

The plan was to make the same candles that we had been selling.

"I can get the molds and materials to reproduce the same exact candle," Jake said.

"Good," I replied. "I want the same quality, nothing less."

Hence, we formed our secret candle company, known only to us as "Pirate Candles." I ordered the entire set of candle-making supplies and set up a candle shop in a garage in North Hollywood.

"Get started and let me know how it's going," I told Jake.

"I'm on it," he said. "This is going to be cool."

I had many other businesses to run, so it took me a couple of weeks to get back around to the candle shop. When I opened the door, I saw that nothing was done. Nothing had been opened, no attempt made.

When I finally caught up with Jake, he was too whacked out of his mind on meth to make any sense, and I wasn't buying his excuses.

"Get your fucking act together," I demanded. "I want to see some results!"

"I'll get things going," Jake assured me. "Don't worry. I'm on it."

I handed him money for his electric and phone bills so they wouldn't get shut off. I should have beat the shit out of him instead of giving him more money, but seeing those kids caught in the middle of that mess somehow took the meanness out of my spirit. Having parents like that only reminded me of what wonderful parents I had.

~~

A week later, I stopped by the candle shop to see if any progress had been made with the candle business. Jake's phone had been disconnected.

I opened the door, and the candle shop was empty. I went to Jake's apartment, it was also cleaned out. I should have known that once a thief, always a thief.

I hated to fail at anything, so I re-ordered all the candle-making supplies.

Since I had no idea what I was doing, I started talking with Scott Meziner at General Wax in North Hollywood. He was a really cool dude.

"Here's a book on making candles," he told me. "If you have any questions, just ask."

"Thanks. If there's ever anything I can do for you, just ask."

"Got a doobie?"

"Matter of fact, I do," I said, opening my gold case. "Here's a couple."

I had never made a single candle in my life or had any interest in burning candles. During art classes back in high school, I had spent more time throwing clay than learning art. I really had no clue how to create a color scheme.

This time, I set up shop in my apartment, placing cardboard over my dining room table and melting the wax in the kitchen on the electric stove. I wasn't going to let the supplies out of my sight again.

The first time I poured the wax, I didn't know that it was necessary to check the temperature. I didn't read all the instructions. I was in a big hurry to start full production without learning to walk first. I thought, Just melt the wax and pour it into molds. Easy -- any dipshit could do it.

I was wrong.

"What the fuck is going on with these pieces of shit molds?" I finally yelled.

"You must be doing something wrong," Jennifer replied.

"No shit. Think so?"

"Did you read the pouring instructions, or just start melting wax?"

"Fuck no!" I knew she had a point, but I was too frustrated to think.

I started out with a recipe that called for two-piece plastic molds and a pouring temperature at 185 to 190 degrees. Once I got a thermometer, I realized I was pouring the wax at 300 degrees. That was why the molds were melting and spraying hot wax all over the dining room. I had a lot of nice furniture and wasn't prepared for a mess like that.

Once I got the molds to stop melting, I didn't know what additives to add, so I didn't add any. When the candles were dry, I couldn't get the candles to come out of the molds without breaking the candle or tearing the mold. I got so frustrated, I began throwing candles across the apartment.

"Why can't I get these goddamn candles out of the molds?" I yelled.

Jennifer asked, "Did you finish reading the instructions?"

"Shut up!" I knew she was right again. What made me angrier was that she knew it and was messing with me.

After reading the instructions, I started using silicone mold-release spray and adding stearic acid to the wax for a slicker, smoother surface. If I had just read the entire candle-making book to start with, it would have saved me a lot of trouble, but that would have been the smart thing to do. Instead, I had destroyed my apartment in the learning phase of my new trade.

The more candles I made, the better I became and the more my apartment resembled the Hollywood Wax Museum.

Jennifer suggested, "Let's put the plastic candle molds into the dishwasher to clean them."

That sounded like a great idea on paper, but the dishwasher only got halfway through the cycle before it froze from wax buildup and started smoking.

While messing with the dishwasher, I took a pot of boiling hot wax off the stove and set it down on the cutting board next to the sink. The front doorbell rang, and I went to answer it. I let a stripper in the front door, and she rushed into the kitchen to smell the scented wax. Slipping on her high heels, she knocked the thirty pounds of melted wax into the sink.

The stripper screamed, "Oh, I'm sorry! I didn't mean to do that!"

Looking into the sink, I said, "That's going to be a problem."

"Oh shit," said Jennifer. "Try to plug it up."

"Fuck that!" I wasn't going to stick my hand into a sink of boiling hot wax. It went down the drain, clogging the plumbing for everyone in the building, all the way down to the first floor. I received a bill for $4,000.

After six months of costly mistakes and extensive damage to my apartment, I finally got the hang of making candles and was able to start my own original line. I decided to keep the name "Pirate Candles."

Chapter 36

Dr. Doom, my speed supplier, went to jail for forgery, computer hacking, and drug possession. Then my second meth connection, the Skinheads, were shut down by the CIA. That was the rumor, even though it didn't sound right. Why would the CIA be out in Sunland?

Either way, I was forced to look for new sources until they came looking for me. Kerry, my partner in the carpet-cleaning business, had a connection with the Valley bikers. He would set me up, but it was hardly enough to keep everyone happy. Plus, he was always late with the product, and it was always short, pissing me off.

It seemed like I was one of the few who could do meth and still stay in control of my actions. That meant still being on time every day and keeping all my promises. I noticed real quick that weak people would fall victim to the meth. The strong people only got stronger if they could handle the chemical stimulant without a mental meltdown. The drug was definitely weeding out the weaker users. It was a real test of the strong minds to be able to handle meth on an everyday trip. When we were snorting the meth I called "Glass," we thought of ourselves as super-humans who could stay awake for five days straight, staying busy the entire time, just like worker bees.

When doing the meth I called "lemon drop," all I wanted to do was have kinky sex. It affected the strippers the same way, so finding someone to fuck wasn't a problem. Sometimes we would be locked in the bathroom for an hour, screwing our brains out high on meth while people were knocking to get in.

~~

Late one night, I got a strange call from two bad-ass bikers whom I knew to be Kerry's meth connection. They told Jennifer they wanted a sit-down meeting that night within the next hour, so I told Jennifer to tell them to come over, since I didn't talk on the phone.

I wasn't sure what they wanted, so I strapped on my two pistols and alerted Shane to stay ready for any kind of confrontation. Unless that happened, though, I told him he should be silent and out of sight. He hid behind his bedroom door with his ear pressed to the wall, armed with an Uzi.

Without explaining a damn thing, I asked all the girls at my apartment to go sit by the swimming pool for the next hour.

Sliding my long knife into my boot holster, I heard the buzzer from the front door go off, so I buzzed my guests in. They didn't need directions. They already knew where I lived.

Dressed completely in black leather, all the way down to their combat boots, they both stood well over six feet tall, with hair halfway down their backs.

Entering my apartment, they introduced themselves: "I'm Rickie Dee, and his is my partner, Buffalo Paul."

I shook their hands. I already knew Buffalo Paul, but I hadn't seen him in five years. I knew it was a friendly meeting when I recognized Paul. All of us had changed names so many times, it became confusing when someone talked about you using your past name.

Rick D. said, "We're not too happy about the way Kerry is running the business. He's too weak and can't handle the pressure. He's always late with your product and always late with my money. He's slowing the process."

I knew what he said was true. The carpet cleaning business was almost ready to fail, and Kerry wasn't making the appointments on time.

"You're in charge of this part of the Valley," Rickie Dee went on. "You got North Hollywood and Studio City and all the way to Sherman Oaks. If you want to supply Kerry, that's fine, but we are done with him. Anything you need, we can handle."

The deal was done.

~~

Every day that passed, I was getting drawn deeper and deeper into the underground world of Los Angeles. Every known criminal group was trying to recruit me into their circle because my reputation was solid as steel. Everyone knew I was honest and easy to deal with, but when push came to shove, I didn't back down. People talked very highly of me in conversations; I did everyone favors and was considered to be the best friend of hundreds of people.

I was lucky that I had two people I knew I could trust to a certain point, and they both lived at Club California in apartments I had set up for them. At Jean's apartment, I kept a safe containing the meth and scales for weighing the product. If I needed anything out of the safe, I had twenty-four-hour access. I had set Jean up with a fake name to get the apartment, and I kicked her down free stuff whenever she wanted.

At Jennifer's, I had another safe with all my money and paperwork, including titles to my cars and my family's phone number. In case I got whacked, she was to call them.

Chapter 37

Knowing the FBI had placed hidden transmitters throughout Club California, I had my place checked regularly. I didn't want to get caught saying anything incriminating. Shane introduced me to an expert in electronics named David Laser.

David worked for an electronic security company that handled all the local major events in Los Angeles and Orange County. I gave David free meth, and he swept my apartment for bugs and phone taps once a week when he came to get his weekly stash. It took him half an hour to check both my living room and bedroom, along with the phone lines. I found out that law enforcement weren't the only ones using bugs. Sometimes other criminal groups wanting secret information about someone's personal life and business also used them to get the right information for blackmail.

Even I used them.

So far, my apartment had always been clean. Doing his weekly electronic sweep, David finished checking my bedroom and living room.

"How's it looking?"

"I found nothing so far, but I still have to check the phone line."

David put his headphones on, plugged the box into the phone line in the kitchen, and suddenly got a serious, distraught look on his face. He motioned for me to come, holding his index finger to his lips for me to be quiet.

David took off his headphones and placed them on my ears. I could hear everyone in my living room talking and blabbing. The bug was in the telephone.

David took me out into the hallway and said, "You have an infinity transmitter in your telephone."

"I find that hard to believe." I never left my apartment empty. Someone was always there, and if I was gone, it wasn't for very long. "What the hell is an infinity transmitter?"

"It's a very nice piece of surveillance equipment," David explained. "Once I take it apart, you can use it later for your own surveillance."

The way the infinity transmitter worked was very simple. It used the phone line to carry all the voices in your apartment to another location, where someone was listening. All your incoming telephone calls went through this listening device so it could monitor both sides of your conversations. The person controlling the infinity transmitter could literally take over your phone line and listen to your apartment with the phone still hung up on the hook.

I was freaked out, wondering how long it had been there and what they might have heard. I wondered what they were after -- putting me out of business or whacking me.

David Laser said, "This isn't government or law enforcement. If it was, there would be a tap on your phone like with the Russians. The FBI has no idea I check the box all the time. This is another criminal group spying on you.

"Besides, the government has a huge computer system that can do this without coming into your apartment. The government computer can call any phone in the United States without the phone ringing by sending an oscillating tone down the phone line, generating a certain tone. The tone then activates the microphone in the mouthpiece of the phone, allowing them to listen into any household they wish while the phone is still on the hook."

I remembered a guy in the early days of computer hacking called "Captain Crunch," who proved that by blowing through a cheap plastic whistle into the mouthpiece of a pay phone and making the right sounds over the phone line, he could get free phone calls. Everything having to do with the telephone system is activated by sounds and tones like notes on a keyboard.

David Laser continued, "All the telephones sold in the United States since the early seventies are set up for government eavesdropping, kind of like televisions with the V-chip for parental control."

"Is there any way to trace the infinity transmitter?"

"No, it's clean of any numbers. Someone was very careful so that if this was found, there would be no way to trace it or get any clues as to where it had come from. Very professional, but not law enforcement."

With that on my mind, I went down to the private workout room behind the pool tables in the recreation center to work off some stress. I took my shirt off and laid my 9mm pistol on the bench, covering it with my shirt, before I started my workout.

Spinning my sys, and then my karmas, all I could think about was who could be interested in my personal activities, if it wasn't law enforcement. Who would have access to surveillance equipment like that? I wondered if it was my new meth connection, but it could be many different groups. I knew for my own sanity and personal safety that I had to find out fast, before they made their next move.

I had set down my three-piece staff and was picking up my four-foot ninja sword when two elderly men with long grayish blonde ponytails entered my private workout room. They appeared to be twins, with ghostly looking skin. They were dressed in street clothes.

I knew they weren't there to dance or sweat, so I clenched my sword very tightly, sizing up the intruders. Hidden in the handle of my sword were two throwing knives. I loosened them with the palm of my right hand as one of the men spoke.

With a tone in his voice that implied he knew something I didn't, he said, "We admire your skill with weapons and your ability to operate right under the nose of the FBI. My name is Cain, and this is my brother Abel."

"Thanks, I guess," I replied. "I'm not really sure what you mean. Who are you?"

They both smiled. "We've been watching you for some time."

"Why would you be doing that?"

They both smiled again, and Cain replied, "We're both on the same side."

"What side is that?"

"The wrong side, made up by those who are criminals themselves."

I looked at him curiously, wondering what the hell that meant. Taking my eyes off Cain for a second, I noticed Abel putting the heel of his combat boot against the bottom of the door to prevent anyone from bursting in.

Cain pulled out a sealed bag of glass, pure crystal methamphetamine, uncut, top quality, and tossed it to me. I let the bag hit my chest and drop to the ground. I didn't know who these guys were.

Turning sideways quickly, I put the blade of my sword to Cain's neck without cutting, but close enough for him to taste the steel.

"I hope you're not stupid enough to think I would take drugs from someone I don't know. Surely you're joking, right?"

"You've made your point," Cain said. "Let's stop fucking around." He pulled out a vial of meth that had been crushed into a fine, glass-looking powder. With a confident look on his face, he carefully tapped the glass vial along the edge of the sword's blade, laying out a sparking line of pure crystal methamphetamine.

He plugged his left nostril and snorted the meth right off the end of my sword's blade. He stepped back and kept his eyes on mine. They began to water.

"I left some for you. Give it a try."

I took three steps backward and snorted the line.

"What do you think?" asked Cain.

"Pretty good. Top grade shit."

"The best. It's made with P2P, military grade."

"It does have a certain kick above what I get from the bikers." I wondered how these two had gotten ahold of military grade.

"Good," Cain responded. "Drop the defense, and let's get down to some serious business."

I stared at Cain. "How did you know I wouldn't cut your head off?"

"We know all about you. We know who you are -- everything, all the way back to high school pranks -- so we knew you wouldn't do something like that unless you felt threatened."

"You think so, huh?"

"I'm not brandishing a weapon, so I knew it was all a tough act."

Abel added, "Stuffed a dead skunk up anyone's ass lately?"

How would they know about that?

"In Hollywood, that might start a new trend," I replied.

"You were the first new recruit who has ever found one of our hidden surveillance devices. It was us who bugged your apartment, just to see and hear what type of man you are. You passed."

Pissed about them bugging my apartment, I snapped back, "Pass what?"

Cain answered with a smug look, "We're here to recruit you into our group of freedom fighters called G.O.D., Government Of Decency. We believe you can be fully trusted."

Cain looked at Abel and said, "Tell him the nickname we've given him."

"You're known to our company as the impeccable Godfather of Club California."

I laughed to myself. It had a nice ring to it.

"How did you get into my apartment and switch the phones?" I asked.

Abel spoke up. "That's for us to know. I hope it's a lesson that you will learn. Just because a woman is screwing you, doesn't mean she's true."

I winced inside. "I already know that lesson."

Abel added, "Believe us, Big Brother is alive and well and will be after you one of these days soon. It would be in your best interests to have us as friends."

I didn't know it all, and I wanted to be further educated. I dropped my sword and shook both their hands like I was the soldier they had been looking for. In reality, I was just a farm kid from Indiana playing the part of a ruthless criminal. Or was I actually a ruthless criminal still in denial?

From that day forward, the twins started schooling me on government operations, letting me in on some of their worst fears and paranoia. They had grown up in the deep South, and their father was a Baptist preacher named Moses Gideon. The twins didn't fear the Holy Spirit or the Satan; they feared -- or should I say hated -- the Trilateral Commission, nicknamed the New World Order.

I asked, "Who and what is the Trilateral Commission?"

"The Trilateral Commission is a group of very rich and evil men," Cain replied. "They want to enslave all Americans in a certain way so they don't even realize they are slaves."

"How would they do that?"

"By running the banks and the court systems and anything else that has any type of influence over the common taxpayers -- or as they call them, 'suckers.'"

I said, "You know who they are?"

"Look at this list we've compiled over the years."

According to the list, the members of the Trilateral Commission had spread through so many major U.S. companies, I didn't see a way they could

181

be stopped, short of executing all of them, which would be damn near impossible.

The list of companies with active members showed that they had people everywhere. I understood how they placed people. They had people working for the press and media to spin everything in their favor, while their members at the oil companies and automobile companies were making deals with members of Congress and the Senate. They in turn made deals with members of the banking systems to make the rich richer and the poor poorer. The only purpose I could see was simple greed.

"What can I do about this?" I asked.

"You can join us in the fight," Cain replied, "or you can sit back on your ass and do nothing."

I joked, "What do you want me to do, drive a truck full of explosives into one of their meetings?"

Cain looked at Abel and smiled eerily. "We got that covered already."

"What the fuck does that mean?" He didn't answer the question, so I said, "What's the plan?"

"We're spying on all the members of the Trilateral Commission," said Cain, "trying to counteract the damage they're causing. If we can get dirt on them, we can use it to bring them down. By exposing the corruption in their daily lives, it might slow the beast."

"So," I asked, "what does this have to do with meth?"

"The meth finances our secret operations. The money isn't traceable."

Now I was starting to understand.

~~

Out in the desert, G.O.D. had several huge meth labs that ran twenty-four hours a day, seven days a week in underground bunkers. The labs were equipped with state-of-the-art ventilation systems to hide their secret operations. The smell of crystal methamphetamine being cooked is very noticeable and can't be made in a populated area.

When the shipment of meth was brought from the desert into North Hollywood, it required three vehicles that would leave the compound in five-minute intervals. The lead vehicle would speed ahead, looking for any signs of law enforcement. It was equipped with radar detectors and police scanners. The middle car, a black Mercedes, driven by an elderly couple with diplomatic immunity, carried the meth. They traveled five miles above the speed limit to avoid looking suspicious. Following behind the middle vehicle was a van with six men carrying assault weapons. Their brains were completely wired on meth, so they were prepared to take out any type of law enforcement if they tried to stop the flow of the meth.

After many months passed, I was finally brought to see a meth lab in action, although I was not allowed to know the location. I had to sit in the back of the van as we drove seventy or eighty miles out into the desert.

The lab appeared to be seven old school buses all linked together. They had buried them underground in a straight line, directly under high-tension power lines. They were using the power lines to hide from satellite surveillance that might pick up the heat with sensors.

I had to wear a mask as I walked through the lab. I could hardly breathe, the chemical smell was so overpowering. The illegal aliens that were making the meth were called "cooks." On the cooks' skin, I could see a buildup of chemicals that were eating right through the outer layers of tissue. The cook was so high, he wasn't feeling anything. He just kept mixing chemicals.

We didn't speak. Matter of fact, I don't think he noticed we were there, considering the blank stare on his face.

The meth lab produced so much meth, they had to dry the wet speed in huge satellite dishes out in the desert sun. Once it was dry, they scooped it into huge trash bags that weighed many pounds. If they spilled a pound, they didn't even care. They just stepped all over it.

By the time I got out of the lab, my shoes were ruined. I would throw them away when I got home.

During the ride back to North Hollywood, Cain said, "What do you think about that?"

I thought it was pretty fucked up, but I replied, "That's out of this world. How did you build such a place without anyone noticing?"

"We monitor everyone."

"What does that mean?"

"We know how to hack computers. We're into intercepting government satellite transmissions and corporations' secrets."

"That takes a lot of talent, and a lot of high-tech equipment."

"All the secret information is out there in the air, just waiting for us to hack into the computers for our intelligence network."

I had some time to think during the ride. I had heard of the Trilateral Commission a couple of years earlier, but I'd thought it was just some paranoid idea that some whacko had made up. But these guys showed me proof that the New World Order really did exist, just like some evil organization in a James Bond movie.

This was just the beginning of the militia movement of the early '90's. The movement was sparked when the Department of Defense began building secret detention camps all across the United States, authorized through the Federal Emergency Management Agency (FEMA). The plan was passed with the 1991 fiscal budget and was partly financed by money from the Trilateral Commission. It was assumed that the D.O.D. were planning something big against the people of the United States, but what we didn't know was why and for what reason . . . We just had a lot of theories.

Each detention camp could hold between 3,000 and 4,000 people at a time. They were equipped with crematoriums that could burn a thousand bodies every six hours. Three of the biggest camps were in my home state of Indiana, with another four in Ohio, three in Michigan, three in New York, three in South Dakota, three in Wyoming, and two in Texas and Alaska. The biggest camp was in Oklahoma City, right in the middle of the United States. It could handle a hundred thousand people.

The detention camps were first discovered by commercial airline pilots who started taking pictures of the camps and asking questions. That brought attention to what was going on, and after that, all flight paths over the camps were rerouted to prevent anyone else from getting an aerial view. One of the talk shows was going to do a show about the detention camps, but it was shut down and never allowed to air. Just to discredit anyone talking about the detention camps, they ran articles in all the fake tabloids. That way, if anyone with evidence came forward, they would be laughed at, since the story had already been discredited for running in the <u>Weekly World News</u>. That was one of the biggest ways of debunking a real story -- make fun of it first, and that way no one took it seriously.

The members of G.O.D. also got hold of a survey that was given to the Marines on May 10th at the Twentynine Palms Marine Corps base, located on the southeast corner of the Mojave Desert about seventy miles due east of San Bernardino, California. The U.S. Marine Corps was asking all the soldiers questions regarding their willingness to serve in various capacities under the command of the United Nations, the One World Government. But they also asked as a final question, <u>Would you as a Marine of the Unites States be willing to fire upon U.S. citizens who refuse or resist confiscation of the firearms banned by the U.S. government?</u>

That made everyone in the underground think the government was planning to enforce a confiscation act of all non-sporting firearms. They would provide a thirty-day amnesty period, and then anyone refusing would be considered a criminal and hunted down like a wild dog, and either killed or taken to one of these detention camps.

It was hard to believe that our government would be so bold and evil, but the twins reminded me that the same thing had happened just forty years ago in Germany.

Unfortunately, no one was able to get the results of the Marine Corps survey, but it was rumored that they didn't get the responses they were looking for. Most of the Marines said they believed in the right to bear arms, like it says in the Constitution, and only a handful said they would shoot Americans.

I lost many nights of sleep thinking about what was going to happen. We really appeared to be nearing the "end times," just like a prophecy out of the Bible, unless we could do something to stop it. I swore to G.O.D. and

gave my word I would give my life to stop the evil that was coming.
I was now part of the revolt.

Chapter 38

In the eyes of the United States government, I would be considered a criminal and a traitor along with everyone else believing in G.O.D., but two hundred years ago we would have been called patriots.

Cain said, "The government has developed a computer program that can distinguish one voice from another and is able to identify the person if their voice pattern is on computer file. That means anywhere in the United States, the second that person picks up a phone and speaks a single word, he will be located instantly."

"You're shitting me," I said. "Is that possible?"

"Every single word said on a telephone line goes through a computer system at the phone company, and they have what's called "word activation." It's a computer with an artificial intelligence comport that enables the computer to start recording any telephone call if a certain word is said over the phone."

~~

Between dealing with the bikers, my new friends, and with the candle business, I only slept twice a week for a ten-hour period. The rest of the time I was active, running on pure meth like a superhuman from the master race.

Meanwhile, Brittney had no idea what I was involved in. The way she talked when she was drunk, she seemed to think I was some small fry digging for scraps, and that was all I wanted her to think for my own safety.

I always told Brittney I was broke.

~~

Cain stopped by and said, "I want to give you a counter-surveillance device to protect you, since you're a valuable asset to our cause."

Looking at what he had in his hand, I said, "A smoke detector?"

Cain shook his head and opened the unit. Hidden inside was a transmitter detector, which would go off the instant anyone wearing a transmitter or hidden video camera entered my apartment.

"Mount it above your front door," Cain instructed. "It will beep once, then flash red if it detects a signal, alerting you to a spy entering."

I told no one about the smoke detector, not even Jennifer. I was learning real fast that no one who lived in the city limits of L.A. could be trusted. Anyone could be a friend, and anyone could be an enemy. Sometimes they were both.

Cain also instructed me, "Duct-tape small fish pumps to all your windows, facing the outside, as a counter-surveillance measure."

"Why in the hell would I do that?"

"The constant vibration from the fish pumps against the glass will disable other types of listening devices, such as the shotgun microphone and laser listening device."

"I don't get it."

"The vibration of the fish pumps against the glass ruins it. The laser will only hear the fish pumps buzzing away, and the same with the shotgun microphone." That made sense. So I set up fish tanks near all the windows.

The more I learned about the government, the more concerned I was about getting videotaped or recorded saying something stupid, so it became a full-time job watching everything I said . . . even in my own bedroom and bathroom. You never knew until it was too late. I had to play the game full-time if I wanted to stay a player and not an inmate.

It was a strange life I was leading. I figured we were getting close to that final battle between Heaven and Hell. I was glad to have G.O.D. on my side.

Chapter 39

As far as hanging out with close friends, for the most part I still hung out with Gary and Shitfield. Shitfield was much like me; he stayed on the honest path and never screwed anybody over, so he was always welcome with open arms wherever he traveled.

Gary, on the other hand, was scamming everyone, from his drug connections to the women who dared to love him, falling for his boyish charm. I tolerated his bad habits because I had promised his mother the day we left for Hollywood that I would take care of her baby boy.

Just so he didn't have to work, Gary married a woman named Judy, who paid him $5,000 to marry her so she could stay in the country. That meant he got to live with her for free to pull off the charade. Gary took full advantage of the situation and wouldn't even let Judy use his car to support his lazy ass. He made her ride the bus to work, which smelled like a moving outhouse and was filled with the mentally ill. Since I wasn't blind and could see what was going on, I felt sorry for Judy.

I said to Shane, "Can't you get her a deal on a car from one of your buddies in Hollywood? It's shameful that she's riding the bus. She told me someone was urinating in the back of the bus yesterday."

"I'll look into it," Shane replied. "How's her credit?"

I laughed. "She's a foreigner. She has no credit and no money to put down."

Shane shook his head. "You're not making this easy, but I'll get her hooked up. Fuck Gary, that's no way to treat a women."

"Thanks."

As soon as Judy got the car, she and Gary stopped coming around. Before I knew it, three months had passed and no money had been paid to Shane.

I could tell by the way Shane was acting and the comments he was making that it wouldn't be much longer before he did something very violent.

I called Gary several times and always got his answering machine. He was screening his calls and wouldn't answer for me.

Gary was my friend, but that pissed me off!

"Fuck him!" I said. "Do whatever you want," I told Shane. "Just don't kill him . . . Please."

"Relax," Shane replied. "I'm just going to take the car back. I kept an extra set of keys."

That was a load off my mind. I didn't want to attend Gary's funeral . . . at least, not yet.

I dropped Shane off at Gary's place, and he drove the other car home. By the time Shane and I got back, Gary had already called twice and left messages.

Shane said, "Give me the phone."

I tossed Shane the phone, and he dialed Gary up.

"Hello, asshole! You can have the car back when you pay me. If you don't like that, you can go fuck yourself!" Shane slammed down the phone so hard, it bounced off the hook.

I thought Gary had gotten off lucky without Shane throwing him a beating, and I thought that was the end of it.

~~

For once, I was getting along with Brittney. We hadn't had a fight in weeks. We had dinner plans, but before we left for dinner, Rudy dropped off some weed.

Usually, I would run it over to my safe at Jean's apartment, but this time, to keep the peace, I tossed it on my bed. I pulled the wrinkled satin sheets over the weed in the briefcase and locked my bedroom door. We were already going to be late, which meant a possible fight . . . so I was rushing.

Shane was the reason we were running late. I wasn't going to leave my apartment until I had someone there to make sure nobody came in while I was out. When Shane finally walked in the door almost two hours late, I said, "Where the hell have you been? I'm going to be late!"

"I had to follow this guy seventy miles out of town, before he finally pulled over to get gas."

"Who were you following, and why?"

"The motherfucker cut me off in traffic and gave me the middle finger. When he pulled into the gas station, I circled around so that I was facing out. I got out of my car and walked over and decked him, knocking him over the hood of his car!"

Finding what he had said somewhat disturbing, I still had to laugh along with him. I asked, "What would you have done if he had pulled a gun?"

Shane looked at me and said, "I would have probably had to kill him."

~~

While Brittney and I were having dinner, I started getting weird pages that I didn't recognize. The pages kept coming, so I excused myself to the bathroom. I returned the page on my phone.

"North Hollywood Police Department, Detective Division," answered a voice. "Can I help you?"

I hung up and returned to the table. I couldn't tell Brittney about the call; I knew it couldn't be good. I kept thinking, <u>Why is the police</u>

department paging me?

I had a really bad feeling about it. The pager wasn't in my real name, so I thought about just throwing it away, but I needed to know what they wanted. I practically swallowed my entire dinner in one gulp and rushed Brittney through her meal. I knew she was getting pissed, but I couldn't discuss this with her.

On the way home, Brittney insisted on stopping for a milkshake. I was doing everything in my power short of causing a fight to get home and settle my paranoia.

We got the shake and then sat in traffic on the 101 for half an hour before I could finally jump off and take side streets, driving like a madman.

Pulling into the underground parking garage at Club California, I noticed five cop cars parked out in front of the apartment complex. Looking across the street, I saw Gary sitting in his car, listening to the radio.

I told Brittney, "Go up to my place. I'm going to talk to Gary."

Approaching his fully restored blue 1968 Camaro from behind, I slapped Gary upside the head like Benny Hill.

"You weren't dumb enough to call the cops about the car, were you?"

Just by looking in his surprised eyes, I knew he had just done something that would cost him our friendship and probably his miserable life, too.

"You're a piece of shit," I said as I walked away. "You're dead meat!"

With my heart nearly pounding out of my chest, I rushed back into the apartment complex as calmly as I could through the underground parking lot and met up with Brittney at the bottom of the stairs. She pointed out the eight cops standing in the lobby, talking with the apartment manager.

Brittney and I darted up the back stairs to my apartment at light speed. I opened all three locks as fast as I could, then rushed into Shane's bedroom and yelled, "The cops are on their way up!"

Shane didn't hear me. He was in the shower with the stereo cranked up to ten, playing Pantera. I could hear him pounding out the drumbeats on the wall. I had to pound on the door to the point of almost knocking it in before he finally opened it.

"What?" he screamed, sticking a gun in my face.

"The cops are on their way," I yelled. "You better split!"

Shane already had a couple of warrants for several serious charges, along with a rap sheet for drug dealing and weapons sales. The LAPD still wanted to question him about the counterfeit operation and the slaying of Uncle Paul.

Before rushing out the door, Shane yelled, "That motherfucker Gary called the cops! I'm going to fucking kill him!"

Still soaking wet, with just a light blue towel wrapped around his body, Shane tossed me his 9mm and took off down the back stairs.

I didn't want his pistol, so I wiped it clean and tossed it into some bushes below. I ran into my bedroom and grabbed the briefcase with the weed. Before I could get the key out of the third lock, the police were tapping me on the shoulder.

"Do you live in this apartment?" They had a warrant for Shane.

"He's not home, and I was just leaving."

I had a milkshake in one hand and the briefcase containing five pounds of marijuana in the other. Once again, I was almost defecating in my dress pants, but this time it wasn't caused by the milkshake, since I had taken four Lactaid Ultra pills.

Eight police officers were standing at my door. The lead officer said, "We want to see inside. Open up and let us take a look."

Once I got the door open, they pushed past me like aggressive photographers at a car accident.

I thought, <u>I'd better do a fine job of acting. Who knows what they'll find in Shane's bedroom?</u>

A lesson I had learned in the past was that cops always picked up on fear, like bloodhounds just waiting for the chance to bully a civilian. But I was no civilian, and I was still armed to the teeth. I was armed with three guns and two blades that I kept concealed from the police officers.

My ability to act normal gave them the impression that I was harmless as they walked around with their backs turned to a fully armed man who had had shooting skills since he was seven.

Nothing in the apartment was in my real name, and if I did have to shoot my way out, it would be better than going to prison. I knew this was the crank talking. Out of habit, I checked to see who was wearing body armor and who wasn't.

The lead officer finally said, "What's your name?"

"Peter Gozenyu." <u>Goz-en-you</u>. "I hardly know Shane," I explained. "I met him by the swimming pool a couple weeks ago. I just happened to need a roommate. But that was a mistake. I was getting ready to kick him out -- he drives me nuts. Actually, I'm kind of scared of him."

"You should be," replied the police officer.

The police officers knew exactly what I was talking about. They all knew about Shane and his violent behavior. That was why there were eight of them.

"That's my bedroom," I said, pointing to the left, "and that's Shane's room through the door to the right. But he's not home." I wanted to make sure I got the point across. "I don't go in his room ever. He scares the living hell out of me! I've been trying to think of a way of getting rid of him."

I knew they were probably going to find something illegal in Shane's bedroom; there was no doubt in my mind for a second. I was trying to come off as a pussy, and I didn't want to seem to be in league with him.

"What did Shane do?" I asked. "Am I in danger?"

"Do you know anything about a stolen car?"

I shook my head. "No idea. I have nothing to do with Shane's business. I own a carpet cleaning business and a pool cleaning service." To explain the mess in the dining room, I added, "I'm also trying to start a candle company."

The police officers walked around the living room. Sure enough, Shane had left his pot tray out on one of the stereo speakers. I was hoping they wouldn't notice it. He did.

There was only a little bit of weed on the tray, with a small black marble oxy pipe. One police officer picked up the black pipe, smelled it, and put it down, but said nothing.

"Could you open your bedroom door?"

My bedroom was always spotless, other than my bed giving the appearance that I was normal and sane. They took a quick look around and walked out. I shut and locked my bedroom door as they headed for Shane's bedroom.

Shane had been busted for meth several times, so the cops knew why everything in his bedroom was spray-painted black. The smell of sweat put a foul look on their faces as they entered his room.

Shane's bedroom looked more like a medieval dungeon or the staging place for a Charles Manson reunion. Clubs, lead pipes, baseball bats, and knives of all sizes lay scattered around his room. Original hand-written lyrics on white paper were tacked to the bedroom wall, looking like the writing of a serial killer. All Shane's songs were about death and gloom and anything that was dark and evil. Even though he was a good-looking blonde guy, his brain was dark and very twisted ever since he had been beaten as a child by his drunken truck-driving father.

"What the fuck?" I heard several officers mutter.

Handcuffs and chains hung from all corners of his bedposts. They were for late-night sex with strippers, but if you weren't into kinky sex, it might look more evil.

Next to the bed, I noticed, was a huge mirror with a big Bowie knife and a pile of meth. I thought, Fuck! My stomach rumbled, but I kept my cool and pretended not to notice the meth. I never made eye contact with any of the police officers as they perused the room, and for some reason they said nothing. I couldn't believe it -- not a single word. It kind of gave me the creeps, as if they were just waiting to pounce on me all at once. I knew they had to see the pile of meth, which was out in plain sight. The huge knife shining in the light was a dead giveaway; even a rookie would have seen it.

Walking out of Shane's bedroom, one of the officers noticed the wet footprints on the carpet leading from Shane's bathroom.

"He might be down at the pool," I said, knowing he wasn't there. I was just hoping to get them out of my place and avoid going to jail.

The officer asked, "Will you walk us down to the swimming pool and point Shane out?"

"No problem, be glad to."

There I went, as bold as day, walking through the swimming pool area carrying five pounds of weed in a briefcase, with eight police officers following behind me in a straight line like baby ducks following their mother to the cement pond.

Everyone sitting around the swimming pool lifted up their sunglasses and stared in amazement, thinking I was finally busted. But I wasn't in cuffs, and I was chatting with the officers.

For the next ten minutes, I took the North Hollywood police on a wild goose chase, until they finally got sick of being in the hot sun. They thanked me for the help.

When Shane came home a couple hours later, he made his feelings perfectly clear. "There's no way in hell you can talk me out of doing Gary and his whore."

I didn't say a single word in protest; I could have been in big trouble.

I couldn't believe that Gary thought calling the cops about the car had been a smart thing to do. I thought we were friends, and this was how he had repaid me. The stupid thing was, he didn't get the car back. Worse, not only did he lose me as a friend, but he was now marked for death by someone who was crazier than anyone I had ever known. Gary knew that about Shane, too; we both had seen him covered in blood once before.

When Shitfield heard what happened, he tried to get me to stop Shane, but I refused. "Gary has it coming," I said. "Even Rudy agreed."

"You got to do something."

"Shitfield, I know Gary's been your friend since you were kids. He was my friend, too, or so I thought. We had a lot of good times together. But he ended that when he brought the police to my apartment. This time, I'm not protecting him. I put up with him writing me a bunch of bad checks that he never covered. I also found out he was the one stealing money out of my dresser drawer and blaming it on Vic. I also let him go for stealing Reo's snake, and I covered up his tracks when he opened that fake loan company using my friend's name and numbers. Rudy isn't backing Gary anymore. He scammed him, too."

"If I were you, I would stop hanging around Gary. Shane doesn't leave witnesses. Shane will be back to settle the score. Right now he's just relocating. He knows the cops will be looking for him at Club California."

Shitfield knew this was very serious and convinced Gary it was time to leave Hollywood. Gary and Judy skipped out of Hollywood that night and moved back to Indiana, out of the reaches of Shane's deadly hands. Shane wanted Gary, but he wasn't going to travel two thousand miles to get him.

I was glad Gary got away, and I finally just paid Shane the 2,000 dollars to just drop it. I thought it was really sad, too. Gary was just another friend I

193

had lost during this California adventure.

Once Shane moved out, I cleaned up his bedroom, repainted all the walls, and set it up as a guest bedroom for when my brother came out for a visit.

Since Shane was gone, I needed someone to help me with some of my business affairs. Shane suggested a younger guy named Strong. Strong was in his early twenties and from a small town in Ohio. He went to college on a football deal, but ended up in Hollywood bailing his sister out of trouble time and time again. Strong had just started partying a couple of years earlier and was still in the process of growing his hair long. I took an instant liking to him; he was a Midwest boy much like myself and seemed sincere.

Chapter 40

All kinds of amateur criminals were trying to produce meth in Hollywood, cooking their meth in the bathtubs of hotel rooms, giving it the street nickname "bathtub crank."

The cooks would seal a hotel room with duct tape and spray a white sealing foam over any opening to the outside world, locking themselves in for days while the drugs were being made. But their temporary labs were very unstable and would either get busted or blow up, taking out a few other hotel rooms in the process.

I can remember listening on the scanner to a DEA raid going down in Hollywood on Western Boulevard. They had to blow the door off with small explosives. They said it was like cracking open a giant rotten egg. The room were sealed and the guys inside the makeshift lab had to be hosed down with high-pressure water to remove the chemicals before they could be put into police cars.

Some of the guys making speed in Hollywood were really whacked out of their minds. They would booby-trap the doors to their labs by building two small shelves on either side of the door and placing bottles of cyanide gas in glass containers on each shelf. They would run a line across the door, connecting the two bottles. If someone pushed the door open, the bottles would drop and shatter, creating a lethal gas that would rise from the floor instantly. I heard that trap took out two DEA agents. The first two through the door were killed, and the others were sickened enough to stop the raid, giving the cook time to blow the lab and escape down a rope into the back alley.

People on meth became dangerously insane and creatively sinister. The meth started to overtake the original personality, leaving only an outer shell of the person. They might have looked the same, but what was going on inside their heads was truly frightening.

Within a year and a half, I had gotten almost everyone in the Valley and Hollywood off cocaine and switched to crystal methamphetamine, making it the new drug of the early '90's. But I was starting to have trouble with my biker connection. Ricky D. was smoking so much with strippers that he was starting to cut the product to make up for his use. By the time I got the biker meth, it wasn't fit to give to lab rats, compared to the supply I was getting from G.O.D. It pissed me off! I stopped buying from the bikers, even though I knew that would cause waves.

One afternoon, just as I had feared, I heard an extremely loud knock at my door. Looking through the peephole, I could see it was Jawn. I had known he would eventually show up. Although I had never met him, I had heard of him and recognized him by his description. He was the enforcer for the bikers. He supplied Rickie and Paul, and when he gave you a visit, it could go either way.

Since I didn't have a choice, I invited Jawn in. I grabbed my pistol.

Every person I met in this business was huge, making me feel tiny, but I could never once show an ounce of fear, even if I was scared shitless. I always thought, I should have been an actor. When dealing with these meth freaks, I became the "Little Big Man," creating the illusion that I was bigger and tougher. I wanted to stand 6'5" in their minds, even though I only stood 5'10" at best.

Jawn was six foot seven, and a former musician turned enforcer. He also claimed to be the younger brother of Phil, the lead singer of Pantera.

Jawn was quite intimidating at first, with nose rings, eyebrow rings, and double-pierced nipples. He wore only cut-off shorts with combat boots. On one side of his head, he wore his hair extremely long, while the other side was shaved. Under the stubble on the shaved side, I could see a tattoo of what his brains might look like, with snakes and barbed wire twisting through the membranes. Jawn was the perfect example of a big farm kid who had gotten possessed by Satan or his son Crystal Meth.

Jawn showed me respect and asked, "What's the problem?"

"The stuff is crap by the time I get it," I said. "I have a reputation to uphold, and my customer only gets the best. I won't move the shit. It's full of cut." I showed him what I had gotten from Rickie Dee.

Jawn understood and worked everything out in a calm manner. "I will personally deliver the meth," he assured me, "and it will be pure."

"It had better be. I won't take any more crap."

Rickie Dee and Paul were out, and I took their place, climbing the ladder.

~~

The candle business was starting to run smoothly, but the meth business was always having problems because of the knuckleheads I needed to run it. Nobody with any brains would have been in this business, so the help wasn't always the best.

Joey the Mumbler was just another gnat in the horseshit of people who thought they could steal from me and get away with it. Joey was one of Dr. Doom's junior hackers who had recently joined my crew. I used him to run meth out to Shane on the other side of the Valley.

Since I was a really nice guy, lowlifes who didn't know my past would take my kindness as a sign of weakness. I was learning real fast that nice guys finish last, but I was trying to hold on to being a nice guy as long as "they" would let me.

Jawn overheard about my problem and said, "You're too valuable to take any stupid chances. With the money you're making, it would be wiser to let a real professional handle the problem. Believe me, Joey won't be talking to the cops after my friend gives him a personal visit."

"I would be interested," I said.

"We have several people that do this type of work, but I have one guy in mind. I know he's available and needs the extra work."

"Good," I replied. "I want someone professional."

"I'm going to introduce you to my friend, Mr. K. He's a licensed bounty hunter. He'll track him down in no time."

I had heard about his tactics; he was somewhat of a legend in the underworld of Los Angeles. He was well respected and outright feared. Mr. K had been shot eleven separate times and stabbed twice. He was a hard man to kill.

I didn't want Joey killed, just taught a lesson. I didn't give a shit about the money he owed; it was chump change. I wanted to make a point to others: Stay in line, or I will make you. My kindness must not be taken for a sign of weakness.

~~

On July 24, 1993, my friends decided to throw me a birthday party. I took the precautions of nailing everything down and hiding all my valuables. I left nothing outside my bedroom that I couldn't live without. I had locks on all the cabinet doors in both bathrooms and the cabinets in the kitchen, and believe me -- it was necessary.

I also set up the fake chair, which was a party joke for newcomers. This chair appeared solid and firm, but the legs would collapse under the slightest weight. The second somebody sat down, they would usually drop their beer and end up on their butt. Girls without underwear usually showed more than they intended. It was a great party gag.

The first time Otis Day saw that gag, he said, "You are the craziest white boy I have ever met. Animal House has nothing over you."

I took it as a compliment.

~~

The doorbell rang around five o'clock. I looked out the peephole, but someone was holding their finger over it.

"Stop fucking around," I yelled through the door.

I heard a weird vibrating sound out in the hallway. Starting to get a bit jumpy, I drew my pistol.

Finally the finger moved away from the peephole. Jawn and a blonde-haired man in a three-piece suit were standing out in the hallway with a twisted birthday present. I opened the door.

A tiny plastic blow-up sheep with a vibrator shoved up one of its many love openings jumped up and down on all fours. "Happy birthday," Jawn said. "Hope you like your present. I pray you will never use it." We laughed.

The man with Jawn laughed, too. He wore his long blonde hair in a ponytail and had a full beard, neatly trimmed. In his casual three-piece suit, he looked well groomed, right down to his snakeskin cowboy boots.

"I would like you to meet Mr. K," said Jawn.

For some reason, I had pictured Mr. K as being taller, but he wasn't much bigger than myself. I extended my right hand, and we shook.

Mr. K turned out to be a Leo as well. Although he was forty years of age, he looked much younger. He spoke in a soft, intelligent voice that carried authority, much like myself, making us instant friends once the respect was given both ways.

For my birthday, Mr. K gave me a bottle of Japanese sake in a wooden holder. I thanked him, and we toasted a couple of shots to future business deals. I wasn't a huge fan of sake -- I thought it smelled like feet -- but I did the shots out of respect.

During the party, everyone tossed the plastic sheep around the room. Every drunk who came in contact with the sex sheep had to insert a finger or a tongue as proof that they were nuts. I didn't need the proof.

As the evening progressed, more people showed up than I had expected. I spent most of my time patrolling my party to intercept any conflicts before they could get out of hand.

One of Mad Max's friends showed up drunker than a skunk. The stupid son of a bitch started head-bunting some of his friends and being rowdy and spilling other guests' drinks. I asked him once, nicely, to stop what he was doing, and he replied, "If I don't?"

"I will toss you out on your ass."

"So you think so?" he replied as Mad Max Mason got in the middle, trying to defuse the situation. Instead, the drunk grabbed Max by the throat and stuck a switchblade under his chin.

"I'm leaving, and I'm taking hostages!" he yelled.

Mr. K and Jawn jumped up.

"Relax," I said. "I can handle this asshole." If those two got involved, someone was going to get killed.

I tried the nice way first by saying, "Cool down. Let Max go before someone gets hurt."

"Fuck you," replied the drunk. "I'm going to cut this traitor's throat!"

Jawn took off his do-rag and, being a smart-ass, said, "I got a tourniquet ready. Hit that asshole in the face and be done with him."

The party came to a halt.

All my guests followed the action into the hallway.

I pulled my Colt .380 and pointed it at the guy's face.

"Hey, stupid fuck," I said, "put the knife away, or I'll shoot you between the eyes." I was done fucking around.

I pulled the hammer back with my right thumb. Seeing I wasn't joking, he lowered the knife to his side. I let the hammer back down and stuck my pistol back in my belt.

I put my hand out and said, "Give me the knife."

He pushed Max out of the way and took a wild swing at me with the knife, cutting open the knuckle on my right hand and sticking the blade through my right palm until it came out the other side. Looking at the blade sticking through my hand, he pulled it back out, and the knife slid right through my hand like it was a stick of butter.

Besides hurting, it really pissed me off.

I grabbed the hand holding the knife with my left hand and placed my bloody hand across his face. Twisting his wrist, I broke it over my knee with a loud crack! He dropped the knife.

I stepped back and kicked him under his chin so hard, his feet actually came off the ground. He landed on his back --out cold.

"Nice kick," Jawn said. "He's going to feel that in the morning. How's your hand?"

"He got me good."

"Yeah. You're dripping blood all over the hallway. You need stitches."

I picked up the switchblade, wiped off my blood, and put it in my pocket to add to my collection. Jawn picked up the drunk and carried him out to the curb like a piece of trash, remarking, "No charge for the removal."

Mr. K took my hand. "Let me have a look at that," he said. "He got you good. It's all the way to the bone on the knuckle and all the way through the center of your hand."

"What a mess," I replied.

"I can fix your wounds without going to the hospital."

"Do it. I don't want to go to the hospital."

"I have to run across the street to 7-11," Mr. K said. "I'll be back with the items I need. Keep the wound covered and apply pressure until I get back."

Five minutes later, he returned.

"Let's go into the bathroom," he suggested.

I followed him into the bathroom and held my hand over the sink.

"This might sting a bit," he said as he poured rubbing alcohol over the wound and dried it with a paper towel.

Mr. K pulled the two pieces of skin together over my injured knuckle, wiped the blood off, and applied superglue across the top of the skin. He held it for a few seconds while blowing on the glue. Once the glue dried, the bleeding stopped and the wound was sealed tight.

He did the same with the holes through the center of my hand.

For extra protection, I put toilet paper over the wound and wrapped gray duct tape around my hand to protect the injuries.

"Superglue is one of the best things you can use to close a knife wound or bullet hole," Mr. K said. "It seals up real tight and prevents infection."

"Are you sure?" I asked.

Mr. K lifted his shirt and pointed to three bullet hole scars. "I glued those." We both laughed. I wished I had known that the last time. The cigar burn had hurt like hell!

Before I could even finish a single piece of birthday cake, another asshole showed up uninvited. Being the fly on the wall, he had overheard about the party at the FM Station. Like a stray dog, he had followed people back.

As soon as the guy came in, he started driving me nuts. "Nice pad. I'm really impressed. Who is Bill? I wanted to wish him a happy birthday. Do you know where I can buy some drugs?" He couldn't shut up for a minute. Shane looked at me, and I could tell he wanted to choke the life out of him.

I was thinking, If you don't know me, then you shouldn't be here, and asking for drugs isn't too smart either. This guy was one of the stupidest motherfuckers I had ever met -- and I knew a lot of stupid motherfuckers. Or he was an informant.

An informant was a likable person whose job was to hang out and have a good time, blending in with people and involving themselves in everyone's lives. An informant was usually someone stupid who had gotten caught doing something illegal. To stay out of jail, they had to spy on everyone else and report on what they were doing, never actually busting anyone or testifying in court. They just gathered the information like flies on the wall.

There had been many cases in which informants had built a case and falsified evidence to make themselves look good or as revenge against someone who had rubbed them wrong. In fact, sometimes informants talked people into committing crimes just so they could rat them out to get favors and get the authorities off their backs. It was much easier to set up someone stupid than to go after dangerous criminals to produce real results.

The guy I suspected of being an informant was wearing an AC/DC T-shirt and a red bandana wrapped around his head. He looked like Beavis without Butthead, so that became his nickname.

I told everyone under my breath, "Don't let Beavis see you doing meth. You can smoke weed and drink all you want, but nothing else."

I hated to be a complete asshole to anyone, even a dipshit, but Beavis began asking everyone at the party for drugs. He wanted to buy anything anyone had to sell. I decided it was time for him to go.

So I had to ask Shane to take care of the problem.

I told Brittney, "I'll be back shortly. Don't get too damn drunk -- it's too early."

"Shut up!" Brittney replied.

"I mean it. I will be right back. Don't get too fucked up."

I didn't want to be in my apartment when things went down. I wanted to be the hero.

Bastard Ben and I walked down three flights of stairs to the underground parking garage below my apartment. It was chilly for a summer night.

"What the hell are we doing in the garage?" asked Bastard Ben.

"Just wait," I replied. "It won't be too long, with Shane's high-strung personality and the sick pleasure he gets out of hurting people, especially once he's been given the green light."

"What's going on?"

"Just back me up in whatever I do."

"No problem." He pulled out his Glock 9mm, pulled the slide back, and cocked it.

"No, put that away," I said. "That won't be necessary."

I learned later from Shane that while Bastard Ben and I were downstairs, Beavis sat on the couch in my living room and began bothering Jamie St. James, lead singer of Black and Blue, and his girlfriend, "Meatwalker." Inside joke.

On purpose, Shane tripped over Beavis's feet, spilling his beer. "You stupid motherfucker," Shane said. "Why don't you watch where you put your goddamn feet, you asshole!"

Having no idea what type of person he was dealing with, Beavis responded, "Fuck you!"

It was over before it started.

There were three rooms full of people, and if Shane had killed this guy, not a single one of them would have opened their mouth. But that didn't happen. After smacking him around a bit, Shane tossed Beavis down three flights of stairs.

Lucky for Beavis, it appeared that Bastard Ben and I were at the bottom of the stairs to pick him up and brush him off.

I reprimanded Shane in front of Beavis. "What the hell is wrong with you?"

"He's lucky I didn't kill him," said Shane. "He told me to fuck off. And he's doing drugs."

"No I wasn't," Beavis whined. "No one would give me any."

I laughed to myself. Bastard Ben also smiled.

Beavis was grateful I had saved him from a further beating. I truly seemed to be the hero of the hour.

"It's time to leave and get off drugs," I stated. "It's going to get you killed!"

While Bastard Ben and I were helping him to his car, we patted him down for a wire but found nothing. He must have been just a stupid moron, but that just goes to show that you couldn't approach anyone about drugs without a credible introduction. The paranoia that went along with the business could get you killed that easy.

Bastard Ben and I traveled back up the stairs, barely able to contain our laughter. The incident had actually put me in a rather good mood, despite my throbbing hand. I had been worried that the superglue wouldn't hold, but it did, and the wound healed with no infection.

Entering my apartment, I couldn't believe my eyes. My birthday party was turning into a nightmare. It seemed like there was no shortage of stupid assholes. I wasn't having any problems with people who were using meth or smoking weed; it was the damn drunks who couldn't hold their liquor.

Standing at my front door, I saw another drunken moron I didn't know pouring beer into my saltwater aquarium. The tank contained thousands of dollars worth of rare fish I had collected over the years.

I didn't say a damn word. I just walked over and grabbed this loser by the back of his neck. With my other hand, I grabbed the back of his pants, lifted him up, and dunked his face into the fish tank all the way up to his chest.

"Open the front door," I yelled to Bastard Ben.

I pulled the guy's head out of the fish tank, spun him around, and sent him flying with a single kick to the back of his pants into the outer hallway.

"See ya!" said Bastard Ben cheerfully before slamming the door.

Just then, Strong came strolling out of the back bathroom, zipping up his pants. "What's going on?" he asked.

"Where have you been?"

Jennifer walked out behind Strong, licking her lips.

"Get anyone I don't know out of here, pronto!" I demanded.

"Yes, boss!"

Before I could take two steps, there was a loud crash of broken glass in the outer hallway, followed by a loud beating on my solid steel front door. I knew what it was immediately.

Mr. K stood up and said, "For Christ's sake, enjoy your party. I will handle this problem. It's my personal pleasure! Happy Birthday!"

"Be my guest."

Mr. K went to the front door, looked out the peephole, and looked back at me. "I'm going to shove that fire extinguisher up his ass. The hallway looks like a Chicago blizzard just went through."

"Beat his ass!"

Mr. K opened the front door with a single motion so quick that the loser didn't see it coming until it was too late.

The fire extinguisher bounced off his head with a loud <u>bong</u> sound. The sound made me grit my teeth. The loser was out cold before his head even hit the ground. A lump the size of a goose egg started to appear in the middle of his forehead. That put a smile on my face as I looked at the mess in the hallway.

Once again, Jawn picked up another loser and threw him over his shoulder. "What do you want me to do with him?" he asked.

"Put him out front with the other guy. I don't know him either."

Mr. K remarked, "It sure looks like you could use my services. I've only known you for four hours, and in that time you were in two life-threatening situations. What does the rest of your week look like?"

We laughed.

I yelled for Pat McCormick, "Fix my fish tank!" He started cleaning the water and fixing the chemicals to save my fish, who were like part of my family. They had been traveling with me for the last six years. I never lost a single one in the many moves.

I heard some girls screaming and thought, Now what? Looking over, I saw that it was just my cat Boots attacking some of the guests who were in her way.

"Brent, that cat is after me," yelled Otis Day. "Help!"

"You look like a big drumstick," I said. "Were you eating chicken earlier? That's her favorite."

"Fuck you," Otis replied with a laugh. "Get this Land Shark away from me!" Everyone who heard the conversation was laughing.

Everything cooled off for about an hour until the intercom for the front door went off. I asked Mad Max Manson to answer it.

"Hello -- who is it?"

"This is the North Hollywood Police Department. Let us in."

Max looked at me, and I thought the same thing: someone is fucking around. It was the oldest joke in the book. I had heard it at least a dozen times already tonight.

Mad Max responded, "Yeah, right. Go fuck yourself!"

The intercom barked back, "We are the police. Open up, now!"

Max replied, "Sorry, I didn't hear you the first time. By the way, go fuck yourself!" We all laughed.

The cellular phone in my pocket started ringing, so I answered. "Hello. What's up?"

It was the guard at the front desk in the main lobby of the complex. "The North Hollywood Police are on their way up to investigate someone being thrown down the stairs."

"Thanks." I hung up quickly. Beavis . . . that fucking asshole, I thought.

I quickly started rushing people down the back stairway and told Brittney to go in my bedroom and close the secret wall.

After the police had come for Shane, I'd had my friends who were working on the set of <u>Deep Space Nine</u> create me a fake wall. Once the fake wall was closed, my two-bedroom apartment became a one-bedroom apartment.

I handed Jennifer my briefcase containing anything that was illegal, and she was gone like the wind. Strong went into the bathroom to wipe any loose drug powder off the countertops and floors. I quickly broke out the air-freshener and sprayed the entire place with Ozium until it smelled sweet. I told everyone who was still there to remain cool. It was show time.

I opened my front door on the first knock, greeting the North Hollywood Police with a friendly smile.

"What can I do for you?" I asked.

The officers looked in and saw everyone in my place just sitting around, drinking beer and watching television like well-mannered, law-abiding citizens. Everyone was smoking cigars and cigarettes to cover the smell of any other type of smoke that the air fresheners hadn't eliminated, along with the air purifiers that ran constantly.

Since I was dressed nicely and appeared somewhat intelligent, the police officers were very cool.

"Beavis showed up here uninvited," I explained, "and started bothering everyone for drugs. Some people got offended."

"Who threw him down the stairs?" the police officer asked.

I shrugged. "I wasn't here when the fight started, but I stopped it and helped the guy to the car. I told him to get off the drugs. He was so drunk he probably fell down the stairs."

Since the security guards were backing up my story, the police didn't give me a hard time. They had no idea a hundred people had just gone down the back stairs seconds before their arrival, and another twenty-five were hiding in my bedroom behind the fake wall.

I said good night to Mr. K and told him we would speak soon.

"You're in charge," I told Strong as I retired to my bedroom. It was still my birthday, and what was a birthday without a birthday spanking? I was in the mood to give Brittney one that she would remember forever. It included the chocolate whipped cream special.

I ended up having a really great birthday after all, despite getting stabbed, shaking a local narc, bouncing out a fish killer, and dealing with the North Hollywood Police.

Chapter 41

Two days after my birthday party, I had a five o'clock meeting with Mr. K. I knew he would be on time, so I jumped in the shower. I wanted to look alert and have a clear mind.

The shower didn't snap me to, so I filled the sink with ice-cold water and dumped several trays of ice cubes into the sink. I submerged my face several times for ten seconds. That really brought me back to life and took the redness and swelling out of my face, removing my hangover appearance.

Drying off, I wiped the steam off the mirror. Standing there, I took a close look at who and what I had become. I was completely surrounded by criminals all the time. Some of the people I called my friends were cold-blooded killers for hire -- and they were the honest ones.

I knew every day that passed I was getting sucked further and deeper into the underground world of Los Angeles. Soon I would never be able to escape. As of now, I could still walk away a free man without anything on my record except the memories that had been burned into my mind to haunt me for all eternity.

Nevertheless, this lifestyle of mine was still safer than the welding job at Thrall Car Manufacturing, before coming to Hollywood.

~~

Mr. K showed up right on time and was dressed professionally for business. Before we could even speak, he reached into his pocket and retrieved an audio jammer about the size of a pack of smokes.

Mr. K set the jammer on the smoked glass coffee table in front of us. The audio jammer emitted an irritating white noise, which was actually composed of twenty-eight random frequencies. The frequencies jammed all types of listening devices, including lasers, tape recorders, and hidden transmitters. All they would hear was a white noise that couldn't be filtered.

"What do you want me to do with him when I find him?" asked Mr. K.

"I don't care about the money -- its chicken feed. This is all about respect. Destroy him, but don't kill him. I want him left with absolutely nothing but the shirt on his back. I want him to tell others what happens when someone disrespects me after I've treated them well."

Joey the Mumbler had really pissed me off. I had given him meth up front and trusted him alone in my apartment while I made a run. Later, I had caught him on hidden surveillance cameras going through my belongings while I was gone for just five minutes. He also stuck a couple CD's in his jacket pocket, thinking I wouldn't know. I monitored everything. Trusted no one.

When I confronted him, instead of paying me back and returning the items, he had told me to fuck off. I had to make sure he knew that no one who had betrayed me was going to tell me to fuck off.

Mr. K nodded. "I fully understand the situation. I'll handle it in my own special way. The K isn't for kindness."

I laughed.

~~

A couple of days later, Matt The Ratt stopped by and asked, "Did you hear what happened to Joey the Mumbler?"

"No . . . Enlighten me." I hadn't yet talked with Mr. K.

"By the time Joey saw the fire, most of the house was up in flames," Matt said.

"No shit."

"His neighbors saw the fire and called 911."

When the police arrived, according to the story, the front of the house was on fire. They saw Joey jumping out his bedroom window. Since he looked like a criminal trying to escape, they grabbed him and started giving him the third degree. Joey, high from smoking speed, couldn't give proper answers to the cops' questions. He failed to produce any type of identification to prove he lived at that address.

The police got sick of his mumbling and searched him, finding hacker toys, stolen credit card numbers, other people's checks, eight-ball of meth in his front pocket, and the pipe in his back pocket. Wearing only a pair of cut-off shorts, he was taken away to L.A. County Jail for arson, breaking and entering, credit card fraud, and drug possession.

The rest of his belongings went up in smoke. By the time he got out of L.A. County, his rectum was puckered to the size of a silver dollar.

When I got into this business, I thought I would never have to get rough with anybody because I was only dealing with friends. I was also naïve, and this was no longer my choice.

I paged Mr. K from a pay phone in Hollywood. When he called me back, I said, "That was quick work. I'm very pleased with the outcome."

"I'd like to take credit," he said, "but it was an accident. I knocked over a lit candle climbing in the back window. It fell into some drapes and went up so fast, I was barely able to escape the way I came in . . . The rest was just karma."

Chapter 42

Trisha's father had passed away, so she gave up her apartment and went to Northern California to help her mother out. When she returned, I let her move into Shane's old bedroom temporarily.

Trisha made almost as much noise as Shane, and my neighbor Pool Table Joe and Club Kevin was really starting to dislike my crazy roommates. I had never met people like Shane and Trisha, who stayed up for weeks at a time and for some odd reason felt compelled to tear things apart and slam closet doors at all hours of the night, keeping everyone up.

As soon as Trisha moved in, I couldn't keep a lighter for more than a couple of hours before it came up missing. It got to the point that I had wrapped candlewick around my last lighter and duct-taped it to the coffee table. I suspected Trisha was smoking the speed, so the lighters were disappearing into the unknown realms of her back bedroom.

One night, while I was attempting to get some sleep, Trisha took the spray-painting thing to the next level. When I got up that afternoon, I could smell paint throughout the apartment, reminding me of Shane's last days.

Trisha appeared and said, "Can I use your bathroom? Mine's still wet."

"Still wet?"

When I saw the bathroom, I felt like a high-school principal uncovering one of my pranks. She had spray-painted the entire guest bathroom, including the walls, floors, ceiling, and everything but the toilet and bathtub, in a shade of neon green. She had replaced the light fixture with a huge black light, which I worried would catch the room on fire.

With real excitement, Trisha said, "Looks really cool, huh?"

I just shook my head and was damn glad this apartment wasn't in my real name. Trisha gave me a kiss on the cheek and bounced out the door to work.

When Trisha did work, it was at the world famous Hollywood Tropicana, owned by Michael Peters. She was a professional mud-wrestler and was one of the girls on the back of the <u>Hollywood Press</u> for many years. Trisha had pictures of herself mud-wrestling with O.J. Simpson. She had taken the Juice out with her famous "69 Slam."

~~

The next evening, Trisha said, "My mother is coming down from Northern California for a visit. Can you take care of her drug needs?"

I thought I had heard it all. I was shocked to hear that someone's parents were on drugs. I knew my parents would never ask such a thing. I felt weird and guilty while handing Trisha's mother some lemon drop speed, a bag of killer green buds, a bottle of Valium, and a bottle of Xanax.

Trisha's mother looked nothing like Trisha. She was short and fat, with dark hair and dark circles under her eyes. She barely passed for the living. After meeting her, I had a better understanding of why Trisha acted so strange.

"Thanks for taking care of my mother," Trisha said. "We're going out to dinner. See you when we get back."

"Have a nice time," I replied.

They never came back. She hadn't taken any belongings, not even a change of clothes. After two days had passed, I had Matt the Ratt do a computer search of all the local hospitals for anyone matching Trisha and her mother. When that didn't pan out, he searched all the police stations' computers to see if they had been arrested, but he got nothing. They were gone without a trace.

I couldn't call the police; I didn't even know Trisha's real last name. I only knew her by her dancing name. Plus, I had already checked the police computer system, and they had nothing of any help.

To try to find some clues, I paid Trisha's phone bill. That kept the phone line in her bedroom active. I was hoping someone would eventually call and give me a clue as to where she might have gone.

Two weeks passed before I finally heard a message on the answering machine. It sounded threatening. Rod Long, a Hollywood gangster, had gotten set up and taken down by the FBI three weeks earlier, and he was extremely angry with Trisha. His phone call made it sound like he was accusing her of being an informant.

Chapter 43

I greased the right palms and was starting to get a lot of custom orders for specialty candles from movie studios. I made the candles in the opening scene for <u>Tales from the Crypt</u> and for several MTV videos. Strong, Jennifer, and I were currently working around the clock trying to finish an order for the movie <u>Geronimo, The American Legend</u>. It had taken longer than I thought to have the custom molds made, so we were running out of time.

For a saloon scene, Sony Pictures needed specialty candles with three wicks twisted together to produce a foot-high flame. The flame had to be bright enough for the cameras to pick up. But with three wicks, the candles lasted only a couple of hours, so the studio needed hundreds. If I didn't get the order done on time, it would delay the shooting of the movie.

Once I got the custom molds made, it took ten straight days to finish the order. We did line after line. I didn't sleep one second until the order was finished and delivered to the movie set on time. I was trying to establish myself as a legal businessman and wanted to keep my word. The order was done on time, but almost at the expense of my sanity.

After being up ten days straight without any sleep, I began having hallucinations out of the corner of my eye. I would see fast-moving shadows and what appeared to be lost souls walking around the room, which no one else could see, except for Silva.

"Where are you going?" I asked with a laugh.

"Fuck you. I'm going to get some sleep," Silva replied. "I'll probably have nightmares. Thanks for sharing that with me."

By the time we finished the candle order, my kitchen and dining room were completely destroyed. Everything was covered in wax.

"We need a bigger place," Strong suggested.

"No shit, Sherlock," I replied.

I didn't have the time, so I put Strong's younger sister, Cheyanne, in charge of finding me a new house. She was very intelligent and had a great derriere -- two nice assets.

After I got back from Sony Pictures, I just wanted to sleep, but Kelly stopped by with Traci the nude model to score some meth. They were friends of Jennifer's from Florida. When the girls entered my apartment, the smoke detector immediately went off, alerting me to the presence of a hidden transmitter being brought into my apartment by one of the girls.

I didn't freak out; I took the warning without blinking and excused myself to the next room. I asked Mr. K to follow.

When I returned, I told Kelly I was out of meth. "Let me make some

209

calls," I said, giving the girls a single line to appear normal before leaving.

Mr. K followed the girls as they left. By tuning into the hidden transmitter they were carrying, he could hear their conversations. They both went back to Kelly's place, did some of the meth she had stashed, and ate each other out like they didn't even know they were bugged.

Sitting outside Kelly's apartment building, Mr. K continued to listen for an hour until a black Corvette pulled up across the street. The driver put an earpiece in his ear and looked toward Kelly's apartment building. Watching the man in the Corvette, Mr. K realized by his facial expression that he, too, was listening in on the hidden transmitter.

Mr. K quietly got out of his Jeep and crossed the street, coming up behind the black Corvette. Catching the driver by surprise, he stuck a pistol with a silencer to the driver's head and said, "What are you listening to?"

The guy turned out to be Traci's boyfriend, not law enforcement. I was dealing with a jealous boyfriend who didn't trust his stripper girlfriend . . . Go figure.

There was a cheap but effective hidden FM transmitter in the bottom of Traci's purse. It had probably been purchased at some spy shop in Hollywood.

Chapter 44

Whenever I slept, I needed someone to stay awake and watch the place to make sure everything was in order, much like Dracula hiring a member of the living. I never slept at home anymore. I found different places to sleep each time and didn't tell anyone where I went so I would feel safe.

Everyone on meth was armed to the teeth at all times, living on the very edge of sanity, clinging to memories of normalcy. In a normal week, if there was such a thing, it wasn't uncommon for me to see an assortment of small sub-machine guns, pistols, and knives in all sizes. None of the weapons had serial numbers, making them ready for murder in the first if anyone was dumb enough to push a meth user one degree the wrong way.

Everyone treated their weapons like they were their pride and joy and wouldn't part with them until death. In the meth circle, respect was measured by the firepower you had on hand. Your firepower kept the other criminals in line.

I had built up a nice arsenal. I had an M-16 with laser sighting in the wall above my couch, hidden behind a hinged painting of a pirate ship, making it easy to retrieve in an emergency. For fighting in close quarters, I had a 12-gauge Mossberg sawed-off pistol-grip shotgun mounted under the kitchen sink for easy access. I had pistols of all sizes to fit any type of clothing I wore.

Over the next few weeks, Cheyanne found me different houses to check out, but none of them seemed right because of location. Location was very important.

Cheyanne was a real blonde knockout; I always joked with Strong, "Maybe someday I will hook up with your sister."

Strong just shook his head and replied, "I can't handle you as a brother-in-law."

The seventh house we looked at was the house of my dreams. I fell in love with it the minute I entered the front door, as if it had taken possession of my soul. It was the mansion I had dreamed about since childhood.

"I'll take it," I said, even before I heard the price.

The new house was on Sutton Street in Sherman Oaks. It was set back into the side of the hills, just east of the 405 Freeway. It seemed too good to be true. The rent was only $3,500 a month, and it came with a giant swimming pool, matching Jacuzzi, and totally enclosed back yard with lemon trees, rose bushes, and many flowers, making it look like the Garden of Eden.

The guy renting the house was named Robert Collins. He fancied himself as a ladies' man, talking to the girls with his Hollywood full-of-shit accent and dressing in his fancy clothes and Melrose Boulevard shoes. I guessed he was around thirty-three years old, and I knew I had seen his face before, maybe in a low-budget movie or a commercial.

I could tell right away he didn't like Strong and myself. Either he hated long-haired white men, or we just intimidated his weak personality, but I wasn't going to let that stop me from getting this house.

"I'm just living in the house until I rented it out," said Collins. "I'm fixing it up for my uncle."

But by the looks of the empty beer cans and whiskey bottles I saw in the trash, I knew he was partying his ass off. I started to look for other signs of substance abuse.

Once I got a good look into his eyes, I could tell he was higher than a kite on cocaine, so I started looking at the countertops in the four bathrooms as we walked through.

Without much effort, I spotted dropped cocaine on the floor and countertops. Very sloppy, I thought. As I talked with Collins, the bells in my head started going off, telling me he was more than just a drug addict.

But I didn't listen. I wanted his house no matter what.

Collins wanted to know if I could afford the house, because he didn't want to get scammed like the people in the movie Pacific Heights.

"Yes, I own three businesses."

"Okay," said Collins. "I want first, last, and a deposit today to hold the house. I have other people interested."

I had $5,000 in my front pocket, but I wanted to appear normal, so I said, "I'll run down to the bank and be right back."

I drove around the block and checked out the sights before returning and handing him $3,500. I shook his hand and thanked him for the new house, although I didn't trust my new landlord one bit.

As I walked to the car, Collins said, "See you later, 'Ben Dover.'"

I chuckled to myself. I was glad this asshole wasn't going to get my real Social Security number.

I knew that I couldn't conduct business out of my new house because it was in a rich up-scale neighborhood. Plus, I wanted a break from the game to relax and not think about getting busted or killed. I put eight people in charge of running Club California and North Hollywood, whom I called the "Fiendish Eight." I wanted the location of my new house to remain a secret as long as possible. I wanted none of my criminal associates, with the exception of Rudy, to know where I lived. I always meet Cain and Abel back at Club California.

The more I thought about my new landlord, I had a funny feeling that he didn't have a damn thing to do with the house and I was somehow getting screwed.

I had Matt the Ratt hack into the records at city hall. The records showed that the house had just been purchased in July by a Robert Harding, who was supposed to be Collins' uncle. Collins said that his uncle lived in New York, but the Sutton Street location in Sherman Oaks was his only residence and nothing was mentioned about anyone in New York being an owner on the deed. Some of Collins' story wasn't jiving. I should have just pulled out, like in sex before it was too late, but I wanted that damn house. I had developed an instant fixation with this mansion. It reminded me of Scar Face.

Collins wanted another $3,500 a week before I moved in, and then he would give me the keys on the third payment. I decided I wasn't going to give Collins any more cash. That was too untraceable, and if this was a scam, I wanted a paper trail so I could find this asshole later. I instructed Cheyanne to give him a money order in the name of Robert Collins so I could trace it to a bank.

Collins got extremely upset when he received the money order. "I wanted cash for tax purposes, and since I just moved here from New York, I don't have a bank account yet."

I knew that was a bunch of bullshit.

I told Cheyanne to tell Collins to meet her at my bank the next day, and she would get the check cashed. But I went there instead.

Once Collins saw me, he started acting all sheepish and didn't have the balls to get angry. I wasn't a woman, even though I had long hair. Knowing how the game was played, I had Big Rich Foreman with me for the fear factor. Foreman stood 7'2" and was also a black man; it would be one black man beating another, canceling the race card. I didn't want another Rodney King riot.

I took my sunglasses off and demanded, "Why couldn't you cash the check? You live in a mansion, and you can't cash a check?"

Collins came up with some lame story that he had just gotten his wallet stolen and didn't have any type of identification. I knew he was lying through his freshly whitened teeth, but I kept my cool. I had been around enough liars that it was getting easier and easier to spot them. The more Collins talked, the faster he spoke, trying to convince me everything was cool. He could tell I wasn't buying what he was selling. It was actually insulting to think I would believe such a cock-and-bull story.

"All right," I replied, "but you're not getting another dime until you can produce a deed to the house, proving ownership. If you can't, I'll be wanting my thirty-five hundred dollars back." I looked into his eyes and let him know I wasn't fucking around.

It took Collins two days to produce a deed, but that still didn't prove to me that he had anything to do with the house. I could have gotten a copy of the deed myself from the hall of records.

I drove into Hollywood and picked up $3,500 in counterfeit that I had stashed away in a safety deposit box. I had been saving it for several years, never wanting to use it. I paid Collins with thirty-five hundred in fake money. He wasn't going to be depositing it in any bank. He was so high, he took the money with a smile. We were both smiling for different reasons.

In the meantime, I continued to pack boxes secretively back at the apartment, not wanting to let on that I was getting ready to split. When I finally left this place, it would be clean of any evidence that I had lived there, other than the bathroom Trisha had spray-painted and the wax melted into the countertops, walls, ceiling, and carpet.

I was all set to move at midnight, September first. There were going to be six of us moving into the house: Strong, Jennifer, Cheyanne, Donna, Jerry, and myself. They were all close, trusted friends with regular jobs.

A couple of days before the move, I went to the new house to get the keys from Collins. Instead, he informed me he wasn't ready to move out and wanted to stay until the first of October. I wanted to tear his head off, but I remained cool because my new neighbors were outside working in their yards.

I expressed my anger to Collins in a mild roar. "That's a bunch of bullshit. We've all already given up our apartments." I wasn't letting this fucker back out of any deal at the last minute, especially since I had given him $7,000, sort of.

While arguing with Collins at the front door, I realized I had interrupted his cocaine binge. He was all strung out and craving the next hit off his glass pipe. I could tell by the way his eyes were shaking and his speech pattern was broken. He couldn't wait to end the conversation.

"Fuck you!" he said. "If you don't like the deal, I'll just rent it out to someone else!" He slammed the twelve-foot door in my face with such force it blew my hair back, missing my nose by mere inches.

I kept my cool, put my sunglasses on, and waved to my new neighbors while taking down Collins' license plate number. Then I made a cell phone call. Within the hour, I met Mr. K at the Red Lobster in Studio City to make arrangements to handle my current problem.

"I need this handled quickly," I told Mr. K. "I need to get out of my apartment at Club California."

Mr. K assured me, "I'll find everything out about this Collins guy. I will know his real name and where his mother lives, if we have to go that route, within twenty-four hours, so rest easy. I'll have the problem handled and will have you sitting by your new swimming pool drinking strawberry margaritas before you know it."

"That sounds cool."

"It sounds like an easy job," he replied. "I needed a break from Chinatown. It was getting a bit hairy."

A couple of days prior, on a bodyguard assignment, Mr. K was entering a nightclub in Chinatown when an Asian kid around thirteen unloaded a sixty-round clip from an Uzi sub-machine gun while hanging out of a speeding car. The kid hit everything but Mr. K as the car chased him down the block like they were mowing grass.

"Lucky for me," Mr. K remarked, "the gun was bigger than the punk-ass shooter, and he couldn't control it because it was fully automatic."

We both laughed.

~~

Sitting at Red Lobster, I explained to Mr. K. "I don't want Collins killed or the house burned down. I want to live there. I just need to know what I'm up against. Information is the key to winning this type of game."

"Like I said before, this job will be a breeze, I can assure you of that."

~~

Mr. K, wearing his phone company jumpsuit and fake identification badge, parked at the end of Sutton Street, climbed the telephone pole, and opened the phone box. Checking each phone line with a headset and line tester, he finally found the line on which Collins had been arguing with me. The phone was then tapped with a voice-activated tape recorder.

Mr. K ran Collins' license plate with one of his buddies at the Department of Motor Vehicles, and it came back as a rental car under some woman's name -- probably a result of a stolen credit card number. Mr. K called a friend at the rental car company and got them to activate the low-jack tracking system on the rental car so Mr. K could track him if he lost sight.

Mr. K followed Collins to five different addresses that day and into the late evening, and he also grabbed the incoming and outgoing mail. It appeared that all the paperwork having to do with the house was in fake names, only proving my suspicion that Collins was a professional con-artist.

On the second day, Mr. K returned to my apartment at Club California and played me a conversation he had gotten off the phone tap. When I heard Collins selling cocaine and making illegal transactions, I couldn't have been happier. Now that I was sure that he was a criminal, I could deal with him in any manner I wanted. He was already in my world, where I was the boss. When you choose to live outside the law, you have to be twice as careful. If something goes wrong, you can't go running to the police for help, unless you're a complete moron or you want to be their snitch bitch for the rest of your miserable life.

Within two days, just like Mr. K promised, he delivered me everything I needed to know about Collins, including his mother's home address in Georgia. I was really looking forward to the next encounter. This time I didn't have to be pleasant. Matter of fact, I was planning on being the world's biggest prick. I was sick of all the scammers in Los Angeles trying to rip me off from the first day I had arrived. Lucky for me, I could do something about it now. I wasn't fresh off the farm anymore. Boone Grove was barely a memory.

Mr. K said, "You want to get your money back and rough him up? Teach him a lesson he won't forget?"

I looked Mr. K straight in the eye and replied, "I want it all! I want the house and everything in it, including all his furniture, for causing me all this pain-in-the-ass trouble. That way, I can leave all my furniture at the apartment, since it's covered in wax, and move only a few boxes at a time."

"Do I need to dig a hole out in the desert?"

"No, that shouldn't be necessary. This guy is a pussy. He will probably shit himself when we arrive."

~~

Later that day, Mr. K and I drove out to my new house to evict Collins. I had Strong sitting down the street as backup, and Krazy Kurtis at the other end of the block watching for any signs of trouble.

Mr. K and I parked around the corner and walked up the driveway quietly. Mr. K rang the doorbell as I stood to the side, but Collins didn't answer. Noticing that the side gate to the house was open, we walked around the back to the swimming pool area. No one could see us, so Mr. K picked the lock on the back door and let us into the sunken living room. Collins wasn't home.

Leaving our weapons holstered, we went upstairs to the master bedroom. It was a mess, with dirty clothes thrown everywhere. A wooden pipe containing marijuana was lying on the bed on top of yesterday's newspaper. Lines of cocaine were laid out on a mirror next to the bed on a nightstand, out in plain view. I hate cocaine, I thought.

I opened the drawer to the nightstand and found several bottles of pain pills and downers. He was probably having a hard time sleeping with all the cocaine he was putting up his nose. Then I found what I thought was a gun, but it was just a replica, a fake gun made out of hard black plastic. I tossed it to Mr. K, and we both laughed.

"I might have to whack this guy just for being so damn stupid," said Mr. K. "Anyone that dangerous to themselves doesn't deserve to live."

I started going through Collins' paperwork while Mr. K downloaded his computer files. In his records of previous addresses, he had used similar names, such as Bill Collins and Colin Roberts. I recognized the pattern of a scammer. It took me a few minutes to figure out how Collins was getting all the fake names and numbers he was using to scam. He and unknown friends had set up fake law offices and were advertising to help immigrants establish credit. In reality, they were stealing their new Social Security numbers and maxing out their new credit lines in the American system.

I also found a list of other houses Collins was currently renting out; they appeared to be properties that were going through foreclosure.

I noticed Mr. K yawning as he went through Collins' belongings. "Didn't get any sleep last night?" I asked.

"No, I went ahead and dug that hole out in the desert just in case you decided to whack this asshole." We laughed again.

But maybe Mr. K was right. Collins wouldn't give me any choice in the matter if he got seriously stupid. He had probably been pretty sharp at the game at one time, but after using that much cocaine, he had lost his edge. If he hadn't been so high when I first met him, I might have fallen for his house scam.

This wasn't his house; it was mine for the taking now.

Looking around the inside of the house, I noticed things were missing. All the brass fittings in the bathroom had been removed, along with anything else of value. He was stripping the place. Both of the downstairs toilets had been removed, and he was working on removing the indoor Jacuzzi.

"What are you going to do?" Mr. K asked.

"I want to move into this house for a short while," I replied. "Stay a couple of months. I know one thing -- Collins won't be staying here another night. Let's do some lines and wait for him."

"Sure . . . Let's wait."

We exchanged wicked smiles.

Chapter 45

Finally, around seven o'clock, Krazy Kurtis called and said, "Collins is on his way up the street."

I ran to the front window and watched him pull into the driveway. He jumped out of his car completely oblivious, thinking he was home and safe. Mr. K hurried downstairs and hid in the library next to the front door while I stood at the top of the stairs like I was the owner of the house. As Collins jiggled his key in the lock, I noticed Mr. K grinning with excitement and almost started laughing.

Collins stepped in and shut the door behind him. He started up the stairs with his head down, going through his mail, until he finally noticed me standing at the top of the stairs. I stared back at him with a sinister smile. Collins froze in his tracks. Mr. K stepped out of the library and quickly came up behind Collins, trapping him halfway up the stairs.

With sudden panic in his eyes, he attempted desperately to frighten us with loud words. "Get the hell out of my house now, and I won't call the cops!"

"Go ahead and call the police," I yelled back. "It'll be a little hard with your head shoved up your ass, motherfucker!"

Collins' eyes widened, and he turned white like Michael Jackson.

"By the way," I said, "my name isn't Ben Dover -- it's Mr. B!" Collins didn't know what to say. He stood there trapped between the two of us. I added, "That distinguished looking gentleman behind you is Mr. K . . . and the K isn't for kindness!"

I liked saying that. I found it funny, although Collins didn't seem to.

Collins was finally realizing he had screwed with the wrong person, and I let him know I was onto his scam. Mr. K cocked his silenced .22 and placed the barrel of the silencer to the back of Collins' head. I kept my pistol stuck in my belt in plain view for further intimidation.

"March your ass up the stairs and keep your mouth shut!" I ordered.

Collins couldn't stop talking as he begged for his life. "Don't kill me. I'll do whatever you want."

"I know," I replied. "You will do what the fuck I say or you will not see another day."

Collins was on the verge of crying as I sat him down at his desk and slapped a lease down in front of him.

"Sign it in your real name," I told him. Since Collins was a lying sack of shit, I took his wallet and found his driver's license. Just as I suspected, his real name was Haywood Collins, not Robert Collins. From that point forward, I would always refer to as him as Dickwood.

I made Dickwood give me the keys to the house and all the outside locks. Mr. K changed the codes to the security system. The house was wired with hidden motion detectors on all the windows and had laser beams going across the floor in three locations.

I told Dickwood, "I'm going to keep your driver's license just in case I have any further problems, so my friends will know who to look for. Got it, smart-guy?"

With a gun to his head, Dickwood signed the lease, and I made him dip his fingers in ink and print them onto the lease, just in case Haywood Collins wasn't his real name, either. The way I saw it, I was going to live in this house until someone could prove to me that they were the real owners. I would deal with them if and when that time came. I would just blame the whole mess on Dickwood so they could go after him legally, and I would take my time moving out.

Once the lease was signed, I said, "Thanks for the house. If I never see you again, it will be in your best interests. Show him to the front door!"

Dickwood walked down the long hallway with his head hung in shame, knowing he had been caught red-handed in a scam and had been scammed in return.

When Dickwood realized I wasn't going to kill him, he said, "What about all my belongings?"

I looked at him incredulously. "You can have the clothes on your back," I said as I slammed the front door in his face like he had done to me. It felt damn good to be on the inside of the door this time.

I said to Mr. K, "I'm going to tell everyone to move in. Can you stay here and make sure Dickwood doesn't come back before the locksmith gets here?"

"No problem." He opened the trunk of his car to retrieve a black case containing a shotgun and an AR-15 assault rifle.

"Thanks. I'll return in four hours or less with my moving truck."

I wiped the bathroom counter clean of cocaine and tossed down a pile of meth. "That should hold you until I get back."

Mr. K nodded his head. "See you in a few."

~~

I never told Cheyanne or Donna how I settled the problem with Dickwood. I just said, "Don't worry about the rent."

I spent the rest of the day packing, and everyone joined in to help. It would have gotten done faster if I hadn't had Ann Marie in my way, driving me nuts with her annoying behavior. The day before the move to the new house, one of the famous "Dark Brothers" had dropped Ann Marie off at my place without warning, so I had to take her in the moving truck to the new house until someone came to pick her up for another movie shoot.

Ann Marie was a major porn star. She had done a couple hundred films under her screen names Brooke Ashley and Fantasia. She was part oriental, with long dark black hair, and looked good enough to eat, like a fortune cookie ... until her constant babbling wore my dick soft. Ann Marie was my connection to the porn stars; I supplied most of the top stars through her. She made the drop-offs because I knew the Feds were constantly watching adult filmmakers. I was too paranoid to go to the places where they shot the films in Van Nuys.

Everyone in the porn business was using meth. They made better, sleazier movies while under the influence of crystal methamphetamine. The meth was a much better sex drug than cocaine, which is why a porn star can be sodomized by a ten-inch penis and still seem to enjoy it. The meth allows pain to be interpreted as pleasure. Those girls in bondage scenes getting whipped and paddled are all high as hell on meth and are really getting off. The filmmakers don't show the amount of drugs being done off camera. I'm not saying they all do it ... but most.

Ann Marie was one person who never should have done meth. She was already on the verge of a total meltdown, and the meth only made her whackier. She would camp out in my bathroom, packing and repacking her suitcases at least twenty times in a row because she was so high she couldn't stop. I had a hard time getting her out of the bathroom once she got into this mode. Then, before doing a movie shoot, she would make a mess of the bathroom with her enema bags.

Ann Marie could give head, have lesbian sex, and do meth, but driving a car or managing a household was impossible. Most days she spent a hundred dollars at 7-11 every couple of hours purely out of boredom.

When I was younger, I thought porn stars must make a lot of money. In reality, Ann Marie got paid a flat fee of only $500 for doing an all-girl scene and $600 for an anal scene involving two well-hung studs, who drove her tiny Eastern back road into a major six lane highway with a passing lane.

But Ann Marie loved every minute of it and was damn proud to show anyone her movies.

She told me that the small girls in the business would use pro-canine so they could handle the well hung studs. But often, after the numbing effect of the pro-canine wore off, they would need medical attention to fix tears and fissures from various huge objects being inserted. Some female stars had sued several porn producers for going overboard and causing serious damage, really wrecking their rectums.

~~

Once we got all my belongings into the moving truck, I ran a scan over the truck to make sure there weren't any tracking devices. It was clean.

When I checked my red sports car in the underground garage, the scanner showed that my car was emitting some sort of signal, even though it wasn't running. Someone was interested in tracking me once I left Club California. I disconnected the battery and it was still giving off a signal.

I couldn't take my car to the new location until I had time to remove the tracking device, so I parked it a few blocks away in a friend's underground parking garage until I could deal with the problem. When I had time, I would create a fake sale of the car, remove the tracking device, and bring it home.

Once I was moved into the new house, people started to actually realize how big I had become and how ruthless I could be to survive in Hollywood.

That wasn't the image I had come to Hollywood to portray. In my mind, I was really just a hick kid from Boone Grove, walking tall. But now everyone was calling me Boss and Mr. B, and music was never brought up in any conversations. I really just wanted to be a rock star, like the guys in Mötley Crüe. But the guitars had been put away for many years, and the cases were instead filled with high-powered weapons.

Chapter 46

While working in the candle shop, I saw a black BMW with tinted windows pull into the drive. A skinny man I had never seen before, with yellowish skin and jet black hair, got out of the car.

"Can I help you?"

"Yes, I'm looking for Pirate Candles?"

"Yes, come in. I'm Brent."

"My name is Darken."

We walked down the hallway to my downstairs bar. "Can I get you a drink, or something more dangerous?" I asked. That was always a good ice-breaker.

The man laughed a wicked giggle and replied, "A Bloody Mary, please."

I grabbed a bottle of Smirnoff vodka, opened a can of tomato juice, and dumped a cup of ice into the crusher. I shook the vodka and juice and poured it over ice, then added a pepper and a stick of celery. It looked so good, I made one for myself.

"What can I do for you?"

"I need some specialty candles."

"Yes . . . What do you have in mind?" I asked, not wanting to hear him ask for dick candles. "I've made candles for several motion pictures. I can do anything you want. I'm an expert mold-maker, taught by someone in the special effects department at Sony."

"Do you make black wax?"

When I heard that question, I knew then that he was a warlock wanting candles for evil practice. My opinion of him went down the toilet.

"I can make any color you want," I said irritably. "What do you exactly have in mind?"

"I want black heart candles . . . and I want you to add pieces of hair and certain personal objects, like pictures and jewelry."

"No," I replied. "I'm not into that shit, and I'm not going to be part of any black magick spells. If you want to do that, I would suggest you go buy some molds and wax. You can go right over here in North Hollywood, and they'll fix you up." I could tell I had insulted him, but I didn't give a flying fuck.

He pulled out a wad of money and said, "Are you sure I can't get you to change your mind?"

"No, you can't. Please leave!"

He set his drink down and headed for the front door, but he stopped and said, "Either you're with us or against us."

"Is that a threat?" I thought, <u>One more word will be your last.</u>

Instead of answering, he hissed at me like a cat. He was lucky I was in a good mood, or he wouldn't have made it to his car without my foot in his ass.

As he drove away, I wondered how in the hell he had found my house as the phone rang. I answered, "Hello, Pirate Candles, can I help you? The unfamiliar voice said, "Can I speak with Brent?"

"Speaking."

"My name is Ira Weinstein, I work for "Hard Copy," are you also the Brent they call Mr. B.?

I hesitated...why?

I'm doing a story about the death of actor River Phoenix.

"Ok, how can I help you?"

I have been talking with a guy that claims he was working with River on a script about the CIA experimenting with meth on occult groups within Hollywood, he claims the CIA killed the actor to stop the production.

"What does this have to do with me?"

"I was told you would be someone that would be able to answer any questions regarding meth and the occult."

I was silent for a brief second before answering, "no idea what you're talking about. Unless you are interested in ordering candles, the conversation is over."

"The guy claims the CIA paid a Hollywood drug dealer to give River a hot load to shut him up.

I slammed the phone. I knew nothing of this, but I asked Cain. "If the CIA was in Hollywood, I would know. The guy is fucking nuts."

"That's what I thought."

~~

The next day, I was up in the bedroom fooling around with a stripper named Sweet Cheeks. She was well known for having D.T.P. "delicious tasting pussy." She was just about to sit her lovely behind on my face when I heard a loud commotion out by the swimming pool. I stopped what I was doing, pulled up my pants, wiped my face off and stuck my pistol in my belt. I also retrieved my M-16 assault rifle from the gun safe.

Rushing through the huge house to the outside pool area, I found Strong arguing with a huge black guy who looked like he had been pumping weights for many years. The black guy was talking shit that he was a boxer and had just gotten out of prison.

"Where's the fucking rent money?" he demanded.

I pointed my assault rifle at his head, which was so damn big I didn't need the laser sight to hit it. I told Cheyanne to call the police.

"That's not necessary," said the black guy.

"I want them here to tag your body after I shoot you through the head for breaking and entering with a weapon."

"I don't have a weapon!"

I pulled the clip out of my M-16 and cocked it, sending the chambered bullet skipping into the pool, before tossing it to the black guy.

He caught it with a strange look.

I pulled out my Colt .380, cocked it, and pointed it right at his head. I explained that the M-16 wasn't in my real name and I would just wipe my prints off later, so he knew I wasn't fucking around.

Once the guy realized I wasn't going to be punked and he stood a good chance of never leaving the house alive, we set up a friendly line of communication.

That resulted in drinking beer and smoking weed at my bar on the second level of the house a half hour later. I knew how to talk to criminals. I chopped out lines of meth with my Bowie knife while Strong stood there armed with the assault rifle.

"Why are you working for a loser like Dickwood?" I asked.

The guy laughed. "Haywood -- no, you're right -- Dickwood told me to collect the rent and he would split it with me. So here I am! He's my brother-in-law."

I laughed. With a cocky smile, I said, "I know damn well that Dickwood has nothing to do with this house. It will be a cold day in Hell before I give him another dime. He's damn lucky he got what he's gotten so far; he should feel lucky I let him live."

He believed me.

Still wanting money, the brother-in-law said, "I can have everything replaced that's missing in the house in a few hours. Everything will match perfectly, since I'm the one who removed everything."

I reached into my pocket and pulled out a wad of cash, just like my first criminal boss Mickey. "Will two thousand dollars cover it?"

"Yes sir!"

In a couple of days, the house was back in perfect working order, with everything replaced. The brother-in-law couldn't tell me who the real owner was, so I became obsessed with figuring out what was going on with this house and why I couldn't find a living owner.

I asked Cain, "Can you use your computers to do some searching?"

"Not a problem."

Cain did as I asked and uncovered a larger scam being run by another criminal group not related to Dickwood.

"What a fucking mess you've gotten yourself into," he said. "Move out!"

Unknown criminals were bouncing the house back and forth between two banks and a fake mortgage company. They kept filing bankruptcies every year, changing the ownership of the house, and in the process rapidly reducing the mortgage by $80,000 every year. Each bank was absorbing the loss each year.

The first record showed the price of the house in 1987 at $1.7 million. Now it was down to $530,000, and no one had paid a dime on it so far -- it was all just numbers on a computer page. The person running the fake mortgage company was playing both banks.

I figured that Dickwood must have found out about the ongoing scam and decided to cash in, making me the last man on the totem pole. I didn't know who owned the house, but I was sure I would eventually have to deal with them. Until then, I would enjoy the free mansion, since I'd had the balls to take it.

Chapter 47

October 1993

When I had first discovered meth a couple of years earlier, I thought it was a gift from Heaven. It had gotten everyone I knew off cocaine. At first, there seemed to be no side effects other than wanting kinky sex all the time. Everyone could go to work on meth and do their jobs twice as fast. After a certain period of time, however, the fatigue that accrued after never sleeping caused them to lose the ability to function in normal society. Everyone I knew who was using meth had eventually lost their jobs and were now involved in some type of criminal activity to make money off the meth. Meth was the most important thing in their lives.

The whole Hollywood scene had changed over the course of two years. The once-friendly atmosphere was now gone, and everyone was copping a real shit attitude. Cocaine was dead, and meth had become the drug of the '90's. That was a huge mistake; I had no idea what door I had opened. If I had known, I would have closed it very quickly -- and nailed it shut.

All the Hollywood musicians from the glam days had gotten rid of the makeup and hair spray and had grown beards and goatees and added a lot of stupid-looking tattoos. The grunge look was in, the dirtier the better, and instead of wearing make-up, it was better to roll in dirt before hitting the stage. Everyone in the music scene, which I wasn't a part of anymore, was trying to look like bad-ass bikers. In the '80's, you couldn't tell the real musicians from the "posers," and now you couldn't tell the bikers from the musicians. I was sick of the whole Hollywood scene and backed away.

At times, I missed playing in front of thousands of screaming fans. But I hadn't even picked up a guitar in two years.

~~

By the end of October 1993, I was already in the process of finding a new house. I figured if any more serious trouble started, I would jump ship to avoid any attention from law enforcement.

Since I was going to ditch the new house, I decided to throw a Halloween party and invite everyone from Club California. It wasn't my house, and if it got totally trashed, that would be cool -- Animal House all over again.

It was a good thing I waited until Halloween, because otherwise my new neighbors would have been scared shitless. The Halloween costumes made my friends look normal for one day out of the year. Most of the female guests were strippers or adult film stars, so they all came dressed as kinky sex kittens or horny-looking Playboy bunnies.

Ann Marie and one of her girlfriends got trashed on bourbon and meth and recreated a scene out of her latest porn film on my bedroom floor, inserting objects into both her below-the-belt love-openings for whoever wanted to watch. As the crowd of onlookers cheered, it seemed I had everything a man could want. But I still had someone else in the back of my mind.

Even though it had been a couple of years, I still felt I was in love with Angel. She was the last normal person in my life and the only person I had met in Los Angeles who wasn't a drug addict. For some reason -- probably insanity -- I wanted Angel to see that I was still on top of the game without her being in my life. But I was told me she was engaged and getting married.

It hurt, but I didn't dare show it. I was a Leo.

As I looked around at the people who now surrounded me, I realized that even if Angel were to call me this very day, I wasn't the same person she used to know and might have loved. Because of the meth, I was a mere shadow of my former self, something of a legend among criminals and outlaws of the Valley. With a failed music career and several broken hearts, I just didn't give a fuck anymore, living in the badlands beyond anything Angel could possibly overlook. The way I was living would have scared the hell out of her. If I had been in my right mind, it would have scared the living hell out me, too, but it didn't. It was starting to seem normal, it really did.

But I couldn't spend too much time pondering over my lost love. There seemed to be an endless list of problems that needed my personal attention. I had two sources of meth that I used to supply the demands of my faithful followers to keep all of them happy and tweaked out of their minds twenty-four-seven. G.O.D. always delivered on time, like clockwork, and the product was always pure and clean.

My biker connection, on the other hand, had sold me two bad batches of product in a row. Both batches had been made wrong in the lab and, within hours of exposure to fresh air, had started to turn into a sticky liquid. I wasn't about to unload this crap on anyone, knowing it was made from several poisons.

I told Jawn, "You owe me my money back, or a new product." He never came through, so I stopped dealing with the bikers. By this point, I wasn't scared of them. If push came to shove, I would shove right back.

However, I had to be very careful who I talked to or dared to deal with. For some reason, the government was taking a very serious interest in the meth industry. As far as I could tell, the government hadn't lifted a finger to halt the cocaine trade, but they were pulling in agents from all over the country to crack down on the meth business. G.O.D. was constantly tracking as many government agents as possible, and they let me know that heavy concentrations of agents were being pulled into the Los Angeles city limits. The government knew someone had opened Pandora's Box, and the nightmare had finally begun in Southern California. They didn't want the meth to spread to the rest of the country like a plague.

Chapter 48

I had cut almost all my ties with my friends and family back in Indiana, knowing they wouldn't come close to understanding my life -- nor would they approve. My brother had stopped coming to visit because he didn't like the company I was keeping, which was understandable.

I also knew that at any given time, especially when I was sleeping, a law enforcement agency could bust down my front door. Or I could be out on the street and someone from another crime group could just walk up and blow my head clean off, for no reason other than greed or jealousy over some woman I was banging.

I wasn't worried about the LAPD. Rudy had inside people who would tip us off to any problems, so we could operate in front of them as if we were invisible. If anyone was to bring me down, it would be a government agency like the DEA or the FBI. I figured I would ultimately get shot in the back by someone I trusted who was trying to take over my business. This was my worst fear and the hardest to guard against.

Every time I moved, I had to leave someone behind to run the buildings I had taken over. The Fiendish Eight, as I called them, already had between eight and ten people working for them, creating a new crime family of my own with membership growing every day. Everyone made plenty of money.

The more time I spent with G.O.D., the more I learned about counter-surveillance and government operations. When I moved into the mansion, my bedroom had too many large windows to properly secure it for privacy. But I had a huge walk-in closet that was probably bigger than some people's bedrooms, so I turned it into a soundproofed room where I conducted all my business transactions. I put my safe and all my firearms in there because it had no outside walls, which was very important for ensuring privacy.

I constantly drilled everyone I knew never to talk in front of a window, whether it was closed or shut. If the government was investigating you, it didn't matter. I told them to imagine the entire glass window being a huge microphone once it was hit with a laser listening device from a couple of miles away, or even from a helicopter in mid-air.

I warned everyone never to talk on any telephone or around a telephone if it was plugged into an active phone line. People could listen through the telephone while it was still on the hook, and you would never know they were listening. It was also very important that when we hung up the phone, we didn't discuss what had just been talked about in code. The government had long ago figured out that the best time to listen was after a conversation was finished.

The average citizen had no such thing as privacy because they had no clue what was going on, but all of us in the underground world knew and fully understood and how to avoid being part of the unsuspecting masses.

The longer I did business with the Valley's computer hackers, the more amazed I was by their ability to break into any system, anywhere, anytime, without much difficulty. The internet was like the Wild West, with no law or order. Seven years earlier, I hadn't even heard the meaning of the term "hacker"; I would have just assumed it was someone with a nasty cough. Now it appeared that the Valley hackers had control of the electronic world at their fingertips. They were light years ahead of any computer security experts. This was just the beginning of home computers, and I could see the potential for a variety of new crimes.

All the top hackers in the Valley did meth and drank Jolt Cola to stay up for weeks at a time, attacking a system until they finally broke the code. The government couldn't figure out the motivation, but it was the meth making them obsessed with gaining access.

Most of the hackers I knew hacked for profit, but some liked to play cruel pranks to get revenge on their enemies. Some hackers could create total havoc in peoples' lives by ruining their credit and anything else that was in a computer database. The more clever hackers would take only a few dollars from each account they gained access to or add a couple of purchases to the accounts of shopaholic rich people who didn't pay attention to their billing statements. That way, the hackers could milk the accounts for years, using their numbers for a long time in small amounts, instead of wiping out an account in one mighty stroke. The hackers had P.O. boxes all over town under fake names, where they had items sent that they bought over the telephone with other people's credit card numbers.

Matt the Ratt was the youngest of the hackers, only twenty. His specialty was printing up other people's checks and cashing them at department stores for products he could sell later. Matt stood 6'2", but he was thin as a rail from all the meth he smoked. His second nickname was "Propane" because he used a blowtorch to smoke his speed through a glass pipe.

Matt had a shaved head and wore his baggy jeans low, showing off his dirty underwear or the crack of his ass. Matt was white, but he thought he was black, so we called him a "wigger." He loved to listen to rap music, even though he really didn't get it and would have gotten his ass kicked in any rap scene. Matt also drove a brand-new four-wheel-drive truck that he had obtained under a fake name. He drove it like a madman, knowing he wasn't responsible for anything that happened.

During his junior days of hacking, before getting his truck, he had traveled around the Valley from store to store, by bus and by skateboard, with a pager in his back pocket and a laptop computer and cell phone in his backpack. Matt had no shame; he went through dumpsters behind office buildings to find receipts and old bank statements, which enabled him to print up other people's checks. Being wired on meth, Matt could put shredded documents back together, even if it took days.

After watching all these different hackers reproduce documents, I began to look twice at all legal forms, even if they had an official-looking seals.

Dr. Doom had taught all these guys what to look for regarding information. Another person's trash can was their gold mine. Silva the Irritator would go to gas stations one after another and put new trash bags in the trash cans, taking the full trash bags with him. He would wave at the gas station attendant and leave, knowing he had gotten valuable information from people who threw personal items into the trash while cleaning out their cars or paying for gas.

Dr. Doom went as far as getting a job at a credit card company under a false name, just so he could steal a machine that could re-program the magnetic strip on the back of any expired gas card with good numbers they found in the dumpster dives. Once that business was set up and running, Silva would fill your gas tank up for five bucks and a soda pop.

Dr. Doom was quite a character. He reminded me of a villain out of a James Bond movie with his round-rimmed glasses and dark curly hair and the way he was constantly plotting his next scam. Dr. Doom created a new computer program entitled Code Thief, which allowed his computer to be routed through some college on the East Coast and make calls twenty-four hours a day to databases containing information about people's credit. For every automated call, the computer generated a new series of tone codes. It kept calling until it finally got a match, getting at least one good number per hour.

Every time Dr. Doom got busted, it was under a different name. After he bailed out of jail, he just moved and started over fresh under a new alias, like a techno-ghost hiding from law enforcement computers.

While studying counter-surveillance with the members of G.O.D., I learned that the National Security Agency, "NSA," had at last count over 12,000 listening posts spread all around the globe, gathering information at all times. These listening posts used satellites, aircrafts, and ocean ships to constantly feed information into central computers for a variety of reasons. They had computer systems that could monitor one million telephone conversations at once. The cameras installed at most stoplights and bridges could scan license plates on cars and keep track of targeted individual movements. They had programs for these computer cameras that automatically photographed or videotaped the occupants of the cars selected by their license plates as they passed through the intersection. These computer cameras would eventually be able to scan a crowd as large as the one at the Super Bowl and find that person in the crowd if they were present.

When a person was stopped for a traffic ticket or routinely questioned, the National Crime Information Center performed a quick computer search right from the police car. With only the vehicle's license plate number, the police could perform a computer search without even stopping the unsuspecting motorist. Even if a driver was not stopped by the cop, there would be a record of the cop car doing the search on the driver's record.

Books checked out of libraries and personal information from computers that were being monitored were all part of a "life file" that the government was keeping on many individuals. It seemed pretty damn close to mind-monitoring to me, and I felt sorry for those who were unprepared to guard themselves. I always guarded what I said, knowing that my own words could be used to convict me later . . . even if I was joking.

Chapter 49

Strong and I weren't seeing eye to eye on several issues. Since we had moved into the mansion, he had done nothing but play big shot with the neighbors and had the nerve to print up business cards saying he was president of my candle company. When I found that business card, I knew it was time for me to put him in his place. He wanted to be me . . . but that wasn't going to happen.

I was extremely angry. It was almost comical.

Jennifer was one of my best friends and knew my business inside and out. I trusted her above everyone else, but I could see that she was losing her mind. Considering how much stomach trouble she was suffering, I figured the meth was finally burning her to a frazzle.

To make things worse, as soon as we moved into the mansion, Kelly started screwing Strong behind Jennifer's back. They were supposed to be best friends. When Jennifer found out about Strong and Kelly, she blamed me for not making Strong love her.

"Jennifer," I said, "I can do a lot of things, but I can't force someone to love you. I can't even find someone to love me."

Jennifer didn't deal with it. She stopped coming around the mansion and had a nervous breakdown in a bathroom at Club California. Her family had to fly out and take her home for rehabilitation treatment, since she wouldn't talk to me anymore.

I was extremely furious at Strong and even more pissed at Kelly, so that was the last straw. I fired Strong and kicked him out of the mansion, losing two key people in my crew.

To replace Strong and Jennifer, I let Mia and her boyfriend Chance move into a downstairs bedroom until they got back on their feet. They were homeless and had been staying with different people every other day.

Chance had just landed a small part on the sitcom Saved By the Bell, but he hadn't received his first check yet. The Christmas season was coming up, so they were going to help with the candle business.

Matt the Ratt called from county lock-up to say he would be out after the holidays. He was doing a couple months for writing bad checks.

"That's cool," I said. "We'll do lunch."

"Anything is better than the slop they're feeding us in here," Matt replied.

After hanging up the phone with Matt, my ex-girlfriend Brittney called out of the blue. Someone had given her my new phone number, and she wanted to see me after several months of no contact. I wasn't sure if I wanted to give her my new address, but I did. I watched as her sports car pulled into the driveway.

The look on Brittney's face as she walked up the brick sidewalk toward my twelve-foot front door was worth all the trouble I had gone through.

Being a smart-ass, she lowered her sunglasses and said, "What, no valet?"

"No," I replied, "but I do validate."

"Take me on the tour, Mr. Rock Star."

We started with the library, with a nice fire burning in its impressive stone fireplace. Then we went outside by the swimming pool, which was surrounded by beautiful flowers and an assortment of fruit trees. The sun was still shining and the air was warm on our skin. I picked two fresh lemons right off the tree for our beers and picked a single red rose off a bush, placing it in Brittney's blonde hair. I knew she loved romantic stunts. Brittney smiled, and I remembered what I liked about her personality.

We went back inside the house and sat at the downstairs bar to finish our beers. We spent the rest of the evening having wild, passionate scx in the hot tub in my master bedroom.

Brittney stayed the weekend, and we got along fine. When we went to sleep Sunday night, she dragged out one of my alarm clocks from the days when I had worked a normal job. She was bartending at the Star Garden in North Hollywood and had to get up to go to work Monday afternoon. Paying no attention to what she was doing, Brittney plugged the alarm clock into the only open outlet, which was on the other side of the bedroom, thirty feet away.

The alarm clock went off around ten in the morning and scared the living hell out of me; it wasn't a sound I was used to. Brittney wouldn't get out of bed to shut it off. She promised that she would get up next time and leave for work, so I hit the snooze and jumped back into my heated waterbed, crashing out instantly. It was a cold morning for Southern California, dipping down into the forties, and it had been four days since the last time I had slept, so I was extremely tired and cranky.

When the alarm went off again, Brittney just rolled over, so I got up one more time and hit the snooze before jumping back into bed. When it went off the third time and she didn't get up, I was done. Instead of losing my cool and yelling, I took a different course of action.

I carefully reached into the Bible on my headboard and retrieved my Colt .380 from its secret hiding place. Grabbing my lucky rabbit's foot, I pulled the hidden silencer from under the white fur and screwed it on.

I cocked and chambered the first hollow-point round and put one bullet into the buzzing alarm clock, silencing it forever. With a smile on my face, I took the rabbit's foot off and put the gun back into the Bible. Brittney didn't hear a damn thing.

A few hours later, when Brittney finally woke up, she was furious because she was going to be late, and we got into a fight. She drove off pissed.

I went back to sleep for two more days.

Chapter 50

Prying myself out of bed, I looked at my adult-themed calendar and noticed it was Ginger Lynn's birthday. I wished I was the one giving her a birthday spanking. She was my all-time favorite.

Many years ago at the Rainbow, I had struck up a conversation with porn legend Ron Jeremy. He had been hanging out all week like his second home.

After drinking a six-pack, I decided I had to ask him something I had always wanted to know. I walked over and said, "What does Ginger Lynn's pussy taste like?"

Ron smiled as he ran his finger through his mustache, quickly flashing back in time. "It tastes better than Mom's sweet apple pie." I knew it.

I had once picked up a stripper who looked just like Ginger Lynn, but her pussy tasted so nasty that I had to turn her over and lick her asshole just to get the taste out of my mouth.

I had slept for eighteen hours straight, waking at 2:30 in the afternoon.

Cheyanne said, "Slocume has been waiting patiently downstairs since eight o'clock this morning for you to get up."

"Tell him I'm up."

I had one rule besides never talking on the telephone: never wake me up. It was dangerous and sure to put me in a foul mood.

I tossed Slocume a small bag of killer green buds and said, "Roll one." I pulled out my Bowie knife and proceeded to chop out my breakfast lines of meth. Every day started with meth.

Most people using meth didn't eat, but meth made me eat faster. The greatest part was that I could eat all I wanted and not gain a single pound.

"Do you want to go to the Great Wok and get some food?" I asked.

"Sure," Slocume replied, "you're buying?"

"Don't I always?"

Descending down the staircase toward the front door, I noticed my sawed-off shotgun lying on top of my black marble bar outside Jerry's bedroom door. Jerry had been feeling spooked by some of the things that were going on around the house, so every night I gave him a weapon so he could sleep a little better. I figured he must have carelessly forgotten to bring it back up to my bedroom before he went to work.

After Dickwood attempted to scare me, to no avail, weird things had started happening to my roommates. Cheyanne was getting threatening calls on her private line, and someone called in a bomb threat where Jerry worked as a sign of intimidation.

I told Slocume, "Wait at the bottom of the stairs. I'll be right back. I want to put the shotgun away."

Entering my bedroom, I noticed the door to the balcony was open slightly. I thought I locked that for sure. Must have spaced it off.

I walked through the bathroom, opened the door to my safe room, and entered without flipping on the light. I tossed the shotgun down on the extra bed and walked back out until I heard a noise that sounded suspicious.

I paused and turned around to see what appeared to be the shadow of someone picking up the shotgun. I quickly flipped on the light switch.

"What the hell are you doing here?" I yelled.

Things sped up real fast as the intruder pointed the shotgun at me. I rushed him as he pumped it and managed to grab the end of the shotgun barrel with my left hand. I pulled it down toward the floor before the shotgun went off with a loud explosion, sending thirty-two molten hot pellets flying in one direction.

Since we were in my soundproofed room, the explosion was especially loud, and I was instantly deafened. My left hand burned like hell from holding the hot end of the barrel. Everything seemed to be moving in slow motion for a brief second . . . and then it became real time, real quick.

I pulled the shotgun from the intruder and hit him in the jaw as I fell backward. My head hit the black marble floor, and the smoking barrel got shoved back in my face, burning the tip of my ear. Blood was splattered all over the wall to my left.

Looking down in disbelief, I realized that part of my left leg had been blown clean off. Only shreds of skin and shattered bone remained.

I couldn't believe my eyes. My leg was gone, and what was left looked like a piece of shredded beef smothered in hot sauce and catsup.

When I looked up again, the intruder was gone. I turned my head in time to see him going out through the balcony door.

Fuck!

Believe it or not, the first thing that came to my mind was, There's no way in hell the police won't be involved this time. I'd better be prepared to tell them something feasible . . . if I live.

No one else in the mansion had any idea what had happened, since I was in the soundproofed room. It all seemed like a terrible dream. But I knew if I wanted to live, I had better do something fast, without hesitation.

Trying not to panic, I grabbed a dirty sock off the floor and wrapped it around my leg above my knee. I pulled it as tightly as I could, hoping to slow down the bleeding. Blood was spurting in the air!

"Help!" I yelled.

The harder my heart pumped, the faster the blood spurted, creating a terrifying and horrifying visual effect.

I thought, <u>Don't lose it.</u> I had to come to grips with it, or I wasn't going to make it.

Thinking I had better dump what I was carrying, I crawled over to my briefcase. Somehow I remembered the combination to both locks and threw my pistols and knife into the briefcase. I locked it and slid it under some boxes.

Looking around the floor, I found another dirty sock and wrapped the meth I was carrying into the sock, tossing it on the floor by some other dirty clothes I hadn't picked up.

The pool of blood I was sitting in was getting bigger, and I was starting to feel a little bit chilly. I had to crawl back through the pool to get through the bathroom and into the bedroom, where the telephone was located.

Pieces of splintered bone fragments and pellets that had gone through my leg began sticking in my hands as I crawled through my own blood. The blood was still very warm, reminding me I was losing a lot.

When I got to my bedroom, Slocume was just walking in. When he saw my leg, he freaked out.

I started yelling, "Call 911! Call 911!" My ears were still ringing from the shotgun blast, so I couldn't hear my own voice.

Slocume was so freaked out by the sight of my missing leg that he couldn't find the phone. He ran around my bedroom like a chicken with his head cut off.

"I can't find the goddamn phone! Where is it?"

I started yelling for Cheyanne. "Help, Cheyanne!" I knew she was in her bedroom only a few feet away.

Lying there, I flashed back to the time when the foreman at Thrall Car had kept the trapped man in the jig-fixture from bleeding to death. I grabbed a bandana off the dresser, quickly wrapped it above the dirty sock, and pulled it as hard as I could. I pulled a pillow from my bed and put it over my stump.

Blood was all around me. Everything I touched left a bloody handprint. The sight of the blood made me sick to my stomach, and I was covered with a cold sweat that dripped down my forehead and the back of my neck. I assumed I was going to die. What else could I think?

I could hear my teeth grinding so hard from the pain that the enamel was turning into a nasty-tasting powder in my mouth.

Cheyanne walked in calmly and said, "What's all the yelling about?" When she saw me, she took off for the telephone.

Slocume was still running in circles, trying in vain to find the telephone, so I yelled, "Jackass! Grab a pair of num-chucks out of my martial arts display cabinet!"

"Why?"

"Just do it, and bring 'em to me, now!"

When he returned with the num-chucks, I shoved one of the wooden ends under the second sock and twisted it tight. That slowed the bleeding down to a mild spray.

During the chaos, Tony, the guy who had been banging Cheyanne, came in to help Slocume.

Everyone was yelling at everyone else in a panic, while Cheyanne got on the telephone with the 911 operator, getting instructions on what to do before the paramedics arrived. The operator instructed Cheyanne to have Tony lift my leg to slow the bleeding, so he did. But by the repulsed look on his face, I could tell it was making him ill.

By now, I had really started shaking and was literally dying of thirst. The 911 operator told Cheyanne not to give me anything to drink, because I could choke. But I didn't care.

"Give me something to drink!" I demanded.

Cheyanne grabbed my hand and asked, "Do you want to pray to Jesus?"

I was so mean from the meth, I stuck to my hard-ass image, not wanting to show fear, even though I was staring death straight in the face.

I gritted my teeth and replied, "Fuck, no! Get away from me with that religious crap! I'm not begging for help from some guy who lived in the desert over two thousand years ago."

I had given up on prayer many years back. The last time I had prayed was for Eve.

Meanwhile, I was thrashing around as everyone tried to hold me still and comfort me until help arrived. But nothing they did seemed to make it any easier. I had a burning, stinging, throbbing feeling, like the end of my leg had been stuck into a bucket of boiling water. No matter how I twisted or squirmed, I couldn't escape it. I kept hoping the shock would take over and I would finally just pass out, but the crystal methamphetamine I had done just minutes before kept my nervous system completely aware of everything that was happening. The only thing I could say was, "Fuck! Fuck! Fuck! Fuck! Fuck!"

Slocume said, "Hang in there."

"Just hit me in the head with anything to knock me out," I begged.

He couldn't do it.

I was saying whatever wild thoughts came to my mind. But I was still there enough to think somewhat straight, and I had to continue playing the game.

I instructed Slocume, "Go over to my closet and get my gun-cleaning kit." He did as I asked. "Open it and put it in my safe room."

I planned on telling the police that an accident had occurred while I was cleaning my gun.

Slocume agreed, and handed me his leather belt to bite down upon. The grinding of my teeth was finally getting to him.

Just as I was about to give up all hope, Cheyanne came running in and said, "The ambulance is here!"

But the paramedics wouldn't enter the house until the police arrived because there had been a shooting. Since the riots, the paramedics always wanted police protection.

I yelled, "Tell those assholes this is more like Beverly Hills. They're not down in the Hood! Tell them to get their asses in here now!"

They didn't listen and stood outside about two minutes waiting for the police while I lay there bleeding to death. It was frustrating that help had arrived, but they were waiting outside with their thumbs up their asses.

When the police finally arrived, Slocume said, "I want to stay, but I have warrants, and the police are going to ask to see everyone's identification. I have to bail before they get here. Hope you understand."

I nodded. "Just wipe the fingerprints of the intruder off the shotgun for me."

Slocume wiped the gun clean and made sure his prints weren't on the gun either. He pumped out all the extra shells and was gone over the balcony as the police came up the front stairs. Tony stuck by my side until the paramedics took over.

Without cracking a smile or revealing a worried look, the paramedics started working on me -- and so did the Sherman Oaks Police, with their by-the-book questions. I was prepared, and I knew how to answer everything they threw at me in my current mental condition. I was still playing the game.

There must have been at least ten police officers, and they were everywhere, taking this opportunity to look over my entire house -- and believe me, they were looking for anything. But they found nothing. I kept my place totally clean, just in case something like this happened. I had always known I wouldn't have time to clean when the moment came.

I never left any drugs lying around and didn't use straws or razor blades to do my meth. Every time I did a line of meth, I made a new snorting straw out of a piece of magazine paper. Then I would rip it up and flush it down the toilet. Every time -- no exceptions. I didn't have pipes or bongs lying around like Dickwood had; I rolled joints and hid the papers out of sight.

Once the cops saw Cheyanne, they all pounced on her like stray dogs in heat, looking for a rear end to sniff. Cheyanne covered for me well, and I was totally surprised. I had never drilled her on this type of situation. She was a civilian, but with her good looks, she was convincing, the police were cool.

Cheyanne told them, "He owns a candle company and is a former Hollywood rock star. He also studied martial arts." That explained the weapons display cabinet and the various swords hanging on my walls.

The police couldn't see anything else different, and they bought my gun-cleaning accident story.

The paramedics couldn't believe I hadn't gone into shock. Little did they know I was wired on meth, which prevented me from passing out. I should have told them, but I didn't.

I watched as one of the paramedics cut my shoe off my detached left foot and stuck the detached limb into a huge ice chest for transport. I wasn't sure where I would end up -- the hospital or the morgue -- but I knew I would receive two toe tags.

The paramedics worked on me for a few minutes, sealing my devastated leg in some type of plastic cast that filled with compressed air, and then lifted me onto a stretcher. They almost dropped me down the stairs while tripping over my fat cat Boots.

I was then transported to Sherman Oaks Medical Center, where they stabilized me and finally knocked me out. It was around forty-five minutes before I got anything for the pain, but before I went under, I realized my Heaven had become a living Hell. From that day forward, my life as I knew it was over.

I hoped I would just die. I couldn't go through life without my leg. I had been through more bullshit and had still walked away in one piece, but this would be a new lesson in survival amongst the most ruthless.

Chapter 51

I awoke some time later to see my younger brother and Strong standing above me, looking down. For a brief moment I feared that I was in a coffin and they were paying their last respects. Then I spoke, and my brother responded, letting me know I was still among the living.

"Where the hell am I?"

"You're out in the hallway waiting to go into surgery," he said. "There was a gang shooting, so a bunch of bangers are in the operating room ahead of you."

Looking around, I saw medical staff rushing back and forth. I wasn't sure at times whether I was awake or still dreaming. I was lying on a cold steel table with several IVs in each arm. I tried to move, but I was strapped down.

My brother yelled at one of the nurses, "This ice in the bucket with his leg has completely melted!" My detached leg was floating in the bucket like a piece of driftwood.

The next time I woke up, I was in the trauma ward with fourteen other guys. Many days had passed, and I was surprised to see that my leg had been reattached. The medical staff had put what was left of my leg into a monstrous steel cage that hovered over my bed like a steel cocoon. I didn't have the strength to lift myself up, and if I tried, it caused more pain and injury. Metal screws held some of the pieces of my leg in place like a puzzle, and tubes had replaced my blood vessels to get blood flow to my toes. There must have been at least seven inches of bone missing between my knee and my foot, and most of my ankle had been completely blown away, making it unrecognizable.

The doctors had seen so many gunshot victims that it was no big deal to them, but it was all new to me. The smell of the hospital gave me the chills.

My physician was Dr. Frank Nathan Stein. "You're far from out of dangerous waters," he told me. "Even though your leg is still somewhat there, I can't say for sure if I'll be able to save it. Only time will tell."

I had already accepted that my leg was gone, but to see it on again and to be told it might have to be taken back off was a real mind-fuck. I didn't even want to think about losing it; I would be a freak by Hollywood standards.

I couldn't actually see my leg because the cage covered it, so I asked Rudy, "Can you hold a mirror over the wound?"

Rudy gave me a look. "Are you sure you want to see it?"

"No, but I have to."

It looked like a shark had taken a huge bite out of my leg. There was no way they were going to be able to fix that.

The doctor explained, "My staff of students and I will take bone from your hips and skin from your back to graft it back together as we try to rebuild your leg."

By reading between the lines, I got the impression that if he could save my leg, he would be considered a god . . . and if he couldn't, I would serve as good practice for the next guy.

"If everything goes well," he continued, "it will be three years or longer before you can even think about walking. You might need to have as many as forty-five operations."

Forty-five operations.

A different doctor told me it might not work, and the bone could just snap under my body weight during my first step. If that happened, they would have to amputate it after all the operations.

Those were my two choices.

That was a lot of mental pressure, and in the condition I was currently in, with all the chemical changes going on in my damaged body, I could hardly think straight. I was more scared of looking like a freak than dying, so what else could I say?

"Try to save it."

As I was getting off one drug, I was becoming addicted to another. Days would pass that seemed like nothing more than a bad dream, punctuated by small glimpses of reality.

As soon as Brittney found out what had happened, she dropped everything and rushed to my bedside to be with me for the long haul. When I saw her, I smiled. She looked like she was looking at a dead body in a coffin.

She wiped tears from her eyes as she reached down and gave me a hug. I looked really bad and was doped up on morphine. My usual witty, smart-ass personality was no longer working. I had nothing to say . . . I just hugged her back with tears myself.

Brittney said, "You look like death warmed over. You're scaring me. Are you all right?"

I could barely answer her. "I've seen better days."

~~

The hospital was so overcrowded that I had to share a room with fourteen guys, seven down each side. I was the only one of two white guys in the entire ward, so Rudy came every day during visiting hours to make sure nothing went wrong and no one gave any of my friends any Latin bullshit. He let everyone in the room know that I was with him, and I was to be treated with respect.

"Relax, Bubba," he said. "I got your back. You're in good hands. I'll be here every day."

"Thanks, my brother."

When Rudy wasn't there, he would leave a bodyguard to watch over me twenty-four-seven. The nurses didn't like it at first and started to protest, but Rudy convinced them to take the money and look the other way.

I had no idea where I was, but based on what Brittney said, it was in a really bad part of Los Angeles. The hospital had metal detectors at the front door entrance to keep out armed gang-bangers, who in the past had come in and shot their way out with a fellow injured gang member. The front of the hospital was the hospital they showed every day in the opening credits of the soap opera General Hospital, it looked nothing like it did on TV.

In the bed directly across from me was Big Daddy, a long-time gang leader from the 18th Street gang. Big Daddy knew Rudy, so we became instant friends as soon as Rudy introduced me and verified that I was cool. Big Daddy was in really bad shape; he had been shot three times with a .45, in the chest, hip, and upper thigh, just missing his heart.

The guy next to Big Daddy was Tommy, an overweight white guy in his forties. He had stolen a car and crashed it during the chase on the 101 freeway and was now a prisoner of the State of California. Tommy was handcuffed to the bed by his wrist and ankle to make sure he wasn't going anywhere, even though he was in a full body cast.

Next to Tommy were two young boys around fourteen or fifteen from Brazil; they had only been in Los Angeles for a couple of days visiting their uncle. They had been standing in front of their uncle's house somewhere in East Los Angeles when some gangbangers drove by and mistook them for someone else. They turned their stolen car around and rammed into the boys, pinning one boy by his knees and crushing both his legs. His brother was thrown over the top of the car and suffered fewer injuries.

The brother whose legs were crushed was told that his legs were so badly damaged, gangrene had already started to set in. I could hear the doctors explaining what was happening from across the room.

"I'm going to have to cut both your legs off just above the knees," said one doctor. "Sorry, but there's nothing I can do to save them."

"No!" He cried for two days straight.

I knew how he felt, but I still had some hope.

Chapter 52

The more time I spent at the hospital, the more I realized how ruthless and uncaring the doctors appeared to be. The only reason I could figure was that it was a county-funded hospital so they thought they could treat everyone like lab rats. All the evil criminals I had dealt with hadn't come close to the cruelty and pain these doctors could inflict with a smile as they stuck their fingers into the wounded areas of the body, probing for what, I don't know, other than to make a patient squirm.

Every night -- or should I say early morning -- I would wake up at 4:45, dreading the visit from the doctors when they made their morning rounds. At 6:00, bright and early, two doctors and six students, armed with scissors and the willingness to follow orders no matter how loud the patients screamed, made their rounds.

Twice a day, morning and night, the bandages on my leg had to be completely changed to prevent infection. At night, the nurses would wet the bandages with warm water and loosen up the dried blood so they wouldn't stick to the open wound and cause me extra pain. After the gauze was pulled out, the nurses would clean the wound, then stuff the huge hole with more gauze and wrap my leg from my knee to my toes like a mummy, until it was completely covered for another twelve hours. The whole process took forty-five minutes or longer, and I would be jumping around like a fish on a rusty hook, trying to get away . . . but I was trapped. Even when the nurses wet the bandages, it still hurt like hell when the gauze was pulled from the open wound.

In the morning, the doctors were in such a big hurry that the students would pounce on my leg like a bunch of starving vultures and start cutting and pulling the gauze out of my dry wound to investigate. When I protested the treatment, they looked at me like I was nuts for getting pissed. I finally yelled one day, "Stick your finger in my wound again, and I will have you killed! Or better yet, I'll stick my finger in your eye and see how you like it!" Big Daddy felt the same way.

The worst one was an Asian doctor who didn't even speak English. She had everyone in the room screaming every time she did her rounds.

~~

My brother stayed for two weeks, and then my parents flew out the day before Christmas to spend the holidays with me in the hospital, which I knew sucked for them. I was wondering what my parents were going to think when they saw the mansion in Sherman Oaks. My bedroom alone was the size of the top floor of their house in Indiana. My brother put all my weapons away and cleaned the house from top to bottom, trying in vain to remove the huge bloodstains from the carpet in my bedroom.

Rudy said, "Relax. I'll make all the arrangements, and I will personally take good care of your parents to make sure their trip is as smooth as silk." I trusted Rudy with my life and the lives of my parents, whom I loved dearly.

The longer I was in the hospital, the braver the rats became. I knew that would eventually happen. As soon as Strong heard that I had been shot, he and Kelly rushed back to the mansion to see what they could find. He knew the ins and outs of my business, being my most current right-hand man.

Strong had told me that he would take care of everything around the house, I shouldn't worry about anything. But he only came to see me once and didn't stay long.

Cheyanne told me, "Strong found the stash of speed you hid in the sock, and your stash in the hidden safe under the Jacuzzi."

"What?"

"He's bossing everyone around in the mansion and packing your favorite gun."

"My Colt .380?"

"That's the one," she answered. "With the black handle."

That really burned my hide. That gun was like a woman to me. We were so close, I could have shot an apple off someone's head at thirty feet.

~~

Rudy picked up my parents at LAX in his new black Lexus and gave them the royal treatment. He showed them around Los Angeles and brought them to visit me at the hospital.

The looks on their faces when they saw me lying there was heartbreaking; I felt the concern in their eyes for their first son. I had always wanted to make my parents proud, but it hadn't worked out in my favor this turn in the game.

After a visit, Rudy took my parents back to my mansion to stay while they were in town. I hoped they would be comfortable. They had never slept on a waterbed with satin sheets; it would be quite a change. I told them to enjoy the swimming pool and the Jacuzzi in my master bedroom.

My parents thought I lived in Hollywood because I had only given them my P.O. box address on Sunset Boulevard. They were rather shocked when Rudy drove them up into the hills overlooking Sherman Oaks and the Valley. They were especially shocked when Rudy pulled into the driveway of the biggest house on the block.

The first thing my parents saw when they opened my front door was a huge pile of dog shit on the tile floor. Then the dogs jumped all over them.

Then Rudy took them up to my bedroom to find Mia and her boyfriend Chance sleeping in my bed. My parents already knew Mia from many years back, so they didn't freak out. Boots, the mean cat they had heard so much about, greeted them by biting my father on the ankle and hissing at my mother for being an invading female.

My parents didn't like sleeping on my heated waterbed. It made them seasick, so they slept on the two couches I had in my bedroom instead.

When I heard what was going on around the house, I was furious!

My mom told me, "We only saw Strong twice and Kelly once. They hid in their bedroom and acted like complete weirdoes."

I couldn't believe the lack of respect Strong had showed by having the nerve to attempt to take over my meth business while my parents were staying in my bedroom. He also hadn't had one ounce of brains to unplug the phone in my bedroom. People were calling after midnight who didn't know my parents were there, waking them up.

My parents weren't born yesterday and caught on real quick as to what was going on. All the years of keeping my eccentric lifestyle a secret from my family were over. The anger in me was starting to boil.

I had to send Rudy back to the mansion to straighten Strong out. "Clean up the dog shit like your life depends on it, because it does."

Strong got the message. It was received.

Rudy added, "If I hear about any more bullshit going on while his parents are here, you will disappear."

What finally blew my mind was that Brittney had been at the hospital every day since she found out what happened, but on Christmas Eve she came early and had to leave early.

I asked her, "What are your plans for tonight?"

"Nothing major," Brittney replied. "Hanging out with friends."

She sounded like she was telling the truth, but something about the look in her eyes made me think differently.

After finding the infinity transmitter hidden in my phone at my apartment in Club California, Cain and Abel had showed me how to use it. I had given the phone to Brittney before I moved out of Club California.

I thought about it all night. I didn't want to know, but I already knew.

I picked up my cellular phone and called the infinity transmitter I had placed in Brittney's bedroom. I was afraid to make the call, knowing what I would probably hear, but I did. I punched in the four-digit code before her phone rang even once, turning on the listening device. I listened for a few seconds as a tear came out of my eye. I really wished I hadn't made that call.

This was the worst Christmas yet.

Chapter 53

The doctors were so busy tearing at my leg and poking at my open wound, they forgot to have the nurses change the IV in my arm. It was supposed to be changed every two to three days. It had been weeks.

One day, late in December, I woke up with no feeling in my right hand. The vein had collapsed, and a very serious infection had started in my arm. By the time they caught the infection, it had reached my eyes, and I could tell by the way the doctors were talking it was very serious. They patched my eyes shut for a week while I ran a fever of 104 to 105, causing damage to my lungs as they filled with fluid.

While the fever ran its course, I soaked the bed sheets in sweat while my parents looked on in horror. They had no power, other than their support, to help me through the worst time of my life.

Considering how I felt, I figured that if I fell asleep, I wouldn't wake up. I couldn't believe I was going out in this fashion -- a warrior, drowning in my own sweat. They strapped me tightly to the bed so I couldn't move, and with my eyes already patched, I was in complete darkness, just waiting for the Grim Reaper to make his final visit.

Barely able to understand what was going on, the medical staff packed me in ice as a last-ditch effort to break the fever. It finally worked, along with all the antibiotics they pumped into my veins. I endured it all with the help of two grams of morphine every ten minutes.

They kept my eyes patched for a week, leaving me with somewhat blurred vision. The doctors couldn't explain it, but I was just glad not to be blind.

~~

Once they got rid of the infection, I started going under the knife every three days for what they called "cleaning operations." I had no idea what they were cleaning. I didn't see any repairs being done, and the anesthesia was really starting to take its toll. Every time I woke up from surgery, I was in an old back room with no windows, filled with stacked tables and chairs. My recovery after each operation was becoming more and more difficult. I was getting weaker and losing more weight because of all the drugs. I couldn't eat, and the IV could only provide so much nutrition.

In the middle of the tenth cleaning operation, I woke up. What I saw freaked me out. I tried to get up, but they quickly knocked me out again.

The next day I asked, "What was with the roomful of people watching behind a glass wall, and why were they staring down at me?"

The doctors gave me funny looks.

"I know I didn't dream it. It was real, god-dammit!"

The doctor replied, "relax. It's a county-funded hospital . . . a learning school for medical students."

"I don't want people watching!" I yelled. "I'm not a lab rat, asshole."

The doctors left the room after I got pissed and I threw a bedpan at one of them for being so sneaky.

"Cleaning operations, my ass!"

~~

Out of all the doctors, only one was truly honest with me. "I'm going to give it to you straight," he said. "Your leg is so badly damaged, that in my professional opinion, it will never work again."

I knew it, but I didn't want to hear it.

"If the grafts take and the bone re-grows, that's only half the battle."

"Why is that?"

"Your ankle is fifty percent gone. At best, you will need a cane or crutch and will have a really bad limp."

I didn't want to hear it.

The doctor continued, "You will walk like a crippled man. Sorry, but that's the truth . . . or maybe a miracle could happen. You have to decide. They will cut on you as long as you let them. The pain will be constant, and when you get older, it will only get worse."

"So what are you saying?"

"I would suggest amputation."

No! I thought.

"With today's new prostheses, you will walk normally."

I wasn't sure what to believe. Was this one doctor right, while the rest were meat-cutters, using me because they knew I had been addicted to meth when I arrived?

"Tomorrow I'll bring an outpatient in to see you," the doctor added. "He's gone through three years of operations. I want you to talk with him before you make any decisions."

~~

The next morning, bright and early, the honest doctor brought the other human guinea pig into the trauma ward. Before he introduced himself, I knew who he was by the way he came hobbling into my room. I watched in complete horror as I realized I might be walking that way for the rest of my life.

It was mind-blowing.

The guy showed me where they had taken skin off his back, veins out of his good leg, and bone from his hip to rebuild his leg. I didn't like what I was seeing; this guy was a mangled mess of scars, and with his shirt off, his back looked hideous. He walked like a retard and would never gain respect from anyone he didn't know based on how he carried himself. I could tell that every step he took was extremely painful, and he was still using crutches after four years.

The doctor let us talk in private. The guy looked at my leg and said, "Mine wasn't as bad as yours. I'm hooked on pain pills, and they really don't work anymore. I think about suicide all the time, wishing I would have just let them take it off four years ago and gotten on with my life. But they won't take it off now; they've put too much time into this mangled mess. Don't let them do it to you!"

Chapter 54

The meeting with the crippled guy sent me into deep depression. I knew the leg would have to go; no way around it. I would just have to get the strength and courage to tell them to take it off. I wished they had just taken it at the beginning and not forced me to make this decision. It was the hardest decision I ever had to make, but I knew that I didn't want to walk like a retard, even though I acted like one sometimes.

The thought of having a part of my body removed really fucked with my male ego. Life in Hollywood was very superficial, and looks seriously counted. People only noticed personalities after looks were established.

It was also very hard on my parents as they watched me lying in the hospital bed, withering away to a skeleton of the son they had once known.

My roommate Jerry's last visit propelled me into making the final decision that would change my life forever. Jerry had just gotten back from his Christmas vacation in New York.

"I have some more bad news that I should probably bring to your attention immediately," he said.

I winced. "Let me hear it."

"I know you put Chance and Mia in charge of your candle business, but I have to tell you, they sold your entire inventory. Plus, Chance tried to make more candles and wrecked all your equipment in the process. He almost burned the candle shop to the ground . . . along with the mansion."

"You're shitting me!"

"There's more," Jerry replied. "Chance also pawned all my CD's, and most of yours are gone also. He even had the nerve to make a necklace out of one of your bone fragments he found in the bathroom."

"Where was Mia while all this was going on?"

"They split as soon as I got home and haven't been back. Chance also lied about getting the part on <u>Saved By the Bell</u>. It was all bullshit."

"What do you mean, bullshit? I dropped him off at the studio several times."

"He was just doing extra work, that's all."

"Did Mia know?"

"I don't know, but she let him do whatever he wanted in your house."

I was shocked and pissed. I had taken Mia off the streets of Hollywood twice, giving her a home with no strings attached -- and this was how she paid me back. I felt betrayed once again, and I knew it would only be the beginning. The rats were already jumping off the ship they thought was sinking.

~~

Later that afternoon, just before visiting hours were over, Neighbor Dan and Ann Marie stopped by for a visit while my parents were still in the room. Ann Marie brought me a few gifts, and "subtle" wasn't one of her qualities. She had brought boxes of autographed movies from porno stars I had supplied with meth. They all wished me well.

All the guys in the ward couldn't wait until movie time. Whenever I put in a movie and the FBI warning about copyright laws flashed across the screen, all the gangsters would boo.

Ann Marie babbled on like they weren't even my parents. The look on my mother's face couldn't have been removed without plastic surgery. My dad just smiled, he was still one of the guys, he pretended not to hear what he was hearing.

"You'll love this one," Ann Marie said, holding up a porno movie. "Debbie Diamond takes it up the ass, good and hard!"

I thought, Please shut up!

Ann Marie continued, "In this one, Debbie fucks me up the ass with a strap-on. I couldn't poop for two days."

I just smiled and pretended I wasn't hearing her either. Neighbor Dan finally put his hand over her mouth, which wasn't rude, since a dick was usually inserted to shut her up.

~~

The next morning, when the doctors and their team of student butchers arrived, I told them to get their hands off me. No more tearing at my leg. Never again would I endure their lack of kindness or tolerate another second of their medical cruelty.

"I want this piece of dead meat removed from my body," I ordered. "I want to get the hell out of this place as soon as possible, before I die from another infection!" When they all looked at me in disbelief, I said, "Give me twenty grams of morphine and a saw, and I'll do it myself."

That made heads turn. They were way beyond looking shocked.

I copped a real shitty attitude. I already had one foot in the grave and was sure the other would soon follow . . . but not before I straightened out a few ungrateful people. The things going on at the mansion were pissing me off. I wanted to get home and start beating people with a baseball bat.

But I had to wait a few days before they could schedule the final operation, giving me plenty of time to think it over. The waiting was the worst part. I kept asking myself over and over again, Am I making the right decision, or am I just pissed? I thought about every option. Maybe they could fix my leg. Should I change my mind? But every time I thought I was making the wrong decision, I only had to look at what was left of my leg when they removed the bandages.

The amputation was scheduled for Friday morning at 7:00. I didn't sleep a wink the night before. It was the longest night of my life; I felt like I was on death row. By tomorrow afternoon, I assured myself, it would be over.

Unfortunately, because of the overload of shooting victims who started to pour in late Thursday night, I didn't go into surgery until Monday, waiting the entire weekend on stand-by. As the days passed and I couldn't eat, I kept thinking, Maybe it's a sign . . . maybe I should change my mind. I had thought it would be over by now; I still had a chance to back out.

Then I thought, Who am I fooling? There will be no sign. As a kid, after a crippling injury, I had made a vow to become a priest. I had promised the Lord that if he let me walk again, I would be a priest when I grew up.

That was the only promise I had ever broken, and now he was going to take my leg back. "Then take it," I thought.

~~

On Monday morning, as they finally loaded me onto the table, I took one last look at my leg. It was sickening. My toes were curling under and losing their shape, turning a shade of yellow-green. With that on my mind, I laid back down and said, "Let's get it over with."

As they rolled me down the hallway, I felt like I was on my way to the electric chair. Everyone I knew kept saying, "I'll be praying for you."

Then the nurse changed the IV in my arm.

The next thing I knew, I was in the recovery room. That was the part I hated the most: waking up in that ice-cold room all by myself with the monitor beeping. I looked around to see what I could see: nothing. Just complete darkness, other than the monitor with my heartbeat beeping across the screen.

As in the past, I just laid there and shook for hours until they came to claim my body for the next room.

Chapter 55

I thought once they removed the damaged portion of my leg, the pain would finally stop, but I was wrong. Instead, the pain got worse. The bone they had cut was fresh and undamaged. They had needed a clean, straight, flat cut so the leg would heal and a prosthesis could be worn. They had taken off more leg than I had expected.

When the anesthesia finally wore off, I felt almost naked without the huge metal cage that had encased my lower body for almost two months.

Once the leg was gone and the pain was still there, I began second-guessing my decision. By this time, though, my amputated leg had been burned up in the hospital incinerator deep beneath the hospital with other discarded body parts left over after surgery.

Early one morning, several days after my last operation and before visiting hours, I noticed a priest speaking in Spanish to some of the other guys in the trauma ward. Not wanting to be bothered, I shut my eyes, put on headphones, and cranked up the volume, hoping the sounds of Anthrax would discourage anyone from wanting to save my soul.

I was getting into the music until I felt someone tapping on my shoulder. I opened my eyes and saw the priest staring at me with a somewhat sinister smile. It creeped me out. What's his problem? I thought.

I stared back into his eyes. I didn't have my contacts in, so I struggled to focus for a minute before recognizing those eyes. It was Louis Anthony Furre, but I knew him as Chino.

Without saying a word, Chino handed me a Bible and said, "Read, my son, and everything will be made perfectly clear. Fear not -- God's former right-hand man shall avenge you if that's what you wish."

In a dark tone, I replied, "I wish."

I looked down at the page in the Bible, pretending to be interested. The page read, Sorry it took me so long, but I just heard about your situation. It wasn't really an accident?

I shook my head no.

Chino nodded and reached down to hold my hand. "Be well, my son. We will meet again very soon."

Chino walked into the bathroom and closed the door. I figured he was ripping up the note and flushing it down the toilet. When the bathroom door opened, he walked out with a poker-straight face, nodded, and left the room unnoticed.

~~

The two months I spent in the hospital, I was fed a constant supply of morphine through a machine called the "drip machine." Every ten minutes, it would give me a boost of two grams of medical-grade morphine through my IV.

That was 288 grams of pure medical-grade morphine being pumped into my veins each day for fifty days straight. I was completely hooked, like a back-alley Hollywood junkie, but I didn't realize it until I got out of the hospital.

The day I was to finally check out of the hospital was the day they cut me off cold-turkey. Two hours before being released, the medical staff unhooked me from the drip machine and handed me two Tylenol 3's with a glass of water.

"That's it," the nurse said. "That's all you get for pain. Take two every three hours. That should be enough."

Once all the machines were unhooked, I could finally move. My back and thighs were covered with bed sores, and I reeked of body odor. I hadn't had any type of bath or had a way to wash my hair in two months. My scalp itched something horrible, and I would draw blood with my fingernails, trying to get relief as I scratched nonstop.

The first time I tried to sit up in bed was rather discouraging; my muscles were stiff and weak. I seemed to be lifeless from lack of movement or chemical stimulation. I had no muscle mass and was nothing but skin and bones.

Sitting up turned out to be the easy part. The next hurdle was actually getting out of bed and standing on one leg with a walker. I had to be able to walk to the bathroom on the other side of the room and back before they would release me from the hospital.

I thought, No problem. I would do anything to get the fuck out of that hellhole. I was dying to smoke a joint.

The first time I dropped the end of my stump off the bed, all the blood rushed to the stump, and the pain was so intense that I blacked out and fell backwards, shaking. I instantly relived the day my leg had been blown off; the pain was similar.

I didn't want to try a second time and probably wouldn't have, but Brittney coached me. "You have to keep trying," she said.

She helped me stand up on one foot and grab the walker. I gritted my teeth and shook, dealing with it the best I could . . . without looking like a total pussy.

It took me twenty minutes to get across the room to the bathroom and back. I couldn't have done it twice if my life depended on it. I was that weak.

Fucking pitiful.

I was at the bottom of the food chain, easy prey. Without help, I wouldn't survive in the jungle I had once roamed as proudly as Leo the Lion.

Chapter 56

Rudy and a couple of his crew carried my big-screen TV, stereo system, and the rest of my belongings to the black limo waiting downstairs. Brittney pushed me down the hallway in a wheelchair, making my departure none too soon.

Waiting to check out, I couldn't wait to get home to see Boots. We hadn't spent a day apart since I got her; she was my fat little black shadow.

My parents had already left, and my brother wasn't coming back for another two weeks. My father and brother had jobs to maintain in Indiana. So, for the time being, I was completely dependent on other people to help me through the worst time in my life. That truly frightened me; I was very weak and frail. I wasn't even sure if I was strong enough to use the toilet on my own, but anything was better than using a bed pan. It had been very humiliating not being able to wipe my own ass.

As soon as I got in the car, Rudy handed me a giant joint of K.G.B. -- killer green bud -- and his gold Dunhill lighter.

"Welcome back to the living, Bubba," he said. "Spark it up and let's get you home."

"Sounds good."

The weather was absolutely beautiful. The sun was shining, and the fresh air, minus the chemical hospital smell, made me feel I was still glad to be alive. The sight of the California sunshine always put a smile on my face. I truly loved Los Angeles.

I had paid my dues. I've earned the right to live here, I thought as I stared out the window at the mountains.

~~

As we drove up to the mansion, Jerry and Mr. K were standing in the driveway, waiting to help me into the house. I was too weak to get out of the car, so Jerry just threw me over his shoulder like a sack of potatoes and carried me up the stairs into my bedroom.

The first thing I said to Strong was, "Give me my fucking gun, now."

He gave it to me unloaded. I guess he had learned something.

For the next couple of days, I laid on the couch in my bedroom in front of the television. My waterbed was too mushy, and I couldn't hold my head up when I tried to sleep on it.

I was really paranoid about my enemies trying something while I was down. I knew if anyone was ever going to take me out, this would be their best shot, so I was armed to the teeth at all times. After I fell asleep, Brittney would pull the covers over me and find a pistol in my hand.

"Why in the hell do you need a gun?" she demanded.

"Mind your own business," I snapped.

It started countless fights, but I wasn't going to be a sitting duck. I knew what I had to do to protect myself in the world I had created.

Brittney still thought I had shot myself cleaning a gun, and I wasn't about to tell her anything different, so she couldn't understand why I would still keep a gun around.

One intruder had already climbed my balcony and entered my bedroom. I knew it could happen again. I wanted the balcony doors shut and locked. Everyone thought that was strange, but I demanded, "Just do it."

Lying on the couch, on my forth day home, I noticed Boots enter my bedroom. She gave me a look, like, What are you going to do to stop me? Then she knocked the trash over and started going through it.

She paid no attention to me yelling at her. That made me mad -- my own cat was disrespecting me because she knew I couldn't chase after her.

The next day, I was prepared. I threw part of my hamburger into the trash as bait.

Boots entered my bedroom and once again gave me that look. She reached up and grabbed the wastebasket, but before she could pull it over, I pulled up my blow-dart gun and blew.

She howled and took off running down the hallway.

That will teach you, I thought.

A few hours later, Boots returned. She had pulled the dart out and didn't even look at the trash can. She walked around the room very cautiously before finally jumping into my lap with all the love in the world.

I was still her master. She was just testing me.

~~

After many days had passed, I finally regained some sense of order, so I ventured back into my safe room, where I had been shot. I could see they had tried to remove the huge bloodstains from the carpet, but that only reminded me of what had happened . . . as if I could actually forget.

I pulled out my briefcase. Somebody had broken into it, and several thousand dollars were missing. That was the only money I had on hand, so it would be a while before I could venture out. The more I looked around, the more angry I became. I could tell someone had gone through all my belongings.

I ventured back into my bedroom and opened my sock and underwear drawer. Most of my underwear was gone, and only a couple pairs of old socks remained. My airplane tickets to Las Vegas were also gone.

I was pissed beyond belief and blamed Strong completely.

I started yelling for him from the top of the stairs, but he stayed out of my way and out of sight, hiding in his bedroom with Kelly. I couldn't make it down the stairs, so he felt safe.

Later that day, Strong went outside with the dogs. I took a shot at him with my crossbow from my balcony, missing his head by a few inches. The arrow stuck in the fence.

I can't remember now if I missed on purpose or not.

Strong didn't say a word. His eyes widened, and he hurried back into the house before I could reload.

Since I couldn't trust Strong, Rudy and Brittney took turns taking care of me. I wouldn't have been able to get along without their help.

The normal everyday things I had always taken for granted were now impossible tasks that I couldn't do on my own. I felt completely helpless and frustrated with my life. I couldn't even get from the wheelchair to the toilet without someone watching. The first time I wheeled myself into the bathroom and shut the door for some privacy, I stood up on my good leg but somehow got twisted around and fell between the glass shower stall and the toilet with my pants down around my ankles, yelling for help. Rudy had to pick me up like a flipped turtle, and it was embarrassing looking so helpless in front of my peers. In the future, I had to sit like a woman to urinate, and bowel movements were very painful, since all the muscles were connected to my amputated leg. It almost brought tears to my eyes. The morphine had turned my stool to rock.

An even more difficult task was getting clean; I hadn't taken a shower in almost two months.

Brittney said, "You're taking a bath or a shower, or I'm leaving. You smell like a homeless person dipped in cat litter."

"Thanks," I replied.

I couldn't smell anything but the smell of the cursed hospital. Nevertheless, I agreed. Like it or not, I was more than ready for a nice hot shower. The problem was, I couldn't get my stump wet because it was still wrapped in hospital medical wrap. I finally thought to wrap my stump in several garbage bags and duct tape it to make it watertight.

Brittney put a small plastic chair in the shower stall for me to sit on. I tried for five minutes to get from the wheelchair to the shower stall, but in my weakened condition I wasn't able, so Brittney just picked me up and sat me in the shower. I only weighed ninety-eight pounds.

The shower felt like a million bucks. I could smell the hospital odor as it washed out of my hair and ran down my face past my nose, reminding me I had barely escaped death by a pubic hair.

It took Brittney countless hours to comb all the knots out of my hair, leaving a huge pile on the bathroom floor.

The shower really brought me back to life. On the flip side, though, once my skin was clean and was able to breathe, the symptoms of morphine withdrawal set in, and they were devastating. The withdrawal started slowly, and I wasn't sure what was going on at first. I kept smoking weed and drinking beer, but that didn't work for too long. Soon, my body was shaking uncontrollably.

Then I started throwing up everything that went down and my entire body went into painful spasms. I couldn't even sit in the wheelchair; I was literally curling up into a ball of muscle knots pulling in all directions against the muscles in my amputated leg. All I could do was roll around on my bedroom floor, once again trying to escape the pain.

Rudy called the hospital, and they said to bring me to the emergency room. But I told Rudy I wouldn't go back to that house of pain. I began getting ice-cold sweats and shook so violently that it was disturbing for anyone to watch. In an effort to warm up, I climbed into my waterbed and cranked up the heat all the way. I covered myself with thick blankets in hopes of getting warm. It was seventy-five degrees outside, but my teeth were chattering so hard I couldn't complete a sentence. I bit my tongue more than once. I couldn't sleep a wink.

This went on for many days of Hell on Earth. I prayed for death many times. My body craved the morphine from the steady diet the hospital had supplied. My body was putting me through a nightmare, begging for a fix, and no amount of pills or booze was going to help.

Rudy would sit in a chair and watch, replacing the blankets with dry ones when necessary, while Brittney did constant loads of laundry downstairs.

Looking up from the floor where I was lying, the outside world looked like it was crumbling again as I appeared to be sinking into the carpet of my bedroom floor.

After the sixth day of withdrawals, I finally passed out for an entire day, resting on the seventh.

When I awoke, it was the middle of the night. No one was awake, and the place was completely dark. It was weird to see my bedroom dark; I hadn't slept at night in years. It took a while for my eyes to adjust and for my brain to activate the night vision program. My brain was still being scrambled by so many chemical changes.

I was still in a lot of pain but felt a little better. The chills and sweating had briefly stopped, so I climbed into my wheelchair and rolled myself into the bathroom. I turned on the light, grabbed a beer out of the small icebox, popped a couple of pain pills, and fired up a joint.

After sitting alone for a while, I got bored. I rolled back out into my bedroom and turned on the television. It lit the room up, and I noticed Rudy was sleeping at the foot of my bed, passed out while baby-sitting. I lowered the volume, trying to be extra quiet. I was glad Rudy was getting sleep, but someone was supposed to be up and on guard.

The intruder hadn't been dealt with, and he knew I would be coming after him. I had learned how to find anyone, anywhere.

But I still had to recover. One problem at a time.

~~

Around five o'clock in the morning, just moments before sunrise, I heard my roommate Jerry strolling in from an all-night drinking binge in Hollywood, breaking the silence.

Jerry noticed I was still up, so he came in and sat down on the floor with a six-pack. He handed me one and opened another for himself, bragging about the strippers he had double-teamed. By the time we finished the six-pack and my pain pills had kicked in, I was feeling a little crazy, and so was Jerry.

"Why don't you go down to the candle shop," I said, "and retrieve a couple of life-size skull candles for target practice?"

"That sounds like a good idea," he slurred.

My bedroom was big enough that we didn't bother Rudy. He slept soundly while we shot solid-steel darts across the room at 120 miles per hour into the skull candles, splitting them in half.

After we ran out of candles, we started looking for new targets. A huge moth caught my attention as it flew in from the balcony and landed on my Naja painting, which hung near the foot of my waterbed.

Jerry laughed and said, "I bet you can't hit that moth, William Tell."

"I'll take that bet," I replied drunkenly, forgetting that Rudy was sleeping directly beneath the painting.

I took the wild shot, missing the moth by inches, but I hit the painting dead center. The glass shattered and the painting fell off the wall onto Rudy. He sat up abruptly, yelling, "What the fuck is going on? Have you finally lost your mind, Bubba?"

"Sorry," I replied, trying not to smile or laugh. About ten seconds passed before Jerry and I finally started cracking up.

Rudy was happy when Brittney came to relieve him. He was glad to get back into the Hood, where he was safe from crazy white boys with dangerous toys.

After Rudy went home, I wheeled myself to the edge of the stairs to yell for Strong. Because my vision was still blurry and I was doped up on a combination of pain pills, I rolled too close to the edge of the first step -- and down the stairs I went.

The chair flipped end over end, and I went with it, crashing down the stairs. I landed at the bottom with a loud thud, and the wheelchair crashed on top of me.

I yelled for Brittney, who came to the top of the stairs looking for my wheelchair. When she saw me lying at the bottom of the stairs, she yelled,

"What happened? Are you all right? Oh my God!" She rushed down the stairs to my rescue.

I started to panic, thinking I had broken the stitches open in my stump. "I think I feel bleeding," I said. "I banged my stump a couple of times really hard on the way down."

"Let me have a look."

Brittney assured me I was fine, and that everything was dry. But my stump started to swell, and the throbbing was so intense I thought I was going to lose my mind. I started throwing up again.

Brittney tried to re-wrap my stump tightly with an Ace bandage to stop the swelling, as she had been instructed at the hospital. They had been worried about me lying on it wrong -- not going down a flight of stairs.

The hospital once again told Brittney to bring me to the emergency room, but I refused. No way were they going to get their hands on me again. Instead, I took drastic measures by calling one of my associates named Gabriel, who was in a wheelchair permanently after a motorcycle accident. He was a former Hell's Angel and his entire back was covered by a tattoo of broken angel wings. He dabbled in heroin for his pain control; it was Lucifer's drug of choice, he claimed.

I was surprised his cell phone number hadn't changed. He answered and said he would send one of his fallen angels over right away to help me through the withdrawals.

~~

A short while later the doorbell rang. Brittney answered and let in a skinny, dirty white guy with both arms completely covered in tattoos. "I'm here by request," he said. "My name is Bones. I've been sent."

With a look of fear, Brittney asked me, "How is he going to help you?"

I didn't answer as Bones wheeled me into the bathroom. I told Brittney, "Wait outside." I shut and locked the bathroom door. "Give me anything that will stop the pain," I told Bones.

"No problem. I was told to take care of you." He laid out a couple of lines of powdered heroin, then handed me a bag as a welcome-home present. "Gabriel says, 'Welcome to the circle,'" Bones added with a snide sinister smile. I tossed him a grand.

I stared at the heroin. Never in my wildest dreams had I thought I would ever consider trying heroin. But at this point, I would have eaten dog shit out of the ass of a dead dog if I thought it would have helped.

I snorted the first line, and then the second without another thought. The wet, sticky brown powder tasted somewhat like Sweet'N Low. It made me instantly sick to my stomach, and my nose started to bleed slightly. Within minutes, though, there was no pain . . . nothing. My whole body was numb with a wave of pleasure that flowed through me once I stopped throwing up. I felt like I was back in the hospital, but with the comforts of home and without the constant smell of death.

Then I watched Bones do it like an old pro. He tied off a vein in his left arm, which looked like a pin cushion. It took him a few seconds to find a vein that wasn't collapsed. He grabbed my can of Right Guard deodorant spray, spraying his arm and then the needle. Then he wiped off both with a piece of toilet paper.

"Here I go," he said, and stuck the needle into one of the broken blood vessels in his arm, hidden by the tattoos. He let the blood run into the syringe, then pushed it all into his arm, emptying the entire syringe.

As the wave of pleasure came over him, Bones leaned against the bathroom wall, then fell off the toilet seat to the black marble floor with a thud.

We both looked into each other's eyes, knowing the same feeling: Heaven.

I thanked Bones while he wheeled me back to my bed. I was finally able to lie down and get some sleep.

"What the hell did you take?" Brittney asked.

"Some pain pills that really kicked ass."

Chapter 57

I got a few hours of restful sleep before the drugs began to wear off. Then the withdrawals started again, causing my muscles to ache. I tried desperately to lie still so I wouldn't wake Brittney, who was dead tired from dealing with my problems.

As I tried to figure out a way to get up without making waves in the waterbed, so I could sneak into the bathroom to do more lines, I heard what sounded like a runaway train in the distance, coming closer every second.

What the fuck is that?

Then the 7.2 earthquake of 1994 shook Southern California, releasing evil spirits that would cause havoc in the Valley for years to come.

When I felt the force of the impact and the way the house was shaking, I thought it was The Big One. When I had last looked at the clock, it was around 4:30 in the morning. Then everything went pitch black. I could hear things crashing to the floor around me.

When the frame of the waterbed collapsed, I almost started laughing from the insanity of it all. I thought for a brief second that we were falling through the floor into the living room below. I grabbed Brittney and the window frame next to my waterbed, hoping for something secure to grasp, but instead we rolled with the waterbed mattress. The mattress, full of water, felt like a giant boulder as it pinned us against the entertainment center on the other side of the bedroom.

Brittney had no idea what was going on and started freaking out. We were in the dark, and the earthquake had awakened her from a dead sleep. But I knew I wasn't going to die in an earthquake -- not after all the other bullshit I had gone through. No one's luck could possibly be that bad . . . not even mine.

Working together, we pushed the waterbed mattress off of us. Unfortunately, the mattress rolled into the martial arts display cabinet, knocking it forward. One by one, razor-sharp swords started falling. I managed to catch two out of three, but the third escaped my grasp and sheared through the waterbed mattress. A small tidal wave of warm water flooded the bedroom.

All six of my aquariums, filled with sharks and rare fish, smashed to the bedroom floor, along with the television and stereo system and anything else that wasn't nailed down. Loose fish were everywhere. Brittney and I had no choice but to sit in the water and wait for the earthquake to stop shaking the house. There was no way I could save my fish. There were no lights, and the place was a disaster. Most of the water poured off my balcony and into the back yard. I watched helplessly as each of my fish took a dive.

The house shook hard for almost a minute, and then silence fell, except for the sound of every car alarm in the city going off.

I couldn't believe that out of ten people living in the house, not one person had a flashlight. Then one of the girls suggested that someone light a candle.

"Are you nuts?" I yelled. "I think I smell gas fumes."

I sent Jerry outside to shut the gas off on the side of the house. It was a good thing he did, because several gas pipes had broken, along with the water pipes.

I tried the phones, but they were out, along with cellular phones and pagers. We had no means of communication. It was every man for himself.

When the sun finally came up a few hours later, we saw the massive damage. The corner section of the house next to the library had collapsed, crushing my barbecue grill and the neighbor's cat. The kitchen was a mess, with every cupboard emptied of its contents. The icebox had also dumped the milk, eggs, beer, and fruit into a big scrambled mess on the tile floor. Jerry took a shovel and started filling trashcans with the ruined food, leaving us with only dry cereal to eat.

Trying to get around the house in the wheelchair was impossible. I was basically stuck in one spot unless I could get Jerry to pick me up and move me around. The floors were covered with junk, and in many places the floor had buckled like a speed bump. I didn't have the strength to wheel myself over them and got trapped in the hallway.

Brittney still lived at Club California, which had been only slightly damaged. They still had water and power, so I went to stay with her for a few days. My roommates said they would clean up the mansion.

~~

It seemed to take forever to get to Club California. It was only thirteen miles away, but there was so much damage to the freeway system that we had to take side streets, which was risky. There was no law and order, and we were forced to travel through neighborhoods that were out of our element.

Ventura Boulevard looked like something out of an old news clip from Beirut after a bombing. In my distorted vision, it seemed like the end of the world was at hand. Everything around me had been destroyed, including my physical body, and I was sure my mental state would be only a few steps behind.

My favorite local restaurant, the Hamburger Hamlet, was on the verge of crumbling, and my bank was on fire. I wondered if my safety deposit box full of money would still be there when I returned. Many other fires burned out of control because there weren't enough firemen to handle all the fires at once. Mother Nature had proved she had more power than everyone in the

Hood, making the Valley look worse than Hollywood after the 1992 riots.

Brittney wasn't easy on me while I stayed at her apartment. She wasn't about to let me sit around doing nothing.

"I can't take care of you for the rest of your life," she said. "You're going to have to get stronger and learn to do things on your own, or you're not going to make it."

I knew she was right, but I didn't want to hear it.

Whenever we went somewhere, Brittney refused to pull the car up to the elevator. Instead, she made me use the walker to walk the same distance as she did. Sometimes it was quite a distance, and I didn't think I could make it. I often begged her to get the car, but instead she just waited patiently. Sometimes I hated her for it, but someone had to be the bad guy and push me to the limit.

I didn't want to go out into public with my leg missing, even if I was in a wheelchair, but she insisted.

"Sitting home all the time is no good," she said, "and who gives a shit what people think? You of all people have never cared." She was wrong; I did care. I was a Leo and took great pride in my appearance.

Before, when I had entered a place with Brittney, I felt the looks of jealousy and sometimes hate. Now, when Brittney wheeled me into the restaurant on Ventura Boulevard, I felt pity, and I didn't like it. I didn't want their pity; I wanted their respect. Without respect, life wasn't worth living.

Some snooty-looking lady asked me, "Did that happen in the earthquake?"

I could tell that Brittney wanted me to go along with that notion, probably because it would gain me sympathy. But since she had made me come here, I replied, "No, I got blown away with a shotgun."

The look on her face was priceless and worth the ticket for coming down. That cheered up my whole evening. Sometimes it feels good to be a shit.

~~

It took a week to restore power to the mansion, and that was only because Rudy sent a couple of his crew to repair everything while the rest of the neighborhood was down for a couple more days.

"I have some bad news," he said. "I couldn't get ahold of anybody at the hospital. It was hit hard and sustained a lot of damage. The room you used to be in collapsed, so I couldn't get you any pain pills. I tried everywhere and couldn't score any. But here's some more weed, a bottle of whiskey, and a 12-pack of beer."

I thought about what Rudy said: the room I had been staying in collapsed. If I had kept messing with my leg, I probably would have been crushed.

By afternoon on Super Bowl Sunday, I had been out of pain pills for almost twenty-four hours and was starting to lose my mind. The pain was so intense that I couldn't complete an entire sentence without gritting my teeth.

I was almost out of powdered heroin, I couldn't get ahold of Bones because cellular phones were still out. I was saving the last three small lines for the end of the day so I could sleep through the night, giving everyone a break.

The air in my bedroom was as thick as fog with marijuana smoke, choking out Brittney and causing fights between us.

"Do you have to smoke so much?" she complained.

"Shut up," I snapped back. "Yes, I do."

I knew I shouldn't talk to her that way, but at the time I was in so much pain I would have bitten off anyone's head if they showed even the smallest amount of defiance.

To get me to relax, Jerry carried me downstairs to watch the football game in my living room. Somehow the room had stayed intact and all the equipment functional. It was great to get out of my bedroom. The living room was spacious, with a thirty-foot ceiling, black leather couches, and a full-size entertainment center. Twenty-foot-tall French doors led to the swimming pool and back yard. Around half-time, the doorbell rang, and Jerry let Trisha in. I hadn't seen her since she had pulled her disappearing act when we lived together back at Club California nine months ago.

Trisha came floating in with her tits bouncing in every direction and lowered her sunglasses to check out my house. I was glad to see her, but Brittney freaked out -- and I mean freaked out.

"Relax," I told her. "She's just here to visit. Maybe she can get me some pain pills. She has a lot of criminal friends."

"No way," Brittney replied. "Tell that silicone slut to get the hell out of here, or I'm leaving -- right now."

Remembering what I had heard on Christmas Eve, I said, "If you want to go, then go, but I'm not asking her to leave. Chill out."

A few years earlier, Trisha had tried to be friends with Brittney, but she wouldn't have any part of it. After that, every time Trisha came around, she would somehow manage to rub her tits or ass in my face just to get under Brittney's skin like an Alabama tick.

It worked really well.

In Trisha's own slutty fashion, she came over and gave me a hug. Brittney got up and stormed out the door, slamming it behind her.

Trisha just smiled and said, "I guess I still have that effect on her."

"Don't worry about it."

She didn't.

"I'm so sorry about your leg," she said. "I just got back in town after doing another dance tour in Japan, or I would have been by your side sooner."

I wasn't sure if I believed her, until she showed me a tape of an interview she did for <u>Hard Copy</u> while shaking her ass in Hawaii.

After the football game was over, Trisha handed me a couple of blue Xanax. "I'll check with a few people about some pain pills and be back in a couple of hours to make you dinner."

"Don't worry about dinner," I replied. "I can't keep anything down, so just come back and hang out. We have a lot to talk about."

As Trisha was leaving, she turned and caught me checking out her butt. "If I can't find any pain pills," she said with a seductive smile, "I'll come back and sit on your face."

She gave her money-making backside a little slap, and I smiled.

As soon as she left, I didn't want to be downstairs anymore, so I had Jerry carry me back upstairs and put me in my wheelchair, giving me time to think about what had just happened with Brittney. I was angry but sad.

Wheeling myself into the bathroom, I grabbed my sixth beer and glanced in the mirror. I looked like shit, like death warmed over and I felt the same.

I shook my head, cracked opened the beer, and looked at the pills in my hand. After thinking about it for a moment, I took all three blue Xanax and downed the entire beer within seconds. When I was finished, I threw the bottle at the wall, shattering it.

The different pain medications I tried and mixed only caused more chemical imbalances in my bloodstream, affecting my nervous system and causing me to act out with violent mood swings. I was very angry at the world and at life, I saw everyone as the enemy.

I sat there thinking for a moment, with my hands over my face, and then dumped the rest of the powdered heroin onto the table top next to the shower stall.

I cut out three lines and did one, then a second one before setting down the rolled-up piece of magazine. I leaned forward to do the last line when I fell out of my wheelchair and knocked the top off the table, spilling the rest of the heroin onto the bathroom floor. I got down and licked up the heroin from the bathroom floor. I had to wipe pieces of lint and hair from my tongue, but I didn't care. None of my problems seemed to matter. I felt as free as an eagle flying over the mountains as the heroin and marijuana mixed in my bloodstream with the Xanax and alcohol. I knew this wasn't the answer to my problems, but for the present time, it was my way of escaping from reality.

Before I knew it, daylight had turned into night, and I was staring at the ceiling of my bathroom. The way the light was hitting the water in my Jacuzzi created an optical illusion of angels flying over the water. It seemed very real to me . . . In fact, I was sure it was real.

After many hours of staring at the illusion, I finally started to come back down to a place I didn't want to be. The angels slowly disappeared, and the throbbing pain in my stump came back. I was alone, and the more I thought about everything that was happening, the more depressed I became.

I scooped what was left on the table into my hand, put it to my nose, and then licked my hand clean. Instantly, I felt like I had to throw up. Struggling to get my face over the toilet, I fell out of the wheelchair again. I kicked it away, it slammed into the shower stall with a loud crash.

If any of the animals back on the farm had been in this kind of shape, I would have put them down immediately. My life was over.

Eventually I finished puking, and the dry heaves stopped contracting my stomach. I wiped my mouth, seeing the blood that I had spit up. My ears rang of different high pitched tones.

I reached into my holster and drew my Colt .380. Checking the clip, I saw that the first two bullets were hollow-points. One was more than enough to blow off the back of my head.

I cocked the gun and put the barrel in my mouth, holding it there for a moment as I quickly flashed back through my life. It had been one hell of a ride. I was twenty-nine and had lived longer than quite a few of my friends. I knew that it was truly over now and that it was time to end the game. How could I live like this? What was the point?

I remained still for a few seconds as a single tear trickled down my cheek. I knew how this would affect my parents. I had already put them through enough; they didn't deserve any more grief. I prayed they would eventually understand and be able to forgive me.

Then, before I could change my mind, I clenched my teeth around the cold steel barrel and pulled the trigger.

Chapter 58

The hammer fell, but nothing happened. I was still alive.

I trembled with frustration. Checking the chamber of the gun, I confirmed that it was loaded. The hollow-point should have blown the back of my head off. I put the clip back in the gun and ejected the chambered bullet, sending it skipping across the bathroom floor, assuming it must be a dud.

Without thinking, I repeated the action: <u>click, click, click</u>, again and again. I ejected one bullet after another, but nothing happened, and I got really pissed. In anger, I threw the pistol through the mirror above my sink. The gun didn't work, and it was the only gun the police hadn't taken.

Death wasn't going to let me out of the game just yet.

Dwelling on the situation, I became even angrier that I was still alive. Climbing up from the bathroom floor and returning to the wheelchair felt like a failed prison break.

Coming out of the bathroom, I grabbed the door frame to propel myself into the next room just as Boots happened to step in front of me. The wheelchair hit the fat cat at top speed, and she let out a cat scream as she derailed me. I fell out of the chair onto my stump. The pain was so intense, I lay curled into a ball on my bedroom floor for the next two hours. No one in the huge mansion could hear me calling for help.

~~

After examining my gun many hours later, I found out why it hadn't worked: the firing pin was broken.

If I'd had two guesses, they would have been that Strong had sabotaged the gun out of fear of getting shot or after walking around all day on meth, dry-firing it and acting like a big shot, fantasizing that he was Tony Montana it broke. If he had been my friend and shown respect, he could have had it all, just like he wanted. I would have been dead and out of the way.

That only made me angrier. I had been driving around the Valley after the earthquake with a gun that didn't even work. I might as well have had my dick in my hand.

The next day, Matt the Ratt showed up. He had just gotten out of county lock-up and paid me a visit out of respect. I asked him to drive me to a friend's house further north in the Valley to buy a new AK-47 with six thirty-round clips and a crate of 7.62 ammo. I also got my Colt .380 fixed.

"Damn, you're really pissed." Matt said.

I looked at Matt and replied, "I'm done talking. The next motherfucker who even looks at me cross-eyed is going to be Valley Swiss cheese. No more Mr. Nice Guy. I tried that method, and it didn't work."

Heading north on the 405 freeway, I noticed that Matt looked healthy and had put on some weight after quitting meth. I thought that was a good thing.

"How bad was jail?" I asked.

"I handled it for the most part, since I didn't have any choice. It was a hard come-down. I thought my skin was going to peel off as I came down off the crystal meth."

As we were getting out of Matt's truck, he spoke again.

"I'm really sorry about your leg. When I heard what happened, I went nuts because I was locked away. I couldn't do anything to help. But I'm here now, and anything you need, I'll be there to return all the favors I owe you. You have truly been a good friend."

"Thanks. That means a lot."

Matt reached out and hugged me like a brother.

"That's cool," I said. "Enough mushy crap. Push this fucking wheelchair, and let's get down to business."

"Sure, Boss. Whatever you say."

Chapter 59

Whenever I got stressed out, my blood pressure would rise and cause muscle spasms and sharp, throbbing pain in my stump. When these spasms started, I had no control over my actions and would jerk around, unable to speak. It wasn't pleasant for anyone to watch, unless they hated me. Trisha could tell I was seriously hurting, and she apologized for not being able to find any pain pills.

I knew this day would eventually come, when anything was better than the way I felt. The depression was settling in real quick; everything looked very gloomy. I had been off meth for twelve weeks, but I was hooked on everything else and felt like hell. Which was worse?

Trisha finally said, "I know you shouldn't have meth, and I've been ordered by Rudy not to give you any . . . but what do you have to lose? It might help you feel better. I hate seeing you in this condition, physically or mentally."

"I don't know," I said. "I hate to think of the muscle cramps it could cause."

"I remember how great you felt the first time I gave you some meth, and how it got you off the cocaine. Remember?"

I did remember. <u>What the hell</u>, I thought, <u>I'm going to Hell anyway.</u>

I watched Trisha chop up and smash the glassy substance into a fine powder that sparkled on the smoked glass coffee table like rat poison. I recognized the familiar chemical smell instantly. Again, at this point in my dysfunctional life, I would have eaten the ass out of a dead rat if I thought it would helped.

Trisha rolled a straw out of a hundred-dollar bill that she pulled from between her breasts and handed it to me.

I asked, "Did you get this from Christ?"

Trisha nodded while holding up the mirror.

I snorted the line through my nearly repaired virgin nose, and it started burning like hell. My eyes crossed and a tear ran down each cheek like a trickle of blood as I gagged and coughed.

"Are you all right?" she asked.

I nodded, and she did her line without flinching.

An hour and a couple more lines later, the pain was completely gone, and I had almost forgotten about my leg. The drug seemed to snap me out of my sinking depression and suddenly gave me the energy to get out of the wheelchair and try to use my walker so I could be more independent.

I was so wired and high on life that I couldn't sit still any longer. I got down on my knees and boxed with my cat, then jumped up and tackled Trisha. We wrestled like a couple of morons until she pinned me to the carpet.

"How much weight have you lost?" she asked.

"Around seventy pounds."

"You're not joking. You have no muscle mass and no ass, literally. You're a bag of bones."

"Thanks."

Later that evening, Trisha helped me bathe. As she got me out of the shower, I gave her ass a little squeeze. Since she was wearing only a g-string.

"Hey," Trisha said, "this isn't a bakery. Stop handling the buns." I laughed.

After the shower, the only way to get the garbage bag and duct tape off my leg was to pull the tape real fast, ripping out thousands of hairs all at once. It was better to do it that way than to pull at it slowly, only dragging out the pain.

Dreading what was to come, I turned my head away and said, "Pull it." RIP! DAMN!!

Once the plastic bag was removed, we had to re-wrap my stump in fresh medical gauze. This had to be done twice a day to prevent infection.

My stump was still swollen to five times its normal size. The doctors had told me to keep it wrapped tightly or else it would heal out of shape and make it harder to fit a prosthesis properly. Basically, I was reshaping my leg during the healing process.

Since I wasn't into self-torture, someone else had to wrap my stump. I still couldn't face the reality of looking at my stump and always kept it covered.

Trisha took care of me for a few days until she finally had to leave. Then Ann Marie came to visit and decided to move in so she could help me recover. I thought that was cool at first, but instead, she drove me totally insane with her bizarre behavior. Once she moved in, the phone never stopped ringing. Every porno producer in the Valley was calling to set up shoots, along with all her female lovers. They were driving me nuts.

~~

Before I knew it, my brother arrived. I sent Rudy to pick him up at LAX. My brother hadn't seen me since my amputation. The last time he had seen me, I was still hooked up to the machines in the hospital. He was surprised that I was up and around, but not too happy about me using meth ... or about Ann Marie living with me.

Rudy provided my brother with a truck so he could get me around. I could throw the wheelchair in the back.

With all the chaos, I hadn't seen a doctor since I had gotten out of the hospital, so my brother took me to a private doctor who was very concerned about my stump.

"The steel staples are overdue to be removed and on the verge of getting infected," he warned me. He snipped them out and gave me some antibiotics, along with some excellent pain killers. "The best thing for your leg would be for you to sit in really hot water."

"Perfect," I replied. "No more garbage bag wraps."

I sat in my Jacuzzi for what seemed like weeks on end, which sped up the healing process at an unbelievable rate. Using the phone next to my tub, I reordered candle-making supplies and attempted to restart my candle company. I was counting on my brother's help and encouragement, but instead I got negative input and sarcasm.

"Why don't you move back to Indiana and give up this stupid idea of having a candle business?" he said. "Get a regular job driving a truck or welding -- something legal."

I shook my head. "That's not going to happen."

~~

When the candle supplies finally came, I found out it was extremely hard to work from a wheelchair. I had a few accidents in the beginning, setting the shop on fire and dumping hot melted wax into my lap while trying to fill molds. I even ran over my own foot while trying to maneuver the wheelchair.

Still, I wasn't going to give up. I got three wheelchairs and put one on each level of the house. I was able to hop up and down the stairs on one foot to get to each chair so I could get around.

The first week I worked in the candle shop, I kept smelling a horrible odor, like a dead animal was decomposing somewhere in the shop. I asked Silva to help me look. We moved boxes and looked around, but couldn't find anything. Then I opened the top of the shop vacuum. Inside was a dark brown substance with fuzz growing on it that stunk like rotten ass.

We looked at it for a few seconds before I realized it was my own blood. They had used the Shop-Vac to clean up the blood but had never cleaned out the vacuum. They had just put it in the candle shop.

Looking closer, I could see pellets, bone fragments, and a whole world of bacteria starting new life in my blood. I almost lost it.

I put the lid back on and told Silva to take it out to the trash. Luckily, it was trash night.

When Silva left a couple of hours later, he returned and said, "Guess what? Someone stole the Shop-Vac. It's gone."

We both laughed.

I thought, Wait till they get that home.

~~

I assumed all my business accounts knew what had happened to me, since Chance said he had taken care of all my candle accounts for the Christmas rush. But each phone call I made was a disaster. Not only had Chance stolen and ruined all my equipment, he had taken advance for candle orders he never filled. The possibility of remaining a legal businessman was looking darker by the hour.

If I wanted any of my old accounts back, I would have to make thousands of dollars worth of free candles to regain their trust and prove to them that I had really lost a leg. It was insulting that they didn't believe me. I guess it just sounded too far-fetched, since it had been months since Chance had ripped them off.

After getting off the phone with all my accounts, I went into a rage and put four holes in the wall. I wanted to kill Chance.

After my brother had pulled the walker out of the wall, he said he couldn't see any reason why I would want to live around such back-stabbing low-lifes. But something made me want to stay in Los Angeles. I would have rather died than move back to Indiana.

Now I had nothing holding me down. My legal business was destroyed, and the money I had saved wouldn't last forever.

I hadn't seen Brittney in weeks. She had already moved in with another long-haired musician. They were living in Burbank and had even bought a dog together. I was sort of jealous at first, and then angry. She had been my girlfriend for two years, and now she was already living with someone else. But since I had acted like a complete ass, I couldn't say a thing. I couldn't afford to look weak, so I pretended it wasn't bothering me.

The following Sunday night, I went out for drinks with Traci at a small local pub just south of Ventura Boulevard. It had a nice fireplace and a warm ambience. I had really enjoyed the bar in the past. But now everyone was staring at me. I was on crutches, with one pant leg safety-pinned up to keep from dragging the ground like a mummy's wrap. I could see the pity in the eyes of strangers, and I didn't need it. I could slowly feel my friendly personality slipping away. I didn't like the thought of being considered handicapped, but there was absolutely nothing I could do to stop that until I got an prosthesis. I decided this would be the last time I went out looking like I looked.

As soon as we had downed a couple of drinks, I just wanted to leave. The more people who came into the bar, the more difficult it became to get to the restroom on crutches. I wanted to go home, so we did.

Once at home, high and feeling no pain, Traci and I watched <u>The Last of the Mohicans</u> on the big screen in my bedroom. I loved the movie, but it depressed me, reminding me that some things were in the past. I was certain

275

I would learn to walk again, and maybe even run, but running through the woods and jumping from bank to bank over creeks was something that wouldn't happen again.

Chapter 60

The information about the intruder finally came back. He was working with another meth lab in a small desert town. If he had gotten out of the meth business, I wouldn't have found him so easily. At present, however, the only people I knew to get off meth were either dead or in prison.

It was hard to conduct business with my brother around. I didn't want to involve him in any of my criminal acts of revenge, so I decided to hold off on everything until he went back to Indiana.

My brother was scheduled to leave on Monday, and it was Friday night. I knew he wasn't having a good time, so I asked one of the hottest blondes I knew, Debra-Do-Wrong, to take him out on the town and show him a good time. Her new nickname was Butt-Lips; some doctor in Beverly Hills had taken fat out of her butt and put it in her lips so they looked plump. Other porn stars were going as far as getting their assholes bleached to get that perfect un-touched look.

While my brother was out having a good time, I had a secret meeting with Chino. He pulled up in his black Mercedes with tinted windows. The car sported paper dealer plates that changed whenever he felt it was necessary.

Chino was dressed in a black suit, and his Italian shoes were shined, matching the sparkle of his gold Rolex. I smelled Polo as I reached out and shook his hand. He looked like a million bucks, and in many ways he was worth his weight in gold to the right client. He made things happen and changed the course of many people's lives. The way the rest of the free world would see it, he was nothing more than a cold-blooded killer -- a murderer for hire. But he was my friend, a good friend. I trusted him, and he trusted me. Both of us knew the outcome of betrayal, so respect was always given.

Chino never told me whether he liked his work or not; he was just good at it. His reputation as a professional was well known among the Trilateral Commission.

"We have to make this short and sweet," he said. "Do you have the information I need?"

"Yes," I replied. "I need two problems to go away. Do I have enough on account to handle it?"

Chino laughed. "Yes, you have enough on account."

"Excellent," I said, handing him two separate folders containing all the information.

Chino opened the first folder and pulled out the photograph. "What's the story with his asshole . . . trying to look like Tony Danza, or Al Pacino?"

I laughed. "He's become a real problem. If you have time, give him a visit. He's not a priority, but it would be nice to shut his fucking mouth."

Danza was a drunk who had been arrested several times for causing problems on movie sets. He liked to stalk actors he thought he resembled. For some reason, he had been prank-calling my house, calling me "peg leg" and screaming other nonsense ever since I got back from the hospital.

I had kicked his ass a few months earlier. When I first moved in, he had followed Silva from the pool hall to my mansion. He was so drunk upon arrival that he ran into the neighbor's car while we were unloading the moving van in the driveway. Danza got out and told my new neighbor to fuck off. I had never liked this asshole and was pissed that he was drawing unwanted attention, so I walked over and knocked him out with two punches. The neighbor thanked me and called the police. Danza was arrested.

I had acted like I didn't know him, so now he was fucking with me. He showed up drunk at four in the morning and drove through my front yard, tearing up the grass. The cameras captured his idiocy.

Chino opened the second folder with the picture of the intruder and said, "This guy looks a little more challenging. Finally, someone who's not a pussy."

I smiled.

"Do you want everyone to know you had it done so it will instill fear in anyone else who might what to fuck with you?"

"Yes," I replied. "Could you wait until Tuesday, after my brother leaves? It would be a load off my mind."

"No problem. Consider it done."

We shook hands, and he gave me a hug, reassuring me that everything would be taken care of promptly.

We laughed. We were as demented as Republicans. In my mind, that was being fueled by hate and revenge, I felt it was my right. I would show the Valley and members of the Hollywood elite that I was someone not to be messed with. Wheelchair or not, I was still able to reach out and touch someone. My power had not diminished. I just used the evil at hand more loosely than in the past. Life wasn't as precious anymore.

After setting things in motion, I felt a twinge of remorse, until I looked down at my stump. That made the guilt disappear very quickly.

In front of everyone, I pretended to be taking everything well, but in reality I wasn't handling it at all. The mere sight of my leg caused serious mood swings that interfered with normal brain activity. I spent a lot of time thinking about suicide, and the only thing I found to take my mind off it was the knowledge that there were plenty of people I would rather do in then myself.

At the time, it seemed like rational thinking . . . it really did.

Before he left, my brother made one last attempt to get me to move back, but I refused. I had Trisha take him to the airport.

~~

Chino never got to visit Danza; by Tuesday, he was already in jail. In a drunken rage, he had stabbed his roommate Johnny in the neck with a pair of scissors. He was being held at L.A. County for attempted murder and cocaine possession.

The Wednesday newspaper had a story that interested me. A meth lab out in Palmdale was hit late Tuesday night. The people were executed buckwheat-style, and the lab was blown sky high. I smiled. Biker conflict was suspected.

Chapter 61

<u>March 1994</u>

Most of the swelling in my stump had gone down from using the Jacuzzi and the use of meth. I was going to receive my first prosthetic leg within the month. They had already taken the measurements, and it was being built at a lab in downtown Los Angeles.

Only a couple of months out of prison, Matt the Ratt had already flunked his first drug test and was on the run from the law for probation violations. I let him crash downstairs on the couch.

After the earthquake, FEMA had condemned hundreds of apartment complexes all over the Valley and hadn't allowed residents to return because the buildings were on the verge of collapse. But that didn't stop Matt the Ratt, Silva the Irritator, and Ara from climbing over police blockades to dig through deserted apartments. They found plenty of material for starting a new illegal business. Based on what I was told, Ara's garage was stuffed with boxes of checks, credit cards, jewelry, and women's underwear -- all the loot from their scavenging.

My candle business wasn't making any money, and my nest egg was starting to run low. The people I thought I could trust had fucked me over, really putting me in a bind. I knew if I didn't come up with some cash real soon, I would be forced to move back to Indiana to recover with my family's help. I wanted to avoid that at any cost.

The fact that I had been shot didn't mean a damn thing to those who were on meth. Everyone I knew wanted me to get back into the business; they were all in debt to other meth dealers because they weren't getting the deals, the way I took care of everyone.

Matt the Ratt was heavily in debt to a Nazi who called himself the Ice Man. I paid Matt's debt so he could work for me and not worry about a bunch of speed-crazed Nazis.

Other friends were heavily in debt to the bikers, but I wasn't going to pay those fucks.

I began contemplating running my meth business from a wheelchair. Would I be able to keep control of the jungle and the savages that came along with the territory? After doing a few more lines of meth, I put some more thought into it. I knew that a one-legged man had taken on a killer whale and that a president of the United States had had the courage to run the country from a wheelchair during war time. General Santa Ana had taken the Alamo with a fake leg. If I was half the man I thought I was, I should have the balls to take back the business I had started. It belonged to me.

I knew if I was going to run the meth underworld again, I would have to be brutal right off the bat. I heard through people who were trying to score favors that someone who owed me money was talking smack and making fun of me. I wouldn't have allowed it before, and I wasn't going to start now. He was one of the Fiendish Eight, so I made up my mind that he was going to be the example. I would do it right out in the open for all the others to see. I was back in town. <u>No more Mr. Nice Guy.</u>

I called a meeting with the Fiendish Eight. Rudy and Mr. K were covering my back, but even they didn't have any idea what I was going to do. I wasn't sure myself, just yet.

Steve the Big Mouth showed up as I had requested. The meth had given him a serious attitude, and he had brought two bodyguards. Everyone in the room was armed to the teeth with enough steel to build a railroad track through the house.

"I hear you want to see me?" Steve said.

"Yeah," I replied. "Why didn't you come to visit me in the hospital?"

"I was busy," he said. "I kept trying to get there, but you know what it's like."

"Yeah, but where's the money you owe me? I shouldn't have to ask. It's been months."

"I don't have it," he answered arrogantly.

"Oh really." I knew he was holding out and that he was using my money to buy meth from the bikers. Enraged, I clenched my teeth. The meth-induced anger was building. "When are you going to have it?" I demanded. "This isn't the Bank of B."

Showing no respect, he said, "I have no idea. It could be this week, or it could be a month. What's your problem? You're not going anywhere." He looked at his bodyguards for a chuckle. They both looked at me and knew it wasn't funny. They didn't laugh, letting me know they respected me -- or at least feared me more than their boss. I was the boss of bosses in this group.

Now that I was in a wheelchair, Steve the Big Mouth was talking to me like I was some chump on a bus bench in Hollywood. I didn't think that was funny.

Two years ago, Steve had been a computer consultant, but now that he was using meth and had bodyguards, his balls had grown three times their original size . . . or so he thought. I figured if he was going to act like he had big balls, I was going to show him that they weren't as big as mine . . . now or ever.

I rolled closer in my wheelchair and, without warning, punched Steve directly in the stomach. The punch was so hard I heard the air rush out of his lungs. While he was bent in half and on the verge of throwing up, I grabbed him by the throat with both hands and pressed both thumbs into his windpipe. His legs started to shake as he ran out of air. I pushed him backwards. Using the wheelchair as a brace, I kicked him under the chin with the tip of the Doc Martens combat boot on my one foot. I heard his teeth clatter as he fell back.

"Got anything else smart to say, smart guy?" I yelled as he lay on the floor.

The remaining Fiendish Seven, along with the other fifteen people watching, stared in amazement. I was going to get respect, even if I had to take it back.

"Fuck you, peg-leg." Steve the Big Mouth moaned.

The disrespect sent me into a full rage. I turned around and grabbed the wheelchair by its handles, raising it over my head. Standing on one leg, I slammed it over Steve's face as he cowered into a ball. I repeatedly hit him with the wheelchair until it bounced off his head and I fell backwards, losing my balance.

This wasn't how I had planned to behave. I would have loved to come home to a welcome home party, but instead I had to take back everything people had stolen from me and were still trying to steal.

Rudy helped me up while Steve the Big Mouth moaned on the floor. His bodyguards just stood there in disbelief after watching their boss's ass get kicked by a meth-crazed handicapped guy.

"Get this asshole out of here before I fucking kill him," I yelled. "You have two weeks to get my money, or next time you'll need that wheelchair, I promise you that!"

I got my point across.

Chapter 62

By April, everyone in Hollywood who had known me over the past ten years began coming by to visit. My mansion was no longer a secret to anyone. It was like Grand Central Station, with people bringing by get-well gifts and home-cooked meals non-stop, twenty-four hours a day.

I went back into the business to survive. Cain and Abel set me up, and I restocked the Fiendish Eight. I had to replace Steve the Big Mouth. The ass-kicking hadn't gone over too well, and he returned to civilian life. The way he had been acting, it probably saved his life.

One evening, unexpectedly, Raquel stopped by and asked to hang out for a while, just like old times back at Club California. She was currently working as a nude stripper at the Seven Veils on Sunset Strip in Hollywood. Not a real classy joint, but times were rough for everyone in Hollywood.

"I'm renting a house in Hollywood with a new roommate I just met at the strip club," she explained.

"That's cool. So how have you been?"

"Things have been good. I got a new boyfriend, and he loves me. How about you?"

"I'll probably never date again. I hardly fit the Hollywood look anymore."

"Stop talking like that," Raquel insisted. "My roommate's boyfriend has a leg missing, too, and it doesn't bother her. Stop worrying about women looking at you in a different way."

"Yeah right." I thought about it for a moment and said, "Do you think her boyfriend might come over and answer a few questions? That would cool."

I really did need to talk to someone who had been there and done that. I hadn't gone through any type of rehabilitation or counseling because everyone thought I was hard as a rock. Inside, though, I was scared to death -- scared of becoming that dorky kid back in high school whom the girls wouldn't give the time of day to.

"My roommate parties, but her boyfriend doesn't," Raquel said, "so keep it a secret from him when they come over, okay?"

"I don't like doing that," I replied. "I really don't want to start lying to someone who's coming out of his way to do me a favor." But I understood and granted Raquel's request under protest.

~~

When Raquel arrived the next evening, I had a full house of people, so I asked Matt the Ratt to answer the front door. Matt led them up to my bedroom while I waited on the other side of the room in my wheelchair, talking on the telephone with my parents letting them know everything was all right.

When Raquel's roommate's boyfriend walked through my bedroom door, I thought, Deja vu.

When the doctors in the hospital had told me I would walk with a limp and would probably have to use a cane, the first thought that came to my mind was a picture of this guy. I had met him several times at the Rainbow back in the glam days, but I didn't remember his name. He always wore fancy clothes and walked with the help of a fancy walking cane with a wolf's head. He was part of the older crowd who had been in the criminal business at the Rainbow before I got there. What he did I wasn't sure, but it involved some sort of scam. He was friends with Alexis and Nick Stanley.

Now that he was dressed in plain clothes and his hair was short, he looked very normal.

I thought for sure he would recognize me, but he didn't, probably because my hair wasn't spiked and I weighed only half my normal weight. I hardly recognized myself when I looked in the mirror.

Raquel made the introductions. "This is Eric Heinz and AnnaLiesa Scribner."

Liesa also looked familiar, but I couldn't remember where I had seen her before . . . somewhere in Hollywood, I was sure. I didn't find her very attractive at first. She wasn't wearing any make-up and had her long black hair pulled into a ponytail. Matter of fact, I thought she was kind of scary looking, like Morticia from The Adams Family.

Reaching up from the wheelchair to shake Eric's hand, I said, "Hello, I'm Brent. Welcome to my house."

"I made you some home-cooked food," said Liesa.

I lifted the lid and gave it a smell, "Thanks a lot. It's been a while since I had something other than Carl's Junior." She smiled.

"When do you expect to get your new leg?" asked Eric.

"In a couple weeks."

"That's cool."

Eric wasn't bashful about his leg; he sat down on the edge of my waterbed and pulled off the prosthesis in seconds, without any trouble or hesitation. I was amazed that he could touch and look upon his stump so easily. That wasn't something I could do yet.

Our legs were missing from the exact same location; we had identical amputations. It was amazing. Eric put his stump next to mine for comparison. They looked the same, except that his leg had huge scars on both sides of his knee from traumatic nerve damage.

"My leg was crushed in a motorcycle accident on Sunset Boulevard nine years ago," he explained. "I went through nine months of surgery, trying to save my leg, before they finally amputated it."

In the process of removing his prosthetic leg, a small .25 caliber handgun fell out of a secret location and tumbled to the floor.

"Oops," he said, putting it in his pocket.

I wasn't threatened. "Don't worry about that little old gun," I said. Everyone in the room was carrying three times the firepower . . . including myself.

"If you like guns," I suggested, "come back into my safe room, and I'll show you some guns."

Eric was a smooth-talker with a lot of confidence in his voice, giving me a new outlook on the future. I took an instant liking to him. I had never known he had a leg missing during all those years of seeing him at the Rainbow. I figured the cane was just for looks or concealed a hidden dagger, but Eric said he needed it when he was around a crowd of people to keep his balance.

I took Eric back into my safe room so I could show off my new AK-47.

"Why do you need all this firepower?" he asked.

"For the next asshole who tries to fuck with me in any way." I said it with a smile as Eric handed me back the assault rifle. I then picked up the Mossberg shotgun and added, "This is the gun that blew my left leg off."

"You kept the gun that blew your leg off?"

"Yes, and on a few occasions, I even slept with it to show everyone that I'm not afraid of anything."

Eric gave me a strange look, wondering if I might be crazy. "Crazy" was the nice term. While we were discussing weapons, the subject changed to women.

"Don't be too concerned if a woman doesn't want to go out with you because of your leg," he said. "Fuck the cunt. She's not worth your time. It's a good way to eliminate bad women right up front."

I nodded. Now that I thought back, I had seen Eric with dozens of beautiful women over the years, and none of them seemed to mind in the least -- considering the way they hung all over him like a second set of skin.

I asked Eric, "How long have you been dating Liesa?"

"Off and on for a while. We're both Hollywood sluts." We laughed like old friends. He added, "I just got back in town when Liesa asked me to come over and talk with you."

"Thanks," I said, and meant it. "It really helped me out. If I can ever return the favor, don't hesitate to ask. Anything, seriously -- anything."

After Eric had gotten to know me a little, he realized that Liesa wasn't all dressed up. The Leo in his nature wanted to impress me, so he showed me a business card that included a semi-nude picture of Liesa bending over in a black g-string. She looked like the poster girl for "All girls bend over." I couldn't believe it was the same girl. Talk about an ass hand-crafted by the master . . . and now it had been brought to my attention.

Eric and I rejoined the rest of the people hanging out, but this time I took a second look at Liesa. I could see the girl in the photo hidden in her loose-fitting clothes.

As we were speaking, Matt the Ratt entered my bedroom with the police scanner running.

"Not you, too," said Liesa. "Eric's nickname is Scanner Boy."

Matt replied, "That's cool," and the two started talking scanner talk.

Eric picked up the scanner and said, "Very impressive. Do you want more secret government frequencies?"

"Sure," Matt replied. "Whatever you know would be great."

Eric pulled out a notepad and started writing down secret FBI frequencies. I wondered how he had access to such information. That tripped my paranoia a bit, but I kept it to myself.

In the meantime, I gave Liesa and Raquel a tour of my candle shop. To show my gratitude, I gave both of them a couple of candles to take home.

"What were you and Eric talking about in the back room?" Liesa asked.

"Oh, nothing," I replied. "Just male bonding." The girls laughed.

"We also want some meth," Raquel said, "but you can't let Eric know."

I frowned. "That's not cool, especially after he's been so cool."

But I did it for them anyway, always being a sucker for women's wishes. They both leaned over and gave me a kiss on the cheek, reminding me how nice women could smell when they want something.

Returning to my bedroom, I was faced with a potential problem. Matt was arguing with Eric about police entrapment, and I didn't like the way the conversation was turning.

I hated to interrupt, but I called Matt into the back room and said, "Shut the fuck up. I don't know Eric from jack shit. How did the conversation go from scanners to police entrapment? Shut the fuck up and pretend to be stupid. Don't offer any knowledge of what I'm doing or what you're doing. I'm serious."

As Matt started to walk away, I grabbed him by the back of the neck with my cane.

"By the way, Eric doesn't do drugs. Keep that cool, too."

Having a cane was like having permission to walk around with a weapon in my hand at all times.

As time slipped by, Eric said, "Nice meeting you, but I have to go. Good luck with your new leg."

"Too bad," I replied. "I was really enjoying your company." I shook his hand again. "If you're ever in the neighborhood, feel free to stop by. If there's ever anything I can do for you, just ask."

"Thanks. I might take you up on that."

Before they left, Liesa said, "I'll stop by to get some more candles in a few days and pick up the dishes when you're finished with the food." Standing behind Eric, she winked at me. I thought that was odd -- maybe a secret code to let me know she wanted more meth.

"That would be fine . . . anytime.

Chapter 63

Rudy took me to get my first prosthetic leg around the beginning of April. The therapist promised that in time I would walk normally.

The prosthetic leg didn't fit worth a damn. My stump had already shrunk in size because of the meth and was now smaller than when they had cast the inner sleeve thirty days earlier. To make up the difference in size, I had to wear several pairs of very thick thermal socks over my stump to get it to fit snugly. I also had to wear a wide belt around my waist with supports straps that connected to the leg like garter belts for support in lifting the new leg when attempting to walk. Finally, to make things even more uncomfortable, there was a leather strap that went around the top part of my leg like a belt, buckling just above my knee.

I was extremely frustrated. I thought I would be able to walk the first day. The meth had triggered my brain to think it would be easy.

Putting my injured leg into the socket of the fake leg was insanely painful once I tried to put some of my body weight on it. The end of the stump was very sensitive. There were a few inches of gap between my stump and the bottom of the fake leg. My real leg was held in place by grabbing the side of my stump all the way around, so it was sort of suspended in air when the fake leg was connected to my real leg.

I couldn't believe they had said this fake leg would work like a real leg; I didn't think it was possible. My brain couldn't make it work. It was stiff and lifeless -- constructed of steel and hard plastic. It didn't seem natural, and I dreaded walking like a cripple. It was going to be a lot harder than I had thought, but I had to try to make it work. I had no choice: walk or drown.

It was like learning to walk all over again. But I had seen Eric walk with the same leg like it was no big deal. If he could do it, so could I.

~~

A week later, Liesa stopped by to pick up her dishes. This time she had on some makeup and was dressed sexier.

"Thank you for the food," I said. "It was delicious. You're a great cook. If you ever want to make me anything else, I'll eat it." I gave her a seductive smile.

Liesa smiled back. "You're welcome. Maybe I can find you something else to eat."

We both smiled at each other as the innuendoes flew back and forth. I kicked Liesa down some meth, so she took me out to lunch. We talked over burgers at the local malt shop on Ventura. I felt comfortable around her, probably because I knew she was used to being around someone in my condition. I felt like I didn't have to hide it.

"Where's Eric?" I asked. "Tell him to stop by anytime, and if he ever needs anything, just ask. I have a lot of influence in the Valley."

Liesa shook her head. "He's out of town, and for your own sake, don't get involved with him." She wouldn't explain why, so I didn't push the subject, not wanting to ruin the mood.

I really liked Liesa's personality. What a cool chick, I thought, very level headed and hot as hell. She would make a great girlfriend. Eric's lucky.

As I picked up the bill, Liesa remarked, "You got a good first impression of Eric, but believe me, he's not a nice guy by any means. He broke up with me once for cutting my one-length hair into bangs."

I didn't say anything; I just shook my head and smiled.

Driving back to my mansion, I wondered what Liesa knew about me. I just wanted her to think I was in the candle business and that I had some extra speed I was sharing with her.

~~

Later that day, I asked Raquel, "What did you tell Liesa about me?"

Raquel shrugged. "I guess . . . everything.

"What is everything?"

"I just told her that you were a boss."

I exhaled and asked, "A boss of what?"

Raquel shrugged again. "I guess a boss of everything. I told her how you always got me my smog checks and how you came at three in the morning to remove a denver boot. I told her you could make anything happen."

"In the future," I snapped, "don't tell anyone a damn thing."

"Fine," she said. "But Liesa is really interested in dating you. She thinks you're really cool. You're the only thing she can talk about."

I was flattered, but thought, In my condition, she must be crazy. I look like death warmed over. Why would she want to be with someone who's in a wheelchair and can't even walk? She could have her pick of men or women.

"Absolutely not," I said. "I'm not stepping over my boundaries."

"What does that mean?"

"Liesa is Eric's girl."

Raquel spoke to me in a patronizing tone, as if I was a child. "Liesa already told you -- they've been broken up since November, and it's now April. He just stops in to see her when he's in town. He lives in Texas."

"I still wouldn't feel right about it." It would be bad karma.

"She's my very best friend and a real down-to-earth girl," Raquel added. "She's not like the rest of the strippers at the Seven Veils."

"That's another thing," I said. "Don't take this the wrong way, but I don't date strippers. I just have sex with them when I get horny."

After living in Hollywood and dealing with so many strippers, I knew they were nothing but trouble -- heart-breaking trouble -- and I'd already had enough of that. I loved the way strippers looked and tasted, but to trust one was beyond me. In my mind, when I looked at a stripper, I saw a demon trapped in a sexy body, using the outer shell to do its bidding.

~~

As time slipped by, I got back into the swing of things. That meant a full house of people on the weekends.

Around midnight Saturday, Raquel and Liesa stopped by on their way to the Rainbow, driving twenty miles out of their way to make the visit. They both were dressed to kill. I hardly recognized Liesa, who towered over me in her six-inch come-fuck-me high heels. She had spared no expense in her look tonight. The thigh-high stockings complemented her long legs, leaving just a few inches of bare flesh between the top of her stockings and the bottom of her low-cut dress. Her entire body was a solid mass of muscle after years of dancing. Once I got my eyes off her derriere, I noticed that she also had the most seductive, mystical green eyes. They were mesmerizing, like Elisabeth Taylor's when she was young. She was a hell of a package, bringing my male hormones to a boil. And she was flirting with me.

I invited the girls into the safe room to do a couple of lines. While I was chopping up the lines with my stainless steel double-edged blade, Liesa wouldn't stop smiling at me, putting me under some sort of spell. She really had a look about her, and I was very attracted. All I had to do was give in, and she would be mine. But it would be wrong, and I still knew the difference.

I set the mirror down on the table, rolled a hundred-dollar bill into a straw, and handed it to Raquel. Raquel did her line, coughed, gagged, and then passed the bill to Liesa.

"Batter up," I said. "It's your turn."

Liesa smiled and stepped forward in her high heels. Turning around, she bent over just enough to flash me a peek of her gorgeous ass in a black thong. From that moment forward, she had me under her spell. I was thinking, Eric who?

~~

Around 3:30 in the morning, everyone decided to split to a rave in Hollywood, but I declined. I planned on soaking in the Jacuzzi.

Everyone left except Liesa. She wanted to stay and join me in the Jacuzzi -- if I wanted her to. I wanted to tell her to leave and was trying my best, but instead I heard myself saying, "Stay."

I was thrilled, but I still felt self-conscious about my physica Knowing that she had already dated a guy with a leg missing mad easier, although I still felt extremely guilty.

My bathroom could be quite romantic when the lights were set low and the scented candles were lit. I could feel a magical presence. The blue neon moon in the window overlooking the Valley gave the air a certain electrical sensation. The bathroom was all black marble, including the Jacuzzi with its brass fittings. In front of the Jacuzzi was a large-screen television and a VCR with a library of adult entertainment provided to me by the actors in the movies. To the right was an icebox filled with beer and ice-cold sodas. The towel rack to the left of the tub was stacked with clean towels, lotions, bath oils, condoms, and a box of sex toys Ann Marie had left behind.

I rolled up a couple of joints and chopped us out a few lines, setting everything on the shelf next to the Jacuzzi along with a few sodas. When I was doing meth, I wasn't into alcohol.

I asked Liesa to lock the bedroom door. While she was gone, I quickly climbed into the tub, hiding my leg under the water.

To finish setting the mood, I inserted the new Nine Inch Nails CD into the player and hit play.

When Liesa heard the music, she smiled, locked the bathroom door, and started a slow, seductive striptease, using years of dance skills to cast her spell.

I sparked up a joint and enjoyed the show.

For a brief second, when Liesa's hair fell across her face, she looked like Angel, my ex, sending chills down my back. Although I hadn't considered Liesa attractive at first, I certainly thought differently now. This would be the first time I'd had sex since being shot.

"If we're going to have great sex," Liesa said, "you have to stop worrying about your leg. It doesn't bother me. You know I dated Eric for several years."

"Are you sure?" I asked. "I feel weird, and to be honest, I still can't touch certain parts of my stump without jumping out of my skin."

"Yes, I'm sure," she replied.

Liesa got down on her knees in front of me as I sat on the edge of the Jacuzzi. She took my manhood into her mouth with a loving kiss and began to massage my injured leg at the same time. I couldn't believe she was actually touching my stump without being disgusted. I couldn't even do that, and it was part of my body.

The up-and-down motion of her luscious lips and the gentle loving care of her hands made me feel glad to be alive. It was the first time in months I felt absolutely no pain of any kind . . . I felt like a man. I was in Heaven.

When the sun finally started to come up, Liesa and I collapsed in each other's arms in the hot water. I could hear the rest of the drinking crew returning as they stumbled through the front door.

"Too bad everyone had to come home so soon," Liesa said. "I was hoping you could teach me about anal sex."

I looked at her perfect behind and remarked, "You're telling me that no one has tapped that fine piece of backdoor real estate?"

"That's right," she answered. "I've been waiting for the right guy. If you keep fucking me like that, you'll be the first to knock on my back door."

I had never been the first for anything with any of my past lovers. I smiled, feeling I still had the sexual charm to romp with a breathtaking woman.

My real advantage was the meth.

Even in my weakened condition, I could last for hours under the chemical influence, pretending to be a mindless jackhammer operator.

As I climbed out of the hot tub, Boots gave me dirty looks from across the room. She hated all other females. In fact, she had bitten me the first time I was with someone other than Angel.

"Get out of here, Boots," I yelled, throwing a towel at her. Boots scurried away.

Liesa was amazing, the best yet. Never in a million years had I thought I would meet a woman who could turn me on and push the right buttons the way she did, especially considering the condition I was in.

Nevertheless, I had a strange feeling that something just wasn't right. It felt too damn good. Maybe it wasn't real.

Liesa had said certain things that were too close and personal while trying to make conversation about things we supposedly had in common.

Sitting on the edge of the Jacuzzi, I looked at my naked self in the full-length mirror surrounding the hot tub. What the hell is this hot-looking chick doing with me? I asked myself.

I was at the lowest point in my life, and physically I was out of shape and hardly attractive enough to be having great sex. Maybe it was the meth, or Liesa was Mother Teresa . . . Not.

I pondered these things as I watched Liesa get dressed.

Liesa gave me a kiss on the cheek, and said, "I'll call you."

"Sounds good," I replied.

Liesa walked halfway out the door and stopped. "If you continue to fuck me like that," she said, "I'll love you forever."

I smiled ear-to-ear.

Liesa blew me a kiss over her shoulder and bounced away, her hips swinging.

I didn't know what it was, but a voice in the back of my head was saying, Let her go. It's not worth it.

I didn't listen.

~~

Trisha made me breakfast and brought the food up to my master bedroom. We sat outside on the balcony and enjoyed the early morning sunshine as we ate our steak and eggs.

"You know, Liesa only has one thing in mind," Trisha said. "She either wants your money or your meth. Please don't be tricked into being a trick."

Not wanting to hear it, I said, "Don't worry. I've got it handled."

I could never figure Trisha out. She didn't want to have sex with me, but she seemed disappointed and hurt when I had sex with other women. I knew that what she was saying could be true, but I wanted to believe that I still possessed the charm to have a woman like Liesa -- a woman like I'd had in my past, before the amputation. A woman other men wanted.

As we finished our breakfast, the neighbors on our left side started fighting in their back yard. It seemed pretty heated, considering the tones and the words being used.

"Want to listen?" I asked Trisha.

I grabbed my shotgun microphone, a super-directional microphone with a special amplifier and a voice band filter. I could pick up conversations a football field away with great ease, if the conditions were right. I had special adaptors that allowed me to listen through doors, ceilings, apartment floors, and walls.

Trisha and I passed the shotgun microphone back and forth, listening. The couple was really going at it about their daughter's behavior. Their daughter had the sex drive of a porno star, I knew; I had heard some of her phone conversations come across the police scanner when I was tuned into the cordless phone-mode.

Eventually, my neighbors took their fight inside. Before I could turn off the shotgun microphone, I heard an unfamiliar sound -- a rustling noise, mixed with a breaking sound. I grabbed my auto-focus binoculars and scanned the tree lines and back yards of the surrounding homes.

Two houses down the hill, a man in a gray jumpsuit was climbing a telephone pole. The man was almost to the top, just below the power lines, when he stopped. He was using climbing spikes with a safety belt, but I didn't see a company logo on his clothes, and he had passed the cable-box junction.

He was moving rather quickly, like Spider-Man, but it was Sunday, and no one worked on Sunday in Los Angeles -- except people who were up to no good.

"What do you see?" Trisha asked.

"Wait a minute," I replied. I didn't want to take my eyes off him for an instant.

The guy in the gray jumpsuit pulled some equipment up with a nylon rope and proceeded to set up a tree stand in a tree next to the telephone pole, right under the cover of the thick greenery. The tree stand hooked onto the front of the tree with stainless steel claws that cut into the tree at a sharp angle. To support the seat, a thick rubber strap wrapped around the tree, securing it tightly.

Before disappearing, the guy in the gray jumpsuit pulled up a mesh screen that was decorated with camo paint and sticks and leaves. The screen blended perfectly with the tree, similar to a deer blind. Once it was in place, I could hardly see him. If I hadn't seen him before he got behind the blind, I would never have spotted him.

I hadn't been able to see the guy's face; he always had his back in my direction, so he had no idea I was watching.

It appeared that someone on the ground was helping, but I couldn't see the bottom of the tree because it was behind my fence and a few yards over.

Using a rope, the guy in the tree pulled up some surveillance equipment, including what looked like a spotting scope and a listening device with a parabolic dish. I watched as he set up his equipment and pointed the device directly at my bedroom balcony doors.

~~

I picked up the phone and dialed.
"Rudy, we have a serious problem."

Chapter 64

By the beginning of May 1994, the mansion was almost empty. I kicked out Donna, Strong, and Kelly; I'd had enough of their crap. Jerry, Cheyanne, and Tony were still living at the mansion, but I hardly saw them.

I let Matt the Ratt move into Strong's old bedroom. He drove me anywhere I needed to go and served as my bodyguard whenever Mr. K wasn't around. I liked Matt; he was always clowning around and making me laugh with his crazy jokes.

I had been seeing Liesa for over a month now, and she had turned out to be everything Raquel claimed: a perfect girlfriend and a great lover, all rolled into one. She didn't mind my friends hanging around, either.

Every night after she got off work, she came over and helped me with the candles. I had set up the shop and was starting to get new accounts. Liesa was skilled at hand-painting, so she helped me do much of the fine detailing.

She also gave me a lot of positive input and a new zest for life. Having her at my side wiped away all thoughts of depression. I actually told her, "I'm glad I lost my leg. If I hadn't, I would have never met you."

Liesa smiled and whispered into my ear, "I will love you forever."

I was content.

~~

On the third of May, I got a collect call from Liesa. She was very upset and crying.

"I need a place to stay," she said. "Raquel and I got into a huge fight. She kicked me out, and I have nowhere to go."

"You can move in with me."

Have trunks, will travel.

I had forgotten that Liesa had a dog, and when Boots saw her dog, it launched a three-day fight.

Liesa's eyesore of a car, which was probably worth only twenty bucks with a full gas tank, broke down in front of the mansion the night she moved in. I had a hunch that it had been planned out, but I kept my thoughts to myself.

Trying to be cool, I said, "You can drive my sports car."

I couldn't drive it because it was a stick-shift.

After Liesa moved in, I asked, "Does Eric know about us?" I still felt some guilt.

"No. I told him I'm dating a woman to keep him off my back."

I wasn't sure if I believed her; something in the tone of her voice didn't sound right. That added up to two things that didn't seem right. So instead of wondering, I put a tape recorder on the phone line going into my bedroom. I wanted to see how honest my new girlfriend was being with me.

I had a lot of female friends and had seen all of them lie to their boyfriends over the years. They were all very clever and very believable.

Debbie Do-Wrong was a high-class call girl, but her boyfriend of three years thought she was a buyer for a Beverly Hills clothing store. Joanna's boyfriend of two years thought she was a first grade teacher. Instead, the beautiful blonde worked as a dominatrix, beating rich guys for big bucks. Ginger was married with children, but had rich male clientele who paid her to squat over a glass coffee table and take a dump while they lay underneath, masturbating.

Basically, anything was possible. Nothing would surprise me.

I debated for a week about tapping the phone line. Part of me didn't want to know, but the other part had to find out.

Well, I got what I asked for.

Sadly, within the first week of tapping my own phone, I found out that Liesa had a pager I didn't know about. She also had voice mail. The tap on the home phone picked her up checking her voice mail. She had daily messages from Eric. Since she was in the same room with me most of the time, she frequently made up excuses to leave so she could go use the pay phone at Ralph's Supermarket.

I wouldn't have had a problem with her talking with Eric, and I had told her that. I liked the guy and felt guilty for being with her. The problem was that she was lying about it. There was no need to, but she did anyway.

A couple of days later, I asked, "Have you heard from Eric?" I already knew the answer.

She looked me straight in the face, eye-to-eye, and lied through her pearly white teeth: "No."

If I hadn't known better, I would have believed her without a doubt. That really bothered me and made me wonder what else was a lie.

Another thing I found weird was that in the course of two weeks of personal phone calls to her girlfriends, she had never once mentioned my name. She had just moved in, and I figured it would be something they would talk about. I had made Liesa's life real easy; she didn't have to strip anymore or do any type of work, other than putting up with me. She had promised that she would help me get my candle business started again.

Then, while listening to one of her conversations, I heard something that truly bothered me.

One of her girlfriends asked, "How are you holding up?"

"I gave him some sex last night," Liesa replied, "so that should keep him off my back for a while." They both laughed wickedly.

I didn't want to believe I was being played, but looking at my torn-up body, how could anyone find me attractive?

I had been right the first night. Even for a boss, that hurt. Still, I didn't let it show. I kept it all bottled up behind the distant look in my eyes.

The more phone calls I listened to, the harder it became for me to treat Liesa the same way. I pretended I was buying her act, and now that I knew it was an act, it was much easier to see through.

I couldn't believe that all the time we had spent together had been meaningless. She had helped me learn to walk with my new leg; it had seemed so real. Now I felt betrayed.

If it hadn't been for the phone tap, everything would have seemed really cool. So I got what I was looking for, and now I was in denial.

Looking for a second opinion, I discussed my thoughts with Mr. K. We took a drive through the Hollywood Hills so we could talk in private.

He suspected something more sinister. "She's some sort of undercover agent," he guessed. "Might even be related to the guy in the tree."

I didn't want to believe it, even though I already suspected it.

"Has she tried to buy any meth from you or asked any questions about meth?" he asked.

I shook my head. "No. Nothing of the sort."

Liesa never asked for money, and I never gave her any. As far as the meth went, she usually had her own stash -- a different brand than mine. I could never get a straight answer from Liesa about where she was getting her meth, other than someone had given it to her.

"I want a full investigation into Liesa," I said. I wanted to know what her intentions were regarding me.

I also had a meeting with Cain regarding Liesa's ex-boyfriend Eric Heinz. I handed Cain one of the business cards I had found among Liesa's belongings.

The business card read, <u>Counter-surveillance, electronic-debugging, and phone tap detection.</u>

I knew if someone could "de-bug," they could also plant bugs.

Cain looked at Abel and said, "This guy was in your house, and now you're living with his ex-girlfriend?"

"Yes to both," I replied.

"Do you know who Eric Heinz is?"

"No. That's why I'm asking you to do a background check on both of them."

"This guy Eric Hentz is a computer hacker turned FBI informant, I can tell you that for sure. The government hired him to bring all of your Valley hacker buddies down. His real name is Justin Tanner Petersen."

I was incredulous. "You know that for sure?"

"Yes. We thought about recruiting Eric many years ago, but unlike you, we found out he couldn't be trusted. Eric's greed is stronger than his convictions or loyalty."

I just shook my head.

Cain said, "I'll put together a file on Eric for you to check out, and we'll run a background check on Liesa."

"Thanks."

"Here's the device you requested," he added, tossing it to me as I went out the door.

Since I was letting Liesa drive my car everywhere, I had Mr. K install a tracking device called a "bumper beeper" so I would be able to keep tabs on her location.

While I was playing I Spy with Liesa, someone else was starting an investigation into me. I started seeing strange white Chevy Blazers and vans with tinted windows parked down the street with people sitting in them for hours, watching my mansion. All the vehicles had paper dealer plates. I asked Rudy to trace the plates. When his connection ran them, red flags went up all over the place, and he was suspended from duty.

"What are you doing with these numbers?" the LA police Commander asked him. He didn't have the proper answers, therefore shutting down that information channel.

Rudy wasn't too happy.

~~

One day soon afterward, Mr. K told me, "Someone tried to tail me home from your house, but I gave them the slip through the canyons at a high speed."

I had heard from other people that they had been followed after leaving my house.

"One Cherokee Indian to another," Mr. K said, "I feel the presence of evil white men closing in on all sides . . . So it might be time to run for the hills."

We both laughed.

Chapter 65

One night as I sat alone in my wheelchair, I shut off all the lights in the house and scanned the back yard and surrounding yards for any sign of surveillance. At the same time, I scanned through all the government frequencies on my police scanner until I finally locked onto a strong signal at 418 MHz. It was one of the new secret frequencies Eric had given to Matt.

I found four guys talking on that channel from different locations. I had been lucky enough to catch them in the middle of a conversation regarding myself, probably because they had seen me sitting outside. According to my information, the frequency 418 belonged to the ATF.

I also locked onto another channel used by cheap walkie-talkies, the type you find at Radio Shack. The walkie-talkie users were also watching the house but didn't sound like government agents. They sounded like "brothers," making me think it might be Dickwood and some of his criminal friends still pissed about me taking the mansion.

Switching back and forth between the two frequencies, I realized that the guys talking on channel 418 were not only watching me, but also the guys using the walkie-talkies.

The guys talking on channel 418 were stationed in two different locations. One was hidden behind my house, looking into my bedroom. Another was across the street on the road above, watching the front of the house from the hill. These guys didn't say much and were very professional.

Based on what I gathered, the other guys messing around my place were from a house down the street, probably another house Dickwood was scamming. I had no idea who my neighbors were past the second house on either side, so anything was possible.

~~

Since I had figured out where everyone was, I was still able to run my business around them, pretending not to see them. Playing dumb worked really well. They weren't that slick.

Mr. K told me that Liesa must be an inside agent, and I had to agree. I knew from the first night in the Jacuzzi that something wasn't right about her.

While Liesa was gone, Mr. K and I shut all the drapes, locked all the doors, and went through her personal belongings, which were stacked in my walk-in closet. I wanted to know more about my pretend girlfriend.

Going through Liesa's trunks, we found at least forty books on the occult and Wicca, or witchcraft. When we saw those books, we both stepped back.

"Do you see what I see?" I asked.

I had so much on my mind, I hadn't even noticed that Liesa had set up an altar in our bedroom. It was supposed to be a make-up table and mirror, but after seeing the books, I suddenly noticed the signs of black magick that had been brought into my house -- again, without my permission. Liesa had set up a two-foot-high table with a black cloth covering, candle holders with black candles at each end of the table, and a ceremonial knife in one of the drawers that were supposed to hold makeup. Under the table, she had stashed several glass containers filled with rotting herbs and flowers soaking in water, which smelled rotten and nasty.

It appeared that my so-called girlfriend was a witch and was practicing the black arts of modern-day witchcraft right under my nose.

In the last box I checked, I found books on casting spells and star charts and mapping locations and dates of the moon to perform witchcraft. Picking up one of the books, I found a tiny piece of paper hidden between the pages. It read "Sorceress" and listed several phone numbers.

Mr. K and I shook every one of her witchcraft books and found many similar small pieces of paper listing names and phone numbers, including Eric's mother's address in Virginia. I recorded all the numbers and placed them back in the books, trying to put everything back as we found it, but I knew Liesa would know. She was very clever.

The phone numbers I found on the pieces of paper didn't match any of the phone numbers she had in her phone book, which she left out for me to snoop through if I desired.

Mr. K picked up one of the black candles from her makeshift altar and said, "Look at this."

Both of the black candles had pentagrams carved into the wax, with my name above them.

"Liesa must be preparing some type of spell to harm you," Mr. K said. "Black is bad. White would be good."

Miserable lying witch, I thought.

Next, I opened the top drawer of her altar and found one of my knives wrapped in a piece of paper. When I opened the paper, I found a spell printed on it, entitled "The Fool."

"Do you know what all this crap is for?" I asked Mr. K.

"I know some, but not enough to say for sure."

I wanted a professional opinion, so after calling in a few favors around the Valley, I was put in contact with the president of the UFO and Phenomena Society -- someone who was an expert in the occult.

~~

Coulee only lived a couple of miles away in the Valley; she said to bring some of Liesa's items over for her to look at. I grabbed a few of the witchcraft books and two jars of rotten herbs I found hidden under the altar.

Coulee looked just how I had pictured in my mind: very thin, with flowing brown hair, looking like a knowledgeable earth witch.

She welcomed me into her home, which was marked with the seal of protection. "Let's see what you've got there in the bag." Carefully examining the items I brought, she remarked, "Liesa is into something very evil. She has no idea what she is meddling in."

That wasn't what I wanted to hear. I wanted to hear that it was all just a bunch of junk, and nothing more.

The more Coulee looked at Liesa's belongings, the less she wanted to handle them, out of fear that some of the evil would wear off onto her soul.

"Liesa has brought evil into your house by bringing these items under your roof."

I nodded my head.

Picking up one of the jars, Coulee added, "This is a rotten rose petal. She is using them to cast a love spell on you. I think the herb in the other jar is Belladonna, which can be poisonous or can be used in small doses to cloud your thinking. It could be put into your toothpaste or eye drops to cause hallucinations."

I found that very disturbing.

I didn't want to tell anybody, but the love spell was working. Every time I looked at Liesa, my heart would melt, even though I knew what she was.

While Mr. K and I had been sweeping my bedroom for hidden transmitters, we had found a pencil drawing of a goat's head with devil horns encircled in a pentagram, duct-taped to the back of the mirror in my bedroom.

I gave the drawing to Coulee and asked, "What the hell does this mean? It gives me the creeps."

"The ram's head is a symbol of Amon," Coulee replied. "It opens the gateway for the spirit of fertility to enter through the mirror, then through your reflection and into your soul."

"What would be the purpose of that?" I asked.

"I don't know. You will have to ask Liesa."

"That's like asking a brick wall."

Mr. K and I both laughed.

I thought about it for a second, then asked, "Wasn't the Egyptian female god Isis once called L'isa?"

"That's correct."

That was fucked up.

I then handed Coulee the black candles I had found with my name carved into the wax alongside the markings of a pentagram.

Looking them over with a disturbed expression, Coulee said, "If she did this work to the candles, then she is out to get you. What did you do to her?"

"Nothing, yet."

"I will fix her," she said. She poured holy water over the candles and said a blessing. "Let her burn them now." She suggested that I should move out of Los Angeles as soon as possible. "You are in grave spiritual danger. She is after your soul or is doing the bidding of others hiding in the shadows."

Figures, I thought.

"What can I do to protect myself?"

"I will give you some magical protection to help fight off the evil that she has brought into your house. The evil realm of spirits is much like the Internet. Once you have logged on, you must log back off, and I'm going to help you do that."

Coulee placed an enchanted crystal cross necklace around my neck and wove a length of blessed ribbon in my long, dark hair.

"When you get home," Coulee explained, "walk around your house and read Psalm 81 out of the Bible to rid your house of any evil spirits and traces of black magick. I also want you to burn sage and place bright white candles in all the windows."

When I got home and opened both of my copies of the Bible, I found that neither one had Psalm 81. Those pages had been removed with a razor blade.

Chapter 66

As time passed, Liesa seemed to suspect that I was onto her charade, but she probably thought she was much smarter than me and I couldn't possibly be that wise. Although she could tell right away that Mr. K and I had gone through her belongings, she wisely never accused me. She just said, "It looks like someone got nosey." I didn't respond.

Before Liesa had moved in, the sex had been out of this world. But as I suspected from the first night, it was too good to be true. Now that we lived together, she gave me sex once or twice a week, and always in the safe room. She would never do it in our bedroom anymore, probably because she knew the surveillance team was watching and they might see or hear us.

I figured if Liesa wanted to play I Spy, I could play the game, too. I set up a hidden camera in my safe room to videotape us having sex and doing drugs, to serve as an insurance policy in case she turned out to be a federal agent like Eric. When I knew the camera was running, I acted fragile and weak for the camera and handed her the meth off-camera, letting her carry it into the safe room.

I never showed anybody the tapes; they were my aces in the hole. I was embarrassed and horrified by my physical appearance on the tapes, only convincing me further that my hot girlfriend was a fake.

~~

A few weeks after Liesa moved in, Raquel stopped by while Liesa was out.

"I've been trying to call for weeks, but I can never get through," she said.

I thought that was odd, since I had call-waiting, but I had been hearing the same story from Rudy and other people. It seemed as if someone had taken over my telephone line and was wreaking total havoc with my communications. But it didn't make sense, since I knew a government wiretap would not interfere with any calls. They would want me to talk to anyone who called.

"I -- I was totally wrong about Liesa," Raquel stammered. "She's not a nice girl, and there's something weird going on with her and Eric. I'm not sure what they're up to, but I feel I have to warn you."

"Slow down," I said. "I'm ahead of you."

"Did Liesa tell you that Eric is a fugitive on the run from the FBI?"

"No, she never mentioned a single word."

"I'm really sorry for making the introduction," Raquel admitted. "It was wrong. I wish you'd get her out of your house before something really bad happens; she's nothing but pure evil."

"Thanks," I replied. "I'm already on to Liesa. I assure you, if anything happens to me, many professionals of a certain trade will never let her get a minute's rest."

~~

The next day, I got the information from Cain about Eric. His code name in the hacker world was "Agent Steal."

I learned that Eric was an only child and that our birthdays were only four days apart -- but four years older and a few inches taller.

Eric was considered one of the most dangerous techno criminals still at large in the United States. He was an expert in electronics, specifically in bugging and phone taps. He was the James Bond of the computer world -- except without morals.

The copies of the court documents said Eric had been arrested in July of 1991 in Dallas, Texas, for possession of a stolen car. During the search of Eric's apartment, the police found more than a dozen stolen credit cards, telephone calling cards, bankcards, five modems, a computer with illegal software, and some two hundred diskettes full of stolen information. Eric was charged by the federal government with eight counts of breaking into the T.R.W. computer systems, as well as several other computer hacking crimes.

While Eric was in prison in September of 1991, serving four months of a five-year prison sentence, he was approached privately by the Secret Service and FBI agents. As part of a deal to get himself out of prison, Eric pled guilty to the crimes he had committed in Texas and to computer-related crimes for which he was still under indictment in California. The government transferred Eric's case to the California courts, trying to make his release look real in case anyone checked -- and they did in the hacker world.

Through an odd series of delayed sentencing, Eric remained out of jail, working for the FBI under direct supervision of FBI Agent Stan the G-man from September 1991 to October 1993. His job was setting up other computer hackers in Hollywood and working his way into the Valley.

The FBI provided Eric with a fancy $1300 per month apartment and $200 in spending cash a week, with a shitload of electronic monitoring equipment and full access to any and all phone lines as he tried to infiltrate the notorious hacker gang known as "Legion of Doom."

Part of Eric's agreement to get out of prison was that he had to educate FBI agents about the art of hacking. But the real reason they needed Eric was to trap and build a case against the Condor, Kevin Mitnick, the thirteen-year-old boy upon whom the movie War Games was based. He was now in his early thirties and thought by many to be a national threat to the security of the United States.

The file said that the heads of many corporate offices were completely outraged by Eric's release. The national director of information security at Ernst and Young in Chicago said that letting Eric out of prison and giving him full access was the dumbest and most dangerous move he had ever heard of.

I read page after page. This guy had an entire world of people pissed at him and completely frightened at the same time. He was a bigger celebrity than myself, but only because he got caught so much.

I did notice that the apartment the FBI had rented for Eric was on Sepulveda Boulevard, only a few blocks from my house, so I knew Eric was familiar with my neighborhood. The FBI had used the Hamburger Hamlet on the corner of Van Nuys and Ventura for the first meeting between Eric and the Condor. I could see the Hamburger Hamlet from my bedroom balcony.

The most important bit of information the file contained was that Eric had stolen one of the FBI's secret phone-tapping computers, entitled the S.A.S. system. It was a laptop-sized machine, and once it was plugged into any phone system, it could literally take over the entire phone system grid. The S.A.S. system had programs that knew all the back doors and secret codes the FBI had compiled, giving the user total access to any computer database that could be reached by telephone or a fax connection. Anyone using the S.A.S. computer could take over any targeted telephone line, making themselves the operator. Eric had already used the S.A.S. system with another computer hacker to take over Los Angeles radio station telephone lines, winning prizes and huge cash giveaways by always being that lucky caller.

The file also indicated that Eric was monitoring DEA operations and warning drug dealers that they were under surveillance. He charged large amounts of money for the inside information. But Eric was suspected of double-crossing drug dealers by turning them in after taking money from them.

When the Kevin Mitnick and his fellow hackers found out that Eric was working for the FBI, they gathered information about Eric's illegal activities and went public, forcing the FBI to revoke Eric's bail and cancel his undercover mission.

In October of 1993, the FBI set up a meeting with Eric, his lawyer, the assistant U.S. attorney, and Special Agent Stan the G-Man. They planned to charge Eric with credit card fraud and several other computer-related crimes.

Liesa drove Eric to that meeting at the federal building on Wilshire Boulevard. During the meeting, when Eric realized he wasn't going to be leaving, he excused himself to use the bathroom and then bolted to the elevator and out the front door of the building, making himself a fugitive.

Reading the file, I better understood what might be going on. I assumed

Eric had found out about me being with Liesa, so he got jealous and ratted me out to the ATF for my fully automatic weapons. That explained the people in the trees and the problems I was having with the phone line. Eric had seized my phone to get more information or just listen to Liesa and play I Spy.

I said nothing to Liesa about the knowledge I had just acquired; I was waiting to see if she would ever tell me any of this on her own.

Chapter 67

I spent a lot of time trying to figure out Liesa, which really clouded my mind. Maybe that was her mission -- to distract me while something else was being planned.

Listening to Liesa's telephone conversations, I sometimes heard her girlfriends say, "So, have you seen Peg-Leg lately?"

"Yes, he's doing just fine," Liesa answered.

I thought they were calling me Peg-Leg, but after hearing them say it in a couple of different conversations, I realized they were referring to Eric. I was never mentioned in any of the conversations, as if I didn't exist.

I knew a lot of strippers in Hollywood, but this bunch who worked with Liesa were unfamiliar to me. I didn't know any of them, and they had never came to the house after the first night she moved in.

I had Cain hack the FBI computers to see if they were watching my house because of Liesa or for any other reason. They found nothing concerning my address or any of my aliases. They checked Eric's file and found that he was still at large, a fugitive . . . whereabouts unknown.

"What have you found out about Liesa," I asked Cain. "Is she a government agent, too?"

"She has many aliases. I'm not sure if her name is even Liesa. I can't find any agency that employs her."

"Did you guys hack the ATF's computers yet?"

Cain shook his head. "We can't get in right now because they changed their codes. But we'll keep trying."

~~

I knew a lot of people who knew Eric, so I started asking around. Everyone I talked to said he was very self-absorbed, childish, and jealous.

Everyone knew about his phone-tapping abilities; he must have bragged about everything he did. That was probably why he got busted so many times. One guy told me that Eric used to charge a sleazy private dick in Hollywood a thousand dollars per phone tap. Quite a few people said that if anything weird was going on around my house, they would be willing to bet Eric had something to do with it.

After hearing everything I had just heard, I called my friend in Hollywood. "Will you come out and do an electronic search of my house?" I asked. "It hasn't been checked since I got home from the hospital."

"Sure," he replied. "See you in an hour."

~~

David started his search downstairs. Right away, he didn't look too happy.

Shaking his head, he pulled me into the candle shop and said, "Both wall outlets have small video cameras. Your living room and the hallway leading to the stairs to your bedroom are covered."

"What the fuck? Are you sure?"

"Yes."

Freaking out, I said, "Check my bedroom right now."

Upstairs, David pointed to the television while standing behind it. A video signal was coming off the television, even though it was shut off. In my bathroom, he pointed to the VCR. After sweeping over it, he determined that it was transmitting, too. David didn't pick up any transmissions in my safe room, but when he popped the hatch leading to the attic, he found a black wire running into the top of the ceiling under the light bulb. It was carrying all the sounds from my safe room to some undisclosed location outside of the house.

Next, David checked the phone in my bedroom and began to take it apart. Liesa had brought the phone with her when she moved in. "It better matches the decor of the bedroom," she'd said, so I let her plug it in.

"The phone has custom work," David said. "It has an infinity transmitter built in so they can listen to your bedroom by way of the phone line. It's just like the one we found back at Club California, but someone else built it. The style is a little different."

"Holy shit," I said. "This is making me sick."

"I can rip everything out, or you can act like they're not there and give out false information, which would be in your favor. At least you know the bugs are there, so you have the upper hand. Who placed them there, I have no idea. The house was probably set up while you were in the hospital.

"I'll take out the one in the safe room, and we can move a few pieces of furniture downstairs to cover the hidden cameras in the wall outlets to block the view."

"That sounds good."

I left the camera in my television alone; trying to remove it would only let them know I knew. I "accidentally" ran into the television in my bathroom with my wheelchair, knocking the VCR to the black marble floor and smashing it. I watched as David took the VCR apart and removed the microchip camera, which was smaller than a pack of smokes.

David also checked my car. Sure enough, my radar detector had been replaced with one that had a hidden camera -- both audio and video.

Just to make sure he found everything, David set up his room analyzer in the bedroom. The room analyzer basically x-rayed the entire room, measuring light, sound, and pulse waves, and could pinpoint any kind of transmission. The device had cost $30,000, but it was well worth the price. Lawyers cost more.

"I'm getting a weird broken signal," David said, "or at least some type of power source coming from a few strange places in the walls throughout the mansion."

"What are you talking about?"

"I'm not sure what they are. Maybe nothing, but I do find it odd. Do you mind if I make a hole in the wall?"

"Knock the damn wall down if you have to."

David walked over and opened my martial arts display cabinet, retrieving a sharp sword. "Are you sure?"

"Do it."

David ran the sword through the wall, opening it up a bit. Reaching into the wall, he felt around and pulled out a device resembling a chip board. It hung in the wall by a thin cord and was powered by three nine-volt batteries.

"What the fuck is that?"

"I have no idea."

We went through the rest of the house and removed thirteen similar devices from all levels of the house, including the candle shop. Anywhere we found an unusual power source, we chopped a hole in the wall. The items weren't transmitters or video cameras, so it didn't seem to make any sense.

"I'll take them apart and find out what they are," David offered.

"Good. Let me know."

While the chip board devices lay on the table in front of us, one device started making a very high-pitched tweaking sound. After two minutes, it fell silent. Then another device went off, making a whistling sound for two minutes. All the devices started going off in different orders making various high-pitched tones that only someone on meth would be able to hear, sort of like a dog whistle for tweakers.

With a look of terror on his face, David said, "These devices are called 'hidden tormentors.' As far as I knew, they were only a myth, something the CIA used in mind-control experiments to fuck with someone's mind while they were under the influence of drugs. They used them on Columbian Drug Lords."

"You're fucking shitting me," I said. That explained the ringing in my ears.

It couldn't be the CIA; that would make no sense.

The idea was almost too much to handle all at once. I felt I couldn't go anywhere private, because someone was always watching and listening. If that wasn't enough, they were trying to tweak my brain with high-pitched frequencies. It freaked me out that someone had been watching me go through the worst time of my life, just like I was under a microscope being studied.

I knew all these secret devices had to have been set up while I was in the hospital. It would have taken a lot of time to place all the hidden devices.

When I looked at my television more closely, I realized it wasn't the original set; this one still had the plastic guard. They had forgotten to remove it when they switched the televisions.

I wondered if they had watched the failed suicide attempt. It made me want to kill someone, but I didn't know who . . . just yet.

Chapter 68

At the beginning of June, I started getting parking tickets in the mail for my sports car. At first I got mad at Liesa because she was the one driving it, but then it hit me as very strange. My sports car was still registered in a fake name, but the parking tickets were in my real name. That wasn't right.

If Liesa had gotten any parking tickets, they would have been mailed to my P.O. box in Hollywood, not my house in Sherman Oaks. There was absolutely nothing in any computer or database to link my name to my current address or my sports car, which had never been in my real name from day one. If the plates were run through DMV, records would show Darren's picture: 6'2", 180 lbs., black hair, blue eyes, Hawaiian-Japanese . . . hardly a description fitting my appearance.

I compared the tickets to old tickets I had gotten a while back. They were identical, except for the address where I was supposed to send the money. The tickets looked damn good, but they were fakes. Some computer hacker had printed them on his computer in an attempt to weasel money out of me in another scam. If the hacker had known anything about me, he would have known I had never paid a parking ticket in my decade of living in Hollywood. I would give up the car before paying a single one.

~~

The following week, I started receiving eviction notices from some mortgage company called Master Mortgage, claiming they owned my mansion. The notices said that the house had been sold and I had ten days to get out. These white-collar criminals had no idea I was already onto their house scam, so I threw the eviction papers in the trash. The eviction papers weren't notarized, nor did they have the proper court seals.

I had always known the scammers would eventually have to show themselves. The house had been sitting empty, so I was staying until I was fully recovered.

I called Master Mortgage and informed them I was on to their house scam. I wasn't moving out of this house until I could walk on my own, without the help of crutches or that fucking wheelchair I hated so much.

"Fuck with me," I told them, "and I will blow the lid off your scam. This is my house for now."

They didn't know what to say.

~~

With the surveillance continuing, I had to play it cool and take everything that was being thrown at me with a grain of salt. It wasn't the time to get violent, since I wasn't sure who was on to me. So, as part of the game, I smiled and pretended nothing was getting to me. I could never show any sign of weakness, no matter how crazy things got. I made up my mind I wouldn't let them get to me; that was my way of getting back at them. They had put a lot of time and money into my fall. I wanted them to think they had wasted both.

To top things off, as part of the game, someone impersonating me called the prosthesis lab and canceled my order for a new, better-fitting prosthetic leg. The impersonator told the doctors I was moving out of state and rudely criticized their ability to handle my care properly. They were trying to keep me from recovering. Once I realized what had happened, it took some talking and filling out stacks of paperwork to get the two-month process moving again.

The prosthetic leg I had now was just a temporary training leg and didn't fit worth a shit. I had to wear twenty pairs of socks over the end of my stump to get the prosthesis to fit somewhat tightly. Wearing all the socks made the leg fit loosely and was very hot. Since it wasn't a good fit, the prosthesis rubbed up and down on my stump, causing huge blisters and unhealed sores that looked like road rash.

Despite having a bad-fitting leg, by the middle of June I had finally learned to walk on my own, without the crutches. I only needed the help of a cane for balance to take some of the weight off my injured leg. When I knew I was going to be wearing the fake leg for a while, I would wrap duct tape around my knee to help hold the prosthetic leg tightly so it didn't slide when I walked.

~~

Liesa and I went out to dinner, but when we returned, I knew an intruder had been in my bedroom. My bedroom door was locked, just like I had left it. But when I left, I pulled out a long strand of my hair, wet it, and placed it across the top of the door hinges. I had seen James Bond do it many times, and I had done it many times in the past. Tonight, the hair was gone. Instead, I found it lying on the floor inside my bedroom.

I pretended like nothing was wrong and didn't say anything to Liesa. I didn't see anything missing, so I had to wait for Liesa to go to sleep before I could check the tape.

The camera caught the intruder crystal clear: it was Matt the Ratt, my right-hand man. He was searching through my personal items, looking for what, I don't know. He hadn't attempted to get into the safe.

It appeared I was surrounded by traitors. I kept thinking, If I can get through this without ending up dead or in prison, it will be a fucking miracle.

I asked Mr. K to tail Matt for a couple of days. I wanted to know what he was doing while he was away from the mansion. Was he just a petty thief, or was he plotting against me, too? I wanted to know if all these people were working together, or if everyone was just taking their best shot.

Mr. K followed Matt for two days straight. He reported that Matt hung out at all-night coffee shops, talking big to impress young chicks by bragging about my million-dollar mansion and arsenal of weapons as if they were his own.

Mr. K added, "Matt has a cellular phone in his toolbox."

I winced and shook my head.

"You're going to love this. Matt had a meeting in Hollywood with your old meth connection and my old friend, Jawn the biker."

Chapter 69

Benny the Mean would stop by every week just like clockwork. No phone calls, just a pre-arranged meeting. Sometimes Benny brought Amy, and she lay out by the swimming pool for a couple of hours while Benny and I took care of business. I started noticing a pattern in Liesa's behavior every time Benny brought Amy; she would go into hiding until they left, or she would leave before they arrived.

One afternoon, before Benny arrived, I tried to delay Liesa from leaving. The situation turned into a shouting match. As Liesa stormed out the front door, she passed Benny and Amy in the driveway.

"Was that your girlfriend?" Amy asked.

"Yes, why?

"I know her quite well. We used to work together at the escort service Body Language, doing private bachelor parties. Anna used to let me tie her up and torture her with hot candle wax and a small black leather whip. The guys really loved it. We made a lot of money together." Amy looked down the road, where the dust from Liesa's car still lingered in the air. "I wonder why Anna Liesa is acting so weird. I haven't seen her since Edwin's mysterious death."

"Who's Edwin?" I asked.

"Edwin was the owner of Body Language. He committed suicide because the government was going to put him away for criminal conspiracy."

"What was so mysterious about his death?"

"The Feds were buying the suicide at first, until they started to investigate. There was a suicide note in his handwriting, making everything seem sad and true, but the shotgun turned out to be in the wrong hand and the angle of the blast was wrong. After some checking, the body with the blown-off head turned out not to be Edwin. He tried to fake his own death to get the government off his back." Amy shrugged. "I've been told not to discuss it with anyone, so you didn't hear that from me."

"Does Liesa's old boyfriend Eric know Edwin?"

"They were friends."

The business card Eric had showed me, with the semi-nude picture of Liesa, was a Body Language business card. This was getting a bit weirder than it had seemed at first.

Liesa obviously didn't want Amy to recognize her, but for what reason? What was the scam? Or was she a government informant like Eric?

The next time Benny came over, he showed me a picture of Amy and Liesa together at a bachelor party to prove it was true.

I knew an escort service typically only employed hookers.

~~

When I got the chance, I asked Liesa, "Do you know Benny's girlfriend?"

"No, but she looks familiar," she said. "I might have seen her at one of the Hollywood nightclubs once."

Seeing the pictures of Amy and Liesa together had made me finally realize where I had seen Liesa before: at "Club Fuck" with Shane a few years back. Liesa had been the femme fatale on stage with the great ass, being whipped. My friend George had warned me about her and called her Anna.

I could feel the conspiracy growing. I knew that shadow players were involved, people who didn't want me to know and were still nameless . . . for the time being.

If I had still been hooked on pain pills or morphine like everyone thought, I wouldn't have been able to handle the problems with all the different criminal groups. But the crystal methamphetamine kept me alert and thinking, instead of being depressed. I was getting stronger as I prepared mentally for whatever they would throw at me next.

Chapter 70

Cheyanne, Tony, and Jerry decided to move out. The late-night harassment and other strange incidents were more than they could take. They thought the eviction papers were real, and I was probably driving them nuts to boot.

"I'll move out when I'm damn ready," I said, "and not before."

One day I was sitting in my bedroom carving candles in front of the big-screen TV when a picture frame hanging on the wall above my waterbed suddenly exploded, sending shattered glass in all directions and scaring the living hell out of me.

The picture was in line with where I had been standing when I saw the first guy in the tree. I looked for a bullet hole in the wall, but only found what appeared to be a burn hole. I had never seen anything like it. It had created a perfect circle an inch in diameter and had penetrated at least a quarter-inch into the wall without catching fire, leaving only a minor smoke trail. I stared at it for a few minutes until I finally realized what I was looking at; it was some type of laser burn. I figured this was just another type of high-tech harassment.

I looked outside and couldn't see anybody, but that didn't mean they weren't out there. I sensed their presence. This seemed like something Eric would be into. His file said he was one of the most feared high-tech criminals in the United States, and this was most certainly high-tech.

~~

The next morning, I went into Hollywood and picked up a new set of night-vision goggles and a game finder. The game finder could pick up body heat up to a thousand yards, so it was perfect for scanning the treetops for hidden assholes with high-tech equipment, bent on driving me insane. Since the collapse of the Soviet Union, the black-market was flooded with high-tech Russian surveillance equipment.

That night, while Liesa was gone, I opened my bedroom door to get some fresh air. I hated being cooped up. Liesa's dog was sleeping next to my bed with her back to the balcony door, when she jumped up and began yelping wildly. I could smell burnt hair.

Once I got the dog to stop running around the bedroom and biting at herself, I checked her for marks. Rolling her onto her back, I found a small burn mark on her underbelly about the size of a dime. Burning the dog was a real chicken-shit act.

In retaliation, I went downstairs and cracked open the dining room balcony door just enough to stick the game finder out and scan the trees. It only took a few seconds to get a positive body heat reading. With the aid of my night-vision goggles, I was able to spot the techno-weenie. He was up in a tree level with my bedroom window; I could see the outline of his body as he moved around.

I retrieved my nighthawk crossbow, cocked it, and slid in a steel-tipped aluminum arrow. The crossbow had one hundred twenty pounds of pull, enough to take a single man out of a tree lethally. I took aim and let the arrow fly.

It hit the dead center of the tree.

There was a lot of rustling afterwards. When I scanned the tree again, there was no body heat. I shut the balcony door and hurried back upstairs to take apart the weapon. I wanted to hide it in my secret safe under the Jacuzzi.

Before I had gotten shot, my friend Wild Brian had built a secret safe under my Jacuzzi. It was virtually undetectable and had a sliding panel. The water had to be drained for it to open. It was foolproof.

I had put Dickwood's driver's license inside with my stash of meth. That way, if the Feds ever found it, I could say it must have belonged to him when he lived in the house. I made sure I never left any fingerprints on the inside of the safe.

Around noon the next day, the doorbell rang, and I saw on the camera that it was a guy from Federal Express with a package under his arm. I had Matt answer the door locked and loaded. I was very hesitant about taking the package. Once again, a piece of mail in my real name was coming to the house.

I examined the package carefully before Matt opened it. There was no return address. Inside, without an accompanying letter, was the steel-tipped arrow I had shot last night at the guy in the tree. They had mailed it back to me as an act of intimidation.

Instead of being scared, I was pissed.

~~

Mr. K came over to discuss some measures to stop the harassment and to improve the security around the outside of my house. We walked around the back yard, examining the angles of the trees and looking for clues. I found plenty once I was actually able to get up and walk around.

We found cigarette butts, chewing gum wrappers, and other items left in the bushes by someone who was spying on me from within my own back yard, only a few feet from the house. That was too damn close.

"This is fucked up," said Mr. K. "I want to rig your back yard with various booby traps to see what we can catch, or at least seriously injure. I know of a company that sells paramilitary supplies in Norcross, Georgia. We just need a credit card."

I called Matt into the room and said, "Normally I wouldn't do this, but I'm at war, so I want you to place an order for me using your skills. I want it delivered next day."

Matt placed the order with Aztec International, ordering electronic alarms, booby traps, NATO trip flares, perimeter alarms, bird control cartridges, and exploding targets.

"Get some sleep tonight," Mr. K said. "I'll stand watch."

~~

The next day, when the military supplies arrived, Mr. K spent half a day planting various booby traps to help eliminate any possible intruders after the sun went down.

Meanwhile, I rigged heavy-duty rat traps with exploding targets to serve as perimeter awareness devices. The rat trap was cocked and the exploding target was set to be struck by the powerful spring jaw of the trap when someone tripped over a thin wire strung across the path. An exploding target was about the size of a pack of cigarettes and contained a highly explosive, percussion-activated chemical. It sounded like a stick of dynamite when it went off. To make the exploding targets more lethal, I dipped them in wood glue and rolled them in brass BB's.

I got some shotgun shells called birdcalls that shot M-80 firecrackers about a hundred meters and then exploded like small hand grenades. It would be perfect for clearing any intruders out of the bushes in the back yard. I was ready to fight a full-on war.

While Mr. K was working on the back yard, my neighbor to the left rang the doorbell.

"What can I do for you?" I asked.

"Was that one of your friends climbing the fence last night? They trampled my wife's rose garden."

I laughed and replied, "It wasn't me; I'm hardly in any condition to be climbing fences and swinging like Tarzan." I laughed again. "I think it's the guy I rented the house from, trying to get me to move. I'm not really sure. But it's hard to get a restful night's sleep."

"I'm going to call the police next time I see someone climbing the fence," my neighbor replied.

"Please do."

He started to walk away, then stopped and turned. "By the way, some guy in a black jogging suit stole your trash the other day."

I shrugged. "Let them steal it. Hope they find something of value." We both laughed.

By this time, my neighbors had a good idea who I was, so we had an understanding: Don't fuck with me.

I never threw anything in the trash anyway, for just this reason, so I decided to set some traps for my garbage diggers. I took a stack of papers from the candle shop and ripped them into shreds until I had enough to fill a black plastic trash bag. Once the bag was completely filled, I emptied my cat's litter box into the bag, scooped in a couple of pounds of dog shit from the back yard, and topped it off by pissing all over everything, making sure it was well soaked. I sealed the bag and set it out for someone to steal. Being that it was ripped-up paper, they would feel compelled to see what I was bothering to rip up. Even wearing rubber gloves and a mask, I would hate to have that job. It was my way of giving them the middle finger without actual confrontation.

~~

My gardener Carlos pointed out that someone had cut the bushes back in several places so they could see through the fence into the back yard. There were climbing marks on the tree right outside my bedroom window, and the screen to my window was gone. The tree branches around my bedroom window had also been cut back.

Then Tim the pool man notified me that someone had been fooling around with the wires to the pool lights and had shorted them out. Without the pool lights, the back yard was extremely dark at night. So I installed huge floodlights on the roof, lighting up the back yard with a couple million candle watts. The floodlights ran off of car batteries so they couldn't be shut off.

I felt like Charlton Heston in The Omega Man, locked in my bedroom trying to fight off creatures of the night. But in my case, I wasn't afraid of the dead; I was more worried about the living.

Liesa didn't seemed to be involved with the people creeping around at night. I had heard her on the phone many times complaining to her friends about all the weird things going on after dark around the mansion.

~~

My neighbors on the right side had small children, and I was used to hearing and seeing the kids out back playing baseball and basketball. When I realized it was the beginning of summer and I hadn't heard a peep, I thought that was odd, so I took a look over the fence.

All the kids' toys were piled up on the side of the house and looked like they hadn't been moved in a while. The last time I had spoken with my neighbors was right after the earthquake, six months ago.

I sent Mr. K over to ring the doorbell a few times, but no one answered.

"I think I heard movement within the house," Mr. K said, "but all the drapes were closed, so I can't say for sure. Something wasn't right." I thought that was really strange, so I turned one of my outside cameras to monitor the front of their house, put a fresh tape into my time-elapse VCR, hit <u>record</u>, and took an eighteen-hour nap.

When I woke and played the tape, I saw strange cars, trucks, and vans coming and going all day. None of the people I saw were my neighbors.

I spoke with the elderly couple who lived across the street, trying to find out whether they had been approached or knew anything about the surveillance. I made a point to take my trash out at the same time they did and struck up a conversation. I invited them into my candle shop for a look around.

"The original house that sat on this lot was a lot smaller," the man said. "They came in with a crew and knocked it down, only keeping one original wall."

"Why would they keep one wall?"

"That way the taxes would be the same when they built this huge mansion on top of it."

"Didn't you think that was kind of weird?"

"We knew right away that the people who built this house were criminals -- Russian mafia, we suspected -- but they had business fronts."

"What kind of business?"

"Real estate, or mortgage broker."

I gathered that the Russian women had to be the ones bouncing the house back and forth -- more Russian criminals. They were flooding Los Angeles by the boatload.

"The Russian couple had all kinds of friends around the neighborhood who also bought houses at the same time," said the elderly man.

"Do you know what houses belong to their friends?"

"No, but they were close enough for them to walk back and forth to."

~~

After talking with my neighbors, I asked Cain, "Can you give me a printout of all the mortgages on the houses in my neighborhood?"

"Not a problem."

I couldn't believe my eyes when the report came back. Twenty-five houses within a couple of blocks were going through the same type of fake paperwork, smelling of the same scam. I appeared to be surrounded by these people. No wonder they were able to come and go through the neighborhood with great ease.

Cain was also able to get into Liesa's voice mail by using a recording I had made of her punching in the tones. He ran the recording through a device called a "telephone number decoder," which decoded the tones and told us what numbers were dialed.

The magic numbers were 3742.

I should have guessed. That spelled out "Eric" on a touch-tone phone.

Chapter 71

One evening, Silva, Robin, Liesa, and I were sitting on my balcony overlooking the Valley. It was very peaceful until someone fell out of a palm tree near one end of the swimming pool.

Thud.

We all froze for a second, and no one said a single word. Then I started to laugh. The man who had fallen out of the tree was dressed in black and wearing black military-style boots. He was stunned for a brief moment and then jumped into the nearest bush, hoping none of us had seen him.

Fat chance of that.

Silva got all excited and said, "Who in the hell is that?"

I replied with a smart-ass tone, "It's probably Eric playing I Spy." Liesa gave me a dirty look, then hit me in the arm like a tomboy.

I knew it wasn't Eric. This guy was much bigger, and I didn't think Eric, with his fake leg, could move after falling ten feet to a hard brick surface.

"I'm going to catch him," said Silva. "He's still hiding in the bushes."

"Go for it," I said. "I'll cover you from up here."

Being very athletic, an ex-pro-racket-ball player, Silva ran out the back door to the pool area and stopped at the end of the pool. He pointed to one of the last bushes.

I nodded. "That's the one."

Silva was attempting to pull back some of the branches when two arms cloaked in black reached out from the thick bush. Silva's eyes widened as the two arms pulled him into the bush. He was there one second, and then he was gone. It happened so fast, I barely saw it happen.

I couldn't start shooting, so I took off downstairs as fast as I could travel. It seemed like it took me forever to get where I wanted to go without tripping down the two flights of stairs. My heart was racing.

Just as I got the downstairs door open, Silva jumped out of the bushes, fighting someone. Finally breaking free, Silva took off for the house, blocking my shot at the bushes. As soon as he ran past, I made sure the silencer was screwed on tightly, and then I unloaded a clip of eighteen .223 rounds into the bushes. I tried to keep my bullets low to the ground. It sounded like a sewing machine as the bullets passed through the silencer, followed by puffs of smoke.

Silva was all right, just scratched up and missing a shoe. Once I got back in the house, I hit the outside floodlights, flooding the back yard with a couple million candle watts.

Not wanting to get my throat slit, I sent the dog into the bushes. She came out empty-handed, without even a bark, so we got braver and went in for a closer look. No one was there. They had gotten away, and there was no blood trail, making me a piss-poor shot.

The next day, I called my gardener Carlos and instructed him to cut down all the bushes and thick greenery to the fence so there would be no more hiding places for late-night intruders. As Carlos went to work, he stopped and called me over to look at the ground trails under the bush, where people had been crawling back and forth, creating a permanent path.

"Has the dog been playing out here?" he asked.

"Never," I replied. "The dog only comes outside for a few seconds, does her thing, and comes right back in. She never gets near the bushes."

We followed the path to the end of the back yard, where we found a small hole that had been dug under the back fence. It was well hidden, and we had to look hard to find it. It led to the alley behind my house, allowing easy access to my back yard.

Silva's shoe was nowhere to be found.

"I couldn't tell what the person looked like," Silva said. "It was too damn dark, and the guy was wearing a mask over his face. Besides, I was fighting for my life."

Now I knew why the perimeter traps Mr. K had set up hadn't caught anybody: they were on the outside of the bushes. We didn't think anybody would be crazy enough to be crawling on their hands and knees.

"You would have to be totally insane or completely whacked out of your mind on meth to be hiding in trees and crawling through spider-infested bushes," Mr. K said. "The cops don't operate in this manner, and as weird as federal agents are, I don't think they're that weird, either."

"You're right. What would be the point?"

Mr. K continued, "This has to be occult people on meth or people trying to get you out of the house by mind fucking with you." I was at a loss.

Chapter 72

It was Sunday, June 13th, Liesa's birthday and the last day the world would view O.J. Simpson as a respectable man. His drug abuse was now public, I wasn't surprised.

Liesa informed me that her girlfriends were taking her to the Troubadour in West Hollywood on Santa Monica Boulevard to celebrate. I had played the club a dozen times when I was in Hap Hazzard, back in the late '80's. Liesa didn't invite me, but I heard through her telephone calls that she had a secret meeting with Eric, her prince of darkness.

I was still connected with the Troubadour; the head bouncer was a former employee of mine. I contacted him and requested that Mr. K be added to the security force for the evening because I needed surveillance regarding a personal matter. I couldn't give him too much information, because he was a friend of Eric's; we had a lot of mutual friends in the club scene. He said it wouldn't be a problem; he didn't even ask any questions.

Mr. K arrived an hour before the doors opened and was handed a flashlight and a set of keys that accessed all areas of the club. Mr. K walked up the dimly lit hallway. No one was around, so he took out his surveillance equipment and set it up in a prime location. From the location he picked, he could see everyone as they entered the club. He was going to be taking surveillance pictures of the shadow players.

Right on cue, Liesa and her girlfriends entered the club. Moments later, Eric appeared, sporting his Italian brown suit and looking richer than everyone else. He wasn't alone by any means. He was with Christ, the leader of the Valley's most sinister motorcycle gang, Heaven's Devils.

Mr. K, standing on the balcony overlooking the crowd, called me on his cellular phone to tell me about Eric and Christ.

I was shocked. "Is Liesa there?"

"Yes . . . She's talking with them."

"I want you to go up to Liesa and just let her know you're there. Then walk away without explaining. That should rattle her cage."

Mr. K did as I ordered. Liesa almost died when she saw Mr. K standing there right in front of her while she was talking to Eric. At first she didn't know what to say, but she remained rather smooth when she noticed Mr. K's flashlight and security badge.

"When did you start working here?" she asked.

"Just doing a little moonlighting," he replied. "There hasn't been much work for me lately." He said it in front of Eric, remaining polite.

Later, Mr. K told me, "The bikers were staring me down, but Eric would never make eye contact."

Christ knew damn well who Mr. K was; his reputation was well-known in the underground world. Mr. K had worked for Christ in the past, so respect was given at the moment.

As soon as Liesa got the chance, she separated herself from Eric. Eric was pissed: all dressed up and no one to go home with. From the file I had read on Eric, he seemed clever, smart, and an expert in the game, but he was very predictable. I could have taken him out of the game with one phone call at that moment. I could have just called the FBI from a payphone and gave his location.

I thought about the situation and found it really odd. Liesa had said many times that Eric didn't use meth, so why was he hanging out with Christ -- the biggest meth dealer in the Valley, and my only competition? That really disturbed me.

I wondered why Eric had been at my house, and whether Christ knew that Eric was a fugitive FBI informant. What was the connection?

While still at the club, Mr. K called me back and asked, "What do you want me to do? I'm a licensed bounty Hunter, and I could arrest Eric the minute he walks out of the club. We could split the reward, it's a 150,000 big ones. Or I could follow him to where his computer systems are located. Or I can just drop him at his car . . . end game."

"Don't hurt him," I replied. "Just follow him until he goes home. I want to know where he's staying so I can keep tabs on him if I need to find him again."

Up to this point, I couldn't prove that Eric had done anything to me other than wanting to see his old girlfriend. I wasn't going to hurt anyone over a woman, not even for Liesa. I still felt some guilt, until now.

I started wondering how hard the FBI could be looking for Eric, if I had found his location twice in the last three months, even though I was still in a wheelchair. The FBI had every method of tracking known to man at their service, and yet they couldn't catch a one-legged man whose flamboyant attitude made him stand out in a crowd like a neon sign. Eric was well known, and I was sure that even his criminal friends would turn him in. From what I had seen, there was no honor among hackers and bikers -- or anyone else in Hollywood, for that matter.

~~

Liesa came home late, claiming that she had gone to the after-party. I found out later that she had fucked Johnny, the singer of the Wild.

"Did you send Mr. K to spy on me?" Liesa asked.

I snapped back, "You wish."

We argued for a few minutes and went our separate ways. I went outside while she sat by the fireplace. Liesa fell asleep around daybreak, but I stayed up to talk with Mr. K over breakfast around eight o'clock.

"Liesa left first, and then Eric a few minutes later," Mr. K told me. "But I couldn't follow him. I had three bikers follow me to my Jeep."

"What happened?"

"When they got within five feet, I turned around and pepper-sprayed all three of them, then pistol-whipped them to the ground. By the time I got in my Jeep, I'd lost Eric. Sorry."

"Don't worry about it."

"However, Eric paid for drinks using a credit card," Mr. K added. "He's using the name Nicholas Probes, and his limit is almost up, so he'll have to change his identity real soon."

I looked at the photos Mr. K had taken. Now I had seen the shadow players. I thanked Mr. K and handed him an envelope with cash and meth.

I remembered seeing a couple of different business cards of Eric's in Liesa's boxes downstairs, so I went to take a look while she was sleeping. I found two cards, one for the *Church* and the other for *Midnight Mass*. Both were rave clubs, which meant they ran from two in the morning until dusk.

"Those are two of the sleaziest clubs in Hollywood," Mr. K said. "There's more meth running through those clubs than the L.A. sewer system."

Holding up one of the business cards, I replied, "This one says Eric was running the club. Hmm . . . An FBI informant running a sleazy rave club, where first-time users are being introduced to crystal meth?" That made about as much sense as anything else I saw in Hollywood.

I took a closer look at the Midnight Mass card and got the creeps. I showed it to Mr. K, and we both shook our heads.

The logo was a woman hanging on a cross, crucified like Jesus Christ. The woman on the cross was Liesa, hanging naked on the steel cross, with blood dripping from her wrists and ankles and a crown of thorns around her head. We both agreed it was Liesa. I kept thinking, What kind of sick and twisted relationship do Eric and Liesa have?

Now that I had an idea who some of my enemies were, I decided to plant a spy in the biker camp to find out more information.

Chapter 73

The next day I slept late into the afternoon. When I awoke, Liesa had cleaned the bathroom, the bedroom, and had dinner ready and waiting.

After dinner, Liesa asked, "Do you mind if I borrow your car to go to Robin's to paint for a couple hours? She's teaching me new methods."

I thought, New methods in what -- clit-licking? But I said, "I don't care. Thanks for making dinner. It was great."

Liesa gave me a fake kiss on the cheek and bounced out the door like Little Red Riding Hood off to see the big bad wolf. I noticed she wasn't wearing panties, when I squeezed her butt.

As soon as Liesa was gone, I checked the phone tap. A few hours earlier, Robin had called and they had a three-way with Eric on the other line. Robin had two separate phone lines in her house, one for private use and the other for her 976 sex line, which she worked on her nights off while doing meth and playing with herself.

Robin was so tweaked on the recording that she babbled on for five minutes about absolute nonsense. I was ready to hit fast forward when she said, "I almost forgot . . . I have Eric on the other line. He wants to talk to you, but he didn't want to dial direct in case Brent answered the phone."

So Robin played middleman between Liesa and Eric. She had the two phones so close together my recording equipment was able to pick up Eric's voice almost perfectly. I could hear the anger in his voice towards Liesa. He demanded to see her tonight, but she didn't think it was a good idea because it was already getting late.

"Meet me around the corner," Eric demanded.

Liesa responded angrily, "No way."

"What the hell is going on over there?"

"Absolutely nothing -- nothing at all."

But after some more whining and begging, he finally convinced Liesa to let him meet her at Robin's house. Apparently Eric had already been there; he didn't ask for directions or an address.

"Whatever you do, if you have to call from his phone, call collect so my number doesn't show up on his phone bill. Here's my new pager number. Don't give it to anyone."

After listening to the tape recording, I lost my cool and snapped. I called Robin's house in a fury, but Liesa was still en route, so I gave Robin a message in a moment of heated anger.

"Tell that two-timing, ass-fucking, lying whore not to bother coming back," I yelled. "I know she's meeting Eric at your house." Before Robin could pretend innocence, I yelled, "Don't insult me by saying I don't know what you're talking about."

There was dead silence.

"I'll send someone to get my car," I yelled, and slammed the phone down so hard it bounced off the hook.

I was tired of playing this sick and twisted game. It was getting harder and harder to suppress my feelings toward Liesa. Most of the time, I enjoyed her company and found her very attractive. I wanted to love her with all my heart, but I had to keep reminding myself it wasn't real. The phone tap told the truth, since the words from her ruby-red lips didn't.

Since Eric had ruined my evening, I thought one turn deserved another. I paged Eric twice using the FBI headquarters phone number on his new pager, followed by Robin's home phone number. I figured that would shake him up. But in case I was wrong, and since I was really pissed, I had Krazy Kurtis watch Robin's house the rest of the night.

Eric didn't show up. If he had, I would have come to visit him.

Chapter 74

After screaming at Robin on the phone, I needed to relax. The way the veins in my head were throbbing, I thought my head might explode like in the movie Scanners.

The water in the Jacuzzi was very relaxing, and the ice-cold beer washed the flavor of the smoke down my throat and into my lungs. Waves of pleasure came over me instantly as I tried to break the spell Liesa had on me. Trying hard not to think about her, I finally relaxed and closed my eyes.

However, asking for peace and quiet was out of the question. Hearing some strange noises coming from inside my safe room, I shut the water jets off, creating silence.

The dog came running in and started growling from the bedroom. The only light in the bathroom was a lit candle, but there was some light shining through the ceiling fan directly above the Jacuzzi.

For a brief second, I thought I could see some type of movement in the attic.

It took me a minute to get the towel wrapped around my waist and my wet hair out of my eyes. Then I wheeled myself into the safe room very cautiously. I had been ambushed there before.

As I entered the safe room, I saw the hatch to the attic closing very slowly.

Directly under the hatch, Liesa had set up some bookshelves, and the intruder had used them as a makeshift ladder to climb down from the attic. He had left two footprints in the dust.

Very calmly, I screwed the silencer on my Colt .380, cocked it, and unloaded ten hollow-point bullets across the wafer-thin ceiling, chasing footsteps. Expecting to hear the sound of a body dropping, I became rather disappointed when ice-cold water started pouring through one of the bullet holes in the ceiling.

There was no way I could climb up into the attic to pursue the intruder. I popped a fresh clip in my pistol and reached for my cellular phone.

"Get over here, now."

"I'll be right there."

~~

"I'll be dammed," said Mr. K from inside the attic. "Someone was up here. I thought maybe you were losing it."

I just shook my head.

328

"Here are a couple of files that someone dropped when you opened fire."

"Toss them down to me."

The files they had been stealing contained information about Eric and the fake paperwork regarding my house.

Mr. K laughed. "You have ten holes in the roof of your house, with moonlight shining through them. That's going to cost someone a pretty penny to fix."

"Fuck it. It's not my house. So how did they get in?"

"I'll have to take a look around. This attic must be over four thousand square feet."

I passed a few items up to Mr. K, including the night-vision goggles, the sawed-off shotgun, and a pack of chewing gum.

"No thanks," he said. "I hate gum."

"Chew the gum," I replied, "and stick it in the bullet holes in case it rains."

We both laughed.

Mr. K looked around for ten minutes and couldn't find anything until he unplugged the exhaust fan to the attic.

"You have an exhaust fan toward the front of the house. I pushed on it, and it came right off. Someone stood on the roof and unscrewed it and managed to squeeze into the attic. They would have to be rather skinny to fit through it, but it's possible for someone in good shape."

"No shit."

"After sunrise, I'll climb up on the roof and secure the fan."

"Before you climb down from there," I said, "tell me if you can look into my bathroom from the ceiling fan above."

Sure enough, all the insulation had been removed from around the fan, and he was able to look directly down on anyone caught off-guard and relaxing. He could see my entire bathroom and bedroom from the attic.

"This is some serious shit," he said. "Someone was watching you while their partner was going through your safe."

I wasn't worried about anything being incriminating; there was nothing on paper that could prove any illegal activities. Through all my years of being in business, I had never once written down anything regarding illegal transactions. The intruders only seemed interested in the house files and the information I had gathered on Eric; they hadn't touched the couple thousand dollars I had sitting on top of the files. That wasn't part of their mission.

But what was their mission?

~~

The air conditioning repairman came later that afternoon, and I sent him up into the attic. Pretending not to know what had happened, I said, "Just fix it," and left it at that.

"It looks like someone stepped on the pipe and broke it in half," he told me after taking a look.

I replied with a smart-ass remark. "Yeah, I ran over it with my wheelchair."

The repairman laughed. "You must have some rather large rats running around to break a pipe like that. And by the way, there are several holes in the roof."

"I know," I said.

~~

Later that afternoon, I got my first report from my spy in the biker's camp. My worst fears about these guys were true. The bikers had a bunch of junior computer hackers hooked on meth working for them like mindless robots.

None of the bikers I had encountered in the past had gotten past eighth grade. A group of cyber-bikers using high technology was something that could only happen in California.

My spy told me, "The bikers have dozens of strippers that work for them as spies."

"Doing what?"

"Gathering information on businessmen they want to blackmail. And you're going to love this: Liesa used to be roommates with Christ's ex-girlfriend, Gold."

I remembered seeing a birthday card among Liesa's things from Gold, signed Love forever.

"Is this the group who's fucking with me?" I asked.

"Maybe. Your name is known to them, and they don't talk about you out in the open. Christ is just as paranoid as you; he's got his dirty hands into everything from drugs, guns, and surveillance equipment to computer fraud and blackmail."

I had no respect for a blackmailer; that was low-down, dirty, sneaky work.

"I did hear someone say something about fucking with someone in Sherman Oaks because of a girlfriend," said my spy. "I think they meant you, but I'm not sure. I'll keep my ears open."

"Have you seen Eric there?"

"No, but I'm not there every day."

These bikers had to be the group Shane was a scout for; I sure could have used him right about now. His services were no longer available. He had finally been put down like a rabid dog.

Chapter 75

After a few days had passed, I piled Liesa's belongings by the front door so that when she showed up, she could just take her stuff and leave. I didn't want to get sucked back into her web of lies and deception.

I didn't mind keeping the dog; she was good company and served as a good second set of high-tech ears to alert me to any funny business. Usually, I left the downstairs doors open to the back yard so the dog could come and go while a camera monitored the open door and I watched from upstairs. The dog always stood at attention when someone moved in the back yard.

The next day, they took the dog out of the game.

The dog started barking in the back yard, so I looked over the balcony to see what was going on. Unable to detect anything, I decided to go down and take a look. As I turned and started to leave my bedroom, I glanced in my dresser mirror and caught someone in the reflection throwing something into the back yard.

A couple of months earlier, the surrounding houses had had watch dogs that would bark whenever one of the intruders started moving around the neighborhood after dark. The barking always gave them away. But the dogs were silent now. A newspaper article blamed "some punk kids" for poisoning all of the neighborhood dogs, but I knew the culprits weren't kids.

By the time I got to the dog, she had already swallowed the object that had been thrown over the fence.

"I saw that, you fucking bastards," I yelled.

They heard me but kept silent. If I'd had two good legs, I would have climbed the fence like it wasn't even an obstacle, but that wasn't possible, and they knew it.

I had been saving one pepper spray grenade since the riots. Pulling the pin, I tossed it over the fence and yelled, "Eat this."

Once I got the dog into the house, she started losing her bodily functions, making a mess all over the kitchen floor. Matt and I took her to the animal hospital in Sherman Oaks.

"Someone gave the dog a rather large dose of crystal methamphetamine in a piece of meat," the veterinarian told us. "It probably would have given her a heart attack."

At least I knew my enemies were involved in meth, as I had suspected. But surely Liesa wouldn't be involved with killing her own dog.

Before setting the trash out that night, I checked the bags to make sure they didn't include anything I didn't want anybody to find. I always dumped the trash out on the floor of the candle shop by the drain so I could hose the floor down afterwards. Checking the trash was a nasty job, but not as nasty as living in a tiny cell with another man. So I did it, knowing it was just another part of the game. I couldn't start slacking at this point.

Good thing I never skipped this chore. This time I found some very disturbing items. First, I found a note on a small piece of crumpled-up paper. It had come from the waste basket in my bathroom, and it was in Liesa's handwriting. It read, "Me and my boyfriend gave my dog meth today, and she seemed to like it. But she lost control of her bodily functions."

I knew we hadn't given the dog any meth, and this note had been written days before the dog was poisoned, so who was she talking about? I certainly didn't want that note in the trash for anyone to find.

Digging deeper into the trash, I found receipts for items Matt the Ratt had bought using someone's stolen credit information. If law enforcement found that in the trash, they could obtain a warrant to search the house for those items, and anything else they found would be extra points in their book. The items included a wireless camera built into a clock and a second one built into a picture frame of a Salvador Dali painting, the L'Apotheose D'Homer, which I had hanging in my bedroom already.

Putting the trash back in the bag, I scooped in more dog shit and soaked everything in piss, making anyone else's job harder out of spite. All the precautions I took were necessary, since I was surrounded by traitors and fucking idiots.

Chapter 76

As the weirdness continued, a lot of my so-called friends who hung out on a daily basis for the free party, started to back away because they saw strange cars following them after they left my house. The possible biker danger also thinned the herd.

I told my friends, "Eric might have had some biker friends, but if he hasn't noticed, whites are the minority." The Mexicans ran Los Angeles, and I was with them.

"You have the full support from the hood," Rudy said. "If push comes to shove and they get nasty, they'll wish they never messed with you. I got your back covered, Bubba."

"Thanks. I knew I could count on you."

~~

While Liesa was staying at Robin's house, Brittney stopped by for an unexpected visit. It was the first time I had seen her since she had walked out of my life seven months ago.

When Brittney and I awoke in the morning, I found something disturbing and quite menacing. I had given Liesa a cute, cuddly teddy bear for her birthday. I had looked at it the night before while it was sitting on the headboard of my bed. But when we woke up in the afternoon, the teddy bear was lying between us with its throat slashed and the stuffing pulled out, as if it had been given a Colombian necktie.

It was an effective stunt; it really shook me up. The perp could have killed me in my sleep, but had chosen not to, leaving only an intimidating message.

Mr. K examined the locks on my balcony door. "They've been picked several times," he said, pointing out the whip marks made by an electric lock-pick gun. "This shit has to stop," he declared. "I can't be here all the time, and you have to be able to get some sleep."

He took an extension cord and cut off one end, peeling back the rubber until the wires were bare. Downstairs, he took the screen off the window to the garage and brought it up to my bedroom. He laid it down in front of the door to my balcony and grounded it to the brass doorknob. A thin rug was laid over it to hide the new doormat. Once he was finished, he plugged it into the wall.

Mr. K smiled. "If someone stands on the screen and touches the doorknob, it will make the connection."

That actually made me smile, too.

When we were finished with the electric door trap, I sat down in my favorite chair to watch television. Then I noticed something interesting on the cover of Liesa's notebook: the impression of an 800 number. She had probably written the number down and then had torn the top page off. I took a lead pencil and brushed over the impression until the number became visible enough to read.

I called the 800 number and was connected to the Los Angeles Train Station Booking Office and Information Center. I thought about it for a minute. If I was Eric, I would know that traveling through the airport was a big risk because of the prosthetic leg. The FBI might have posted his pictures; Eric would never make it through, no matter how clever his disguise. His fake leg would always set off the metal detector.

But if Eric traveled by train, he wouldn't have to go through a metal detector, and he could bring his gun. I knew that Eric had been traveling back and forth between Texas, New York, and Los Angeles, but for what, I knew not.

I wondered how long Eric could stay on the run. Sooner or later, he would need a new prosthetic leg. They only lasted a few years and needed constant repair or complete replacement, which cost $6,000 for the basic model.

I was told that the FBI had sent out fliers to all the prosthesis labs in the country to watch out for Eric. As I thought about it, I realized I was in the same boat if I continued to stay in the business. I could never move about freely, and my stealth trips through the airport were a thing of the past.

~~

Mr. K went home to get some rest, so I shut and locked the front door. It was just me and the pets in this huge mansion. I could hear the echoes of my cane tapping on the floor as I moved through the huge hallways. The one-time party house was now empty.

I really hated being alone; I was starting to feel isolated. But I was doing my best not to let them get to me.

I reset all the motion detectors and set the security system. I made sure all the cameras were operating and punched in the security codes. In reality, I knew it was a false sense of security; any high-tech criminal could get past it. So I took other means of protection. I put four pillows in my bed and covered them with the sheet so it would look like I was asleep.

It had been five days since I had taken off my fake leg, and the sores were open, raw, and oozing. The pain so overwhelming that even with heavy amounts of crystal meth, it was more than I could stand. I didn't want to take it off out of fear of being caught legless, but I had to get some rest. I turned on the television to cover any snoring I didn't want to broadcast to my enemies if they were somehow still listening.

As I took off my prosthetic leg and set it down on the floor, a huge black widow spider came crawling boldly out of the socket. It must have crawled in when I took my leg off in the candle shop. I had left it on the cement floor for about an hour. That had been five days ago.

I hated spiders, and the thought that it had been with me for at least five days chilled me in a new way. If I hadn't been wearing all the socks, it could have bitten me several times before I could have gotten the leg off.

After killing the poisonous spider, I left my fake leg lying next to the bed to make it look even more convincing. Then I pulled the couch away from the wall. The back of the couch had been cut out so I could hide in it and pull it back against the wall tightly.

Lying on the floor inside the couch, with a pistol in each hand, I almost fell asleep. With one eye closed and the other on the way, I heard a thud on the balcony right outside my bedroom door. Cocking both pistols, I lay still and hoped I would be able to take a live prisoner to question -- if not a dead one as a trophy.

I actually forgot about the electric mat until the intruder touched the door handle, making a full connection. I heard what sounded like a small yelp of pain, before the intruder was knocked to the ground with another loud thud. The dog started barking at the balcony door.

While keeping an eye and a pistol on the balcony door, I climbed out from behind the couch and crawled to the edge of my bed to retrieve my fake leg. The swelling in my stump, made putting it back on almost unbearable. It took some time to put on twenty-four pairs of socks over my stump before sliding it into the socket.

Just as I got out on the balcony, I saw a shadow dive into one of the neighbors' bushes on the other side of the fence. He had been trying to clear the next yard, but when he heard the balcony door open, he tried to take cover.

I reached back into my bedroom and retrieved my night-vision goggles. I could barely see what appeared to be a man crouching behind the bush. To make sure, I switched modes to infrared, which revealed the intruder's body heat. I could always sense the people, but I always back up it up with high tech equipment.

I stepped back a few feet and grabbed my blow dart out of the martial arts display cabinet, along with a cartridge that held thirty-two stainless steel darts. I had dipped the darts in rotten onion juice, an old Indian recipe for poison.

I looked around, then pulled up the blow dart and started shooting darts into the bush as fast as I could blow them out, turning the cartridge into a Gatling gun. The intruder was crouched in a fetal position, and the first darts stuck in his lower back around his kidneys. But he still didn't move. So I patterned the shadow with darts until I hit him right behind the ear and several places on the neck and face.

The last dart I blew stuck close to his eye. At that point he got up and ran out into the open across the neighbor's back yard with over two dozen darts stuck in his back like the spines of a porcupine. Laughing, I watched him scale the neighbor's fence to the next yard.

I figured that was the last intrusion for the evening, so I climbed back behind the couch and slept until Mr. K woke me around two in the afternoon.

We went downstairs to make some lunch as I told him how well his doormat had worked. When we got to the dining room, I noticed one of my large Egyptian cat candles sitting in the middle of the dining table.

I thought that was odd; I hadn't put it there. Taking a closer look, I saw that it had thirteen blow darts stuck in its neck. They were the darts I had stuck in the back of the intruder the night before.

They had drawn a pentagram in the dust on the table, placing the cat in the center. Under the pentagram were the letters F-U.

All the doors were still locked, and nothing had been forced open.

Chapter 77

Ten days passed before Liesa showed up. I had known she would come dressed to kill, in a mini shirt, high heels and black stockings, trying to work her sex magick to get me to fall back under her spell.

"I don't know what's gotten into you," she said. "I wasn't going to meet with Eric. You have to stop being so paranoid."

I looked at her and thought, <u>What a lying whore.</u> She spoke with all the confidence in the world. It pissed me off that she was trying to make me think I was crazy.

"If I do talk with Eric," she said, "it's because he used to be someone I cared about, and I just want to help."

"Oh, really."

"Eric doesn't even know we're living together. He wouldn't care, anyway. I told him I was dating a female, he's cool with that."

"That's a bunch of bullshit," I replied. "Who do you think you're fooling?" Taking a deep breath, I pointed my cane at Liesa's face and yelled, "Listen up, if you know what's good for you. Eric has been fucking with my phone line ever since the day you moved in, and if he doesn't stop, I will make him stop. I'm not afraid of Eric or Christ."

"What are you talking about?"

"You tell him to back the fuck off, or I'm coming after him with all the fury that Hell can bestow."

"You're just being paranoid."

"My other business partners are also complaining about the same weird shit going on. They're ready to skin Eric alive, and they're starting to ask about you, too."

Liesa looked worried for a brief moment, but she kept her cocky grin.

I continued, "My partners, who you have never met, think Eric is nothing but a low-life rat and that death would be almost too good for him. As for me, I respect Eric's skills as a hacker . . . but I also think he's a fucking dick weasel for working for the FBI."

Liesa gave me a surprised look.

"Yes, I know all about him."

Her eyes widened.

"I don't hate Eric, and I don't want to fight with him. Don't play the both of us, because you're going to get someone killed -- and it might even be yourself. If you're playing some type of game, let me tell you: if anything happens to me, I can guarantee that anyone even suspected of being involved will be taken out like yesterday's trash -- and in the most unpleasant way

337

possible."

"If you think you can come in here and shake your ass and I'm going to fall right in line, you've got another think coming, Anna Liesa -- or Anna, or Liesa Lynn, or whoever the hell you are."

"You need to lay off the meth," Liesa responded. "I wasn't going to meet with Eric, and nothing weird is going on." She rolled her eyes at me, like I was nuts.

That made me so furious, I exposed one of my secrets.

"Wait right here," I ordered in a mild yell. "I'll be back in a minute. Don't move a single muscle!"

I rushed downstairs, grabbed the recording I had of Liesa speaking with Eric, and came back to my bedroom. Putting the tape in the player, I stared at Liesa with all the fury of hell in my eyes!

Liesa asked, "What is that?"

I just let the tape play.

Nothing is more satisfying than to catch someone in a lie and make them eat their own words -- or should I say, cram them back down their throat. This was the second girlfriend I had caught on tape lying. I could only imagine what I would have heard in previous relationships.

Liesa quickly realized it was a recording of telephone calls, and she knew she was busted. She started crying, and it was a damn good act.

"I'm so sorry, I really am," she said with tears in her eyes. "I'll do anything to get back with you and regain your trust."

Since she had pulled this shit while I was in a wheelchair, that would never happen. I wasn't born yesterday and I wasn't going to die today.

"Why are you with me if you're still in Love with Eric? Go be with him. I don't need this shit."

"You don't understand. If I don't do what he asks, it could be dangerous."

I laughed loudly. "So you're telling me that you're afraid of him? And not me?" I laughed again.

"Yes. You don't know him like I know him."

I thought about that and replied, "If Eric has a problem with me, tell him he can talk to me anytime. But if he pulls any more shit, it will be his own undoing and the undoing of anyone who is helping him."

"Will you protect me?" she asked, looking scared.

"Yes."

Liesa had lied about so much, I wasn't sure what to believe. But the file I had read said Eric was the most dangerous tech criminal in the world. I had never turned my back on anyone being threatened, so I let her stay for a good night of meth-induced sex.

The second day after I let Liesa back into the house, the tape recorder on the phone line stopped working. Not that I thought Liesa would be stupid enough to talk over the phone line again . . . but I still wanted it in place, just in case.

I purchased two more new recorders, but they wouldn't work on my phone line either, so I smashed them in anger.

~~

Standing in an underground bunker in the desert, Cain said, "Eric is probably running a computer program nicknamed the 'tap-buster' through his S.A.S. computer system as it monitors your phone line."

"What will that do?" I asked.

"The computer program will modify line voltage, which will shut off any tape recorder and other type of voltage-activated listening device, making the phone line clear for Liesa to talk over."

That was okay. I had heard enough in the past to know what was going on.

~~

"Eric is about to score two million dollars," Liesa said to Robin, "but I don't want any part of it." They both laughed. "He's going to use his computer to take over the phone line to some bank and re-route a money transfer to another account, so he can withdraw it before anyone finds out. He's going to try to pin it on the Condor."

A joke was even made about blowing up the bank with dynamite to cover his tracks.

I knew that by doing this bank job, Eric would climb even higher on the FBI's most wanted list, once they figured out what had happened. He was probably planning to go somewhere afterward, since hanging out in Hollywood would no longer be an option. I didn't see how he was getting away with it now.

I noticed something else weird about my phone line. Phone calls to numbers in area codes 213, 310, or 818 would go through even if I didn't dial the area codes. That only proved my suspicions that a computer was monitoring my line, remembering the numbers dialed in the past and putting the calls through.

~~

The first week of July, Liesa said, "I'm leaving for the weekend to attend my brother's wedding in Sacramento." I wasn't invited. "My mother doesn't like guys with long hair."

That was a crock of shit. I didn't believe a word she spoke. She said something else that I found strange: she had to go back to Robin's to pack some clothes before leaving.

As far as I could remember, when we had gotten into a fight, she hadn't taken any of her belongings. She didn't come home for ten days. Everything she owned was still at my house, or so I thought.

A couple of hours after Liesa left for the weekend, I asked Matt to drive me by the strip club where Robin worked to make sure she was at work. When that was verified, we headed back out into the Valley.

Matt picked the lock to the side door of Robin's house and opened the garage door. I drove his truck in and closed the door quickly.

I had never been in Robin's house, but I remembered Liesa saying her bedroom was on the second floor. We went up the steps quietly. The bedroom wasn't too hard to find; Liesa's name was on the door in bold black letters. That was odd, I thought, since she had only stayed there a couple days.

When Matt unlocked her bedroom door with his hacker tools, I couldn't believe my eyes. There was an entire bedroom set and a closet full of expensive dresses -- all name-brand and completely unfamiliar to me.

Looking through her dresser for clues, I found a couple of knives that had been missing from my collection, and a large black dildo.

Out of the corner of my eye, I saw Matt stuff a pair of Liesa's panties down the front of his pants. If it had been any other girlfriend, I would have broken his fingers, but in this case I just looked the other way.

Looking around the bedroom, I noticed Liesa had thirty of my hand-painted candles decorating her bedroom, and more downstairs that had been burned in the living room. I couldn't believe that she had been able to smuggle all those out of my house without me seeing. She must have been taking them out to the car in her dance bag while I was sleeping.

"Liesa's had this place for quite a while," I said to Matt. "All this was here before I kicked her out." Matt agreed.

I wanted to remove everything that belonged to me, but I didn't want her to know I had been there, so I just took my knives.

On the way out, I took a final look around the garage. By pure luck, I found a couple of boxes that belonged to Liesa in the corner under some dirty clothes. Inside was an address book with her real parents' names and address, plus phone numbers of countless friends and contacts. When I had first met Liesa, she claimed to have been raised in Kentucky with horses, but this book said her parents lived in Pomona, which was only sixty miles east of Los Angeles.

I also found a few different identifications. One letter on each I.D. was the only change, but in the computer system, that made her a completely different person.

I didn't want her to know I had been there, so I took all the books to Kinko's and copied them, then put them back where I had found them. I also stopped at Ralph's Supermarket and bought a bottle of spearmint oil and rubbed it all over the black dildo. I soaked it in it for a few minutes. It wouldn't be noticeable until it got wet and hot. Sometimes I have to just be a real shit, it helps me with what's being thrown at me in my current mental and physical condition. I never said I was an angel.

~~

Sitting at home, I spent some time looking at all of Liesa's different identifications before sending them off to Cain so he could do a background check.

"None of the names are her real name," he confirmed later.

"What?" I couldn't believe it.

"I found a file on a girl who fits Liesa's description. It says that her parents put her in a mental institution at the age of sixteen. At seventeen, the same girl was dancing at the Pussy Kat strip club in biker territory, using a fake name so she could dance underage.

"I'm finding bits and pieces about Liesa under all the different names, so it's hard to put it all together. From what I can tell, she's still married to a guy named Patrick. She's got to be a black widow who's been playing the game since she was underage, since she isn't showing up in the real world at the age of twenty-four."

"Is she a government agent, or not?"

"I don't know yet, but I see that she spent some time in Seattle. There's a training center there for undercover government agents, called Secret Enforcement Agencies Training Advisement Center, or SEATAC, and I'm willing to bet she spent time there. Have you seen an I.D. with SEATAC on it?"

"Yes, I have."

"What are you going to do about her?"

I thought, I really just want her to love me, but I said, "I'll play the game a little longer."

Cain shook his head. "It's your funeral."

I shrugged my shoulders.

It had to be the love spell; I wasn't thinking right. I should have kicked her ass to the curb. Honestly, for real, I just didn't want to be alone. I hated not having tons of people around all the time.

Chapter 78

<u>July 24, 1994</u>

My parents called to wish me a happy birthday and find out if everything was going well with my recovery.

I lied. "Everything is just perfect," I said.

After speaking with my parents, I ordered a pizza. Cheese pizza was Liesa's favorite. I wanted one day without any problems, if that was possible.

While Liesa had been at her brother's wedding -- or wherever the hell she had gone -- I had discussed with my business contacts what I should do about her, since they would be involved if she turned out to be an undercover government agent like everyone suspected.

I got two opinions. Some said, "Let her go about her business. She must not have anything if she's still hanging around."

Others said, "Get rid of her to make sure your secrets are safe."

If it were up to my ruthless partners, Liesa would start answering some questions correctly, and it wouldn't be very pleasant. But I kept my dogs of war at bay, since I knew the extraction of the truth would not only be bloody . . . it would be a one-time deal. The thought of her being disfigured before bleeding to death didn't sit right with me, so I assured all my partners I had nothing she could find that would incriminate any of us. There were no notebooks or computer disks; everything was in my head. I never left any kind of paper trail. My computer was loaded with a bunch of nothing, not a single name or number, but it was still encrypted. If anyone wanted in, it would take a lot of time and money to crack the code to get nothing but a message saying, <u>Fuck you. You've been had.</u>

As far as Liesa knew, I had only a couple of eight-balls at a time. I never let her see me do any big deals. As a matter of fact, she never saw me hand anybody anything, except for what passed between us, which never involved money. Just sucking or fucking, or a good hand spanking if she was in the mood to have her ass tantalized.

When the pizza arrived, Liesa and I lay on the floor in front of the big-screen television while MTV cranked out Marilyn Manson. I liked his style. It wasn't new, but I liked it.

When we finished eating, Liesa gave me a sexy look, so I asked, "Do you want to get in the Jacuzzi?"

"Sure," she replied, "but only if you're going to tap my rear end."

"Don't I always?"

"Since it is your birthday," she suggested, "how about going to get some drinks? I will be waiting for you in the Jacuzzi in my birthday suit when you return."

That sounded good, so I went into the safe room to get my pistol and my wallet. On a whim, I decided to turn on the hidden cameras. I wanted to see what Liesa was up to while I was away.

Coming down the staircase, Mr. K asked, "Are we going out?"

"Just to the store at the bottom of the hill and back, real quick."

"Are you going to leave Liesa alone in your bedroom?" he inquired. "We just de-bugged it."

"Don't worry," I said. "If she plants anything, I'll know."

He understood.

We were only gone fifteen minutes, but when I returned, Liesa was pretending to be sound asleep, which wasn't possible considering the amount of meth we had done a half-hour ago.

I reached down and shook her.

She rolled over with her hair still wet and said, "I'm not in the mood anymore." Pulling the covers back over her, she turned the other way.

I was livid. What a miserable, lying bitch, I thought, but I kept my mouth shut for the moment.

In the safe room, I checked the video surveillance tape. As soon as I had left, Liesa had started the Jacuzzi. She pulled a slim, studded white vibrator from her dance bag and laid it down on the edge of the tub before climbing into the hot bubbling water. With three fingers in her vagina and the white vibrator shoved halfway up her derriere, Liesa had multiple orgasms for the hidden camera.

The secret video tape didn't make me horny; instead, it only hurt my feelings, reminding me that I was just some stupid amputee to Liesa. She found the toy more sexually satisfying than me. The more I thought about it, the more enraged I became. It was my birthday, goddammit. Stupid slut!

Storming into the bathroom, I reached into Liesa's dance bag and retrieved the white vibrator, which was still wet and smelled of her recent sex. I stopped in the doorway and yelled, "You are a worthless, lying bitch." Then I threw the white vibrator like a punted football end over end across the bedroom.

Liesa wasn't sleeping, so she sat up in my bed to see what I was yelling about just as the sex toy hit her right between the eyes. Double D batteries flew in two directions.

That pissed her off. She rose out of the bed like the Exorcist, with her long, black hair standing on end, "I'm going to tear your fucking balls off."

I believed her, so I slammed the bathroom door and locked it. My laughter only made her more angry.

I let her beat on the bathroom door for a while as I watched on the camera from my safe room, drinking the bottle of champagne we were supposed to share. After a while, Liesa stormed out the front door in a huff. She took my car, but I didn't care, I knew she would be back, her mission wasn't over.

I laughed until I finished the bottle. At that point, I didn't care.

I knew my house would soon be filled with people I could trust, celebrating my birthday . . . people who were actually glad I had been born and whose lives had been bettered by meeting me.

By ten o'clock, the house was packed with strippers, porn stars, hackers, and many other elite criminals of Hollywood, along with celebrities who have asked me not to mention their names in the hope of keeping their clean image. Everyone reminded me they still had my back, but they were all lying low. They seemed to be under surveillance . . . the entire network.

~~

Around five o'clock on the second morning of the two-day party, we were sitting around the pool smoking joints and waiting for the sun to come up, when I decided I'd had enough of sitting in the wheelchair. I couldn't show any more signs of weakness -- no more chair.

Making my final decision with a crowd watching, I put my fake leg on, picked the wheelchair up, and tossed it into the deep end of the swimming pool. As we watched, the wheelchair sank to the bottom like Poseidon, and there it would stay, reminding me to have a heart and to be hard.

The party really cheered me up, and since Liesa wasn't there, Trisha spent the night.

~~

Trisha and I were talking, when the telephone in my bedroom rang. I answered it. I heard a deep, sinister voice asking for Trisha, so I handed her the phone. Like Duncan McCloud of the Clan McCloud, I sensed when I was talking to one of my own.

When she hung up the phone, I asked, "Who was that?"

"It was one of my photographers wanting to set up a shot next week."

"He's calling at six in the morning?"

"Yes," Trisha answered, and excused herself to the bathroom.

Trisha hadn't told me the truth in the past, and I didn't expect her to start today.

I cut her out a couple of lines, and they really spun her out. She immediately went on a cleaning spree in the bathroom, so I let her go while I went to check the full-time tape recorder I had finally hooked up to the phone line to defeat the tap-buster program.

I wasn't surprised by what I had found. The caller had been Christ himself, leader of the Heaven's Devils, warning Trisha not to hang around my house. He knew she was in my bedroom. What really angered me was that Christ referred to me as the asshole who had blown his own leg off. It was very disrespectful, and I didn't find it amusing. I wouldn't be ridiculed by a low-life meth pirate. The way I looked at my life, I already had one foot literally in the grave, so I wasn't about to take an ounce of crap from this piece of shit biker.

Around eight o'clock in the morning, Trisha and I decided to sit in the Jacuzzi for a while, since she had cleaned the entire room with a toothbrush while wired on meth.

Meanwhile, Mr. K went to get us all some breakfast.

~~

Mr. K told me later what happened. As he backed out of the driveway and headed south, a baby-blue BMW pulled away from the curb about a block away and followed him down the hill, past Tower Records and onto Ventura Boulevard. The BMW was hanging back a block or so, trying to look loose. Being a veteran of the Hollywood underworld, he spotted the tail instantly, but he remained cool.

Sherman Oaks just wasn't the same after the earthquake. Many of the businesses were closed and boarded up as a reminder of the evil that had been released into the Valley during the opening of the earth's crust. The presence of evil was at an all-time high. We could all feel it. Something wasn't right.

Arriving in Studio City, Mr. K took an abrupt right turn, up into the hills overlooking the Valley. He sped up and parked in the driveway of an empty house on a dead-end street he was familiar with. Once the BMW passed, Mr. K backed out and blocked the roadway. He popped open his trunk to retrieve a back-up weapon.

The BMW turned around in the cul-de-sac. When the driver saw Mr. K blocking the road, he gunned it and charged -- then suddenly came screeching to a halt.

A well-dressed black man, unprepared for the situation, jumped out of the car with his weapon drawn. He took a few wild shots.

Mr. K, who had taken cover behind his own car, was ready for this situation. A pistol against an AR-15 assault rifle was like bringing a knife to a gunfight.

~~

Mr. K was back before Trisha and I had even gotten out of the hot tub. We found him sitting in my bedroom in front of the television with a calm look on his face and no breakfast.

Mr. K and I went into the safe room, and I turned on the audio-jammer to ensure my privacy. He told me what had happened and tossed down the badge and identification he had taken off the guy: Anthony Purves, NSA -- National Security Agency.

"Fuck. How are they involved?"

"They're not," he replied. "The badge and identification look good, but they're fakes."

I looked at the identification again; the guy looked like one of Dickwood's friends.

"This guy was a professional hit man," Mr. K explained. "He had a custom silencer on his 9mm and a 308 sniper rifle in the trunk of his rental car. He wasn't just following me for information; he was going to try to take me out of the game. It was a hit."

I smiled. "I guess the hunter became the prey."

We both laughed.

"With these fake badges," Mr. K continued, "these guys could have gone around to all your neighbors and said they were investigating you so they wouldn't call the police if they saw them outside watching."

"Shane told me about these guys who were dressing up like cops and raid drug dealers. They were trying to get me a few years back. Shane said they had badges and uniforms."

Mr. K nodded his head. "I think you'd better give up this cursed house and move. That might be the answer to all your problems, or at least some of them. You need a new location. Everyone knows where you are. You're a sitting duck."

I nodded in agreement. Mr. K was right; this mansion was worth a couple million bucks. It made me look like Tony Montana, especially with the Jacuzzi in my bedroom and all the cameras everywhere. Anyone investigating me would think I had something to do with the fake paperwork going on with this house.

On top of my amputation and the amount of meth I was using, my depression over Liesa and her lies had caused me to fantasize about going out in a hail of bullets, like Scarface. I had celebrated my thirtieth birthday, and as far as I was concerned, it was probably my last. I accepted it.

Someone had gone to a lot of trouble to plant all the secret devices in my house while I was in the hospital, and they continued to try to intimidate me. Eventually, it was going to get more physical. If the other criminals didn't gun me down, I figured the government would try to put me away, since the ATF was watching 24-7. It wasn't an if -- it was when.

I had already made up my mind. I would not go to prison. I would rather die than be treated like a wild animal. Dead in a wooden box was better than alive in an iron cage, having to fight every day for the right to live.

I had just watched a movie on HBO called <u>Blood In, Blood Out</u>, about a white guy who got involved with Mexican gang-bangers. To make a long story short, the guy got his leg blown off and ended up in prison. There was no way I would go behind cement walls and have inmates take my fake leg and shove it in my face or up my ass.

The worst thing I would let them do to me was kill me -- nothing more. I would never be taken alive. That was probably the meth talking, but if I couldn't live life to the fullest, then what was the purpose? I had risen from being a dorky kid in high school to being boss. I could never be less then boss.

I made it perfectly clear: "Anybody who comes through my front door by force, no matter what they're wearing, will be met with everything I can unload."

I would save the last bullet for myself. I didn't give a fuck anymore; they had fucked with me to the point of no return.

"Do you think I'm still under surveillance by any real law enforcement agency?" I asked Mr. K. "Or is it just these fake assholes?"

"At this point, I really don't know. It's hard to tell who's who anymore in this clandestine mess."

~~

When the Fiendish Eight arrived for the usual meeting, I couldn't overemphasize how important it was to be on top of their game, since we were all being watched. The Fiendish Eight were new to this game, and I could tell they didn't believe me about the people doing surveillance in the trees.

"I'm probably being watched right now as I speak," I told them. To prove my point, I took my police scanner and started scanning through all the government frequencies, searching for anything regarding Mr. K's confrontation, while listening for the surveillance team watching my house. I knew someone was still watching. Through the scanner, I had heard the surveillance team whistling and whooping earlier when Trisha had done a striptease in front of the window.

Looking through a spotting scope, I scanned the tree line, but I couldn't see anyone. So I grabbed my game finder body heat detector and re-scanned the same tree line until I picked up a hot reading. Zooming into the area with my spotting scope, I could see part of a tree stand wrapped around the tree directly in the path of my bedroom balcony door.

"Do you see him?" Mr. K asked.

"Yes. Do me a favor and start stacking those cardboard boxes up outside my balcony door. I'm going to use them as cover; I'm sick of this shit."

I needed to prove my point to make sure they understood.

Once Mr. K finished setting up the boxes, I took my fake leg off and crawled on the floor so no one would see me position myself behind the boxes. Mr. K and the Fiendish Eight stepped out onto the balcony.

I slid the barrel of the air rifle between two of the boxes, exposing only a small crack in the wall of cardboard to get a perfect line of fire. In the scope on my air rifle, I saw that the guy in the tree was in perfect range. The rifle would be silent and would have a real effect. Five pumps on my Benjamin Sheraton was like shooting a .22 rifle. I figured if I shot him with a real rifle, the bullet could be traced, and if I missed, the bullet would eventually hit something else. But a high-powered pellet gun was just enough to get the message across that I didn't like my privacy violated.

"Sure you want to do this?" asked Mr. K. "This might be going a little too far."

"This is driving me nuts, and this is what a crazy person does. I'm going to take the shot and see what happens."

"All right. You're the boss."

The Fiendish Eight definitely thought I was nuts.

I inserted two pellets and a brass BB, and then pumped it nine times.

Mr. K looked around and then nodded his head, giving me the signal that none of my neighbors were outside to observe the event.

Lying on the floor next to me was Neighbor Dan. He whispered in my ear, "You have finally lost your mind. You know that, right?"

I looked at him and frowned. "Shut the fuck up, greenhorn." Damn civilians have no idea what's possible, I thought.

I took aim and shot.

I hit the guy in the tree dead-center with such surprising force that it knocked him out of the tree backwards, hurling him toward earth. We could hear him screaming, "Damn, fucking damn!" He looked like a giant green bush as he busted through the bottom branches. I wasn't able to see him hit the ground, but I heard the loud thud.

The scanner went crazy as the other agents tried to find out what was going on. The fallen guy was screaming, "I have been shot! I have been shot!"

Neighbor Dan almost swallowed his tongue. He didn't know what to say except, "Sorry I ever doubted your sanity."

I smiled and thought, Told you so.

Mr. K pretended not to notice what had just happened. He lit up another smoke while looking around for any type of movement. I told Neighbor Dan to stay down. They didn't know where the shot had come from.

The scanner was still going crazy with wild chatter when I heard someone say, "If they shoot again, I'm going to spray the balcony."

Then a deep voice of authority came across the scanner: "Everyone stand down. I don't want the local dumbasses to show up and cause a cluster fuck."

I had proved my point beyond any doubt. The Fiendish Eight understood and were freaked out. As they left, I watched all of them on the security camera walking down the driveway to their cars, looking at the trees as they passed.

~~

A few hours went by without any talk on the scanner, so I asked Mr. K to climb over the back fence to look for clues. He was only gone a few minutes before returning with a pair of high-optical Gargoyle sunglasses.

"It looks like you hit him right between the eyes, by the mark on the bulletproof sunglasses. These are standard government-issue . . . so if I were you, I wouldn't be shooting at any more tree people."

"Maybe you're right," I said. "I hope the agent didn't take it personally. It's just part of the game."

We all laughed. I was still glad I had done it.

Chapter 79

<u>August 1<u>st</u></u>

I got a letter hand-delivered from an old friend who wanted to meet me privately at a hotel in Beverly Hills. Eric didn't realize just how many friends we had in common until they had to choose sides.

"I have something for you to read," said Jane Doe, tossing that day's issue of the <u>L.A. Times</u> on the coffee table with a slap.

On the front page was the first page of a two-page article about Eric and the secret talents that had gotten him into trouble with the federal government. The FBI was now offering a reward for any information leading to his capture, but they denied that Eric had ever worked for them. I knew that to be a lie, so I figured the entire article could be just another part of the cover-up. The FBI didn't want to take any responsibility for anything illegal that Eric had done or was doing while on the run. Reading between the lines, I assumed they were just trying to cover their asses because they had let him out of prison.

The article described Eric as one of the world's most sinister computer hackers and said there wasn't a system that he couldn't get his fingers into. The article also mentioned that Eric was known for using the identities of others to serve his own purpose and provided a list of his former aliases.

In my opinion, Eric's real problem was that he thought he was smarter than everyone else. If that was the case, he wouldn't have had a criminal record . . . arrogant dumbass.

Every newspaper in Los Angeles had printed the story.

Once I finished the article, I tossed the newspaper back down and said, "So what? Tell me something I don't know. I had that information two months ago from another source."

"I don't think you have a clue as to what's going on," Jane said. Shaking her head, she struck a match and lit her coffin nail.

Waving the cigarette smoke out of my face, I said, "I'm on to Liesa's game. I think she's a government informant, just like Eric. They used my leg to get in close." "That's a good guess," Jane answered.

"I think Eric is just freaking out because he knows Liesa is a lying slut, and it's driving him nuts that I'm fucking her. Or she's playing both of us for whatever she can get. She claims Eric has threatened her if she doesn't help him."

Jane Doe took a drag off her cigarette and blew a smoke ring. "Liesa afraid of Eric? That's a good one. The rumor going around Hollywood is that you whacked the owner of your house and took it by force."

I laughed. "That's not entirely true, but sort of. I don't want to get into that right now."

Jane took another drag. "If someone was to investigate who owns your house, what would they find? And whose name is your car in?"

"Not my name. There's absolutely nothing around me in my real name."

"You almost made it too easy for them."

"Too easy for who?"

"Dumb shit," Jane said in a frustrated tone. "Eric was planning on using your identity to get a new fake leg, the Feds are watching all the prosthesis labs, so he's fucked. He was also planning on using you as a body double to fake his own death."

"What are you talking about?"

"Eric knows he'll never be free from the government until he's either dead or behind bars, because of the secrets he knows about the federal government. He never wants to go back to the human zoo. He'll do anything to stay out of prison, and if that means you have to die, so be it. He's very desperate and selfish, and since you're a criminal, he doesn't feel bad. You both have similar appearances and the same leg missing at the exact same point. Eric has been planning to crash your car off Mulholland Drive with you in it, burning up your body."

"That's fucked up."

"Since Liesa was Eric's long-time girlfriend, she would say it was Eric in the burned-up car. The FBI would bury you as Eric, and he would be completely free to go about his life with your identity and the two million dollars he's planning on hacking from some bank. He plans to pin the bank job on a guy named the Condor. He pinned several hacking crimes on him already."

"You know this for a fact?"

"Yes. Since you never used your real name, you wouldn't be missed right away. Like I said before, you almost made it too easy for them."

Eric was the evil James Bond of the computer world, and he did have control of the phone lines and computer systems. The story made sense ... He just needed the physical body, since he could reach into any medical lab's computer and change the results of any tests done on the burned-up body to make sure it would match his description. It was actually a good plan.

I had taken my house from a less powerful criminal, and now a criminal viewed me as being weak was trying to do the same thing.

"Do you really think Eric is a nice guy?" Jane said. "So nice he would come all the way out to the Valley just to help someone he doesn't know? Please. Give me a break."

Jane lit up another coffin nail, uncrossed her legs, and re-crossed them.

"Why are you telling me this?" I asked.

"You have always been my friend, and Eric is a real piece of shit. I'd like to see Eric get fucked for once. The last time I fucked Eric, he did some real sick shit to me. He duct-taped my hands and feet, smeared Vaseline all over my body, and literally tore me a new backdoor."

"Do you know where he is?"

"He moves around a lot . . . but I have his pager number."

"I already have it. I've paged him a couple of times and punched in the phone number of the FBI just to fuck with him." We laughed.

"How is Eric involved with Christ?" I asked.

"Eric has been supplying them with secret government information and warning them of any surveillance regarding their illegal activities."

"I understand."

"Christ hates you. He's extremely jealous of your friendship with Trisha, because she prefers your company to his. He's very territorial. Plus, they're mad that you don't do business with them."

"Fuck those assholes! I tried to do business with them."

There was a bump against the hotel door. We both went silent, and I drew two pistols and aimed them at the door. Quietly, I got up and looked out the peephole. It turned out to be some idiot across the hallway who had let his suitcase fall against the door.

"I'm taking a big risk in telling you," Jane continued. "My life won't be worth a cent if you open your mouth. I'm not telling you everything so you can start a war that no one will win. I just want you to get the hell out of Hollywood while you still can. The forces of evil are closing in on you. They outnumber you, so don't throw your life away, and don't let your Leo pride get in the way."

"I'm not running from anyone," I snapped back. "Fuck those assholes. I will go to war."

"Wait," Jane said. "I still remember how you used to be when you first arrived in Los Angeles. You had the kindest heart and helped anyone who asked. Please don't let this city take what's left of your soul."

"It's a little late for that."

"Please," she begged, "use your brain, not a gun. Trust no one. Maybe in a couple years, we can sit around and look back at how fucked-up everyone was on crystal meth. Maybe then everyone will realize how it made all of us insane."

I had known Jane Doe for many years. She was the one person who had never lied or stolen from me. Her word was still good in my book.

~~

After I got back from Beverly Hills, I had Krazy Kurtis drive me over to Robin's place on the other side of the Valley, where I knew Liesa was staying.

The house was completely empty.

Ten days' worth of newspapers were piled up on the front porch, covered with dust from the Santa Anna winds. The mailbox was full.

We drove back into Hollywood and went by the strip club where Liesa and Robin worked. They didn't work there anymore.

Los Angeles was huge, so there were plenty of places to hide.

~~

Things were at a standstill until Liesa showed up around the second week of August, acting like nothing was wrong. She claimed she had been staying with Robin, but I knew that was a lie. Robin's place was empty for some time.

Liesa played with her dog, pretending to be concerned about her well-being while asking me questions about my living situation. She wanted to know if I was going to give up the mansion.

"No. I'm staying right here."

I should have just tossed her out on her ass, but her clothes always seemed to peel off the longer she stayed. It was a hell of a spell.

Around three in the morning, after a few hours of no-holes-barred, meth-induced sex, Liesa climbed into my bed. I decided to sleep in the safe room. I couldn't lie next to her anymore. She had fucked me over worse than anyone else by doing it during the weakest point in my life. I was appalled by the scenario she might be involved with, which was supposed to lead to my disappearance and death.

I shut the door to my safe room and piled some dirty clothes on the floor as a bed. I smoked a joint, cocked my AK-47, put the safety on, and curled up with it like a teddy bear, knowing that I could depend on my weapon more than anything else in my life. It was the only thing keeping the wolves at bay.

While lying there, I realized I was sleeping over the bloodstained carpet where I had been shot only a few months earlier. When I looked up at the ceiling from the floor, I remembered the view and the blood surrounding me.

I dreamed for hours -- maybe a whole day -- about witches and evil spirits surrounding me as I tried to run. But my feet just wouldn't work, and I ran in place for what seemed like forever. When I woke up, I was lying in a pool of my own sweat, and Liesa was gone.

An hour after I got up, Mr. K appeared and slapped an address down on the smoked-glass coffee table.

"What's that?"

"I followed Liesa. This is where she lives."

Chapter 80

Walking through my bedroom, I smelled natural gas. It had been an ongoing problem for the past couple of weeks. This would be the gas company's seventh trip to the house since the earthquake to check for leaks, and the third time this week. I figured the culprit was an underground gas line damaged during the earthquake, but the gas company pressure-checked every line and found nothing.

Finally the gas company man put his nose right next to the ground under my bedroom window and said with a bewildered look, "This might sound a bit crazy, but I think someone is fucking with you. It's an old trick. You go to a chemical supply warehouse and buy a chemical called ethyl mercaptan, which gives off an excellent natural gas odor."

"What are you talking about?"

"At night, you pour it on the ground around a house, and when the sunlight hits it in the morning, it heats up the chemicals and causes the gas smell."

He reached down and picked up what looked like a broken water balloon, stuck it under his nose, and gave it a sniff.

"Someone is fucking with you, all right," he said. "They're filling these balloons and throwing them over your fence."

<u>Fucking bastards</u>, I thought.

As we looked around, we noticed broken balloons all over the place. When I had seen them before, I figured it was something the dog had torn up.

The guy from the gas company left with a weird look on his face, like he was wondering what the hell was going on and why I didn't seem surprised by his revelation.

I knew whatever criminals owned the house couldn't take any legal action; they didn't want to go to court any more than I did. Instead, they were trying every dirty trick in the book.

As far as anyone else was concerned, I wasn't planning on moving. But I got word to my close friends to prepare to move me in the middle of the night.

~~

With all the weird shit going on and Jane Doe's story on my mind, I wanted an extra hired gun around the house until I could get out and into hiding. Krazy Kurtis arrived around four in the morning with a bag of donuts, two greasy hamburgers from Jack in the Box, three burritos from Taco Hell, and a fat line of meth to wash it down. That was enough artificial fuel to keep him alert until Mr. K came back the next afternoon.

Everyone who used meth was a junk-food junkie, eating anything that was fast and full of sugar and caffeine to accelerate the blood flow even more.

"I'm dead-tired," I told Krazy Kurtis. "Don't let anyone wake me up for any reason until the sun sets behind the mountains tomorrow."

"No problem," he replied. "Consider yourself in good hands. I'll stand guard."

Climbing into bed, I retrieved my Colt .380 out of the Bible in my headboard and slipped it under my pillow. I was getting used to having a huge piece of metal under my face when I slept, which wasn't often.

As I settled into bed with my eyes almost shut, a bright flash of light went across the back yard behind the fence, followed by a loud boom!

I sat up and yelled, "What in the name of almighty Jesus Harold Christ was that?"

I jumped out of bed and started going through the process of putting my fake leg on. Just then, Krazy Kurtis came running into my bedroom, laughing.

"What the fuck is going on?" I yelled.

"I was standing on the side of the house with the night-vision goggles, scanning the back yard, when I saw a guy come crawling out of the back bushes. I let him get in real close and then yelled, 'Put your hands up!' He dropped something and took off for the back fence."

"What did he drop, and what was that explosion?"

"I rushed over and picked up the thing he'd dropped. It was a half stick of dynamite, taped to a rock for weight and then dipped in glue, with brass BB's stuck to it. He was going to throw it through your bedroom window."

Motherfuckers, I thought.

"I ran to the back fence, lit it, and tossed it over."

Behind my house was a natural drainage alley running between the houses on the hill, filled with thirty feet of thick bamboo. Twenty feet of it had been blown into tiny pieces of sharp shrapnel. Since the explosion wasn't in my back yard, I played like I had no idea what happened as my neighbors came outside.

I thought for sure the Sherman Oaks police would show up, but nothing happened -- not even a cruiser making a single pass.

When we checked in the morning, we found a blood trail leading down the hill and a dead cat lying in a three-feet by six-feet hole in the ground. Four pieces of sharp bamboo were stuck all the way through the cat's body from the explosion. I hoped the same had happened to the intruder.

Mr. K couldn't believe the damage. But he found something sinister buried under the dirt and destroyed bamboo.

"I found some type of projecting camera and a fog machine uncovered by the massive explosion. These bastards were pulling what's called a "Fantasia Operation." You have some twisted assholes fucking with you, my friend. If you live through this, it'll make one hell of a book."

Mr. K explained. "There was a tube stuck under the back fence from the fog machine, designed to produce a thin white screen, something to shine a projection onto. It took me a few minutes to find this wireless projection camera mounted in a tree on the side of the yard. It was hidden really well."

"What are you saying?"

Mr. K took the projector camera and shone it on my bedroom wall. A gruesome green skull appeared.

"Have you ever seen that when you were alone?"

I nodded. "Lots of times when I was alone. I was afraid to tell anyone, thinking they would think I was nuts. I didn't want to discredit anything real that was going on by talking about glowing skulls."

"I think that was the whole point -- to make you look foolish and weak."

"Usually I heard some kind of noise that drew my attention to the back yard. I would scan the back yard with my binoculars and night-vision goggles and would see the outline of the skull on the back fence. It gave me chills, but I pretended not to see it and wrote it off as a side effect of being up too many days in a row, since it didn't register on the body heat detector."

Mr. K nodded. "I also found this device strapped onto the top branches, buried in the middle of the thick bushes towards the end of the pool area. I thought it was a camera at first, but it's actually a device called a "Bushmaster."

"What the hell is a Bushmaster?"

The device was twelve inches long, with an antenna on the back for remote activation. When it was strapped to the branch of a bush, it vibrated or shook when activated, causing a distraction and giving the appearance of someone climbing or moving through the bushes.

"I also found a piece of clear plastic with a mirrored side attached to a piece of blown-up bamboo. It had a clear nylon cord attached to it, and I think they were using it to reflect light or to cause shadows on the back walls. It's hard to say exactly. Anyway, Krazy Kurtis seems to have taken out their entire spook operation." Walking over and looking out the window, Mr. K concluded, "This reminds me of an episode of Scooby-Do. They're trying to get you to think the place is haunted so you'll give up the property.

Chapter 81

After the earthquake, when broken pipes under the mansion had to be fixed, a Mercedes Benz had been discovered in the crawl space, buried in pieces. The house appeared to be built right on top of it. I had to get out of this cursed mansion, or I would end up dead like the last owner. I planned to live like a gypsy, with no permanent address, until I could figure out this mess.

As we were packing my belongings, I thought about something Liesa had said the last time she came over to the house. She had asked if she had any mail.

I had told her no, but that wasn't true. She never got anything in the mail except past-due bills. Liesa had bills from the gas company, water, power, cable, and phone services. Liesa said they were past-due bills from when she had lived with Raquel in Hollywood.

I found a stack of previous bills in one of her boxes at the bottom of the stairs. I wanted to compare them to the recent bills delivered yesterday.

I said to Mr. K, "Why would she bother to have her bills forwarded to my house if they were in a fake name? The whole purpose of using a fake name is so you don't have to pay bills."

The way the game worked, you stiffed the company out of the last few months of service. Eric had probably taught her how to do that; everyone I knew did that while living in Hollywood. I taught them.

"Look," I said. "The account number changes every month on each bill, and the amount due and current balance also change, like she's making payments. But I know she's not. Here are the return envelopes."

The bills from May and June were under the name Annaliesa, while the new ones were under Liesa.

I called Raquel. "Did Liesa have the utilities at your house in her name?"

"No," Raquel replied. "Everything was in my name before that fucking cunt moved in."

Just to check all the facts, I called the companies from a pay phone, and each one informed me that she didn't have an account with them and they were not sending bills to my address. So who was sending them, and why?

One bill from the gas company was in Spanish, so I asked Rudy to translate it.

"It only looks like Spanish," he said. "I think it has something to do with your Trans Am, and there was a word that kept coming up again and again: cunta, cunta. That is not a word that would be in a bill."

I thought about it for a minute. I remembered one time when Liesa was extremely high, she said Eric were able to write in code if she was under surveillance.

"Eric might be using a drop code system," Mr. K said, "printing up these bills on his computer. It's a known FBI trick of the trade. I think Liesa forgot how to use it, or got too high to follow his codes and caused confusion. That's why Eric had to have Robin call Liesa at your house and you were able to get him on tape. These bills probably give times and dates of locations to meet, if you know the codes."

"Let's see if Matt the Ratt has any bills like this lying around in his bedroom," I said. "He's out."

We opened his bedroom door with a set of lock picks and found similar bills that Matt was getting from some record company. The bills were in Matt's real name, and I knew he never bought anything in his real name.

I pointed something out to Mr. K: all the bills that Liesa was getting had two letter H's overlapping in each corner of the pages, like the trademark of a personal copier. I found the same trademark on Matt's bills. I couldn't imagine the local gas company and a record-of-the-month club from the East Coast would have the same trademark.

"What's Eric's last name?" Mr. K asked.

"Hentz."

While we were discussing the fake bills, Mr. K's pager went off with a 911. Mr. K returned the call; his wife was in a state of panic. Their son was thought to be safely hidden and attending school in Palm Springs. But that day, two black vans with tinted windows had driven by, slid open the side door, and opened fire, riddling his son's house with bullets. His son was shaken up but escaped injury.

A witness said the shooters looked like bikers, dirty-looking white men.

Looking into the mirror after getting back from Palm Springs, I realized that in the past year, I had aged ten years because of the stress and lack of sleep I had endured. My youth had been stolen, my body wrecked by crystal methamphetamine, my heart crushed by love, and my soul lost to black magick.

Chapter 82

I had only one day to go before I was to move out of the mansion. It was around two in the afternoon, and I was sitting in my favorite chair watching an episode of <u>Beavis and Butthead</u> I had taped the night before. The sun was bright and warm, reminding me of why I would die to stay in California. It was the weather -- not the people, by any means.

Before I could spark up the joint I had just rolled, the doorbell rang. I yelled, "Matt, answer the door."

I looked at the outside camera to see who it was, I didn't recognize him.

"Someone wants to talk with you about Eric and Liesa," Matt yelled up.

"Let him in."

I tossed my joint down on the table next to a newspaper with the headline <u>O.J. Goes on Trial for Murder</u>. That was another situation I had a problem with. One of the Fiendish Eight was supplying a guy with meth, who was selling it to O.J. -- or should I say, to his lackey house guest. All rich assholes had gofers to get their drugs and make their runs. They called them "house guests." From what I had heard, the Juice was juiced on crystal methamphetamine. When I heard that, I knew why he had freaked out and developed such superhuman strength, snapping two people in half. I was hardly the athlete the Juice was, but even with a leg missing, I had almost beat someone to death with my wheelchair after being out of the hospital only a few months.

Looking at the feed from the second camera, I could see that the guy walking up the stairs was huge. I turned on the overhead camera in my bedroom and cocked both pistols, sticking each one between the cushions of the chair for easy access. I was on edge, but I tried not to show any signs of fatigue. It had been many days since I had last slept, and I wasn't planning on sleeping again until I moved out.

I didn't have a shirt on and had a red bandana wrapped around my head like an Indian war chief waiting to ambush Custer. I was wearing cut-off shorts with one combat boot, and my fake leg was lying on the floor next to the chair. I didn't have time to put it on, making me feel somewhat vulnerable . . . but it was only one guy, and I was armed to the teeth.

A huge man with a simple smile knocked on my bedroom door and said in a friendly but powerful voice, "Are you Brent?"

<u>He knows my real name.</u>

"Yes," I replied. "Come in. What can I do for you?"

He introduced himself as "Stan, special agent for the FBI, Los Angeles Branch." He held out his hand, and we shook.

My mind froze for a brief second; I remembered his name from the newspaper. I had heard Liesa mention him as the FBI agent in charge of Eric's undercover missions.

Looking into his eyes, I realized this was the head federal agent who groomed all the undercover federal informants . . . and now he was sitting next to me in my bedroom, in the same chair where many of the most dangerous outlaws in the Valley had sat many times. In reality, Stan was no different; he just had a badge.

I'd heard that he and Eric had become good friends, that he took Eric to get his long hair frosted and styled at some Beverly Hills salon while they palled around Hollywood, discussing how to trap the Condor. I had also heard that Stan was very disappointed and embarrassed by Eric's actions while under his personal supervision. Eric had made Stan look bad in the eyes of his superiors and in the newspapers.

Stan didn't look how I had imagined. He wasn't wearing all black, nor did he have on dark sunglasses. He had light, stylish hair and was dressed in jeans, tennis shoes, and a Hawaiian shirt like Magnum P.I. He looked more like he was ready for a cook-out than tracking down hard-core criminals.

I asked to see some identification. It looked as real as anything I had seen, but then again, who could tell anymore?

Stan said in an inquisitive tone, "I hear that you might be having trouble with one of my rogue agents, Eric Hentz."

"That's right," I replied. "How did you know that?"

"That's not important. I'm here to help, if I can."

If Stan had demanded answers or acted rude, I would have said nothing. But he was being very cool, as if we were just two guys talking shop. Stan didn't appear to have any idea who I was. I had gotten good at reading people's facial expressions, and he was looking at me with pity because of my leg and treating me like a potential victim of Eric's conspiracy plan. If he had known anything about me, he wouldn't have come alone.

As the conversation went along, Stan reached into his folder and retrieved a current picture of Eric. "Is this the same guy we're talking about?"

"That's him."

"How long have you known Eric?"

"I really don't know him," I replied. "I met him a couple months ago after I got out of the hospital, through a stripper friend from Hollywood."

"Figures," Stan remarked with a chuckle.

"Eric was really cool while he was here," I said. "He showed me his fake leg and how it worked. We put our stumps together. They were almost a perfect match, same exact amputation. That was the only time I saw him in person. I didn't know he was a fugitive at that time."

Stan paused for a moment. "What problems are you having?"

To play the part of a victim was the right move at this point in the game.

This wasn't the beginning or the end of the game; more players were being added.

I had to say something, so I said, "All my problems started as soon as Liesa moved in. It started with the telephone, when I wasn't able to get through and heard what sounded like people listening in the background. Some phone calls got intercepted and rerouted. Certain phone numbers were blocked, and it was just a plain pain in the ass to try to run a business. I also found an infinity transmitter in my telephone that Liesa had brought into my bedroom. Eric did the custom work, I'm sure."

Stan tried to act surprised by what I told him, as if it wasn't possible. I knew damn well that Stan knew exactly what I was talking about, and we both knew how Eric was doing it.

Stan finally realized what I had said. "Wait a minute. Liesa lived here?

"Yes," I replied. "All those boxes at the bottom of the stairs are her belongings. I kicked her out a couple weeks ago."

Stan reached into his folder and pulled out an eight-by-ten black and white glossy picture of Liesa.

"That's her," I confirmed.

Stan truly seemed shocked. "The last address we had on her was Hollywood Boulevard."

I wasn't surprised. "You guys are way behind. She's moved at least four times since that address."

I was amazed that I knew more about Eric and Liesa than the FBI. Once again, I would have to slip them the information so they could get their job done. It was pathetic.

"Liesa is a long-time girlfriend of Eric's," Stan remarked. "She's trusted by everyone in his circle."

"What's her real name?"

"What name did she tell you?"

"Annaliesa Scribner."

"That's her real name."

Bullshit, I thought. Why is he lying? Stan had already tried to cover up twice and is withholding information, but I was, too, for my own reasons.

Playing the part of the victim, I said, "I've been told that Eric was planning on stealing my identity and faking his own death so he could get a new prosthetic leg, since you guys are watching all the prosthesis labs."

A few seconds of silence passed.

"I heard something about that," Stan answered. "Do you think it's true?"

"I don't know if that's true, but they are in constant contact, and there are weird signs pointing in that direction."

I thought it, but didn't say it: With meth being involved, anything was possible. Nothing was too far-fetched. I had witnessed the strange behavior it was causing across the Valley, like a spreading plague of mental illness.

As Stan and I talked, I wondered if Stan had actually looked around my bedroom. Did he notice the M-16 assault rifle in the corner next to my bed? Or the martial arts display cabinet with swords, knives, and throwing weapons? Or the case with the AK-47 within reach on the other side of the chair? Or the two pistols under the cushion? I know he didn't notice the camera above his head.

Stan seemed like a reasonable guy. He wasn't the rude asshole that Liesa had said he was. But then again, I was meeting him under difference circumstances. I didn't fear him; my frame of mind wouldn't allow it. I didn't have any drugs in the house other than personal amount, which wouldn't be worth the time of a big-shot G-man. It would have been insulting for him to bring it up at this point in the conversation, since he had said nothing about the joint lying on the table right in front of him. I had done nothing to hide it.

Lying next to the joint was the piece of paper with Liesa's new address and all her fake bills.

"All these papers belong to Liesa?" Stan asked.

I didn't want him to have them, but I replied, "Yes, I was going to give them to her the next time she stopped by." I tried to blow it off as unimportant.

Looking at the piece of paper with Mr. K's handwriting on it, Stan got a strange look on his face, and he asked in a stranger tone, "What is this?"

"That's Liesa's friend T.Z.'s address. That's where she's living."

"This address on Ashton Street is only a block from my office. Eric wouldn't have the balls to hide right under my nose."

I laughed to myself and replied, "Eric has the balls to do anything but get a job, from what I have seen."

Stan had no idea I knew everything about Eric or that I knew who he was. I didn't open my mouth or arouse suspicion.

"I would like to take Liesa's paperwork," Stan said. "I'm going to track her down and play hardball until she tells me where Eric is hiding."

"What kind of hardball?"

"Liesa has outstanding parking tickets."

I almost laughed, I thought, Parking tickets? That made no sense. It would take more than that to frighten Liesa.

Stan also picked up Liesa's secret phone book, which I had found at her other place, and added that to the pile.

While talking with Stan, I wasn't too worried. I knew I would be out of the house within twenty-four hours. Whatever Eric will tell him about me wouldn't matter if he was captured. I would be a ghost.

As we continued with the conversation, Stan flipped through his notebook and stopped at a page toward the back.

"I want to be introduced to Matt Barker."

My heart stopped. "Why?" I asked in a near-panicked tone, almost coming out of character.

Stan noticed my reaction and said, "Was that Matt who let me in?"

"Yes," I replied abruptly. "Why?"

"We think Matt is working for Eric."

"How sure are you about that?"

"Real sure."

I already knew it, and now the G-man had confirmed it.

"I want to question Matt," he said.

"I'll get him."

Matt must have been eavesdropping, because he split. I heard him hightail it down the stairs and out the front door, lickity-split. Although I really didn't want to draw attention to my security system, I pointed to one of the outside camera monitors showing Matt backing out of the driveway fast.

"He sure is in a big hurry," Stan remarked.

I agreed but made no comment.

That wrapped up our conversation. Stan handed me a business card and asked me to call him when Matt returned.

"Not a problem. I will."

But there was no way in hell I would let Matt talk to Stan. That was not going to happen.

"Nice meeting you," Stan said, "and good luck with the leg." We shook hands again.

"It's been a real pleasure," I replied, . . . Compared to how it could have been if we had met under different circumstances, I thought. I watched the white Ford Crown Victoria pull away from the curb. It did have government plates.

I'd never had any intentions of getting this deep into the business, but now I was playing for keeps.

The FBI involvement was only going to make things more difficult once they realized who I was.

Chapter 83

After Stan left, I got a call from my accountant on the other side of Los Angeles.

"They ransacked my apartment!" she screamed in panic. "They got your birth certificate, medical records, and your real driver's license."

The phone suddenly went dead, as well as the power to the mansion. Neither was scheduled to be shut off.

I went over to my accountant's apartment.

"When I got home, the door to my apartment was locked from the inside," she told me. "Someone had broken something off in the door lock, so I had to have the apartment manager break the door in. Once we got inside, everything was dumped out of the drawers all over the floor, as you see. All the information on my computer hard drives were stolen and erased. You can see they also flooded my apartment by plugging up the sinks in the kitchen and bathroom, making the place unlivable."

I looked around at the mess. "I'll do whatever I can to help with the situation, but I'm especially disturbed that someone has all my real information."

If they hadn't vandalized the apartment, I would have thought it was the government. Plugging the sinks was something someone on meth would find amusing.

Later, when I returned home from the accountant's, I found the mansion trashed by Matt the Ratt. He had been in a meth-induced frenzy because he knew I was on to him. He had spray-painted bright red gang symbols and Nazi signs up and down the hallways and thrown a huge glass coffee table through the wall into the next room, which was the main bathroom. Shattered glass was everywhere.

He hadn't been able to get into my bedroom. There were huge dents in the doors, but I had reinforced the doors with heavy-duty deadbolts, making my room practically impregnable.

Matt had gone down into the candle shop, piled a huge stack of old newspapers under the water heater, and set them on fire. To my surprise, the fire had gone out.

When I got home and saw that mess, I spent the next six hours searching every inch of the Valley to eradicate the Ratt, but I couldn't find him. It was time to move, so I decided to deal with him later.

~~

That evening, the moving truck backed up to the garage and all my true friends came to help, loading everything while Mr. K and I stood guard. When we finally finished around four in the morning, we sat back on the last few pieces of furniture I had left and partied until dawn. I didn't want to leave until there was a lot of traffic, hoping to lose any sort of tail.

The plan was to leave all at once in six separate vehicles, no looking back -- get the hell out and be done with it.

By the time the sun came up, we had each taken a turn paddling Trisha with the cutting board. The meth always made us act in the most perverted ways, just like the guards at Abu-Ghraib prison in Iraq. To us, the behavior seemed normal, a good time for all, including Trisha . . . especially Trisha.

I hadn't been able to drive my car because it was a stick shift. The night before the departure, I had looked it over and noticed something funny. The door locks were already popped. The car couldn't be locked, and the car would start without a key in the ignition. The ignition would just turn.

It appeared somebody had been working on my car. This could only have been done while Liesa was away from the house. I had almost made it too easy for them to make me disappear, since I never used my real name.

Around eight o'clock, I walked out the front door to get the morning newspaper in plain view of the surveillance team. I wore a shirt with long sleeves and a pair of black sweat pants. My hair was pulled back into a ponytail. I pulled up my pant leg and adjusted my fake leg so I would be easy to identify. I used my cane and walked with a heavy limp, intending to look weak and frail.

When I got back in the house, I changed my appearance drastically in hopes of fooling the surveillance team. In the past, I had never worn jeans because it was too difficult with the fake leg. I always wore shorts or sweats. But today I squeezed myself into a ripped-up pair of rocker Levis with a tank top. I pulled my hair to the top of my head and stuffed it under a hat.

My friend Jeff put on my sweats, my long-sleeved shirt to cover his tattoos, my baseball hat, and dark sunglasses. With his long hair pulled back into a ponytail, he could pass for me as long as he kept his head down. To make it look real, Jeff took my cane and hobbled out to the moving truck. He got in the passenger seat with Neighbor Dan, and they drove to the storage unit.

Trisha walked out the door ahead of me, carrying Boots, and started my car. I put on my dark sunglasses and walked out the front door and down the steps without my cane. I walked absolutely perfect.

I had said I wouldn't move out until I could walk on my own. That day had finally come to pass.

Trisha, Liesa's dog, Boots, and I went one way, and the moving truck went another. The surveillance team followed the moving truck to the storage unit in Van Nuys; I heard them on the scanner.

~~

After finally escaping the haunted mansion, I went completely underground. I dropped out of sight and sold my car to a friend out in Semi Valley, since it was too well known and too easy to spot, being bright red.

I crashed out in Bastard Ben's garage in the middle of the Valley on an old dirty couch with Boots and Liesa's dog, who were freaking out. It turned out to be the hottest day of the year, well over 105, and the garage had no ventilating system or air-conditioning. I thought I was going to dehydrate, along with the animals, who were lying on the floor next to me, panting.

I passed out for three days straight, sleeping hard, tossing and turning in my own sweat. I only awoke long enough to drink some water and then pass out again. Time seemed to stand still. A week seemed like a day, and I had no idea what day it was when I awoke. I realized by looking around that I had become Eric. I had gone from living the high life to living in a two-car garage like an escaped prisoner.

After two weeks had passed and I hadn't heard any chatter on the police scanner, I got a rental car in a fake name so I could bounce around Los Angeles to make sure I wasn't under surveillance. I had picked Bastard Ben's place to hide out because I hadn't been there in over three years, and I knew that anybody recently interested in me wouldn't be aware of his secret garage/recording studio. There was no phone line there, so there would be no tracing of calls to that address. I knew that anybody I had called from my last phone line would be on a watch list. Telephone calls were like leaving fingerprints; there was always a record of the calls stored somewhere.

~~

Once I was sure I had slipped any type of surveillance, I had a meeting with Cain.

Cain played my videotape and said, "Oh yes, that's the famous bull-head Stan-O, all right. He's a real FBI agent, and he's hated all over the Internet by hackers who consider him a real hard-on."

Everyone in the room laughed.

"He was really cool with me," I said.

"I can see that."

We continued to play the videotape. I found a few things Stan said a little strange, things I hadn't noticed the first time we spoke.

Stan said, "Eric hasn't been known for violence. If I thought Eric was dangerous, I would have him in my office so fast his head would spin."

If Stan could have Eric in his office, what the hell was he doing talking to me? As for Eric not being violent, had Stan forgotten about the bondage, clothespins, and homemade torture devices Eric liked to use on his women?

If the FBI had ever looked in Eric's trash cans, they would have found rolls of cut-up duct tape smeared with Vaseline and satanic doodles done in a another state of mind on scrap pieces of paper, along with studded condoms. That was strange even by my standards, and I was kinky.

One of Eric's friends whom I had questioned told me Eric put his gun to a homeless person's head to just scare them. That didn't sound too stable. That was a punk move. I only pulled my gun if I was going to shoot it.

Chapter 84

It was early evening, and I was over at Benny's place in Van Nuys. It was a small apartment building with only thirty units, falling apart because of earthquakes. The front of the building had palm trees like every building in the Valley, but the faded blue paint made it look cheap.

Benny and I were hanging out, playing guitar and attempting to record a few tracks on his home studio while the television was on in the background. One particular news story caught our attention: "Computer hacker was on the run for two years, but the law finally caught up with him. Story at ten o'clock."

"Did you hear that?"

"Yes," Benny replied.

The story was all over the ten o'clock news and in all the Los Angeles newspapers the next day. The FBI had caught Eric coming out of Liesa's place on Ashton Street just one block from the federal building, making the FBI look even more foolish.

I was glad Eric was out of the game and grateful to the FBI for doing my dirty work. That was one more asshole removed from the list, that I didn't have to whack.

The FBI raided Jimmy's house the next day and found most of Eric's computer equipment. When I heard that, I knew the FBI would figure out I wasn't a civilian.

~~

I met with Mr. K at Allison's in North Hollywood a few days after Eric got busted. Allison's place was one of a few I stayed at to avoid detection. It was a small apartment complex in North Hollywood, right next to the old railroad tracks that had been torn out and filled with gravel. Allison had a one-bedroom apartment in the back of the complex, facing the alley.

"I'm out of the business for a while," I said to Mr. K. "I need a break from the game to recover."

I had enough money to keep me afloat and had unloaded my entire stash to the Fiendish Eight. When I told Cain I was shutting down, he was angry.

"I'm sure Eric's completely spilled his guts about you and your many business ventures," Mr. K said. "Your name has probably come up regarding Liesa's involvement. She'll probably be charged with helping a federal fugitive. If the Feds haven't arrested Liesa, that means she's rolling over. She'll probably rat you out in hopes of saving her own sweet ass."

"The only thing Liesa could say is that we both did meth and that I was in the business, but no details other than that."

I still had the videotapes of us doing drugs. On the tapes, I had acted in a way that made it look like she was the one providing the drugs.

"It's going to look really embarrassing for the Feds if the newspapers get wind of your encounter with Eric," said Mr. K. "They'll want you to keep your mouth shut, they're going to be all over you, when they can find you."

"I know."

"Your story, if you wanted to play victim, would scare the hell out of the general public. Everyone would get extremely paranoid about the FBI listening in on everyone's phone calls without warrants."

I nodded thoughtfully.

While we were talking, the phone rang. It was Stan the G-man.

I thought no one knew where I was, but it turned out the FBI did. I hadn't lost the surveillance. As a matter of fact, the FBI had been listening to us through the telephone on the coffee table in Allison's living room. I didn't know it at the time, but that phone had already been rigged with an infinity transmitter. Anywhere I went was bugged after my first visit on the assumption that I would return. In the future, I would always unplug the phone the moment I entered a room.

Stan the G-man was still being cool.

"You were right on the mark," he said. "We caught Eric coming out of Liesa's apartment on Ashton Street."

"Was Liesa with him?"

"If you mean were they still a couple, yes, they were."

"Did you find Eric's computers and files? Did you find anything regarding me?" I was trying to feel the agent out, looking for voice changes.

"No," Stan replied, "we're not interested in building a case against you."

"I was referring to my birth certificate or driver's license."

"No," he replied.

I kept remembering what Mr. K said: Act like a victim. So I tried to act the way the average citizen would under such stressful, mind-scrambling conditions. I ranted and raved. I tried to make the FBI think I was afraid of Eric and that everything he said was a lie.

"I was really relieved to hear about Eric being captured," I said. "I'll sleep better knowing he's off the streets of Hollywood." I almost laughed.

"You won't have to worry about Eric for a long time," Stan replied. "He's looking at forty years behind bars. His trial starts October thirty-first -- Halloween."

I thought, Nice twist for the self-proclaimed Prince of Darkness.

I was glad to hear that Stan wasn't interested in building a case against me, although I wasn't sure if I believed him. I wanted to know what he knew, but I wasn't going to ask. I thought for sure Stan was going to ask me a question about meth, but he never said a single word. I didn't ask how he had found me either.

Before we ended our conversation, I asked Stan for a favor: "Can you tell me who owned the mansion I used to live in?" I let him know I wasn't involved with the scam that was going on at that address.

"Your mansion?" He chuckled. "That's a can of worms I don't want to open."

If Stan already knew about the mansion, then he had already been investigating me. That was twice I caught him lying.

"Thanks for the help," he said. "I'll be in touch."

"Nice talking with you. Be well."

Since the FBI knew my whereabouts and my real name, I decided to play it safe. I took my files of fake names, drivers licenses, and passports into the kitchen. One by one, I burned them on the stove below the exhaust fan and flushed the ashes down the toilet.

Between me burning files and Boots tearing up a bird she had caught in the alley to bloody shreds, we were driving Allison crazy. Her place was getting trashed. Allison's side effect from the meth was constant cleaning, so any mess I made, she was right on top of it . . . knocking me out of the way to clean.

The meth I had with me, I kept in a Kleenex wadded up like a dirty-looking snot rag so no one would find it when I fell asleep. Several times when I woke up, Allison in her constant cleaning mode had picked up my stash and threw it in the trash. I would wake up hours later and search the place top to bottom before realizing she had done it again.

I would call her at work and yell, "Where the hell did you put the trash? Stop cleaning everything."

I would then have to climb into the dumpster to find my stash like a homeless person or wait for someone to stop by and make them do it.

~~

The first night I stayed at Allison's, I thought I was going to lose my mind from a non-stop rhythmical pounding sound. The guy who lived above Allison's was a heavy meth user and his side effect was jumping rope, and I mean non-stop for ten hours while I sat beneath pointing my assault rifle at the ceiling. I finally had to knock on the door to see what he was doing and ordered him to FUCKING STOP IT.

Now that I didn't have my own place, I got to see how everyone I knew lived. I had no idea how bizarre and crazy everyone was acting in their everyday life on meth.

One stripper I stayed with told me that she thought the government had constructed a wind tunnel in her attic for interplanetary travel, and another stripper wanted me to put my ear to the floor so I could hear the children screaming for help who were buried under the house. A truck driver I knew, saw a flying ostrich after being up five days and reported it to the office; she got drug-tested and fired. Allison's boyfriend, Hip, was driving her crazy with his meth addiction. He wasn't going to work anymore and there were many nights he was up bouncing off the walls, claiming to see UFOs landing in the alley behind the apartment building. Other people's apartments were filled with junk they had collected and took apart in a meth-induced frenzy, having no idea how to put the items back together.

I only stayed at one place for a single day, then I would move. I only used pay phones with a digital voice changer so my voice wouldn't be picked up by the computer system scanning the phone lines. Anywhere I stayed, I would mount a smoke detector with thick doubled-sided tape to the outside hallway. Inside the smoke detector was a custom wireless camera that ran on batteries . . . that lasted eighteen hours. Using my laptop computer, I could always see the outside of any door, giving me some extra warning.

Traveling around the Valley, I couldn't figure out how the Feds found me. Anything they found out at Eric's wouldn't hold up in court because of the way it was obtained. But the real problem at hand was the biker threat. It was on its highest level, putting me on edge and ready to pull weapons at the slightest noise, almost blowing away Boots for moving around too fast.

Matt the Ratt had told Christ that I was now working for the FBI. He claimed I had worked out a deal to stay out of prison. None of it was true. Matt made it sound like a bunch of FBI agents came to the mansion and he escaped just in time. Since the mansion was empted the next day, it seemed believable.

The bikers wanted me dead; they believe Matt the Ratt. He had been my right-hand man for six months.

I had treated Matt like a brother, but he had stabbed me in the back just like Judas.

I told Trisha, "I want a meeting with Christ."

Christ told her he wouldn't be in the same room with me. He feared I would be wired by the government, and he didn't want anyone to know his location. When I found out he wouldn't meet with me, it sent me into a rage, so I challenged him to an "Indian knife fight."

I was a man in serious physical and mental pain, so death wasn't too frightening. Under the influence of crystal meth, I would have taken on a pack of wolves with a butter knife -- and actually stood a chance of winning.

"No way," Trisha said. "He's twice your size. Are you insane?"

"I don't give a fuck anymore," I snapped back. "I have nothing and it's just a matter of time before they get the rest of me."

After getting into the verbal altercation with Christ, I was even more on edge, knowing that I could be hit any minute if they found my location. Now I was on the move every twelve hours. With my street reputation, I was more than sure one person wouldn't have the balls; it would have to be many packing high-powered weapons, which I knew they had.

Since I wasn't a musician anymore, I converted one of my base guitar cases into an assault case. I reshaped the case to hold my AK-47 and my sawed-off Mossberg shotgun, along with 1000 rounds of ammo. I never left the case more than two-feet from my reach at all times, including showers and toilet breaks. When I traveled the streets of Los Angeles, I laid the case in the back seat of my rental car so I would be ready to rock at the drop of a dime.

To up the odds in my favor, I took twenty-four shotgun shells and turned them into homemade hand grenades. This was known as a "nut-buster."

I took a shotgun shell and enclosed it in a cardboard roll, then glued on some homemade fins for balance. On the primer end of the shotgun shell, a small cork was glued with a very small hole drilled through it. I drilled through the cork before gluing. Then a roofing nail fit into the cork snugly enough to stay in, but loose enough to plunge into the primer upon impact.

The idea was that if I was being followed by a bunch of bikers, I could throw a handful out of the window of my car, easily taking out someone on a motorcycle. If I was to get into a firefight in a parking lot, I could toss a couple handfuls of shells where someone was hiding, sending pellets flying in every direction.

I was more than ready to take on an army of thugs if I had to, all the way down to the bulletproof vest Mr. K had given me to wear under my loose-fitting flannel shirt. Between my fake leg and the enclosure of my body in Kevlar armor, I didn't feel human anymore. I felt like the bionic man who never slept.

Everything I had once loved about my life was now gone. Who would have thought that first line of cocaine eight years ago would have led to this outcome? It's always that fine line, on the mirror or in a contract, that gets your soul in the end.

Chapter 85

I contacted Cain from a pay phone. "Meeting in twenty minutes," I said. "Location twenty-five."

He agreed.

We had a small window of privacy for a quick chat without anyone seeing us. I told Cain about the bikers wanting to do me in.

"Fuck those greasy bikers," he said. "It's time to put them out of the game, since they don't play well with others."

I agreed.

"Do you know where the bikers make their meth?"

"I don't think they make their own. They steal their supply from other dealers -- they're meth pirates."

~~

As days and nights passed, I moved around Los Angeles to make it harder for any would-be assassins, and I never used a telephone unless it was absolutely necessary.

I couldn't imagine the FBI breaking down my door for smoking a few joints and doing a few lines, since I had already proved that I would let them in. The FBI wanted to catch me with something; they wanted to know if what Eric said was true. Catching me with a mere eight-ball and a few joints would hardly justify all the man-hours and wiretaps, along with a helicopter. Any rookie cop the first day out on the job could grab any guy off any corner in Los Angeles to get an eight-ball.

But the problem was, meth wasn't a luxury drug anymore; it was like medicine that had to be used every day to keep moving. Without the meth, everyone I knew, including myself, would stop dead in their tracks and be paralyzed for five to six months going through withdrawals. This wasn't the time for us to let our guard down, so the meth had to flow.

~~

Sitting in the back of the room, facing the door with my AK-47, I was listening to every sound and every squeak. I thought, How could I let things get so far out of hand?

Checking the clip of my assault rifle to make sure all the bullets were loose and ready, I remembered how my parents had drilled it into my head to not take drugs. They had done everything possible that a parent could do, but the warnings had failed. I don't know what they could have done differently.

I wasn't dead or in prison, but I didn't feel like I had won a damn thing, since everything I had traveled with was in three traveling trunks. One trunk had 10,000 rounds for all my guns, and enough swords and knives to hack my way out of a shopping mall infested with the living dead.

I had truly become one of the lost angels, giving up on all thoughts of ever returning to the real world. I was just like Eric and Liesa: with no real home, just moving from place to place like a gypsy. This was the first time in my life I didn't have a place to call home, nowhere to throw my junk.

~~

The next afternoon when I woke up, Allison said, "A Hollywood agent has been leaving messages for you. She wants you to call her back about a movie deal."

"A movie deal?"

Since the agent didn't use meth, she didn't know who I was. She had heard about Eric trying to steal my identity and wanted to do a movie of the week about it. But I wasn't going to push that story, knowing the problems I would have from the FBI. Besides, I didn't want to play the part of a victim in a wheelchair in any movie of the week, so I turned down $50,000 and the movie.

~~

I had just gotten back from lunch in Beverly Hills with the agent and sparked up a joint when the phone rang.

It was Stan. "How's it going?"

I almost laughed, but I replied, "Things are cool. What's up?"

"Why don't you come down to the federal building on Wilshire Boulevard, and we'll talk about some of the things you asked regarding Liesa, 2:30?"

"Okay," I said, realizing the movie deal had spooked the government.

~~

Mr. K picked me up at Club California; I was staying that day in Neighbor Dan's apartment, facing the swimming pool. That was the second location where the FBI had called me, letting me know they knew where I was at all times.

Boarding the elevator to the parking garage, Mr. K and I noticed a few dirty-looking bikers who had taken their colors off. They were making their way through the brightly lit lobby. We stood back in the shadows and watched as they entered the courtyard, seeming out of their element. The bikers looked around as if they didn't know where they were going, until someone on the second floor waved and called them up. They went into the apartment across from me, which had its drapes closed all the time.

"Are they with Christ?" I asked.

"I'm not sure; it's hard to say. But they were up to no good, that's for damn sure."

~~

Pulling into the parking lot of the federal building, Mr. K said, "Play it cool. If they wanted to charge you, they would have just picked you up, so be cool and play the part of a victim."

"Okay."

Mr. K and I both disarmed, dropping several pistols and knives to the floor of his car, and pushed them under the seat. I went through the metal detector after Mr. K and set it off, so I had to be patted down for weapons.

An armed federal agent took us up to the FBI headquarters, where a preoccupied woman was sitting behind a bulletproof glass window in a secure room. She asked us our business, and I told her we had a meeting with Stan.

"Have a seat. He will be with you shortly."

We sat there for an hour until the lady finally said, "Stan can't meet with you. Something has come up. He will call you." We got up and left.

Once I was back in the car, I felt like Luke Skywalker escaping the Death Star. Before I even got back to the Valley, everyone in the underworld knew I had gone into the federal building, which tripped their paranoia.

~~

The next day, as soon as I walked into Allison's apartment, Liesa called. She wanted to talk with me about something really important, but I said, "I'm not interested in anything you have to say," and slammed down the phone.

It had been two months since I had seen her, but she kept calling back until I agreed to talk in person. Allison's place wasn't a secret hiding place from anyone anymore, so I told Liesa to meet me there.

~~

The front door buzzed, "Who's there?"

"It's me," Liesa replied.

I stepped outside to see her bouncing down the hallway with her hips swinging from side to side. She was dressed to kill. She knew I had a kink for high heels and thigh-highs, and she looked like the evil version of Brittney Spears.

Liesa wasn't in Allison's apartment but thirty seconds before she managed to flash her ass twice, trying to cloud my thinking. I tried to fight it off, but the meth was saying, "Tap that ass!"

I finally said without any finesse, "Enough showing off your ass. What's so damn important, I'm busy. I don't have time for your games."

Liesa wrapped her arms around me, gave me a kiss on the cheek, and said, "I'm pregnant with your baby."

"Bullshit. You don't look pregnant."

"Look at my boobs -- they're already bigger," she said, flashing her tits.

I couldn't really see any difference, but then again, I usually only saw the top of her head or her backside while she was on all fours.

"Are you sure it's mine?"

"It's yours," she replied, looking insulted. "What are you going to do?"

"If it's mine, then I don't want to raise my kid in Los Angeles. We'll have to move back to Indiana to give the kid a fair chance at being normal." I truly felt that way.

Liesa seemed happy I wasn't abandoning her, even after she totally fucked me over. I figured if the child was mine, I had to deal with it in the best way for the child's sake.

"Don't tell anyone that we're going back to Indiana," Licsa said, "or 'they' will come looking for me."

"Who is 'they'?"

Liesa changed the subject. She wanted to go back to her new place to discuss the future. She was sharing an apartment with Robin in Hollywood.

"Okay," I said.

I grabbed my weapons case, and we were out the door. We took Laurel Canyon over the mountain into Hollywood.

When I got into Liesa's apartment, I realized I left my cellular phone in her car.

"What's the security code for the front door?" I asked. "I'll need it to let myself back in?"

Liesa was very hesitant about telling me, but she had to.

"Six-six-six," she replied, looking the other way like there was nothing wrong.

I said nothing, knowing I was being sucked into a witch's den of my own free will. All over Liesa and Robin's apartment were witchcraft paraphernalia like crystal balls, a small black cauldron for burning herbs, and many pentagrams hidden in paintings, along with other goofy witchcraft crap that was completely worthless, in my opinion.

I was sure that when I wasn't there, it was lesbo-licking, toy-stuffing, muff-munching, finger-licking good times. Anybody in their right mind would have known better than to even enter the lair of two bi-sexual witches, but I was far from being in my right mind. Besides, I knew from plenty of experience that none of these so-called witches had any real supernatural powers, other than seduction.

Liesa was evil, but she wasn't stupid enough to lead me into a trap, knowing the firepower I was packing. She had seen me draw many times at the slightest bump in the night.

I spent a few days with Liesa. I really enjoyed her company, once I got past the deceit and betrayal. Her spell seemed unbreakable. I was still attracted to her after knowing everything I knew; I couldn't figure out what was wrong with my judgment.

I wondered if Eric was under her spell, too.

~~

Soon as I got back to Club California, I used my security card at the gate and entered the underground parking structure. As I parked a few spots away from the elevator, I noticed Cain and Abel standing in the shadows. We made eye contact as I got out of the car but said nothing. I took my weapon case out of the back seat and headed toward the elevator.

The elevator doors opened, and we all entered. We remained silent until the doors shut and the elevator rose to the top floor.

"What are you doing?" Cain said.

"What do you mean?"

"You were videotaped going into the federal building. What the hell were you doing there? It's got everyone real paranoid."

"The FBI asked me to come in to talk about Liesa," I said. "It had nothing to do with you guys. Chill out. You need to lay off the gack. It's twisting your brains."

"Sure that's all?" Cain inquired.

"If you think I'd do something stupid, you're nuts. What was I going to do, tell the FBI no? I had to play it off. I think it was a test to see if I would run or come in to talk.

"You were in the building for over an hour. What did you talk about?"

"Nothing. I never got to talk to the agent who called me in; something came up. I just sat there with my bodyguard, staring at the picture of George Washington while picking my nose and wondering what the lady behind the bulletproof glass was typing."

Cain stared into my eyes, trying to see if I was telling the truth. "Why are you with Liesa? She's just trying to find out more information. Don't be so damn foolish. We want her gone, and she is working for the government. Why do you think she's not in jail for helping Eric? She's one of them."

"What do you mean gone?"

"Put your hand out."

Cain dropped a capsule into the palm of my right hand.

"What is that?"

"In the capsule is a hot batch of meth, laced with a special poison. One line, and she'll have a heart attack and drop dead on the spot."

My eyes widened. <u>No fucking way.</u>

"This is what the CIA uses to rid the free world of rock stars who shout their opinions on records."

"No fucking way! I'm not going to kill her. She's not even using meth."

Cain shook his head. "You have to prove yourself if you want any more support from us. This will prove your convictions."

"I don't have to prove a damn thing. I ran this end of the Valley before I even met you guys. If I have to fight everyone by myself, I will stand alone." I pointed my finger at Cain with my teeth clenched. "None of you better lay a hand on her. She's carrying my baby."

Cain didn't hesitate. "That changes nothing. It only makes it harder. Besides, she's probably lying."

The elevator opened, and I stormed out. I knew if I didn't do what Cain asked, this would be our last friendly meeting. The next time, they would come as my executioners.

~~

Sitting on the floor and cleaning my weapons, I figured I would never live long enough to see my child born. I was going to be a father to a child who would only hear lies from his evil mother about a father he would never know.

I knew Liesa would never go back to Indiana, and there was no way in hell I was going to let her step a single foot in my parents' house. So, for the time being, I pretended to go along with her game, and we continued to play.

Chapter 86

The next day, I had Mr. K drive to the courthouse in downtown Los Angeles, just to use the pay phone in the lobby. He took his motorcycle so he could ditch anyone attempting to follow during rush-hour traffic.

Wearing a three-piece suit and carrying a black leather briefcase, Mr. K strolled into the courthouse lobby and went over to a pay phone. He attached a digital voice changer to the mouthpiece in seconds without anyone noticing.

He knew exactly what to say; we had gone over it several times.

The phone rang at Allison's, and I picked up.

The digital voice changer made him sound sinister, but with authority and power in his voice. "Is there a problem?" he asked. "Do you need to be pulled out?"

"Things are a real mess," I replied, "I got the FBI interfering with my operation."

"Is your cover blown?"

"No, but it's getting to be too much to handle."

"I'll let the committee know of the problems."

"I don't want to let them down," I replied, "but I also got this biker threat that wasn't part of the deal."

"I understand and will get back to you real soon. Be careful, and stay on top of things."

"I will."

I hung up the phone with a smile. <u>Try and figure out that one, you wiretappers.</u>

~~

Two hours later, I called a California politician I had done favors for. I wanted to add more confusion to my profile to throw off the FBI.

I had been introduced to the politician at a party eight years back. He was bringing ecstasy into the country from Sweden and needed someone to set him up with strippers/hookers. I just happened to know a lot of strippers, which sparked the secret alliance.

It took three phone calls, but he finally called me back at Allison's apartment. I wanted the FBI to know who I was speaking with, hopefully giving some credibility to the fake phone call Mr. K had made with the voice changer.

My well-connected friend said, "What's up, Brent? I heard what happened. Are you doing all right?"

"I'm holding my own, but I might need some help."

This was a somewhat risky phone call. I had a lot of dirt on this man, and if he felt threatened, I would be making a new enemy who also had assassins.

"What can I do to help?"

"I might need to start my life over," I explained. "I'll need someone to make sure all investigations are cancelled so I can go back to using my real name in Indiana."

"That's not a problem. Whatever you need, just call me." He gave me his private cell phone number. "Keep in touch."

"Thanks a lot," I said, calling him by his first name and ending the conversation like long-lost friends. That phone call alone should have stirred things up at the federal building, adding more confusion to who I was or who I might be in bed with in high places.

~~

Lying in bed with Liesa a few days later, I thought, <u>You stupid bitch.</u> <u>Your lying ass has almost gotten us both killed</u>.

Resting there with her eyes closed, she looked harmless, like a little baby with no worries in the world. Meanwhile, I couldn't sleep a wink; I was afraid to shut my eyes. I feared that the next time I awoke, I would be staring down the barrel of a gun.

Looking around her new apartment, I noticed that none of her belongings were there. Liesa still had another place she called home; this apartment was just the place she stayed when I was around.

Later that day, after lunch, the phone rang, and Liesa answered. I couldn't hear what was said, but someone seemed very displeased with her actions. She hung up and, without saying a word, made a call to her aunt's house in Sacramento.

"Hello, it's me. I'll be coming to stay with you. See you soon." She hung up the phone and looked at me. "I'm not going back to Indiana. I'm going to stay with my aunt. I'll give you a ride anywhere you want."

"I really hate you. I really do," I replied, and I meant it.

It was a cold, silent ride over the mountain and down Laurel Canyon as we descended into the Valley. I kept thinking, <u>I'm risking my neck for this</u> <u>worthless whore. I should just whack her and gain everyone's trust; she's</u> <u>nothing but a low life scammer with an extremely nice ass. Pure sadistic evil.</u> I had heard nothing but lies out of her mouth from day one. But she was carrying a child, mine or not. I handled myself accordingly.

Getting out of the car I had bought for Liesa, I said, "What, no explanation? What about the baby?"

"I'm getting rid of it."

I slammed the car door. "The baby is the only thing keeping you alive."

I stormed into Allison's apartment and slammed the door shut so hard it shook the building like a small earthquake.

But something caught my eye as I slammed the door. I opened it and took a look at the next apartment that was currently not rented. A new third deadbolt lock had been installed. I knew what that meant.

I shut the door and went inside.

Allison said, "You have that look on your face like you're going to kill someone. What's going on?"

"Liesa's gone again."

"Good. I hate that cunt."

Allison hated all the women I dated; she knew they would be my downfall.

"You need some sleep," she noticed. "I have to work on my mid-terms. Why don't you crash in my bed? I'll wake you if I hear or see anything."

"That sounds cool. See you in twelve hours."

When I woke up, two days had passed. Allison was at school, and Mr. K was sitting out in the living room watching television.

"What day is it?"

"Does it matter?" he replied. "You've been asleep for almost three days. It's Monday."

Rubbing my eyes and looking around, I asked, "Anything weird happen while I was out?"

"Something real weird. All the surveillance appears to be gone. No one has attempted to follow me, and I don't see anyone watching this place anymore."

~~

In the three days I had been asleep, Liesa left town. I checked with the post office and found out she had put in a change of address. I changed it again so her mail would go to my post office box first.

Once a week, I would take her mail back to where I was staying and spray the envelope with Freon. The envelope would become transparent for about a minute and then dry, but I would take a photo. I would read it and mail it to Liesa at her aunt's house in Rio Linda, California.

Liesa wasn't getting any weird bills like she had gotten while living with me, just personal letters from friends. But eventually I came across a letter from Eric, written in lead pencil on white tablet paper -- nothing computer generated. The return address was a P.O. box in Los Angeles. Eric didn't appear to know that Liesa had moved, but he knew about her being pregnant.

He wanted her to get rid of it.

Eric mentioned me, something about meth, but no information of value. I didn't forward it to Liesa. Since my name was mentioned, I kept it. I also opened the letter and dusted it for Eric's fingerprints. I wanted a copy for my file I had on him.

Chapter 87

<u>Thanksgiving 1994</u>

I slept through the entire weekend. A local speed metal band called THC recorded a song written about me, titled, "The Man Who Never Slept and Wouldn't Die." It was fast and a very violent song. I felt honored.

Liesa had been gone about five weeks, and I was just trying to lay low, hoping everyone would forget about me if I stayed out of the limelight. After three days of solid sleep, I was awakened by Allison.

"You missed dinner," she said, "and you have company."

Bastard Ben was standing in the kitchen with a weird look on his face, like he had seen a ghost.

"What's up?"

Bastard Ben put his finger to his lips and signaled me to follow him outside. We stepped outside and walked around to the back of the apartment complex, where we talked in private behind the painted brown metal dumpster. The sounds of bees and flies buzzing around the dumpster masked our voices from anyone trying to listen.

"You are absolutely right about everything concerning the bikers," Bastard Ben declared. "They have Allison's and Neighbor Dan's apartments bugged. They know everything you're even thinking of doing."

"Are you sure?"

"Yeah, real sure. I was at this biker party a few hours ago when a strange guy sat down next to me."

"Yeah."

"He asked, "Are you having a good time?""

I said, "What's it to you?"

The strange guy looked at me kind of funny and said, "It's time for you to go."

"What the hell are you talking about?"

"'You don't recognize me,' the guy replied. "I'm Brent's best friend.""

"Then I recognized him. He looked different from the picture you showed me; his hair is much shorter. And there was Liesa standing over in the corner. She must have pointed me out as being one of your close friends.

"You saw Liesa?"

"Yes. When I saw her, I got up and headed for the door and noticed several bikers following me."

"What did you do?"

"I took off as fast as I could and got the hell out of there."

I hated always being right.

"It's not safe to stay here anymore," said Bastard Ben. "I can't go home, either. They'll be after me, knowing I was the one supplying you with information."

"We can go stay with Silva out in Palmdale until we can figure out what the hell is going on," I said. "No one should find us out there."

"That sounds good," he replied. "I'm going back to my place to get some of my belongings. I'll be back in twenty minutes."

I walked Bastard Ben back out to his car, while looking around for any signs of trouble. We saw nothing until he opened the car door.

Lying on his front seat were thirteen white lilies, the flowers that are laid on graves. That shook us both up a little, knowing they were extremely close.

"Give me a gun," said Bastard Ben. "I'm not going home unarmed."

I reached into my waistband and retrieved my Colt .380. "Here's my favorite gun," I said. "It's never let me down, and here's an extra clip of hollow-points."

Bastard Ben took off, and I started packing everything I had into the three trunks, ready for travel. Once I got everything packed, I wrapped my AK-47 in my trench coat so I could carry it under my arm unnoticed in case of sudden trouble. I was locked and loaded.

~~

I sat there while the clock ticked away, and a half-hour turned into an hour and an hour turned into a day, without a word from Bastard Ben. I called Mr. K, and we went to his apartment. He wasn't there, but we found his car a block away, unlocked.

The car was filled with his belongings, and one of the Colt .380 pistol clips was on the floor, halfway under the front seat, empty. It was full when I gave it to him, but it was empty . . . missing ten bullets.

Mr. K said, "It's time to get out of this fucked-up town and give it back to the evil that wants to control the meth trade."

I knew he was right, but I was too stubborn to listen.

Mr. K's wife had just gotten her doctoral degree, so they were going to move to North Carolina, where a position had opened up. He was taking a job in bail bonds.

"Do you want to come?" he asked. "It's really nice, and the people are very friendly. It's time to get off the meth and get away from anyone who's infected."

"No," I replied, "I can't leave just yet. I have unfinished business. But thanks for the offer and for helping me survive the worst times in my life. I will never forget you, and if I live, I'll come visit someday."

We shook hands and hugged.

I watched Mr. K drive off. My crew of people I could trust was getting smaller every day.

It was getting even hotter down in the hood, so Rudy was leaving the country. He was going to stay down in El Salvador in his second house until the government backed off. I also declined to go south of the border.

I got ahold of Silva.

"No problem," he said. "You can stay with me."

Palmdale was on the other side of the mountain in the next valley beyond.

~~

I had never been to Silva's apartment before; he had a three-bedroom on the top floor. I got the spare bedroom at the back of the apartment. There was only a single staircase leading up to Silva's apartment, so I would hear anyone coming up the stairs or see them on the hidden camera I had mounted.

I checked Silva's apartment for any hidden transmitter in the usual locations. Since there wasn't much furniture, it was easy. Then I got to the phone line.

I showed Silva, and he said, "What the fuck is that?"

I unhooked the alligator clips and held it under the light: TX-6/VHF.

"It's a phone tap. Something you can buy out of a spy magazine. Someone is interested in what you have been saying; it's not here for me."

"I bet it's my ex-wife," Silva said. "We're fighting over visiting rights to my son. My ex-wife's father used to work for the phone company."

"Great. Does she have any idea who I am?"

"No."

Silva and I drove out to "Kentucky," a shooting range out in the desert. I wanted to make sure Silva knew how to shoot before I gave him a weapon. We set up body targets on wooden crosses and then walked back twenty-five yards to the stack of weapons. I handed Silva the AK-47 and showed him how to pull the bolt back and load the first 7.62 round of fifty into the chamber.

Silva dropped the weapon to his waist like Arnold Schwarzenegger, all ready to start blasting.

"If you pull the trigger in that position," I said, "it'll recoil and hit you in the nuts." Shaking my head, I added, "This is not the movies, so hold the assault weapon to your shoulder and look through the sights. Pick your target, and don't spray like Machine-gun Kelly."

After the sixth clip of ammo at fifty dollars a clip, Silva had it down. He was no longer afraid of the weapon and blew the body targets to hell.

Once I felt Silva was ready at the end of the training session, I gave him a 9mm and said, "Only pull it if you plan on shooting someone, or you'll look like a complete punk."

~~

Living out in Palmdale was weird. Not much happened under the hot desert sun, but a lot of strange people came out after the sun went down . . . much like in Hollywood.

Silva lived in a huge complex with ten buildings surrounded by a ten-foot cement wall holding back the desert sands and homeless intruders.

One early evening, I sent Silva out to grab us something to eat. The last time I took his car to get food was the last time I would drive it. I had been going through the McDonalds drive-thru when the car ran out of gas with fifteen cars behind me blowing their horns. His car's gas gauge didn't work.

Silva was probably gone ten minutes when the phone rang.

"Is Silva there?" asked a female voice.

"He's not here."

"Is this Mr. B?"

"Who is this?"

"This is Silva's ex-wife. Let me tell you something. The only reason he's helping you is because he's working for the district attorney's office. He got busted a while ago. Bet you didn't know that."

"How do you know he's working for the DA's office?"

"I have a tape recording of Silva talking with the DA."

"I want to hear it."

"I'll give it to Ara," she replied. "He'll let you hear it."

Ara was an old friend of Silva; they had grown up together in the Valley. When Silva returned with the food, I didn't mention the phone call, other than to say she had called. The next chance I got, I called Ara.

"She told me the same thing," he said, "but she never produced the tape."

"Oh really," I replied. "Is she credible at all?"

"She's a female, so take it how you want, but she tried to pay me to plant drugs in Silva's apartment. She wanted to have the police bust him."

"Do you think Silva could be working for the district attorney's office?"

"It's possible," Ara replied. "He's been acting stranger than usual, and someone else said they saw him taking down license plate numbers at this computer hacker party out in the Valley last month."

"No shit."

"Did you know that his apartment complex in Palmdale is a government complex? Everyone who lives there was relocated through H.U.D. after the earthquake eight months ago."

"I didn't know that." I was wondering how Silva could afford such a place when he didn't have a job.

My pager went off, so I ended the conversation with Ara. I didn't recognize the number, but I recognized the code "69 slam." It was Trisha. It had been months since I had seen her; she was living in Palmdale now, too.

Chapter 88

Up until six months ago, I had never even heard of Palmdale. It was nothing more than a desert town a couple of hours north of Hollywood. It was a place I wouldn't have come to by choice.

"I'm staying for free in an apartment complex that my attorney owns," Trisha said. "I'm waiting for a settlement from a car accident."

I remembered the car accident from a few years earlier, which she caused by her reckless driving. Somehow, with the help of her crooked lawyer, she was getting some money out of it.

"Give me an address," I said, "and I'll come over for a visit. I also live in Palmdale." She didn't seem surprised.

Trisha's place was on the other side of town, the shady side. I could tell by the gang symbols marked on the walls.

Her apartment was a pit; I could see why she was getting it for free. It wasn't fit for dogs to live in. The place hadn't been cleaned in years, and the desert heat had baked the crust in the bathroom, so I didn't touch anything in fear of a staph infection.

How could Trisha go from penthouse living to this? I thought. I also couldn't see how she would even feel safe. Everyone in the building had light brown skin except Trisha, with her huge boobs, white skin, and blonde hair, which made her a target of home invasion . . . especially the way she walked around half-naked with the drapes open. As usual, Trisha was fearless.

She was now driving a Jaguar, which wasn't hers, of course. It was quite impressive, except for having a rusty coat hanger as a radio antenna. That made no sense; it made it look like a gypsy-mobile. Trisha had already wrecked the front end, but it wasn't her fault . . . she claimed.

After we had smoked a couple of joints and done a few rails, Trisha said, "You have to get out of Los Angeles, or you're never going to get out."

"I'm not leaving until I get my new leg," I snapped back. "Then I'll think about leaving."

"I can't believe the mess you've gotten yourself into," she said harshly. "There are so many people who are out to get you, and for so many different reasons. It's insane." She walked around the room for a minute and then turned toward me. "I'll take you to all your appointments to get your new leg, and then get the hell out of town, please. The meth is making everyone nuts."

I agreed.

I stayed the night at Trisha's apartment; she was going to drive me to Los Angeles in the morning for the final fitting for my new leg. While Trisha slept, I stayed up on guard. There was no way, no fucking way, I could sleep in an unsecured place.

~~

Sitting in the dark living room with the lights out, I tuned my night-vision goggles to the outside surroundings. I kept my assault rifle pointed at the front door, ready to stop any forced entry, and my sawed-off shotgun pointed in the direction of her front window, which was almost big enough to drive a truck through. My hearing was so in tune, I could hear the bugs crawling through the walls of the building, and every door opening and closing throughout the rundown complex.

Trisha's apartment faced the street, so I could see who was coming and going. Around four in the morning, as tumbleweeds were blowing by, something caught my attention. I started to see weird movement across the street. At first I thought it was government agents setting up surveillance, or a kill team sent to take me out.

I had learned from the past how loud weapons could be inside a small room, so I inserted earplugs carefully. I pulled the slide back, inserted the first 7.62 round into the chamber of my AK-47, and clicked the safety on. I carefully kicked open my weapons case and retrieved a sound grenade and two extra clips of ammo and stuck them into my belt. I stuffed handfuls of shotgun shells into my pockets.

As I got ready, the group of guys outside slowly dispersed in all directions. Some crouched down behind the bushes, a couple more hid behind the wall of another building, and one nut climbed into a tree hanging over the street. I thought, <u>He'll be the first to get blasted.</u>

Leaning over, I snorted a huge rail off the mirror on the side table, thinking, <u>This is it: the final battle.</u> I wanted to be at full-strength, since I was backed in and had no way out.

I watched and waited for their next move, but what they did was unexpected. A line of cars and trucks started pulling up, and the guy in the tree handed down what appeared to be drugs. Meanwhile, the other guy hiding in the bush took the money.

I was relieved. It was a criminal operation and had nothing to do with me. They had no idea a man armed like the Terminator was watching from across the street.

The man in charge was standing behind the brick wall, hiding in the dark shadows; he had the large amount of drugs. Using runners, he would re-supply the front men every fifteen minutes and collect the money, so they never had a lot of money or drugs at once.

When a cop car came patrolling by, they saw nothing; everyone dealing drugs went into hiding. The guy in the tree didn't move, and the other guys darted into the apartment complex. When the cop car was gone . . . it was business as usual.

I grabbed my police scanner and ran through the channels. Sure enough, these guys were using wireless headsets to talk. They had lookouts for the cops at the end of each block. It was very well organized.

The line of cars finally stopped around nine o'clock. I guess everyone had to be at their real jobs. I put the heavy firepower and the surveillance equipment away.

The last guy from across the street -- the one who appeared to be in charge -- entered Trisha's complex. I opened the apartment door and gave him a look that only someone in his business would understand. On the street, you must look people in the eyes; that's how they read you. You must show no fear at all, without being threatening.

The guy stopped and looked at me. I was a crazy-looking white boy with long dark hair and a single blonde streak, wearing dress clothes with Doc Martens combat Boots. I got his attention.

"What's up?" I said.

"Doing my thing."

"I'm staying here," I replied. "I'm not complaining. I just want in."

"My name is Caesar."

"You can call me Mr. B, or the Candle Man."

Caesar was shocked. "The Candle Man from Sherman Oaks?"

"That's right . . . One and the same."

"I know who you are," he replied. "I thought you got killed."

"I got shot," I answered, "but I'm alive and chilling out in Palmdale."

I stuck my fake leg up on the door, then pulled one of my throwing knives at lightning speed, spun it, and thrust it into my prosthetic leg with a bone-crunching sound.

Caesar didn't say anything; I had proved who I was. He handed me a bindle and said, "This one is on me." It was a show of respect.

Graciously, I replied, "Thanks, but I don't smoke crack."

"This is meth. No one wants crack anymore. You saw to that."

At least I was known for that much.

I opened the bindle and saw that it was snow white. It was the same stuff I had seen floating around the Valley. It kept you up with no feeling of being high -- just awake, and ready to tear someone's head off. Cain had tried to unload some of it on me once, maybe even twice, but I'd sent it back.

I invited Caesar in and cut him a fat line out of my personal stash with the double-edged knife I pulled out of my leg.

"This is the real shit," I said. "Have a try."

One hour later, Caesar was knocking on the door, wanting more and wanting to know if I could supply Palmdale.

"I'm out of the business for now," I said, "but when things change, we'll work out a deal. By the way, where are you getting that meth from?" I had no intention of supplying anyone anymore.

"Normally, if someone was to ask me something like that, I would tell them to fuck off," said Caesar. "But since you're the Godfather, I'll tell. Why do you want to know?"

"I want to know who's making this crap," I answered. "You can see it's not nearly as good as what I shared with you."

"That's for damn sure. I'm kicking." Caesar thought about what I'd said and replied, "I'm getting the meth from my cousin. He had a connection after he came back from Desert Storm."

"Tell me more."

"My cousin gets it from some government guy, but that's all I know."

"If you want me to supply you," I demanded, "I must know whose toes I'm stepping on. I'll need a plate number off his car. When you get that information, we'll talk seriously about getting you the good meth."

~~

When Trisha woke up, she said, "Did you get any sleep?"
"Sure," I replied. "It was calm and quiet all night."

Chapter 89

El Nino was in full rage; it had been raining for almost two months straight. Everything was flooded, and mudslides were shutting down all the major highways. The weather report advised anyone who didn't have to travel to stay off the highways leading into Los Angeles.

"I'm going to call the prosthesis lab to cancel my appointment," I told Trisha. "The weather is too bad to travel back into Los Angeles."

She snorted a huge rail of speed off the plate and said, "There's no way in hell you're missing that appointment. Get ready to leave in a few minutes. Even if I have to drag you by your nuts, you're going."

I couldn't change her mind.

The drive to Los Angeles proved I wasn't as fearless as I thought. At speeds of eighty to ninety miles per hour, the tires were hydroplaning seventy-five percent of the time. I finally had to just close my eyes and hope we didn't slide off a cliff as we traveled over the mountain and into the next valley. There was no way of getting Trisha to slow down. She was in a meth trance, locked onto one thing: Get to Los Angeles.

Sitting in the passenger seat, holding on for dear life, I thought about all the events that had just taken place. I knew that if I didn't swallow my Leo pride and get out of Los Angeles, I would be dead. I would probably vanish without a trace.

When we finally arrived in downtown L.A., I felt damn lucky to step on solid pavement, even if the pavement was flooded with three inches of water, because the drains were clogged with the belongings of the homeless.

The leg fitting went well. The new leg would be completed and ready for pick-up in four days. The fitter at the prosthesis lab was concerned about the condition of my stump.

"Why is your stump so full of sores?" he asked. "Why can't you just leave off the prosthesis and use crutches until they heal?"

I couldn't tell him I was at war, that I had to wear the fake leg for weeks at a time so I wouldn't get caught legless. I didn't answer his question.

"You also have water on the knee from wearing it too long," he continued. "You need to stay off the leg and leave the prosthesis off until all the sores can heal. Otherwise, it'll be hard to break in the new leg and get a proper fitting."

The hard part was putting the leg back on. Once the pressure was released from my stump, it would swell, so re-attaching the leg was very painful. Then, after wearing the leg for a week, it would smell and itch really bad. When I finally took it off, I had to quickly wipe my stump down with rubbing alcohol to remove the film of heavy sweat. The alcohol set my skin on fire; sometimes it almost made me scream.

Once Trisha and I got back to her car, I snorted a line of pain control and lit up a joint for the car ride.

I had Trisha stop by my bank to get some money. My bank accounts were hidden all over Los Angeles, so nothing was in one place. I always used the outside versa-teller, but this time it didn't work. As I entered the bank, I got a real bad feeling, but I proceeded up to the teller. I filled out the savings withdrawal slip for a thousand dollars and pushed it to the bank teller.

A few seconds passed, and then she said, "This account has been closed."

I almost freaked out, but somehow remained cool. "I forgot that I closed this account," I said casually. I exited the bank under the watchful eye of the security camera.

I had Trisha drive me to another bank, but that account was also closed and the money gone. A fourth one told me the same thing.

"What's going on?" Trisha asked.

"Drive me to Studio City."

~~

For once, luck was on my side; they had not found my secret drop box. I opened the box and withdrew all the money: $5,000. It wasn't much, but enough to keep me afloat for a little while longer. I threw my old cellular phone away and used the new one out of my box. It would be good for a while until they locked on to the new signal.

Riding with Trisha back out to Palmdale, I felt sick. All the planning and saving for a way out was gone. I was almost broke. I didn't know how they had found the secret accounts; I didn't have anything on paper anywhere for anyone to find. It was all in my head. How could they know, unless they used a psychic or the "Van Eck System" to figure out what accounts were mine?

When I got back to Silva's later that day, I was extremely depressed. I finally realized I was going to lose the game. I literally had nothing. All my dreams had been shattered, and what I knew of love smelled of betrayal.

I kept thinking, <u>Don't let them get to you. Don't let them win by default.</u>

I decided to take a hot bath, hoping that might help me think and reduce the stress before my brain exploded. I drew the bath water and poured Epsom salts and apple cider vinegar into the extremely hot water to help relieve my muscle aches. I lit several scented candles to help mask the smell of the vinegar.

Submerged in hot water, I took a fresh razor blade and sliced open all the sores on my stump, squeezed each one until it was emptied of its poison content. I kept draining and re-filling the tub with fresh hot water every half hour until I got all the sores cleaned out.

Then I had to take care of the water on my knee, which was swollen because of the ill-fitting leg.

I remembered as a kid watching the veterinarian use a basketball air pump fitting to let gas out of a sick horse's stomach. I sharpened the bike pump needle with my sharpening stone and pushed it into the liquid filled area around my kneecap. It hurt like hell, and hot, discolored liquid shot out of the needle for several minutes. I continued to push all around my kneecap until it was "deflated" and I could see the actual shape of my kneecap again.

When I got out of the tub, I dried my stump and covered each sore with a solid, protective clear coat of superglue. I let it air dry for a few minutes and snorted lines of meth. After the lines kicked in, I pulled a nylon over my stump and put the twenty-four pairs of socks on. I slid my stump into the socket of the fake leg, and off I went.

When I came out of the bathroom, Silva asked, "Do you think the FBI took your money, or was it criminals?"

"At this point," I replied, "I really don't know."

I finally decided to swallow my pride. I was out-gunned, almost out of money, and the people working against me had total control of the phone lines.

The next phone call I made was to my brother. "I'm ready to get the fuck out," I said.

"Good. I'll book a flight and be out in a couple of days."

"Thanks."

That night after dinner, I told Trisha I was finally leaving town. "My brother will be here tomorrow afternoon," I said.

"Good," she replied. "Be careful, and don't tell anyone else you're leaving. Here's a going-away present. I want you to have this jam-box."

"I already have one in storage, but thanks."

I tried to hand it back, but Trisha insisted and practically forced me to take it. I put it in the trunk of my rental car with the rest of my things, kissed Trisha goodbye, and gave her firm butt a little squeeze just for memory's sake. She smiled and waved goodbye.

I would miss her.

~~

Traveling back over the mountain into the next valley, I couldn't get something off my mind: What was Trisha doing out in Palmdale? And I hoped the jam-box didn't have a hidden transmitter.

Rule number one: beware of people bearing electronic gifts. As soon as I got back to Allison's, I set the jam-box on the coffee table and stared at it, thinking, I have to know.

I grabbed a screwdriver and tried to take the jam-box apart, but the screws had been filled with superglue so it couldn't be taken apart. I found that very suspicious, so I set the jam-box on the ground, popped out the clip in my AK-47, and hit the jam-box until it had cracked open. I wanted to see the insides.

Sure enough, it had a transmitter and a tracking device with an extra power pack so it would last a while.

I was outraged. I knew Trisha wasn't cable of building such an electronic device. But someone had told her to give it to me. I guessed the bikers had done it, because the government didn't use duct tape to hold devices in place.

I was extremely pissed. I hate being played. I called Trisha, but her phone number had already been disconnected. I didn't have time to drive back to Palmdale, which was a hundred miles away, so I called Silva and asked him to drive by her place.

He called me back in an hour, saying, "She's already gone."

Chapter 90

Allison picked my brother up at the airport while I was out taking care of last-minute business. We stayed that night at Brittney's and she drove us to the hospital in the morning so I could get my new leg.

When I got to the registration desk, I told the nurse I had an appointment. "I'm supposed to be picking up my new prosthetic leg today."

"I'll check," she replied. "Have you stayed at this hospital before? I can't find any records in the computer."

I just rolled my eyes and walked right past. I knew my way around this hospital like the back of my hand. I found the guy who had done my fitting.

"What the hell is going on?" he asked. "I finished your new leg, but I got orders not to release it to you for some reason."

I shook my head in amazement.

The technician looked around and found the leg. "Here it is," he said, showing it to me and sticking it in a black trash bag. "Take it. I'll act like I didn't get the computer memo until you were already gone."

"Thanks," I said, shaking his hand. We both knew something weird was going on, and I wasn't going to try to explain. I didn't have time.

I took the black trash bag and walked back to the waiting room, where Brittney and my brother were waiting.

"Does the new leg fit any better?" my brother asked.

"I don't know," I replied. "Let's just get the hell out of here."

When I got back to Brittney's, I tried the new leg, but it didn't fit worth a crap. My stump had changed shape since the last time I had gotten cast. Every single step I took hurt like hell, no matter how much drugs I used to ease the pain. Nothing worked, and I was forced to put the old leg back on.

I was deeply disappointed and angry. I had been promised that the new leg would be lightweight, with state-of-the-art upgrades. But it was nothing of the sort; it was a piece of crap. The leg was a solid rod with a foot; the ankle didn't move or give an inch. If I wanted another one made, it would cost at least $10,000 to $15,000. I didn't have that kind of money anymore. I was almost broke.

After a few hours of extreme anger, I decided this was not the time. I had to get out of town before something happened while my brother was here. We needed to go.

~~

When we arrived at the storage unit with the rental truck, the security guard waved me in with a strange look. As I opened my storage unit, I could immediately tell someone had rummaged through my stuff. Besides, they had left a calling card.

Draped over my entertainment center, practically hanging in my face, was a piss-stained bed sheet from the L.A. County Jail. Most of my belongings were in sorry shape. All the boxes were open and falling apart from someone going through them numerous times.

"What a fucking mess," my brother said. "What do you want to save?"

I picked out the candle-making equipment and personal items that I wanted to keep to remember the good times in Hollywood. It took us seven hours to load the truck, and when we were done, we were dead tired.

Brittney and I spent one last night together, while my brother slept on the couch. Brittney fell fast asleep as soon as she got under the covers, but I couldn't sleep a wink -- not on my last night in Los Angeles.

~~

In the morning, my brother and Brittney looked well rested, but I hadn't slept in probably two weeks. I was really starting to feel the effects.

We ate breakfast at the Big Boy's in Burbank. When I was done eating, I went to the bathroom and entered the stall with the handicap sign. It was sad but true; I could use it.

I chopped out two huge rails on the back of the toilet and snorted them with a hundred-dollar bill. It still burned like hell, reminding me I was still alive. I was glad I had decided to finally quit and go clean.

I hadn't met anyone who had been able to quit. I had no support or anyone to ask for advice. I would be alone.

Once my eyes stopped watering from the meth, I turned around and lifted the toilet lid, stared at the water, hit the flush, and threw a couple of eight-balls into the swirling whirlpool. That was it. I had no more.

It was hard to flush the last of the good meth; it was the last batch I would ever get from Cain. But I knew I had to do it. I couldn't risk my brother getting in trouble because of my drugs during this cross-country venture.

I said goodbye to Brittney and to the city of Los Angeles, which I had called home for the last decade of decadence. It was hard to leave under these circumstances; it wasn't the way I wanted to go. I wanted to have fond memories of Hollywood, but at the present time, all I could think about were the nightmares.

I had come to Hollywood with dreams of being a rock star, but sadly, I would only be remembered as an eccentric gangster who had had a ten-year party.

~~

Boots was freaking out. She had to ride up front with us in the truck's cab. I knew it was going to be a long four days after she relieved herself in my lap when my brother let out the clutch.

As we were going over the first mountain, leaving Los Angeles on the 210 Freeway, the last lines of meth finally wore off. What would have kept any normal person up for days only lasted an hour at this point. I passed out cold for fifteen hours straight, seat-belted in, and left the driving to my brother. When I awoke, I was in New Mexico. I had escaped Los Angeles alive but had soiled myself from stress.

It was a good trip, with no problems except when the DEA stopped us and searched the truck in Missouri. They had found nothing because I had nothing, and they let us go on our way after Boots attacked the drug-sniffing police dog.

When we arrived in Indiana, it was snowing and looked beautiful. It was a sight for sore eyes, home sweet home. I waved to the <u>Welcome to Indiana</u> sign.

We stopped at my parents' house for a quick visit, and then I went to live with my brother. He had a three-bedroom house in Valparaiso on the north side in a quiet upscale neighborhood. I got the small bedroom, down in the basement across from the laundry room. It was smaller than my walk-in closet at my last house. The room was cold, and the windows of my bedroom were covered with snow, making it dark and gloomy. I felt like I was in a dungeon, which made me miss California even more every day.

I had a lot of time to think. Everyone back here had jobs and families, so I was alone to deal with life. It was really a different scene.

I spent countless nights watching television in the basement with Boots, trying to figure out my next move. This was the first time I didn't have any type of income or any way to make money. There was no way in hell I would even think of trying to get my old welding job back; I literally had nightmares about going back to "Thrall Car."

I really couldn't see myself working for anyone other than myself. There was no way I was going to take orders from any geek or stupid college-educated fuck -- no way. I would end up killing someone. So I basically just dreamed about the life I once had, wanting it back every day while wondering if Liesa was really carrying my offspring some two thousand miles away.

Sitting by myself, I got depressed and then very angry about my current situation. I should have just been happy to be alive and not in prison . . . but every time I looked at the dirty melting snow and the bare trees, I remembered that some of my enemies were still enjoying the warm rays of Southern California. Meanwhile, I was stuck in Indiana during the worst months of the year.

Weeks passed, and I thought I would never hear from anyone in Los Angeles. Then, one afternoon, I got a call from Rudy, who was back from El Salvador.

"Call me back at this number from a pay phone in ten minutes," he said. So I did.

"How are you doing, Bubba?"

"Not good."

"I found out through a certain contact that the government worked on your brother's house before you even got there so they could keep an eye on you. Be careful what you say."

"Don't worry. These people have no idea who I am."

"Good. I'll keep in contact."

"Stay cool."

So the game still wasn't over -- we had just changed locations.

~~

The next day, all hell broke loose in Los Angeles. The Feds mopped up the rest of my crew who were still doing dirt. The Fiendish Eight were no more. The Feds also hit all the skinheads' meth labs during early morning raids all over the north end of the San Fernando Valley, seizing thousands of pounds of meth and untraceable cash and weapons.

By this time, it had been weeks since I had done a line of meth, and I was starting to feel the chemical withdrawals. I caught myself many times walking down the aisles of a drug store looking at the cold medicine, knowing what I could create and share with others. I would be very popular again -- but at what price? I could literally destroy my hometown just by cooking these chemicals together to create meth. Meth was a monster I didn't want to let out of the box in a place like Valparaiso. In translation, Valparaiso means Vale of Paradise.

I knew the government was just waiting in the shadows to see if I would fall back into my old habits, and with the stricter laws in Indiana, I wouldn't see the light of day if I was caught messing with meth. It wasn't like Los Angeles, where you could do anything you wanted. This was the real world.

The more I sat around and thought about everything that had happened, the more intense the withdrawals became. To try to take my mind off things, I began hanging out at the clubs I had played when I was a musician. But every time I ran into someone I hadn't seen for a few years, they would remember me as being a rock star and want to know how many celebrities I had met while living in Hollywood. Movie stars and rock stars were the furthest thing from my mind. For many years I had supplied drugs to many Hollywood celebrities, including low-life rock stars I had once admired, and many of them still owed me thousands of dollars. Their autographs weren't worth the checks they were signed on.

After making a few appearances back in the local Chicago rock scene, the phone started to ring off the wall with offers to jam. But I wasn't a rock star anymore; it had probably been three years since I had even picked up a guitar.

I said, "Thanks, but not right now."

Some people took it as an insult that I didn't want to play, but I wasn't in the right frame of mind. My guitar case were still filled with deadly weapons.

~~

No one in Indiana even knew what "crank" really was; they thought it was called crank because it cranked you up. It had gotten the nickname because bikers had once smuggled the meth across the county in the crankcases of their Harleys.

Indiana's version of speed could be bought at any gas station in the form of a pill called "white cross" or "357 Magnum," but it wasn't even close. I tried three white crosses and two 357 Magnums while downing them with a double espresso, hoping to get a speed buzz, but I felt nothing. I didn't even break a sweat, except when I got an upset stomach an hour later, followed by the shits.

I tried not to think about meth. But when I wasn't thinking about meth, I was thinking about Liesa and revenge. It was a horrible trio of thoughts that wouldn't stop running through my mind the entire time I was awake.

The more depressed I became, the harder it became to get out of bed. I had no energy or motivation to do anything. I was dwelling on the past too much for my mental health.

Finally I called Krazy Kurtis and said, "Why don't you come for a visit?

Chapter 91

I picked up Krazy Kurtis at the train station in downtown Chicago. He had taken the train so he could carry his .45 caliber, along with some goodies. We had learned that trick from Eric.

"I didn't come all this way to sit at your brother's house," Krazy Kurtis said. "Let's go out and raise some hell."

We did a few rails and went out to a bar called McCool's in South Haven, a hillbilly town about twelve miles away, to see a heavy metal band. Since we were on speed, we drank like fishes without feeling any effects of the booze, besides wanting to get rowdy. After the club closed, we partied with some chicks at a motel until five in the morning, then decided to head home, trying to beat the sunrise.

Driving down Route 6, Krazy Kurtis pulled out his .45 caliber and started blowing off mailboxes as we sped by at sixty miles per hour.

"Don't it remind you of the good old days in L.A.?" he yelled, while laughing like a madman.

"Kurtis, this is Indiana," I yelled. "Put that away before we end up in prison. This isn't Hollywood, where you can pop caps off without anyone caring."

~~

The next morning, we went out for breakfast. I told Krazy Kurtis what Rudy had said about my brother's house.

"I'm not surprised," he said. "I have some information that I couldn't tell you over the phone. This is the real reason I made the two-thousand-mile trip -- to talk with you in person."

Before leaving Los Angeles, I had given Krazy Kurtis a list of license plates I had gotten off strange vehicles that I thought were following me around the city. His father was a Texas Ranger, so I knew he could get the information.

"My father flipped," he said. "He wanted to know why I would have these license numbers, and what the fuck I was doing."

Some of the numbers belonged to the FBI, some DEA. They had been gathered around the time Eric was caught and the mess with the mansion in Sherman Oaks. But all the license plates I had gotten while staying with Silva in Palmdale had belonged to a company called E-Systems, out of Dallas, Texas. Even the license plate on the gray van that had delivered the meth to Caesar in Palmdale had belonged to E-Systems.

"Who the fuck is E-Systems, and why are they watching me?" I asked. "Why are they moving in on the meth business?"

"It only gets better," Kurtis replied. "I have copies of a special <u>Sixty Minutes</u> did about E-Systems."

Kurtis put the tape in. <u>Sixty Minutes</u> said that the company was nothing but a front for the CIA. E-Systems were independent contractors the CIA used for surveillance operations. They were already in trouble for shooting a suspected drug dealer and his wife through the walls of a hotel room by accident . . . they claimed. <u>Sixty Minutes</u> could never get a straight answer from anyone.

"I found their location in Texas," Krazy Kurtis said. "It was surrounded by a tall steel fence with barbed wire strung across the top. No one was getting in or out."

That really freaked me out. The CIA was nothing but a bunch of killers for hire, and they truly enjoyed their sadist work. I didn't want to deal with "spooks," but things were starting to make some sense.

I remembered the story about the skinheads being taken out by the CIA, but I hadn't believed it at the time. I just couldn't stop wondering, <u>Why would the C.I.A. even be in the country? And what's their involvement with meth?</u>

~~

After getting back from the train station, I noticed the red light flashing on the answering machine. I pushed the <u>play</u> button. I had been waiting for this phone call for five years, but the message wasn't for me; it was for my brother.

Angel wanted his address so she could send him a wedding invitation.

That really set me off. How did she even have his phone number? Did she know that I was living there? Was she just rubbing it in my face?

I was so angry, I couldn't find words to describe how I felt. Angel had never sent me a get-well card or called my parents to see how I was doing, but she had the nerve to invite my brother to her wedding. That almost hurt worse than what Liesa had done. Once again, love was replaced by hate . . . and the hate always seemed to feel better.

I paced back and forth, walking in circles and stewing to a full-blown rage. To release my frustrations, I started smashing everything in sight. I snapped.

I pulled out my trunks and suitcases; I would only take what I could carry. I wanted to be back in the game, making money instead of living in a basement like some nobody.

I swore I would never date again. I had gotten taken out of the game by the women I had chosen to love. It wasn't the drugs or the government, or even the bikers who had gotten to me. It was the constant broken hearts that had driven me under.

As I packed my suitcases in rage, the room started to spin. I fell to the floor.

~~

By the time everything was said and done, I ended up moving back in with my parents. I was right back where I had started, with less than I had ten years ago, before leaving for Los Angeles full of dreams of stardom and no monkeys on my back.

I was furious with my brother. It would be years before we spoke again.

To finally make my mother happy and hopefully remove that look of disappointment from my father's face, I cut my hair short. I was trying to create the appearance of being normal, but I was far from that. I had had long hair for fifteen years; it was part of my personality. I felt like I had finally sold out and given into society's demands.

When I awoke that first morning in my childhood bedroom, I looked over at the mirror on the dresser and rubbed my face. I had dark circles under my eyes and short hair. I looked like the nerd I had been back in high school. My worst fears had come true. Now I knew how Samson felt after Delilah had cut his hair. I felt weak, and it sent me into a deep depression.

Anytime I was awake, I was obsessed with that same trio of haunting thoughts that would never quit: meth, Liesa, and revenge. Lying in bed, wishing I were dead, I had no energy or zeal for life. I felt like my life was over, and no matter how much my mother tried to get me out of bed, I only sank further into depression. I couldn't believe I was living back at home; I hated being a burden on my parents. They didn't deserve it, and I felt like a loser having to ask them for help.

So I slept for the next six months, only getting up to eat and use the bathroom. I lived in a dream world. I wanted nothing to do with the real world and didn't want to live anymore. Days and nights passed, and time seemed to stand still while I hid under my covers dreaming of a life I had once lived.

My parents hadn't given up on me; they got me a used car and tried to support me emotionally. Since I was free and hadn't gotten busted, my parents had no idea what I had just gone through. I wasn't about to tell them.

I imagined I was like a Vietnam veteran returning from war. No one around me could possibly understand why I was looking in bushes and trees, over my shoulder and around every corner. None of my friends in Indiana had seen me when I was in a wheelchair or how weak I was when I came home from the hospital addicted to morphine. They had just heard wild stories, and then I showed up a year later without even a slight limp.

Since I never wore shorts, no one saw the fake leg. The way I walked around, it appeared to be no big deal, but in my head, it was a huge deal.

Every single step I took reminded me of everything that had happened. Without the meth flowing through my bloodstream, it really hurt to walk, so I didn't. I slept the time away until something brought the fight back into my life.

If I wanted to throw my life away, that was my business. But someone trying to take it . . . That was a different matter entirely.

~~

I was lying in bed when my mother brought in a letter with no return address. It was stamped with California as its point of origin. I smelled Trisha's perfume on the envelope. I would know her scent anywhere.

The letter inside had been computer-generated with no handwriting for me to evaluate.

Christ is sending a hit team to pay you a visit, it read. They still think you work for the government and are being blamed for several raids.

The letter was not signed, but I knew it was a warning from Trisha. She was still my blonde guardian angel.

I knew it was time to get up. The game wasn't going to wait.

Chapter 92

June 14, 1995

The sun finally came out, and I pried myself out of bed. It had been raining for months, only adding to my depression.

Sitting up, I looked into the mirror. I looked like shit. I had let myself go to hell even further, but at least I had been drug-free for six months. I felt like I had grown old in the time I had slept away, like Rip Van Winkle.

I needed a shave. I had grown a potbelly. I was forty pounds overweight, so none of my clothes fit, other than sweatpants. I looked at the leather pants hanging in the closet, which I had once worn on stage, and I just had to laugh. No way would I ever fit into those again.

Getting dressed and moving around the house, I noticed my parents were gone for the day, playing golf. Since I had some privacy, I loaded all my gun cases into the back of my dad's pick-up truck and drove to the back of our property, where the hill met the creek. I drove a few iron stakes into the ground and set up a shooting range so I could blast a stack of targets. I blasted away for hours until I was down to one single 9mm bullet.

I looked at the bullet for a moment and then put it back in the clip. Then I cocked the gun and put it to my head for the second time in two years.

Looking down at my fake leg, I couldn't think of a reason for living. As long as I was alive, I was putting my family in danger. This would be the easy way out.

Then a voice in my head reminded me that it was about time for Liesa to give birth. It had been nine months since she had gotten pregnant.

I took the gun from my head and shot the last bottle. I knew I had two things to do. I had to protect my family, and I had to go back to Los Angeles to settle a few scores.

When I looked in the mirror again later that day, I stared into my eyes, knowing there had once been a very giving and kind soul in there somewhere. But after seeing what I had seen, my eyes resembled those of a great white shark -- cold, with no remorse.

My parents knew I was up to something, but I tried to be very secretive to avoid a fight about my trip. I knew that the "hit team," when they arrived, would come at night under the cover of darkness, so I prepared for their visit.

~~

I trained every day out back at my homemade shooting range until I had regained my skills as a marksman. I had to learn how to stand and brace myself with the prosthetic leg, adjusting my style so the high-powered weapons wouldn't knock me off my feet. I taught myself how to run and shoot at the same time. If anyone had been watching, they would have wondered what the hell I was doing, as I set up targets in all directions and positions to make shooting a real challenge.

For six straight nights, after dark fell and my parents went to bed, I sat outside with my night-vision goggles and M-16 assault rifle, watching and listening. We were out in the country, so it would be damn hard to sneak up on me, especially since I was hiding in the bushes by the driveway. I knew they would drive by to check out the place before attempting an assault.

On the seventh day, I picked up the local newspaper and saw a front-page story about four bikers from California who had been arrested on Route 2, just three miles from my parents' house. The bikers had gone into Wal-Mart and purchased two thousand shotgun shells. On the way out of the store, they shoplifted a few items. Wal-Mart security caught them on security tape, and they were later pulled over by the county and state police. When the cops searched the bikers' van, they found four shotguns, along with two thousand shells, marijuana, and a few ounces of pure crystal methamphetamine.

Shoplifting was a side effect of using meth. Lucky for me, it had never affected me that way. People on meth think they are so fast that they can steal anything without anyone seeing.

Before I could even put the newspaper down, the telephone rang. It was a friend I had gone to high school with, who was currently working as a county sheriff. He wanted to meet at the crossroads to have a conversation.

I got dressed and drove to the crossroads. We shook hands, and I said, "What's up?"

"Did you read about the bikers we caught yesterday right down the road?" he asked.

"Yes," I replied. "What about it?"

"They had your address and an aerial map of your parents' property taken by a surveillance satellite, along with directions on how to get there from US 30. The FBI is coming in to question them. Are these guys friends of yours?"

I shook my head but said nothing.

"Tell me you're not dumb enough to be doing a dope deal."

"Relax," I replied. "You're way off base. They aren't here to do a drug deal; they're here to kill me."

My friend went silent, not knowing what to say.

"Were they wearing colors?" I asked.

"Their leather jackets read 'Prospects.' They're in a lot of trouble, and they all have warrants back in California."

"Thanks for sharing this information. I hope you understand that this is something I can't really talk about right now, but someday I'll explain."

"I don't know what hornet's nest you stirred up, but be assured that law enforcement around here will be interested in why these guys came for you, so stay out of trouble."

"Thanks," I said.

We drove off in opposite directions.

~~

After that, I stepped up operations to go back to Los Angeles. I was going to take out Christ, leader of the Heaven's Devils. If I didn't take out the leadership, other assassins would come and keep coming until I stopped the source. The next time, I might not get so lucky. I was going to show these fuckers what I was made of; I had nothing left to lose. One way or another, Los Angeles was going to get my soul.

~~

I began preparations for my trip by calling my friend Vice Grip. I told him I needed an assault rifle, a 9mm pistol, and a rocket launcher, something that would fire smoke and live grenades. No more Mr. Nice Guy. I had to wire him half the money to grease the wheels of illegal activity.

I took my encrypted computer disk to the Valparaiso library and accessed the information I needed to obtain a new fake driver's license and to set up a line of credit in that name so I could rent a car when I got to Los Angeles.

With my short hair, extra weight, and new contacts, a lot of people wouldn't recognize me, and I could move about more freely.

In the days leading up to the trip, I drove an hour in all directions to use pay phones. I never used the same phone twice, and I always used the digital voice changer. I never used my parents' phone. I was sure it was tapped.

By the middle of July, I had most of the information I needed to return to Los Angeles. Then a friend called, claiming he had talked to Liesa at a rave in Hollywood.

"Was she fat?" I asked.

"No, she still looked hot."

"What did she say?"

"She knew I was friends with you, and she asked where you were. I said I didn't know, except that you had moved back to Indiana. I got her talking, and she said she was caught in the middle between helping Eric and saving you. She said she was some type of undercover agent for some law firm or something."

"Say that again?"

"I was really fucked up," he replied, "but she wanted to talk with you."

Knowing that someone was probably listening to all my home phone calls, I said, "It'll be some time before I can come back to Los Angeles."

I hung up the phone and went straight to a travel agent to book a one-way, first-class flight to L.A. under a fake name. I still had a drop-box at a mailbox place on Sunset Boulevard. I packed some items that I didn't want to take through the airport and mailed them so they would be waiting for me when I got to Hollywood.

~~

The night before my flight, I finally told my parents I was leaving. I told them I was going to Los Angeles to attend the funeral of Miguel, who had been a good friend of mine and Rudy's. That was true; it had just timed out that way. Miguel had died of a rare disease caused from smoking PCP. The drug caused his skin to literally shrink, suffocating him very slowly over the course of a few years.

I left a letter with my long-time friend Johnny Boy, with instructions to give it to my parents if I didn't make it back.

My parents had a royal shit-fit.

"Are you totally fucking nuts?" my father said.

I looked at him and replied, "Yes, without a doubt."

"Why would you even think about going back to Los Angeles? That is crazy."

I didn't want to fight with my parents, since it was probably going to be the last time I saw them, so I refused to talk about it.

"I'm taking the bus to the airport in the morning, I'm not discussing it."

Chapter 93

"We are now making our descent into Los Angeles. Please make sure your seat belts are fastened," the captain announced.

As soon as I got off the plane at LAX, I could feel the presence of evil. I felt like eyes were watching me, but I saw no one as I cruised through the airport. I was wearing my mirrored sunglasses and could see behind me, nothing. I grabbed my luggage and took the shuttle bus to get my rental car, a black Corvette with tinted windows.

So far, everything was going smoothly. It didn't appear that anyone knew I was coming. I hit the 405 Freeway and headed north toward Hollywood, zipping through traffic with "Hell's Bells" playing on the radio at full blast. I had an evil sinister grin on my face. I was back.

I jumped off the freeway a few times to see if anyone followed, but the coast seemed clear. I skipped over to the 101 south and got off on Laurel Canyon to get my weapons.

~~

"It's nice to see you're still alive," said Vice Grip.

"Thanks. Do you have what I ordered?"

"You know it."

"Good man." I looked everything over and remarked, "The rocket launcher is only a single-shot, one-time use. I wanted a multiple shooter. One shot might not be enough."

"This is all I could get on short notice," he replied with a frown. "This isn't 7-11, asshole."

We laughed.

"That's cool," I said.

The pistol was what I wanted. He had added a silencer for free. The assault rifle was a Russian-made SKS-7.62 with two fifty-round clips.

"What are these marks on the gun's butt stock?"

"They're marks made by Iraq soldiers after they kill someone."

I counted over sixty marks. This weapon had already proven itself, just like myself, and was battle-ready.

My second stop was at my P.O. Box on Sunset Boulevard. The box I'd shipped had arrived, containing my Air Taser and a throwing knife.

My third stop was at Tweetie's apartment in North Hollywood, just over the railroad tracks and two buildings up the street from where I had stayed with Allison.

I let Tweetie know ahead of time that I needed two different batches of meth: yellow lemon drop, which was great for sex, and red devil, which made me feel invincible, like a warrior on a crusade to kill Satan himself. Both batches of meth were going to help me go out with a bang.

I had been clean for eight months, but there it was, staring me in the face. The angel on my left shoulder said, "Don't do it. You used to be such a good boy."

The devil on my right shoulder replied, "Don't be a fucking pussy. Have it."

I snorted the first line of red devil through a one-dollar bill, since I was now almost broke. My nose burned like hell, and my eyes watered. "Fuck," I said, coughing and gagging. I actually liked this shit? I remembered that familiar taste and chemical smell.

Within five minutes, I didn't have an ache in my entire body, and I felt like a young man once again. I knew it was only a temporary feeling, but I didn't care. I just enjoyed the moment. I wasn't planning on living forever. It was a one-way trip.

~~

My forth stop was out in Sunland to visit the skinheads who had the custom electronic equipment I needed.

Tattoo Skin said, "I got everything you ordered. Do you have something for me?"

I handed him a thousand dollars and gave him the traditional handshake, holding up my right fist. "White Power!"

I wasn't a racist, and I didn't think the white race was the best. I knew my enemies were white and the most evil of all nationalities. If I wasn't white, I would have been scared to death of white people.

"The cellular phone is chipped," said Tattoo Skin. "It'll be good for a month. The scanner will pick up everything -- cell phones and all law enforcement channels. You're all set."

"Great."

At this time, the only people who could afford cellular phones were doctors, lawyers, and drug dealers. It wasn't hard to catch someone talking if they stayed on longer than a minute if you were in their tower range.

"While you're here," Tattoo Skin added, "you should let Needle Jim give you a tattoo.

A skinny-looking dude without a shirt stood up and said, "It would be a real honor. I'll do a great job. No charge."

He was shaking so hard from the crank, I wouldn't have let him wipe my ass, let alone stick me with a needle.

"Why waste your art on a body that won't be around much longer?" I said.

Everyone in the room laughed.

"I'm surprised to see you with short hair," Tattoo Skin said. "You look less intimidating and half the size. Like a lion without its mane."

"That's the idea. I don't want to look the way others remember me."

"You don't look like such a pretty boy anymore. You look like a man who's been driven beyond his limits. You're most definitely a war-torn veteran of the City of Lost Angels."

"I'm not lost," I replied, "and I didn't come back as an angel. I came back as a messenger."

"What's the message?"

"Hell isn't full enough. There's room for more, and I'm here to collect souls that are overdue."

The skinheads went silent, then cheered me. I was the craziest of all the fuckers, even through these guys' eyes.

~~

Since I had a new credit card to go along with my new identity, I spared no expense. I got a suite in Beverly Hills at the Four Seasons and ordered room service, along with a massage. It felt good to be back in Hollywood, the city of car-jacking, riots, and earthquakes, and probably the home of Satan himself. What I really missed was the women of Hollywood. Even though they were no-good, lying whores, they did the most twisted sexual things, making their other faults seem unimportant.

After my massage was over, there was a knock at the door.

"It's nice to see you," Candy Cane said as she came in. "What name are you going by today?"

"Bond, James Bond." I had always wanted to say that.

She laughed and shut the door.

We did some lines of lemon drop, and I rode her like a cowboy on a ten-day ride for the next two hours. After I showered and got dressed, it was just like the old days. I was armed to the teeth and wired out of my mind.

After Candy Cane left, I went to a party at Brittney's, where a whole apartment full of old friends were very surprised to see me . . . including Brittney. She gave me a kiss and said, "I'm single. Want to spend the night?"

"I would love to."

It was just like old times. I thought it was a good send-off. But I wasn't in Los Angeles for all fun and games. I had business to take care of.

~~

My friend Tom in Studio City had called me shortly before I had left Indiana, claiming to know where Liesa lived. His apartment was my next stop. I parked right up front at the complex, next to the curb. Since I had been up all night, the sun seemed blindingly bright, so I was lucky to be parked under a big tree.

Looking around, I saw no one, so I snorted a line off the blade of my throwing knife. I was instantly alert. My body tingled, and I pushed forward, buzzing the front door of the apartment building.

Tom let me in and said, "I'm glad to see you. How have you been?"

"Things are cool, but let's get down to business. Where does Liesa live?"

"I'll have to show you. It's a little one-story white house on Santa Monica. I don't have the address. I was too wasted to write it down."

"Let's go."

"I can't right now," he replied. "I have to be somewhere. I was just on my way out the door. I'll have to show you tomorrow. I didn't know you were coming."

"No problem. It can wait till tomorrow."

~~

That night, after midnight, I hit the rave clubs, looking for people I knew and for some information. I was hoping I would find Liesa. I saw a lot of new faces, and some I avoided like the plague.

I went into Crazy Girls and the Seven Veils, but none of the strippers working were girls I knew, so I didn't stay for more than a beer. I continued through one club after the next until sunrise, looking for some of Liesa's girlfriends. No luck.

Eating my grand-slam breakfast at Rock 'n' Roll Denny's on Sunset Boulevard, I kept trying to get hold of Tom, but he wasn't answering. I was getting extremely frustrated.

When I finished my breakfast, a waitress from another section walked over and said, "Brent, is that you?"

I looked up. "Do I know you?"

With a scowl, she said, "Yes, you fucked me several times, asshole." She walked away pissed.

I didn't recognize her, and I still have no idea who she was. I thought about it for the rest of the day.

She must look different in the daylight, I thought.

I went back to the hotel for a quick shower and a change of clothes. Since I couldn't get Tom on the phone, I thought, Fuck it, and decided I couldn't wait. I drove out to Studio City.

I buzzed Tom's apartment but got no answer. I glanced around; no one was looking. Letting myself into the building with a credit card, I went up the stairs to the second level very cautiously.

Turning the corner, I saw that Tom's door had been kicked in and was sealed with yellow police tape.

Fuck me, I thought.

Without even tilting my sunglasses, I walked right past his apartment, down the back steps, and back out to my car in case someone was still watching.

That plan was ruined. I was pissed; I would never find Liesa in this huge city without help. But I still drove up and down Santa Monica Boulevard for several hours looking for Liesa's house. There must have been a thousand small white houses. Before going after Christ, I really wanted to know if she'd had my child. If I was a father, it might make me think differently about dying.

~~

After lunch, I decided I didn't feel like sleeping, so I did another line of meth and went to see a lawyer on Wilshire Boulevard who had one of my swords. It had been stolen from my collection when I was in the hospital. I wasn't going to let it get away. It was the prize of my collection: a Marine dress sword, fully inscribed. I had gotten the needed information the day before by using my stun gun on the thief, who admitted he had given the sword to this lawyer in exchange for his services.

I called the lawyer's office and made an appointment. When I said I was involved with meth, they were very eager to take my money and offered to see me right away.

I took Hollywood Boulevard to La Brea Avenue and made a right on Wilshire, going west. When I arrived, I found a handicap spot right out front, so I backed my black Corvette into the spot and hung my blue plastic handicap decal on the mirror. I clicked the remote alarm, leaving all the high-powered weapons in the trunk.

There it was on the marquee: Dickey Freyburg, Attorney at Law. Just knowing he was a crooked lawyer made me angry.

I took the elevator to the thirteenth floor. The door opened onto a black marble entranceway, paid for in blood money.

I was wearing dress clothes with dress shoes and my hair slicked back. I acted like my shit didn't stink, so I fit right in with these snobby assholes. No one gave me a second glance. Without long hair and combat boots, I appeared normal. Now that's frightening, I thought.

I read Dickey Freyburg's name on his office door and proceeded to the bathroom down the hallway. It was spotless. I went into the handicap stall and shut and locked the door so I could do a line of meth.

I was basically a nice guy, but the meth turned me into a ruthless person. You could tell, just by looking into my eyes once the meth kicked in, that I wasn't someone you wanted to fuck with.

I laid my credit card down on the back of the bowl and crushed the red devil, chopping it into a fine, sparkling powder with my throwing knife. It burned like hell as I snorted it. I wiped my eyes and nose and spit into the toilet. Finally, I put on a pair of black Italian leather gloves so I wouldn't leave any fingerprints if things didn't go smoothly using intimidation alone.

I entered the lawyer's office with all the confidence in the world; I was getting my sword back. I hoped I had the right information, but I wouldn't know until I entered the private office.

The girl behind the desk said, "He will see you now," and led me into the lawyer's office. I shut the door behind me.

When the lawyer looked up, I could tell by the look in his eyes that he didn't know who I was. He wasn't frightened. He had a chip on his shoulder and thought he was going to get some of my money, but I wasn't there to give.

There it was, on the wall behind his desk. My sword hung on display like it was a trophy he had earned. I was enraged to my limit just as the crystal methamphetamine kicked in.

"Dickey Fryburg, do you know who I am?" I said.

"Someone in trouble."

"Do you know why I'm here?"

"You got busted with meth," he replied with a chuckle.

"No, I want my sword, the sword hanging on your wall. That's from my collection, and I'm not leaving here without it."

He looked up at the sword with a smile. "I was given that as payment, and it belongs to me unless you have some type of paperwork to prove it's yours."

At this point, I was already irritated, so I made one last attempt at using the Jedi mind trick.

"I guess you didn't hear me right. This is not a court of law, and your legal bull crap holds no magical spell over me. For the last time, while I'm still in a good mood, hand me the goddamn sword!"

"You can't threaten me," he yelled as he kicked back in his leather chair and started to reach for the phone.

Wrong move. I was done talking.

Bang. Two steel-tipped darts shot out of my hand-held Taser and stuck in the middle of his chest, sending electrical sparks flying.

"Hugghhh," said the lawyer.

"Shut up. I tried it the nice way. You wanted to be a tough guy."

I set the Taser unit down on the desk as it continued to shock him for the next thirty seconds.

I reached up and took my sword off the wall, feeling proud of myself. I had actually found it. This sword was for a man, not a crooked lawyer.

Using my left hand, I cleared the lawyer's desk of everything, sending items to the floor with a crash. I opened my briefcase and took out brown wrapping paper, wrapping my sword up so no one would know what I was carrying out of the building. I worked very quickly, I knew the secretary outside couldn't hear what was going on. The high-dollar lawyers always had soundproofed offices for keeping their secrets. He was lucky. I could have shot him, and no one would have heard it.

When I was done, I detached the cartridge from the Taser unit and left the lawyer with the two darts still stuck in his chest. Drool was coming out of his mouth on one side, and his eyes were bugged out. He would be all right in time.

To cover my ass, I said to the lawyer, "Call the police, and I'll tell them that our run-in was over drugs. Your name will be in the paper, with drugs attached to it. Think about it."

"Huuughhh," slurred the lawyer.

I exited the lawyer's office without any problem and went straight to a Mailboxes, Etc. to ship my sword home. I wanted someone in my family to have it.

That felt good.

Chapter 94

Later that night, sitting in my hotel room after a dinner of Mr. Jiffy's chicken, I wished Boots was here to share my last meal.

I was going to the Pussy Kat Club; it was Christ's hang-out.

I changed rental cars, upgrading to an SUV, something with ramming power if push came to shove. I loaded both fifty-round clips for my assault rifle and went over the instructions for the rocket launcher. The Pussy Kat Club was in biker territory. They ran the place and supplied all the strippers with meth.

I snorted a huge rail of the red devil so I would be on the same level and walked out the door, heading for Death Valley.

~~

If Christ were at the club, I would get him in the parking lot without anyone else getting hurt.

Pulling into the parking lot of the Pussy Kat Club, I could see the line of Harley's parked along the side. I did another line of red devil on the glove box and was ready for action. I pulled my baseball cap down over my eyes and made sure none of my weapons were showing.

I passed a bouncer at the front door who looked like a grizzly bear. I knew I would have to get past him on my way out if things went down.

I sat at a table in the back of the strip club, where I could see everyone. I had my back to the wall; I didn't want anybody coming up behind me. I ordered a shot and a beer and kept my eyes peeled. I constantly had to keep saying, "I don't want a lap dance." I never understood why anybody would want a lap dance; it was just a tease.

I had five shots and five beers while sitting through the rotation of strippers and watching the members of Heaven's Devils pinch strippers' butts and deal meth under tables and in the restrooms. I recognized several of the bikers, but no one of high rank -- only grunt soldiers.

After three hours, no sight of Christ, I decided to head out to Palmdale. I would just come back every night until I found Christ at the club; I wasn't leaving Los Angeles until I got him.

While getting into my SUV, I noticed two black vans with tinted windows that were parked across the street with the engines running. They had been behind the Pussy Kat Club when I arrived.

Mr. K's son had said that the people who had shot up his house were driving two black vans, and Bastard Ben's neighbors said they had seen two black vans parked across the street around the time of his disappearance.

I started the SUV and did another line of red devil. My eyes watered, and my nose burned like a volcano, but I was flying high. I pulled the assault rifle out of the case, cocked it, and set it on the passenger seat, tip down.

As I pulled out of the parking lot, the two black vans followed. I floored it, and the black vans gave chase.

I picked up my cellular phone and called East Los Angeles, ringing down into the hood.

Rudy answered. "What's up, Bubba?"

"I'm here in town, out in the Valley, and I've got problems. I need a reception committee for the group following me."

"What kind of trouble?"

"I've got two vans of bad-ass bikers hot on my tail, and I'm sure they're armed to the teeth and wired out of their minds."

"Give me a few minutes, and I'll call you back. But jump on the I-5 south, heading toward me."

While I was talking with Rudy, my police scanner locked onto the conversation the bikers in the two vans were having on their cell phones. They didn't think I saw them and were just waiting for me to make my first stop. Then they were going to open fire, cutting me down in the streets of Los Angeles where I stood, upholding up their reputation as bad asses of the San Fernando Valley.

I recognized the voice in charge as that of "the Coroner," top hit man for the Heaven's Devils. Christ was sending the best, since his last batch of flunkies had failed.

Buzzing through traffic, I kept looking down at the cell phone, thinking, Rudy, don't let me down. If I ever needed you brother, this is the time.

Twenty minutes went by before Rudy called back. I was getting worried because I was down to a quarter tank of gas, and that was my life expectancy.

"Get off on Fletcher Avenue," he said. "Are you almost there?"

"I'll be there in five minutes. It's three exits ahead."

"Get off and go south to the first stop light. Take a sharp right and go up into the hills. When you see my car, make a left, drive to the end of the street where it meets the hill, stop, and get out and run for cover."

"Thanks, my brother."

Jumping off the I-5 south at Fletcher Avenue, I put down the phone and got my right hand on my assault rifle. When I reached the first stop light, I made a sharp right and gunned it up the hill, with the black vans closing in by a few car lengths. I got about half a mile up the hill when I saw Rudy's black Lexus.

The tinted window was lowered slightly to allow the smoke to exit, as a light brown finger with a gold lion ring pointed to my left.

Looking at Rudy, I took my eyes off the black vans and when I looked back again, one van was alongside of me.

When the tinted window rolled down, I saw the Coroner with his shaved, tattooed head. He just smiled at me as the biker with tattooed arms in the passenger seat pointed a sawed-off shotgun at my face.

I hit the brakes hard, letting them pass as the shotgun went off, spraying the hood of my SUV with 32 pellets.

That sent me into a meth-induced rage, so I raised my assault rifle and began shooting right through my windshield at the black van now in front of me. Fuck sticking the assault weapon out the window.

I unloaded the fifty-round clip with glass flying and shells ejecting and bouncing back in my face like a metal rainstorm. The bullets were going through the van into parked cars we passed. The black van finally slammed into a telephone pole on the hill.

I missed the road Rudy wanted me to turn on. I was going to have to double back so I hit the brakes, spinning the SUV around.

The smell of black powder was almost choking me into an asthma attack from firing the weapon inside the SUV. My ears were ringing and I felt I was still somewhat in a state of shock.

I wiped my eyes and teeth of black powder, and then floored it, charging the second van, playing chicken at full speed.

Being all hopped up on crystal methamphetamine, I felt invincible. If I was going to die, I was going to be against many.

The second black van swerved past me, taking several shotgun blasts, shattering what was left of the window shield and sending pellets through the driver's side door.

As soon as I made the turn, Rudy took off. I sped down the road leading into the mountain until I saw the dead-end and the reception committee waiting.

Michael Angelo pointed to a parking spot, so I hit the spot and jumped out of the SUV that was now smoking. I changed clips as I run for cover.

The second black van came screeching to a halt. The back doors opened and five fully armed members of Heaven's Devils jumped out, only to be met by as many as three hundred bullets flying through the air all at once.

When the smoke cleared, everyone collected weapons. I looked around at the men with bullet-ridden bodies that I had never seen before, and counted thirteen of Christ's disciples. I could only hope they enjoyed their last supper.

Michael Angelo was instructed by Rudy to take me anywhere I needed to go except his house; it was too hot for us to be seen together.

Michael Angelo grabbed me by the shoulder and said, "Your pants are smoking," and pointed to my fake leg.

In all the excitement, I hadn't noticed, but they shot my fake leg. That was twice I got shot in the same leg with a shotgun.

I was so insane by this point in my journey, I thought it was funny.

The fake leg was still intact and functional, but really damaged. The cosmetics of the leg were blown away, so when I looked at it and saw the steel bar connected to the steel ankle, it made me feel like the Terminator ... part man and part machine.

Seeing the metal leg seriously fucked with my mind even more as I walked over to the Coroner. He was still breathing.

I opened the van door and threw him to the pavement like the Terminator. I could see three holes where bullets had gone through his back and exploded out of the front of his chest. His pierced ear had been blown clean off.

I didn't feel a bit sorry for him. He had done worse to a lot of people, so I got down close to his face so he could hear me in his last remaining ear.

"I want Christ. Where is the son of a bitch?"

The Coroner, with slurred words gurgling blood, replied, "Fuck you."

"Fuck you right back," I said, flipping him the middle finger, "You bastards started this. I'm just here to finish it." I put my 9mm to his balls. "You can go with them or without. Where is he?"

The Coroner answered, "Christ will be waiting for you, and I will be waiting for you in Hell." He gave me the information I needed, right before his tattooed eyelids closed and the Grim Reaper came for his meth-ridden soul. The Coroner wasn't smiling anymore; I wiped it from his face forever.

As I started to walk away, I turned around and went back to wipe my prints off the van when the cellular phone in the Coroner's pocket started ringing.

I picked it up and answered it. "Funeral arrangements will be needed. We will discuss them when I get there."

The voice said, "What's going on?"

"You're next," I replied, before smashing the phone.

I walked back over to my SUV, which was still smoking with no windows left in it. I grabbed my assault rifle and rocket launcher, putting them in the trunk of Michael Angelo's low rider. Rudy's crew poured gasoline all over the SUV and set it on fire.

Michael Angelo took me to North Hollywood, where I met up with Vice Grip and changed cars.

I had to move quickly, before Christ moved locations. I was sure the phone call had spooked him a bit.

Getting on the freeway, I pulled my pant leg up so I could make some repairs on my fake leg. I filled the holes with wadded-up newspaper and wrapped several layers of gray duct tape around the leg to hold it together for one last mission.

"You look like hell and smell like burnt toast," Vice Grip said.

"That's the gunpowder," I replied. "I need a shower. Pull into the first motel you see before we go back out."

After the shower, I felt better. I kept thinking I heard the cops breaking down the door while I was in the shower, but it was only my paranoia.

"So what's the plan?" Vice Grip asked.

"I've got a location where I can find Christ, so I just want you to drop me off."

"What do you mean?"

"I'm tired of playing the game. I don't care anymore. It's over one way or another today. There is no way I'm getting out of Los Angeles alive. I was meant to die here, so die here I will."

"That's crazy. You sound like Frank White."

"Frank White is a character in a movie. I'm real."

~~

Heading up the freeway into the next valley, Vice Grip said, "I have to make a stop by this chick's house real quick."

"That's cool, but make it quick," I said, snorting another line of meth. He stopped and called her from a pay phone.

We traveled away from the main freeway. Just as it seemed like we were out in the desert with nothing around us, we passed two L.A. County sheriff's deputies sitting on the side of the road with their motors running. As soon as we went by, they hit their lights.

One car pulled in front of us, while the other remained behind. The officers got out charged us very quickly. I knew the game was over.

"Get your fucking hands up now," the lead officer screamed.

The officers' weapons clicked as they cocked them and pointed them at my face.

"If you move a fucking muscle, we will blow you away!" The officer screamed!

"What do you want to do," I said, "give up, or go out blasting?"

"I didn't do anything," Vice Grip replied. "You're the one in trouble."

"Okay."

The officers pulled both of us out of the car at gunpoint, then cuffed us and threw us over the hood and trunk, separating us. When they searched me, they found two double-edged throwing knives, a 9mm pistol, a silencer, an Air Taser, an assault rifle, and a rocket launcher, but they didn't find the meth.

They put Vice Grip in the back of one of the cars, while I stood there with several sheriff's deputies looking over everything they had found in amazement.

"Where did you get a fucking rocket launcher?" asked the lead officer.

"Saddam."

"Shut up, smart-ass!"

Before the lead officer could ask me any more questions, a black GMC Jimmy with tinted windows and government plates pulled up. Several government agents got out and proceeded to pull rank and take over the scene. They took me handcuffed to the back of the truck, where the first guy I had ever bought cocaine from was standing with another government agent.

"What's up, Brent?" Jay said as another government car pulled up with more agents. "You've been really busy tonight."

I'm never going to see the light of day, I thought. This is going to be all over the news.

"Just wait here," Jay said. Another agent waved to the sheriff's deputies. They took Vice Grip out of the back of the car and handed him over.

Both of the deputies' cars pulled away, leaving me alone in the middle of the desert with government agents -- of what branch I didn't know, since they weren't speaking to me.

"Jay, what's going on?" I asked. "Am I going to prison, or are you guys going to whack me?"

"Just sit tight," he replied. "The man in charge will let you know what's going on."

~~

An hour and a half went by while I stood there handcuffed, thinking they were going to kill me any second. Eventually I heard another truck pull up and the doors slam.

It was Cain and Abel. I thought, What the fuck? They faked the local cops out.

Cain said in a harsh tone, "You have gotten really good at counter-surveillance. We didn't even know you were in town until you made the cell phone call to Rudy."

I smiled.

"You sure have listened and played the game well, so you have my respect, along with others. So this is how it's going down."

I stood there silently.

"Your days as Mr. B are done. That name will never be spoken again. We seldom arrest anyone, and we don't put people in jail. We watch and decide if they should live or die. Like it, love it, or hate it, just accept that's the way it works in this country, and there's not a damn thing you can do about it."

I didn't know what to say, so I said nothing.

"I'm sure you have a lot of questions that you want answered. Tough shit. You're going to forget about everything that has happened in California if you want to live another day." Cain looked over at Vice Grip and said, "So, you're Mac Morris, A.K.A. Mac Gun, A.K.A. Vice Grip, a.k.a. D.O.A."

Abel walked up behind Vice Grip and put a silenced pistol to the back of his head.

My eyes widened.

Abel pulled the trigger. Vice Grip's brains came out of his mouth and ears as the bullet penetrated his skull and exited his face. It had to be a hollow point, the way his head exploded.

I just stood there silently, figuring I was next. No way I was getting away this time. My luck, if I ever had any, had run out. My parents would never know what had happened to me. I would just disappear, as if the desert had swallowed me alive.

I still wasn't going to pray to any more artificial gods for mercy.

As I stood there watching and waiting, government agents opened the back of the black truck. Inside were two barrels marked "medical waste." They lowered both and opened one.

Two agents wearing plastic covers over their suits picked up Vice Grip and stuffed him into the barrel like a dead cat being removed from a highway. Then they removed their plastic suits and gloves and put everything that had blood on it into the barrel. As I watched in horror, an agent sprayed some type of solvent over the huge bloodstain in the sand, then scooped up the sand and put it in the barrel as well.

The barrel was sealed and then loaded back into the truck. When the tailgate was closed and the truck started to pull away, Cain finally broke the silence.

"Vice Grip was the one who ratted you out to the bikers," he said. "He was trying to call Christ to let him know he had you in the car, but we blocked all the phone calls going to Christ's location. Otherwise, they would have been waiting for you."

I started to speak, but Cain wasn't finished.

"Shut the fuck up, and just listen."

"Okay."

"I'm going to take you to LAX and put you on the next flight back to Chicago. You will not come back to Los Angeles for a long time."

"Okay."

"You will go straight, get off the drugs, open your business or get a job, something legal. I will not give you a second chance."

"You're going to let me go back to Indiana? You're fucking with me?"

"I don't have time to fuck around. If I wanted you dead, you would be in that second barrel. Don't make me change my mind."

"Thanks. I owe you one."

Cain nodded. "Damn right you do."

"Take the handcuffs off him," Cain barked at the other agents. "Get in the truck," he demanded. "You leave Christ for the FBI. He's not getting away. His days are numbered in single digits."

"Are you sure?" I asked, and realized immediately it was a dumb question.

"Yeah, I'm sure," he said, looking at me like I was stupid. "Things are getting way out of control. We're shutting down the meth business. If these assholes want to get high, they're going to have to sniff cocaine."

Typical CIA move, I thought. They had created a problem, and when it got out of hand, they dropped the burden on the local authorities who had no idea what was going on.

"We're going to run that fake name of yours in the paper so the bikers will think you're dead," Cain explained. "We'll also spread rumors through Hollywood that you were killed, and we've removed any type of investigation of your previous names from the computer systems. Use your real name again. No more fucking around, no more secret missions. This is it; this is your redemption from G.O.D."

While Cain spoke, I watched Abel take my assault rifle and put it in a black bag that was sealed airtight.

"What's he doing with the weapon?" I asked.

"That's our insurance policy. Double-cross us, and we'll drop that weapon with your fingerprints at a crime scene."

"What crime scene?"

"I'll find one somewhere, or create one."

Fucking bastards, I thought. But I said, "I understand."

"Someday," Abel said, "when you're old and gray, you can tell your grandchildren about your joyride in Los Angeles and how some 'spooks' made you leave town before sunrise."

~~

I sat in the passenger seat while Cain drove and Abel sat behind me. I kept waiting for my brains to blow out of my mouth any minute.

"What the hell is going on?" I asked. "Are you really the government? What about G.O.D. and the revolt? What about saving the country?"

Cain and Abel both just smiled a weird smile, finally revealing their true selves. "G.O.D. doesn't exist now, and it never has. It was something we made up to get you to do what we needed done."

"What the hell was that, kill bikers?"

"No, move a thousand pounds of crystal methamphetamine. By spying on you, we knew you actually believed in doing the right thing if given the opportunity."

"As far as saving the country, move to Canada," Cain suggested.

As I thought back over the years, I remembered Cain bringing me different batches of speed every time. Each separate batch had its own mind-controlling effects. Lemon drop made you sexual, red devil made you violent, and snow white made you awake and alert, with no euphoria or any high feeling, other than aggression. The first type of snow white was given to U.S.

troops during the Gulf War, and it contributed to Desert Storm Syndrome because of the one molecule they had removed to prevent the soldiers from being horny, which messed with their nervous system.

First, the Hungarians had used all the Hollywood heavy metal musicians for employees and for revenge and the government had used musicians for an experiment.

"You're much smarter than a lot of people give you credit for," Cain said, "but you're not ruthless enough to belong with us. You don't have the stomach to do things that you think are wrong."

Cain was right; I had never wanted to be any part of this. All I'd wanted was to be a rock star. I was twenty-four years old before I tried my first joint. I just happened to fall into the underworld and somehow ended up being the guy in charge.

"What would have happened if I had given Liesa that poison?" I asked.

"Last question. Like I said before, you would still be with us. That was your last test; you failed and should feel grateful we're letting you go."

"Thanks," I said, but I wanted to say Fuck you.

As I rode in the passenger seat of the SUV to the airport, I stared out the window, looking at the lights of Los Angeles burning through the night. I couldn't believe I had been tricked by the CIA. No one would believe me. All my efforts had been in vain, and everything I knew was a lie.

I felt like the biggest chump in the world, but I was quickly realizing why things were how they were. My mind was still processing a million thoughts per second. The hidden cameras in my mansion hadn't been intended to bust me; they wanted to watch me recover at an accelerated rate because of the type of meth they were selling me. It was unheard of that I was up and fighting after two months in a bed and losing a leg. Without the meth, that wouldn't have been possible. Now it made sense. They were preparing to use the meth on the soldiers of the next war, and they wanted to make sure they had the right grade this time. I was living proof. I should have been a cripple, not a threat to anyone. The meth made me stronger and meaner and able to fight off several criminal groups while being severely injured.

I couldn't imagine what damage a fully trained soldier could do under the influence of meth, combined with heavy metal.

~~

As we pulled into the LAX International Airport, Cain said, "Do we have an understanding?"

"Yes. I won't talk about Los Angeles, and I will stay away."

"It would be real stupid to tell anyone what you did. Plus, they would just think you're crazy. The CIA doesn't even work in this country." They looked at each other and laughed.

Cain said to Abel, "Remember Mike Rupert?"

"Yep."

"What a chump."

They both laughed again.

I didn't know who they were talking about, but I found out later that Mike Rupert was an LAPD narcotics investigator who had resigned in 1978 after attempting to expose CIA drug trafficking. They made him look like a complete fool when he claimed that the CIA was bringing cocaine into the country and were flooding the streets with the drugs for profit. But it was true. The CIA had a pilot dropping off tons of cocaine every few days in Arkansas until local cops caught him. When he claimed to be working for our government, they laughed until agents arrived and took him out of the jail and he disappeared.

The CIA even went so far as to shoot down a small aircraft that was carrying missionaries, claiming it was a mistake. After that, there was a policy of not shooting down suspected drug planes, opening the sky up for drug traffic.

"I don't have a ticket or any cash, other than a hundred dollars," I said.

"Use your fake credit card one more time to book a first-class seat, then toss it away," said Cain. "Don't get caught with it. It might link you to the police investigation of what happened."

I just smiled. "No problem."

Waiting at the curb by baggage check was another government car containing my belongings from the hotel.

"Thanks for not leaving me out there like a chump."

Cain shook my hand. "Have a nice flight. These agents will make sure you get on the plane very quickly."

I grabbed my bags and turned around to speak with Cain, but he was already gone, like a ghost.

~~

When the plane took off and didn't explode in mid-air, I closed my eyes and opened them again. I have to be dreaming, I thought. I should have been dead or behind bars, but instead I ordered a shot and a beer and sat back.

Looking out the window of the plane as we flew over the City of Lost Angels, it finally sank in that my days as Mr. B were over. I noticed that a hole in the airplane's wing had been repaired with gray duct tape, the same duct tape that was holding my leg together.

It was time to go home. Home sweet home.

Epilogue

I wish I could paint a prettier picture of Hollywood, but that would only serve as a web of deception to draw in more victims.

It took two years for the meth cravings to finally stop. I thought they would never go away. The nightmares, on the other hand, lasted forever.

I took the second chance they gave me and made something of my life. I finally used my real name again. The names of my past were dead, as far as I was concerned.

I saw no one following my every move any longer. They kept their word, and I kept mine. My mouth remained shut. They had taught me a lifetime lesson.

In 1996, Christ died in a shoot-out with federal agents. The Heaven's Devils were no more.

The Condor/Kevin Mitnick was also captured that year in North Carolina and spent the next five years in solitary confinement, without even a trial. He wasn't let out of prison until the Trilateral Commission could secure their computers. They didn't want him to blow the whistle on their plan.

~~

In 1997, I reopened my candle business with my parents' help, launching a family-run business that would become very successful. Since my mind had been opened by the stimulant effects of crystal methamphetamine, along with several other illegal, mind-altering drugs, I was able to create a new, original style of candle. I worked hard every day to become a part of normal society, which turned out to be my greatest challenge yet.

After watching cooks make crank, I had gotten a good idea of how chemicals could be mixed and matched. By blending wax, scents, dyes, oil paints, and a few secret ingredients, the special effect I created was out of this world, making the candles appear mystical.

A book was published that same year called The Fugitive Game by an investigative reporter named Jonathan Littman. The book was about Eric and the Condor. Liesa and I were mentioned in the conspiracy, but I didn't come forward. I let the book ride and kept my mouth shut.

But the FBI still followed me around at the time to see how I would react.

~~

In 1998, Ann Marie, the porn star I had lived with, contracted AIDS from Mark Wallace during the filming of the movie <u>Anal Gang Bang</u>. Her career was over, and she became just another fallen angel taken by the city of Los Angeles.

That year, I hooked back up with Otis Day. I heard on the radio station called the Chicago Loop that he was playing at Joe's Sports Bar on Weed Street.

It took me ten minutes to work my way up to the front of the stage, trying to get past all the drunken college kids dressed in togas. No one wanted to let me through, since I wasn't dressed in <u>Animal House</u> attire. But even with a leg gone, when push came to shove, I made it to the front row.

There was Otis, larger than life and doing what had made him famous. This was the first time in the decade I had known him, that I had actually seen him play a live show. I stood there and stared at him, excited and looking forward to seeing my old friend. He danced back and forth, still doing the splits like a young man, but he didn't recognize me. He stopped once and gave me a funny look, then kept doing his thing. I thought what the hell.

Otis jumped off the stage and went through the crowd, shaking hands, until he got to me. I grabbed his hand and said, "Hey, shamalama dick-dong, have you forgotten me already?"

Otis gave me a funny look, as if he had seen a ghost, and replied, "What?"

I said with my usual smart-ass tone, "You know me, dipshit."

"Brent, is that you?" he yelled.

"Who else would have the balls to call you a dipshit in front of three thousand screaming fans?"

"My nigger, you're alive!" Otis smiled wide and hugged me, giving me a sloppy kiss on the cheek.

"Enough," I replied. "Go brush your teeth."

"Shut up, asshole," he said, and then he actually started to cry. Tears were running down his face, and the show came to a halt. Otis said in excitement, "I was told you were killed many years ago."

"I'll explain later."

Otis pulled me up onstage, and his niece, who was also shocked, gave me a kiss on the cheek. He yelled through the microphone, "I would like to introduce you to my best friend in the world, and the Godfather of Hollywood."

The crowd cheered, and the band started a song while I stayed onstage, singing backup with Otis for one song. Everyone in the crowd who had given me a hard time as I tried to get through, all were now looking at me differently.

~~

In November of 2000, the Trilateral Commission finally seized control of the White House and the perks that came along with it, the military. It would go down in history as the first election won by cheating.

~~

On Christmas Eve, I finally tracked down Liesa. She was living in Guam on a military base with a D.O.D. agent named Ted, who was an expert in planting bombs.

We started talking by e-mail after the first phone call, since there was a seventeen-hour difference in time zones. When I did a spell check before sending an e-mail, the computer would always suggest correcting the spelling of Liesa's name as "Lies."

That figures.

~~

In March of 2001, I agreed to meet Liesa in Huntington Beach, California, at a place with no address on a street with no name. I was introduced to my son, Tyler, who was five and was the spitting image of myself. I spent a week with both of them and took him to Disneyland.

After spending that week with Tyler, Liesa and I couldn't agree on anything, so there was no further contact.

Liesa said, "If you try anything in court regarding Tyler, my friends in high places assured me that you wouldn't have one leg left to stand on."

I was pissed, I didn't think it was too funny. I told her to fuck off and that I would never speak to her again. I was no longer under her spell. I would find Tyler when he was eighteen and try to explain.

~~

On September 10, 2001, the CIA made over $100 billion in stock trades, and the product of crystal methamphetamine called snow white, which now had no smell or taste, was put into full production by two companies, one in Texas and one in Florida. The meth I call snow white, is now called Dexdrine, it is a nootropic version. For the soldiers to come down from Dexdrine, they have to take Ambien or Restorial.

On September 11, terrorists were allowed to take control of American Airlines as part of the Trilateral Commission's plan to steal 9 TRILLION in American tax money by creating a new war. Contracts were handed out like dinner invitations. After everything I had seen, could I really believe they didn't know about the terrorists? They monitored everyone.

An FBI agent had filed a report about known terrorists in flight schools, but he was ignored. He flied 70 reports in a four-week period...obviously no one wanted it stopped. The Pentagon is the most defended building in the world, but with 45 minutes notice they failed to stop a jumbo jet from crashing into it. Where were the jet fighters or the patriot missles, nothing. But an AC-130 Gun Ship just happen to be flying over at the same time and the pilot said he said he saw the plane hit the Pentagon. Here's the problem, there is a no fly zone for over a hundred miles above the Pentagon, yet there is an AC-130 gun ship equipment with missles and enough firepower to level the Pentagon flying over it, it should have never been there.

~~

In 2002, Boots died of a brain tumor, and Dawn my horse finally died at the ripe old age of forty-three. She was one of the oldest horses on record.

It was very sad. I had to end both their lives for them because they were in overwhelming pain. I buried them both out back by the apple tree.

Gary and I finally became friends again, he came up to me at the county fair and said sorry for his actions. I accepted. I didn't get my $2,000 nor did I ask. I was tired of being angry with Gary and just let it go.

I also returned to Los Angeles that year -- not for pleasure, but to attend my best friend Rudy's funeral. They had finally gotten to him. The game was over. I could do nothing to save him. I had tried; Lord knows how I tried.

As Allison and I entered Rose Lawn Memorial, I saw Michael, an enforcer from Pico and Union, walking down the hallway in tears. We shook hands and hugged. It would be the last time I saw him.

Seeing Rudy lying there in the casket choked me so that I couldn't speak. I was so broken up that I couldn't even say the things I wanted to say to my dear departed friend. I just stood there.

My days in the Hood were over. No more ghetto-chicken, and no reason to ever go there without my best friend. My legend and ties died with Rudy. I was now the oldest member of a crew that had once stood tall.

I was the survivor.

Sometimes I wished I wasn't.

~~

After I returned to Indiana from Rudy's funeral, I was so upset I came down with shingles and spent a month in bed with a high fever. During that time, while I sat at home recovering, I decided to finally go through all my old boxes from Hollywood. I wanted to get rid of old memories.

When I got to the bottom of the last box, I found that damn Ouija board. I didn't remember packing it six years ago; it had been following me around since 1988.

As I picked the board up, I sensed something strange about it. I actually got a tingling sensation. I set the board down in front of the computer monitor and finished going through the boxes.

When I was done, I took all the pictures of the people I was thinking about and placed them across the Ouija board. Most were dead, and the fates of the others were a mystery to me.

For some strange reason, I placed the keyboard on top of the Ouija board. I closed the drapes, put on a Korn CD, lit some white candles, and smoked a joint. Once the mood was set, I sat down and started typing, while watching Late Night with Conan O'Brien.

By the end of the evening, I sat back and read the pages I had just written. It was so full of detail and style, it almost brought a tear to my eye.

English had been my worst subject; it had kept me off the honor roll every time. There could only be one explanation for this manuscript: the board was channeling my thoughts, as if the book was being written by many ghostwriters. Many of my friends were now ghosts, but they were not English scholars themselves, so there were a lot of spelling and mechanical errors.

Many of the events I wrote about caused horrible flashbacks and nightmares. When I awoke from one of the nightmares, I found myself with a pistol in each hand, looking for demons in all directions. In time, I was able to deal with it.

Even though I was ordered to keep my mouth shut, I was now compelled to tell my tale. After seeing Rudy dead, all bets were off. No one lives forever, and I didn't want to take this tale to my grave. The ghosts of my past wouldn't rest until their voices were heard from the grave.

In 2003, I got engaged and bought a house on a small lake.

In 2005, I looked up several people from my past. That year was the ten year mark of being clean and sober, and off of crystal methamphetamine.

The people who quit when I went out of the business were smart as hell, and all were in high-ranking positions or owned their own companies, creating products only someone with an altered mind could create. They were the elite of the crowd, but like me, they had similar problems and side effects. All of us have insomnia, asthma, and digestion problems, along with nightmares of a past that we're trying desperately to forget. They remember the insane behavior caused by the meth, and how we didn't think there was anything wrong with the way we were acting at the time.

The people who didn't quit had to start shooting the speed into their veins, since their nasal passages finally rotted out and their lungs were so coated they couldn't absorb any more chemicals. They are no longer skinny; they're like blobs, sweaty and smelling of toxic waste. Their livers are so damaged, they can no longer filter the poison. Their bodies stored the chemicals in fat deposits and retained the polluted water, making them walking cesspools. There is no hope for those lost souls. Seeing those victims has only made me appreciate my life even more and cherish the second chance I was given.

As far as me getting away scot-free, that wasn't the case. I got the worst sentence of all: living the rest of my life as an amputee. It's a life sentence as I walked the rest of my time on earth. It's just a matter of time before I'm returned to the wheelchair. Sometimes when I get up in the morning and have to face the process of putting on my fake leg, I wonder, <u>Is it all worth it?</u>

But every day so far, I have decided that it is, and I put on the leg and move forward.

I don't talk about my past. I tell everyone I lost my leg in a motorcycle accident. It's just easier that way. No one would believe me. They would think I was nuts.

In 2007, I caught my fiancé cheating on me. I hacked her computer and went back 5 years in emails to find out I was with another lying whore. I would remain single for the rest of my life. That summer they found Cyn dead in a bathtub with a needle stuck in her neck, the same thing I saw 20 years ago.

March of 2009, I open "No Halo Productions" in Hollywood and the same month they found Eric/Justin Petersen, the hacker who tried to steal my life dead. Someone summered him with a pillow and yes the police came to talk to me.

When I got on Facebook in 2010, I contacted my old singer Bobby Lee from Hap Hazzard. It had been 25 years since we had spoken. He wrote me a four page letter telling me how sorry he was for acting that way and for what happened to me. I responded by calling him every name in the book but a white man and took anyone off my friend list that had him, I was so angry. He took it and understood and said if you can forgive me someday, I will be here my once brother. After I cooled down, I forgave him and we are now good friends again and there has even been talk about a reunion tour.

In all my molded candles, I hide a magic quartz crystal in the wax for good luck. People who don't know me often ask, "Does the crystal really give you good luck?"

With a smile, like I know something they don't, I reply, "Yes. I'm still alive. If that's not lucky, I don't know what is."

You've read the book! Now visit the author!

www.BrentsBook.com

Join the conversation, download pictures, supporting documentation, and to learn more about Author Brent David Schroeder, his other published books, screenplays and much more.

~~

Coming Soon!

THE LYCAN
CHRONICLES

BY AUTHOR BRENT DAVID SCHROEDER

Available in stores Nationwide

August

2012

Made in the USA
Charleston, SC
09 August 2012